D1520757

Wives for Sale

WITHDRAWN

Particular and merry Account of a most Entertaining and Curious

SALE OF A WIFE,

Of a pretty young WOMAN, *who was* Sold *to a gallant young Fellow,*
For FIFTEEN Sovereigns, and a *Dozen of Wine*, this Morning,
Together with the *Wedding* SONG.

AT an early hour a young couple came into the market: The Lady was dressed neat and clean, and so attractive were her rosy cheeks and sparkling eyes, that all the folks in the market soon collected about her, (she being to be sold.)

Well, good folks, says the Lady's spouse here's a rare bargain to dispose off! Here's my pretty sweet Wife, who will try all she can, to please any man, who's willing to take her for life. What have you got to say, Mr Butcher? Oh! says the Butcher she charms my very heart to look at her! here's 17s. for a beginning. That's too little, says Snobby, the Cobler, I will run to my uncle's with some of my customer's shoes, to raise the wind, & give 3s more: Oh-ho, says Frisk, the fiddler, & Friz, the barber, we will join and buy her between us; two shillings a-piece more says they: That won't do, cries Snip the tailor, putting on his spectacles, I have 20s. in my pocket, & I will sell my Dandy collar, stays, busk, sheers, thimble, needles and goose, to raise 15s more. Clear the way, you silly bodies, quoth a Miller, or I'll shave you all with a wooden razor, here's 50s. for my ducky, so mount upon my old mare and let us trot home to the mill together:

Botheration, says a Farmer, I'll capsize you all together, here's 3l. for her, 7s more

says a Tallow-Chandler, 2 more bade the Baker, and 10 more the Painter: A gallant Publican hearing the fun, bounced forward with such haste that he upset the Barber & Tailor in the mud, & almost trod the fiddlers' toes off: He instantly paid down Fifteen Pounds, and took them all to an Inn, where they had a capital Dinner and after emptying a dozen of Wine, the happy couple mounted a gig, and set off in full glee.

The Wedding *Song.*

NOW come jolly neighbours let's dance
    sing and play,
And away, to the neighbouring wedding away.
All the world is assembled, the young & the old
To see the fair beauty that is to be sold.

So sweet and engaging the Lady did seem,
The market with bidders did presently teem,
A Tailor sung out that his goose he would sell,
To buy the fair Lady—he lov'd her so well.

But a gallant young Publican 15l. did pay
And with the young Lady he marched away.
Then they drank, & carouz'd & rejoiced all day
The glass pass'd around and the piper did play

Success to this couple, & to keep up the fun,
May the bumpers fly round at the birth of a son
Long life to them both, in peace & content,
may their days & their nights for ever be spent

(Price One Penny.)
Catnach, Printer, 2, Monmouth-court:
BILLS, CARDS. ETC. Printed on very Reasonable Form

Wife-selling broadside printed by J. Catnach, London, c.1832
(*See page 207*)

Wives for Sale

AN ETHNOGRAPHIC STUDY OF
BRITISH POPULAR DIVORCE

Samuel Pyeatt Menefee

St. Martin's Press · New York

Contents

Illustrations

Maps

Acknowledgements

The author and publisher are grateful to the following for permission to reproduce the illustrations: Avon County Reference Library (pages 107 and 239), Birmingham Reference Library (page 203), the British Library (frontispiece), the Central Reference Library, Manchester (page 296) and the John Rylands Library, University of Manchester (page 140). Some of the discussion in this book previously appeared in the author's article in *New Society*, 26 January 1978.

Preface

This book has grown out of an initial study, 'Some Informal Institutions in British Society'. I am indebted to Dr P. G. Rivière and Dr K. Thomas for their suggestion that I should concentrate on the topic of wife-selling. Their perspicacity is indicated by the result — a collection of over 400 sales far exceeding the textual limits they allocated. I would like to thank my publishers for valued assistance in pruning this study to a more manageable size, combining research with readability. I can only hope that wife-selling has lost none of its colour in the transit from marketplace to the port-stained newspapers of the Bodleian and now to this book.

Mr Roy Palmer once mentioned the resentment he encountered when contacting one wife-seller's descendants, who preferred to forget their 'black-sheep' ancestor. I can only say that I have met with little but help; My researches have indebted me to many people. My supervisor Professor Rodney Needham of All Souls was kind enough to read a complete dissertation draft; he offered helpful comments and suggestions and urged me to publish. In the Department of Social Anthropology both Dr P. Lienhardt and Dr P. G. Rivière took time to supply me with leads. In law I am indebted to Dr J. M. Kaye and and Professor John H. Langbein, and particularly to Dr J. Hackney, who went well beyond any call of duty, meeting with me several times. Professors Richard Parker and David Maybury-Lewis provided much appreciated support during the later stages of my work. Professor Francois Crouzet introduced me to an excellent French source. Professor M. P. K. Sorrenson supplied background on New Zealand wife sales, while Dr K. Danaher wrote to me in detail about the institution's place in the folklore of Eire. The Reverend P. G. Peck suggested several sources for cattle sales, while Dr J. S. C. Riley-Smith supplied information about a manuscript peerage entry in the library of Queen's College, Cambridge. Dr E. J. Hobsbawm and Professor G. Rudé could suggest no written sources for the practice but took time to respond to my letters. Professor John R. Gillis was generous in the best tradition of scholarship, and I am only sorry that the exigencies of time and space have not allowed me to benefit more fully from his unpublished article. And thanks also to Mr E. P. Thompson, whose published works provided general background. Finally, I wish to mention Dr K. Thomas and Dr I. Hamnett whose unusual criticisms of my dissertation have contributed to making this a better book.

Throughout, Miss Christina Hole and Miss Katharine Briggs of the Folklore Society kindly offered information and support. Mrs Faye Roberts and Mr Hugh Oak-Rind took time to copy several wife sales, while Mr Jon Raven answered my queries despite a busy schedule. Mr Tony Deane generously went out of his way to supply typescripts of several Cornish examples as well as a xerox of a Cornish wife-selling folktale that he had collected. Extracts from the diary of the Reverend Henry Bary Knox are due to the assistance of Mr W. A. B. Jones, while Mr Keith Williams and Mr Clifford Morsley went through their notes to supply me with several useful leads. Miss Rosalind Laker and Mr Patrick O'Brian took time to write in detail about the source material for their novels. Mr Robert E. Wilson brought a Dallas example of popular divorce to my attention. Finally, Mr Roy Palmer deserves very special thanks for supplying no fewer than nine wife-selling broadsides and songs. My discussion of wife-selling as it appears in music owes a great deal to his generosity.

Several newspaper editors and their staff took time to supply particular cases. My thanks to Mr N. H. Chandler, Ms Cathy Millar-Smith, Ms Sheila Robson, Mr D. W. Smith and Mr Max Hodnett. I was greatly impressed by the almost universal courtesy that libraries and record offices extended to me. To list those who helped individually would extend this preface by many pages. I can only say to each: look herein and recognize your mark. I must, however, give special thanks to Mr G. Langley, who on his own initiative supplied copies of two broadsides, Mr W. Linneard, who answered several queries, and Miss U. B. Murphy, who continued to supply newspaper references after answering my initial query.

On a more personal level, this work gained from the assistance of many friends. Mr Alan Stokes provided a perpetual calendar, while Mr N. B. Rankov, Miss Ann Taylor, Mrs M. McGovern and Miss F. White supplied expertise in foreign languages. Miss P. N. Rae and Miss Elizabeth Lott translated sixteenth-century calligraphy, while Mrs Roger Walker researched Hertfordshire and Suffolk record offices, and supplied a previously unrecorded oral reference. Mr Doug Cox provided a literary example of popular divorce.

Thanks also to the good typists I encountered. In particular, I appreciate the assistance of Mrs Donald Matheson and Mrs Kenneth Fox, my typing mainstays on both sides of the Atlantic, and that of Brendacopy. Mr Paul Barker, editor of *New Society*, kindly granted permission to use material appearing in my article. The Rhodes Trust provided the funds that made my attendance at Oxford possible; to the trustees and to Sir Edgar Williams, the former Warden, my sincere thanks.

Harvard Law School, 1981   S.P.M.

To my parents

CHAPTER 1
A Popular Institution

'Will anybody buy her?' said the man.
'I wish somebody would,' said she firmly. 'Her present owner is
not at all to her liking!'
'Nor you to mine,' said he. 'So we are agreed about that.
Gentlemen, you hear? It's an agreement to part. She shall take the
girl if she wants to, and go her ways. I'll take my tools and go my
ways. 'Tis simple as Scripture history. Now then, stand up, and
show yourself.'

(Thomas Hardy: *The Mayor of Casterbridge*)

Michael Henchard's drunken sale of his wife in *The Mayor of Casterbridge* shocked Victorian sensibilities. Critics cried that Thomas Hardy had passed the bounds of credible fiction when he wrote: 'I don't see why men who have got wives and don't want 'em shouldn't get rid of 'em as the gipsy fellows do their old horses . . . Why shouldn't they put 'em up and sell 'em by auction to men who are in need of such articles?'[1]

These sentiments, unalterably opposed to the Victorian idealization of womanhood, seemed more suitable to a savage and barbaric society. With lofty interest the Englishman could contemplate African brideprice, by which the wife's family was compensated for her loss by money or cattle. Chinese husbands who sold their wives left Englishmen unmoved, and even Hungarian peasant customs in which the bride-to-be was referred to as a cow were comfortably remote.[2] But that actual sales of *wives* could exist in England? It must be fantasy, an aberration. . . . Nonetheless, wife-selling *was* an established British institution. Wife sales were popularly believed to be a legal and valid form of divorce. The husband, by transferring his wife to a purchaser, considered himself freed from responsibility for the woman.

1

D'Archenholtz, a French traveller of the eighteenth century, noted that in England:

> Among the common people, a method is sometimes practised of dissolving a marriage, no less singular than compendious. When a husband and wife find themselves heartily tired of each other, and agree to part; if the man has a mind to authenticate the intended separation by making it a matter of public notoriety, thinking . . . that his wife is his goods and chattels, he puts a halter about her neck, and thereby leads her to the next market place, and there puts her up to auction to be sold to the best binder [sic], as though she was a brood-mare, or a milch-cow. A purchaser is generally provided before hand on these occasions; for it can hardly be supposed, that the *delicate* female would submit to such public indignity, unless she was sure of being purchased when brought to market. To the highest bidder, the husband, by delivering up the end of the halter, makes a formal and absolute surrender of his wife, and, as he imagines, at once absolves her and himself from all the obligations incident to marriage!

Such conjugal sales were often pre-arranged, taking place at market or in a pub in order to publicize or validate the exchange. The woman was supposed to give her consent; often she was disposed of to a lover. Another Frenchman reports: 'The purchaser, always widower or youth, is ordinarily a connoisseur of the merchandise sold, who knows her; one only presents her at the market for the matter of form.'³ Sales were often accompanied by legalizing actions, including the payment of a market or turnpike toll, the statement of a minimum price, the presence of witnesses or even the drafting of a written agreement. Most notable, however, was the frequent use of a rope or halter, by which the wife was led to the place of sale. The transfer of this lead symbolized the transfer of the woman and underlined the frequent association of the institution with livestock sales.

Wife-selling occurred throughout the British Isles, perhaps as early as 1073, with scattered cases as late as the twentieth century. Many considered the practice to be of extremely ancient vintage. D'Archenholtz called it one of 'those singular laws which evince the barbarity of remote ages', while Pillet claimed: 'A judge has assured me that the formalities of divorce by the sale of the wife, in the lower class, was founded on the customs transmitted by the ancient *Brises* or Britons, before the Danish dynasties.'⁴ One author advanced a theory in *Notes and Queries* that 'the custom originated from the Anglo-Saxon law which compelled every freeman seducing another freeman's wife to reimburse the outraged husband for his expenses in obtaining another spouse,' but concludes that 'this seems somewhat far-fetched.'[5] Christina Hole suggests confused memories of Anglo-Saxon brideprice as an alternative idea, while Wilkinson Sherren proposes Danish barter or Norman serfdom as origins. Jannoc believed that the sales evolved after the Napoleonic Wars, when soldiers and sailors returning home discovered that their wives had remarried in their absence; wife-selling would have provided a speedy and cheap method of divorce. Others have modified this idea, influenced, no doubt, by the numerous sales predating the Napoleonic period.[6] While the custom is undoubtedly ancient, this very antiquity makes agreement on a single origin difficult, particularly when one considers the span of time before the first firmly recorded case in 1553. The Divorce Act of 1857 is generally accepted as a significant external development. Before this date few had the money or knowledge to obtain a parliamentary divorce, and many writers trace the institution's decline from this time.[7]

Wife-selling was never formally sanctioned by law, and many have seen it only as a device to protect the purchaser from an action for *criminal conversation*.[8] Nonetheless, it influenced the minds of several generations. Tales of sales among the navvies and the Sheffield knife-grinders were common.[9] Wife-selling became a theme for comic songs, *bon mots* and several operatic farces. The proverbial phrase 'Smithfield bargain' took on new meaning, and in Liverpool: 'The young bloods of the town, when not engaged in more disgraceful pursuits, deemed it fine amusement to circulate handbills in which young ladies were offered for sale.'[10] Jon Raven claims that the institution 'became a popular cause for the regional press' and that it led to editorial comments denouncing the custom as 'both illegal and barbaric.'[11] This custom typified the English for their old rivals, the French. And just how much the practice was ingrained in the ordinary individual's subconscious may be judged from the following incident:

> A stone mason at Colchester was lately employed by a tradesman there to engrave the following epitaph to his wife: − 'A virtuous woman is a crown to her husband.' The stone, however, being narrow, he contracted the sentence in the following manner: − 'A virtuous woman is 5s to her husband.' − The tradesman refuses to

pay for the stone, the engraver sustains his charge, and the matter stands for the Quarter Sessions to determine. [12]

Yet by the end of the nineteenth century clouds of ignorance appear to have settled around the institution. Hardy's *Mayor of Casterbridge*, published in 1886, was virulently attacked because the opening wife sale was considered unbelievable. A correspondent in *Notes and Queries* wished to know if there had ever been 'any foundation in law for the practice of selling . . . wives, which our neighbours the French persist in believing to be perfectly legal and common [in England] at the present day?' Questions filled the air: 'What was the origin of the custom?'; 'Did either the legislature or judicature touch upon the matter?'; '. . . was the practice widespread on the Continent at any time?' Several newly discovered sales were proudly proclaimed by their finders to be the basis for the occurrence in Hardy's famous novel. [13]

This state of affairs is hardly surprising when one considers the general ignorance prevalent until recent times concerning many sections of British society. Francis Place, a chronicler of eighteenth-century London life, noted in his autobiography

> The manners of the people, have seldom been attended to by writers of any repute, excepting now and then on extraordinary occasions and those generally when they were mischievously disposed, and when something to their discredit could be alleged against them. What is known of them can be gleaned only from a few passing incidents.

Thackeray, writing in *Fraser's Magazine*, agreed: 'an English gentleman knows as much about the people of Lapland or California as he does of the aborigines of The Seven Dials or the natives of Wapping. . . .' [14] Because of the initial failure of many attempts to trace 'primitive customs' in British society to 'logical tribal antecedents', and perhaps because of the very emphasis on this spurious 'primitivism', most British anthropologists reacted by abandoning the study of their butlers and maids for that of more obliging colonial peoples.

It is only recently, particularly with the revival of interest in European peasant communities, that more thorough anthropological evaluation of British culture has enjoyed a come-back. Operating under the guise of 'local' or 'social' history, many historians have employed ethnographic methods to produce studies markedly similar to those of their anthropological brethren. Although more practically oriented, some sociological studies might also be included in this grouping, and the work of folklorists certainly merits consideration. Awakening to the possibilities, anthropologists are increasingly using their talents to consider British beliefs and institutions — witchcraft, land tenure, domestic relations — not in an attempt to see these as part of a predetermined evolutionary structure, but in the hope of understanding their meaning and import within society.[15]

Wife-selling can be seen as one of a number of 'informal' institutions that existed in British society. This is not to say that it was formless, for it is difficult to imagine any custom, usage or organization bereft of definable features and existing at only a single point in time. Rather, its informality should be taken to imply a state of existence independent of the formal social institutions of the day (such as those of Church and State), as an institution without an externally imposed structure. Many informal institutions are seasonal in nature; others represent patterned responses to certain social problems or crisis points within a society. To some extent, the survival of each indicates successful solution or alleviation of problems or the supplying of some need.

A better overall indication of the prevalence of these informal practices might be given by following an 'average' man or woman through life, from the cradle to the grave. At birth a groaning cheese or cake might have been made and presented to family visitors before the christening to bring luck. The dangers of infant mortality may thus have been felt to be averted, or the sharing of food could have served the more practical purpose of introducing the baby to the community and thus, it was hoped, assuring the child of a place in community growth and good will.[16] A special ritual was used to legitimize bastards, in which the guilty mother stood in a shift or sheet and the boy or girl crawled forth in a symbolic rebirth. This ceremony was considered particularly important because social status and rights of inheritance depended upon the community's conception of legitimacy or illegitimacy.[17] In school 'barring out' was a method of protest or of negotiating holidays with the master. This was particularly common in northern England and Scotland in the seventeenth century and provided an occasion on which rules and promises could be set and become known to both parties.[18] Young unmarried men participated in exercising community value judgments through

rough music, mock punishments and chaffing. Transgressors (of various local norms) who were not considered liable to official court action were ridiculed by the banging of pots and pans, the parading of effigies or the strewing of chaff in front of their residences.[19] Many of these practices show strong similarities to those of the mummers, plough-jaggers, soulers and carollers who appeared on doorsteps at various festive seasons, requesting entertainment and good cheer and issuing the implicit threat of less acceptable action were their perquisites denied.[20]

Love divinations could be social in nature. Winding a clue of yarn, 'sowing' hempseed, baking a 'dumb cake' or washing a sark may have been done not only in an effort to summon the future spouse, but might also have served as excuses for social get-togethers or might have advertised the 'availability' of participants.[21] Other informal institutions were directly connected with the change of state implied by marriage. In barring the way, obstructions were placed in the path of a married couple upon their return from church and were removed only upon payment of a small fee. In addition to representing community acceptance, the practice may have been linked with fertility rites or may have served as a test of chastity. Similar sexual and social significance could underlie flinging the stocking or racing for the bride's garter.[22] If a woman was burdened with past debts, her aspiring suitor could protect himself from potential creditors by staging a smock wedding. This required the bride's attendance at the ceremony in an undergarment, as a literal demonstration that she came to the marriage with only the clothes that she wore on her back.[23]

Several informal institutions occurred throughout adult life. Candle auctions regulated the bidding for various lots by the length of time it took for the taper to extinguish itself or for a nail, set in the tallow, to fall out.[24] Some felt that title to waste or common land might be acquired by erecting a house in one night so that smoke passed through the chimney or a pot boiled on the hearth. Far from being impossible, such action suggested the communal help necessary to assure a popularly recognized title.[25] Right of way could be established by the course of a funeral procession; sometimes pitched battles were fought to prevent the progress of a corpse over disputed land.[26] Summoning was a method used for detection in suspected cases of witchcraft. By boiling or stabbing a bewitched object, it was believed that the witch responsible would be brought running, tortured by similar pains.[27] In addition, most occupations supported their own informal practices. 'Crossing the Line' represented a nautical trade initiation celebrating the sailor's first passage across the equator. Elsewhere apprentices could buy their standing by means of treats or fees, thus gaining the acceptance of fellow workers. Even among agricultural labourers informal organizations existed; in East Anglia the Society of the Horseman's Word seems to have had secret methods for handling horses and boasted an admission ceremony said to involve the acquisition of a magical 'Toad bone' through competition with the Devil.[28]

Death too had its informal institutions. Wakes involving feasting, music and story-telling were common in Ireland, Scotland and Northern England. Showing respect to the deceased, these festivities appear to have represented survivals of ceremonies intended to placate the spirit of the departed. The bleeding of a corpse could indicate a claim's veracity; more often it was used to identify a murderer. Bodies could be arrested for debt, using the respect of survivors to secure payment for outstanding sums, while with sin-eating the deceased individual was symbolically relieved of his worldly transgressions when a scapegoat ate bread or salt placed in a dish on the corpse.[29]

As this brief survey indicates, informal institutions were (and are) far from uncommon in British life and society. Often, these practices show resemblances to other customs or to folk traditions and beliefs, but in almost every case each institution represents a unique solution to some human condition or social problem.

CHAPTER 2

Jumping the Broom — and Back

As an informal institution, wife-selling combined reactions to two crisis points in contemporary social relations: marriage and divorce. Marriage was an institution sanctioned by both Church and State — not only a biological but also a social and economic bonding of the sexes. In addition to providing a basis for the conception and rearing of progeny, marriage often involved transfer of property. Children sired by a married couple had greater rights than illegitimate offspring, while the position of a married woman was more secure than that of a mistress. Lawrence Stone, in his *Family, Sex and Marriage*, argues from the small amount of 'hard evidence' available that

> For the rural or urban smallholder, artisan, tradesman, shopkeeper or common labourer, a wife was an economic necessity, not an emotional luxury, while for a woman a husband was also an economic necessity, to do the heavy work and to provide a subsistence income.

Barring exceptional cases, a woman's control of property passed to her husband after marriage, but the husband was in turn obliged to support his wife or run the risk of being classified as a 'vagrant'.[1]

Despite supposed 'community pressures' on couples to be married, many of the unions in the late eighteenth century were common-law in nature. This appears to have been particularly true when the husband had been previously married, as divorce was normally unavailable. Such common-law liaisons were often associated with soldiers, sailors, the criminal element and other mobile individuals.[2] Several descriptions of common-law ceremonies survive. Christina Hole thus describes the broomstick wedding once used in Wales:

8

A birch-besom was set aslant across the open door, either that of the bride's home or that of the cottage in which the couple were to live. The young man leapt over it into the house, and the girl then did the same. Care had to be taken not to touch the doorpost or the broom, or to move the latter accidentally, otherwise the ceremony was void. It had to be performed in the presence of witnesses, and one person, chosen for his standing and importance in the community, acted as officiant.

In north Wales to say a person has 'jumped over the besom' indicates that he or she has been married (a minor change in nineteenth-century matrimonial law was, in fact, popularly known as the 'Broomstick Marriage Act'). The informal ceremony appears to have been widespread in former times. It was used by navvies; at Woodhead Tunnel Cheshire in 1845 one couple jumped over a broomstick in the presence of a roomful of celebrating men and were officially put to bed. Gypsies practised other variations. A besom was held, with one end on the ground, by one parent, and the boy and girl leapt over it. Or a branch of the plant was placed on the ground, and bride and groom jumped backwards and forwards across it while holding hands. A nineteenth-century songbook claims (in the song 'How to be married; or, Weddings all over the World') that 'A soldier and lassie jump over a sword'. That similar practices were resorted to by American Negro slaves suggests an assimilation of the custom from European immigrants. [3]

Symbolic interpretation of these broomstick weddings is possible. A feminine symbol, the broom or besom, was often thrust up a chimney to indicate the wife's absence or was used to mock a henpecked husband. In some areas to call a woman a besom was a grievous insult, as the term suggested sexual immorality. In Yorkshire 'She's jumped o'er t' besom' or jumping 'o'er t'e besom before she went to t'church' referred to having an illegitimate child, and one Lancashire boy accused of murder swore that the girl in question had come up to him as he was crossing the dyke and had asked him if he would take her as a besom. The care taken in Wales not to touch the broom is better understood in view of a gypsy belief that if the girl's skirt touched the branch when she jumped, she was pregnant or had lost her virginity, while if the man's trousers brushed the implement, he would prove unfaithful. It was general superstition that any girl stepping over a broomstick would conceive before she was wed, and, as a joke, many boys tried to trap unwary maidens into doing this. A medieval analogue is found in the Fourth Branch of the *Mabinogion*:

> She was fetched to him; the maiden came in. 'Maiden,' said he, 'art thou a maiden?' 'I know not but that I am.' Then he took the magic wand and bent it. 'Step over this,' said he, 'and if thou art a maiden, I shall know.' Then she stepped over the magic wand, and with that step she dropped a fine boy-child with rich yellow hair.

The above strongly suggests that broom-jumping may have been originally regarded as a test of virginity.[4]

Perhaps the best known common-law ceremony was handfasting. This normally involved an exchange of promises before witnesses, with a joining of hands by the man and woman involved. Although considered only a prelude to a religious ceremony:

> In remoter areas, especially the Scottish border country, Wales and the extreme south-west, the betrothal ceremony itself, the 'handfast', continued to be treated by many of the poor as sufficient for a binding union without the blessing of the Church.

Such contracts were divided into two groups: those *per verba de praesenti* (in which vows were made in the present tense and were therefore considered binding) or *per verba de futuro* (in which the promise was given to marry at some future time). The latter was considered enforceable only if it was followed by consummation, which may be likened to the 'consideration' required in commercial contracts. Witnesses were normally present to ensure legality and enforcement. As one folksong, 'The Blacksmith', puts it:

> 'What did you promise when you sat beside me?
> You said you would marry me, and not deny me.'
> 'If I said I'd marry you, it was only for to try you,
> So bring your witness love, and I'll never deny you.'

Sadly, in this instance no witness was forthcoming.[5]

In some cases the handfasting took on special trappings of its own. At ceremonies at the Ring of Brodgar the spouses clasped hands through a hole in the Stone of Odin, and a similar practice was observed at Campbeltown, in Kintyre. At Teltown in Co. Meath, the site of a famous fair, marriages were celebrated according to the odd manner following. A number of young men went into the hollow to the north side of the wall, and an equal number of marriageable young women to the south side of the wall which was so high as to prevent them from seeing the men; one of the women put her hand thro' the hole in the gate, and a man took hold of it from the other side, being guided in his choice only by the appearance of the hand. The two who thus joined hands by blind chance were obliged to live together for a year and a day . . .

In several of these cases marriages were for a limited period and could be dissolved by mutual consent.[6]

Since Scottish law required only a witnessed declaration of intent to marry, it held obvious appeal for lovers barred under the more restrictive English code. As a border town, Gretna Green in Dumfries thrived on the business thrown to it by the strictures of the Marriage Act of 1753, and the term 'Gretna Green marriage' acquired a reputation similar to that of 'Las Vegas divorce'. Period prints depict irate fathers pursuing daughters eloping to the Scottish border. Should an amorous couple arrive there safely, they could approach any one of several laymen willing to perform marriages. One officiant alone is estimated to have married almost 8000 people between 1811 and 1839! It was accepted that a certificate witnessing the parties' declaration that they were married sufficed, and these certificates are known to have been printed, with a rough woodblock at the top. The questioning of Mr David Laing, one practitioner, in a court case elicited the following information:

Well, what did you do in this affair? — Why, I was sent for to Linton's, where I found two gentlemen, as it may be, and one lady.
What did you do? — Why, I joined them, and then got the lady's address, where she comes from, and the party's, I believe.

.   .   .   .

In fact, you married them after the usual way? — Yes, yes, I married them after the Scotch form, that is by putting on the ring on the lady's finger, and that way.

.   .   .   .

What else did you do? — I think I told the lady that I generally had a present from 'em, . . .

.   .   .   .

What did the gentleman say to you? — Oh, you ask what did he treat me with.
No, I do not: what did he say to you? — He did nothing to me;

but I did to him, what I have done to so many before, that is, you must know, to join them together; join hands, and so on. . . .

Did you give them a certificate? — Oh, yes, I gave it to the lady.

.   .   .   .

Did the gentleman and lady converse freely with you? — Oh, yes; he asked me what sort of wine they had in Linton's house? and I said they had three kinds, with the best of *Shumpine* (Champagne). He asked me which I would take? and I said *Shumpine*, and so and so; while they went into another room to dine I finished the wine and then off I came. . . . — We have done with you Laing.

The opposing counsel takes over — But my turn is to come with you, my gentleman. What did you get for this job besides the *Shumpine?* Did you get money as well as Shumpine? — Yes, sure I did, so and so.

Well how much? 30l or 40l, or thereabouts as may be. Or 50l as it may be: Mr. Blacksmith? — May be for I cannot say to a few pounds. I am dull of hearing.

In addition, there were other, less frequent forms of popular marriage. A Liverpool couple as late as 1867 could not afford the marriage fees and so knelt together and mixed handfuls of meal in a basin, swearing on the Bible not to part until death. It seems probable that this rite graphically dipicted the union of the two individuals, symbolizing that they would be as commingled as the meal they had mixed. [7]

These common-law forms often coexisted with religious marriages. Stone claims that it was not until the thirteenth century that the Church took control of marriage law, not until 1439 that the ceremony was elevated to a sacrament and not until 1563 that a priest was required (by the Roman Catholic Church) for valid and binding nuptials. The Anglican Church at first clung to medieval forms but gradually came to see a church wedding as the capstone of the union. Although most available information concerns the propertied classes, it seems that the religious marriage could be broken down into a written agreement between the parents; the spousals (or contract) between the man and woman; the proclamation of banns; the church wedding; and consummation. Of these, the spousals have often been considered sufficient in and of themselves, while written agreements were probably entered into only when dower or a settlement were important concerns. Banns were normally called three times in church on successive Sundays or, under the Commonwealth, at the market on three successive market days. Individuals possessing information concerning previous espousals or with other valid objections could forbid the banns, in which case the relevant ecclesiastical court would often hold subsequent investigation. Members of the upper-class could avoid public display by marrying with a special licence, and in some cases of uncertain ecclesiastical jurisdiction both banns and licences were dispensed with. Although wedddings outside hours or away from the local church were illegal by the canons of 1604, these ceremonies were nonetheless considered both valid and binding. [8]

Fleet marriages, held in London in an ecclesiastical 'no-man's-land', avoided the heavy taxes levied on official church weddings. Exploitation often resulted in under-age, drunken or otherwise ill-starred unions. Fortune-hunters were quick to see the advantages of a swift, valid ceremony, which put them beyond the reach of family or indeed of second thoughts on the part of their intended. The practice also encouraged bigamy and false marriages for the purpose of seduction. Practitioners were not above back-dating ceremonies or providing husbands for women in debt or in advanced stages of pregnancy. Simon Place, father of the famous radical and autobiographer, was involved in a long court case instituted by a woman who claimed to have been married to him in such a ceremony. Even more notorious is the story of Richard Leaver, charged with bigamy in 1737:

> he denied all knowledge of the woman claiming to be his wife. After a drunken evening he had awakened to find himself in bed with a stranger; 'Who are you?' demanded Mr Leaver. 'My dear, we were married last night at the Fleet,' was the reply.

Pennant notes:

> In walking along the street in my youth . . . I have often been tempted by the question, 'Sir, will you be pleased to walk in and be married?' Along this most lawless space was hung up the frequent sign of a male and female hand conjoined with 'Marriages performed within' written beneath.

The practitioners often worked in collusion with the owners of local taverns: 'Virtuous', in a letter to *Gentleman's Magazine*, complains about the 'drunken swearing Parsons, with their Mymidons [sic] . . . pulling and forcing People to some pedling [sic] Alehouse or Brandyshop to be married'. Lawyers were sometimes present to draw up the wife's marriage settlement.

Marriages by fraud and force were not confined to London; it was reasonably common to find men compelled to wed women who had sworn a child to them, and one bridegroom was observed to be marched to the altar in handcuffs![9]

These abuses, and the consternation created by eloping heiresses, brought about the Marriage Act of 1753 (Lord Hardwicke's Act) abolishing clandestine marriages in England. Stone notes that before this 'Perhaps not much more than half the population were being married strictly according to the rules of canon law, and of those that were at least half had already entered into full sexual relations.' Lord Hardwicke's Act not only reinforced most of the conditions of the canons of 1604 but also declared that a church wedding took precedence over an espousal; that no one under 21 could marry without consent of parents or guardian; and that marriages contravening these rules would be considered invalid.[10]

General marriage statistics for England are at present sketchy, but Stone notes that many appear to conform to Continental findings based on careful examination. In so far as the scope of the institution is concerned (Stone does not differentiate between types of marriage, but his data probably deal primarily with religious forms), 'marriage was the normal condition, applying to about 90 per cent of the children of the lower middle class, the peasantry and the poor and almost all the male heirs of the rich. It was not universal, however . . .' Stone claims that the lower and middle classes appear to have married remarkably late — at age 26 — 30 for the men and 24 — 7 for the women. While this may have been due in part to employment patterns, it seems likely that one major factor in delay was the necessity to accumulate enough capital to support a separate household. Marriages themselves were short. From data available, it appears that 17 — 19 years was the median duration among the poor, rising to 22 years for the late eighteenth century. Stone suggests that marriages were broken by early death, much as divorce later served to sever such ties. 'Occupational endogamy' among artisans and craftsmen appears to have been at a significant level (1:5), which 'suggests, but does not prove, a correspondingly high level of parental control over both occupation and marriage'. Finally, remarriage was common, accounting for about one quarter of the total number of unions. (This appears to have been more the case for widowers than for widows.)[11]

Bigamous unions occurred not only when a former marriage made subsequent divorce unlikely but also in more spectacular multiple forms. Thus three women, each calling herself a wife of the executed criminal Bryant, claimed his body. One wife charged with bigamy was known to have two husbands, with the possibility of two others, and was cohabiting with a Life Guardsman when she was apprehended. John Penson, a carpenter charged with bigamy, claimed that

> he had separated from his first wife by agreement drawn up by a Clergyman, and she gave him 2l. to get married with — both he and his second wife considered this agreement valid, and she declared he should have Counsel to defend him — . . . . — added, that first wife was living in adultery with the said Clergyman!

Bigamy itself, although liable to ecclesiastical punishment, was not made a civil offence until 1603. Stone notes that it was 'easy and common' and was particularly practised in cases of desertion. [12]

More informal sexual encounters may or may not have been counted as *de facto* marriages, depending upon whether or not they involved other elements, such as economic support or social status. A possibility on the list for inclusion might be prostitution, which was practised in both urban and rural environments. This involved an economic interchange of goods and services as well as the more obvious element of sex. Attributable both to poverty and to the general promiscuity of some social groups, prostitution provided one alternative to formal marriages and represented the total range of some people's sexual activity. [13]

It is much more difficult to deal with the whys and wherefores of divorce, but law offers a few possible clues. In Wales laws of divorce in force between the tenth and the thirteenth centuries gave the following reasons for separation:

(a)   mutual consent of husband and wife;
(b)   adultery or other sexual actions by the wife, the husband's being detected in adultery upon three occasions, the introduction of a strange woman into the house;
(c)   non-fulfilment of the wife's dowry agreement;
(d)   the wife's sexual involvement before marriage;
(e)   the wife's barrenness or husband's impotence;
(f)   (the husband's) leprosy or bad breath;
(g)   a foreign husband's removal from the area (if the wife were Welsh).

In Ireland reasons for divorce included:

(a)   mutual consent of husband and wife;
(b)   immorality of the husband;
(e)   the husband's impotence;
(h)   a husband striking his wife, slandering her or satirizing her;
(i)   repudiation of the wife;
(j)   the husband's becoming, 'unarmed' a priest or 'lawless'.

The laws of King Ethelred, promulgated betwen 976 and 1016, were heavily influenced by the Church and entirely forbade divorce; rather, the Roman Catholic Church allowed the annulment of marriages deemed to have been contracted outside ecclesiastical laws. Reasons for this included:

(d)   adultery with a near relative of the partner before marriage;
(e)   the husband's impotence;
(f)   particular physical disabilities;
(k)   marriage within prohibited degrees of consanguinity, affinity or spiritual relationship;
(l)   pre-contract to another party.

After the Reformation annulment in England could only be obtained for one of three reasons:

(e)   the husband's impotence over a three-year period;
(k)   marriage within prohibited degrees of consanguinity;
(l)   pre-contract to another party;

with the added dispensation that (m) if the spouse had removed and had not been heard of for seven years, he or she could be assumed dead, and the way to a new marriage was open.[14]

Stone argues that the failure of the Church to provide for divorce based on (b), the wife's adultery, and possibly on (h), cruelty, was partially rectified by parliamentary divorce, combining the workings of ecclesiastical and secular courts. This cumbersome mechanism of divorce by Act of Parliament was in its turn replaced by the 1857 Divorce Act, which allowed for divorce by reason of (b), adultery by the wife, incestuous adultery by the husband, bigamy with adultery by the husband, adultery; (h), extreme cruelty by the husband, or adultery; and (m), desertion for at least two years by the husband. A further Matrimonial Causes Act (1878) allowed for separation and maintenance for the wife if the husband was convicted of (h), aggravated assault. The Maintenance of Wives (Desertion) Act, passed in 1886, provided for the maintenance of women by husbands guilty of (m), desertion.[15]

In considering the above data, it is necessary to note certain limitations that inhibit their interpretation. All of these divorce laws are class-conscious to some degree; Acts of Parliament in particular were resorted to only by the rich and powerful few. (Even the 1857 Divorce Act appears to have been considered too costly for use by many people.) Additionally, legal fictions often masked the realities of the situation; laws were self-justifying to the extent that a couple who wished to sever the marriage bond usually applied under a recognized heading rather than advancing their own reasons for the union's failure. The cosmetic divorces of the 1920s, so aptly described in Evelyn Waugh's *A Handful of Dust*, are a comparatively recent manifestation of such pretence. Additionally, it is significant to note the husband's preponderant role in divorce proceedings. Even among the upper classes, where the wife's social position was often strengthened by independent wealth, most actions were instituted by husbands, and the first successful female suit to clear Parliament was in 1801, some 130 years after the divorce procedure had been instituted.[16]

Conclusive evidence is lacking concerning the general causes of divorce among the lower classes, particularly from the wife's point of view. Nevertheless sources do provide insight into various individual causes of divorce. A debt disclaimer published in the *Western Flying Post* suggests incompatibility when it notes that William and Martha Farrant of South Petherton 'have mutually agreed to part'. Other advertisements reveal domestic adulterers such as Eleanor French, who

> hath led a very bad life, and had a child in the absence of her husband, about three years at sea, during which time she had credit, and he wrote her letters three or four times a year; and she hath married a second time . . . to Richard Davis, mariner, under her assertion that the said John French was dead, and now continues to cohabit with the said Richard Davis . . .

or Rebecca, 'The wife of one JOHN GIFFORD, of Wellington, in the County of Somerset, Gent.', who

> lately eloped from me without any reason or provocation whatsoever (but I apprehend through the persuasions and ill advice of some person or persons to serve their own bad and iniquitous designs) carrying off plate and other of my effects.[17]

Further examples of adultery (not necessarily connected with separation and divorce) may be deduced from displays of rough music and the skimmington, two informal institutions serving to express community censure of adulterers. As early as 1618 an armed Wiltshire band of three or four hundred men gathered under the leadership of a horned commander, fired guns, played flutes, blew horns and finally seized the offending woman, threw her into the mud and beat her, intending to lead her away to the cucking-stool. In Bermondsey a petticoat was carried in procession to note the infidelity of the wife of an operative tanner. Rough music was practised on a man on Bladon Feast night about 1925 for much the same reason and, as late as the 1930s, on a Coombe woman suspected of immorality. Wiltshire rustics used the Wooset Hunt, a parade featuring the skull of a horned horse, for a similar purpose. Somerset has several examples of effigies made to ridicule such domestic transgressions, while riding the stang was performed for the same reasons in Yorkshire. The records of ecclesiastical courts, too, yield proof of this strain on family relations. [18]

Evidence of barrenness and impotence is less frequent, although non-consummation of marriage does occur as a cause of complaint in ecclesiastical courts. That it was a worry, however, is suggested by the numerous folk aphrodisiacs recommended in country lore and by the warnings given to women and young marrieds about actions that might bring on barrenness. Reports of suspected bewitchment often include barrenness and impotence as resulting calamities. [19]

Proof of cruelty is furnished by the many examples of chaffing, rough music or stang riding connected with wife- or husband-beating or with more psychological forms of cruelty. Often rhymes were used, such as that connected with the *ceffyl pren* in Tenby, Pembrokeshire:

> Ran-dan-dan:
> Betty Morris has beat her man.
> What was it with?
> 'Twas not with a rake, nor yet with a reel,
> But 'twas with a poker, that made him feel.

Ethel Rudkin recorded several Lincolnshire examples from local informants, while William Barrett gives the following background to a case of 'tinging' he witnessed at Brandon Creek in 1904. This was

> directed against a man whom a local girl had married when she was
> in service in London. The marriage had not been a success, so the

girl had returned to her home, to which she was, after a time, traced by her husband, a heavy drinker. Rumours began to spread that he was ill-treating his wife, who often appeared in the village with a black eye or a cut on her face. Then, one winter's night, he came home drunk, dragged her out of bed and threw her out of the house. Two neighbours dealt with him by administering a good beating and then trussing him up with a rope so that the wife could get back into the house. He was quiet for a time after this; then he started to drink again and to treat his wife more cruelly than before, so that the villagers decided it was time to ting him out.

Two years later, a Cambridgeshire woman, believed to have been responsible for her husband's suicide, was subjected to rough music from the neighbours. Similar treatment was reserved for a Shotover husband whose effigy was paraded about to the banging of tins and periodic speeches about his cruelty.[20]

The frequency of desertion is attested to by the large number of debt disclaimers citing this as a source of grievance. Often desertion had economic implications — Richard Ashford, a feltmonger of Somerton, noted that his wife, Suzannah, 'broke open his boxes, and carried away many things unknown to him, and threatens to run him into debt'. Deserted wives in similar circumstances faced the threat of the workhouse. Nor was such separation always voluntary. Francis Place's brother-in-law, Mat Stimson, was transported for highway robbery: 'After Mat had been gone some months, the young man before mentioned the Printer [a former suitor] again visited my mother, then courted my sister and at length married her. . . .' Another acquaintance, James Powell, 'had been married to a woman of the town who had left him and he was now living with a young woman at a small house near Battle Bridge'. Nor does Place appear to consider such cases exceptional. Not surprisingly, therefore, it was widespread belief that seven years' absence freed a husband or wife to remarry.[21]

Incompatibility, adultery, barrenness, cruelty and desertion, then, were major areas of marital difficulty. They involved emotional, physical and economic hardship, and any practice likely to alleviate such problems would have held a certain attraction for members of the community thus affected. Divorce, in any of its forms, could have rectified incompatible marriages, allowing each partner the option of a single life or of a new relationship with someone else. Adultery was not as simple ; but divorce could permit betrayed husbands to cease supporting women who were intimate with other men, enable betrayed wives to remove themselves from an emotionally harrowing position and give guilty parties of both sexes an opportunity to form new relationships with their lovers. The termination of barren unions could be followed by the redeployment of the fertile partner. Cruelty, too, was eased by the physical separation of incompatible spouses. Divorce could formalize the position of deserted husbands and wives, allowing the former to relinquish the responsibility to support their spouses and allowing the latter economic independence or the opportunity to arrange for alternative sources of assistance. Divorce in all its forms was more than a mere means of freeing the participants from present evils; it permitted the parties involved to form new associations, with all the benefits that these were traditionally supposed to bring. Considered in its widest aspect, divorce can thus be held to have included any action or practice leading to the separation of two individuals who lived together as man and wife.

One form of informal divorce was associated with broomstick marriages in Wales. Such a union was sundered by the exact reversal of the form used for marriage. If divorce was desired and twelve months had not elapsed, a broom was again placed in the doorway in the presence of witnesses. The dissatisfied person then jumped backwards over the besom into the open air, making sure neither broom nor door jamb was touched in the process. Or as a nineteenth-century song puts it:

> So let us be married, my Mary!
> If ever dislike be our lot,
> We jump'd o'er the broom, then an airy
> Jump back shall unfasten the knot. [22]

The Scottish-Irish practice of 'handfasting' through a holed stone had several antidotes. In the Orkneys parties desiring a sundering went to church near the Ring of Brodgar, and left through separate doors after the service. A quarrelling couple at Gretna Green were told that they might separate in a similar manner. A. D. Hope notes:

> At Teltown marriages were arranged for a year and could then be dissolved, according to some accounts, by the parties climbing one or both of two adjacent mounds and turning their backs on each other. They could then marry again . . . .

Still another account speaks of spouses leaving through separate entrances of a fort. In each of these cases the couple symbolized its separation by a public and physical cleavage. A further Teltown report mentions only a 'deed of separation'. A completely different procedure for dissolving handfast unions occurs in a 1791 account of the Kintyre region's history:

> [St] Coivin . . . proposed that all who did not find themsleves happy and contented in the married state should be indulged with the opportunity of parting, and making a second choice. For that purpose he initiated an annual solemnity, at which all the unhappy couples in his parish were to assemble at his church; and, at midnight, all present were sufficiently blindfolded, and ordered to surround the church three times at full speed with a view of *mixing the lots in the urn.* The moment the ceremony was over, without allowing an instant to recover from the confusion, the word *cabhag* (seize quickly) was pronounced; upon which every man laid hold of the first female he met with, whether young or old, handsome or ugly, good or bad, she was his wife till the next anniversary return of the solemnity . . . .

This resembles not only the reputed orgies of the early Christians (and later, of pagans and witches), but also the 'Paul Jones' of ballroom dancing, and 'Sadie Hawkins Day' festivities in the United States. [23]

Other accounts of handfasting divorces survive, without specifics. At an annual fair in Eskdalemuir, Dumfries, partners were chosen for the year by the unmarried. The following year at the fair

> If they were pleased with each other at that time they continued together for life; if not, they separated, and were free to make another choice as at the first. The fruit of their connection (if there were any) was always attached to the disaffected person.

According to Martin Martin's account of Skye in the seventeenth century:

> It was an ancient custom in the islands that a man should take a maid to his wife, and keep her the space of a year without marrying her . . . if he did not love her, he returned her to her parents, and her portion also; and if there happened to be any children, they were kept by the father: but this unreasonable custom was long ago brought into disuse.

A. D. Hope notes that this was not quite the case; the 'War of the One-Eyed Woman' (*Cogadh na Cailliche Cairne*) was provoked when the Chief of the MacDonalds returned his handfasted

Macleod bride (who had lost the sight of her eye during the year) on a one-eyed horse and accompanied by a one-eyed dog and groom. [24]

Yet a third type of symbolic break was practised: a wife was freed from her husband by the removal and return of her wedding ring. In some cases, this appears to have extended to loss of the ring as well. In the neighbourhood of Exeter,

> At a Court-leet dinner . . . a few days since, a rather novel discovery was made. The party having disposed of the roast beef, and other parts of old English fare, plum pudding, was introduced, and, on cutting it into slices, it was found to contain that invaluable gem, a *wedding ring*! 'Mine host' was called; and on being informed of the circumstances, began dancing about the room to the astonishment of his guests. The thought, quick as lightning, rushed on the old man's imagination, that his wife had lost the hymenal lock, and he was free to marry a young wife. The amusement this adventure produced among the company may easily be conceived; but the veteran ceased to caper when he found he was mistaken, and must, in spite of this, cleave to his old rib still.

Such a belief was closely related to the esteem in which wedding rings were held. Not only were they used in divinations and cures, but they were also believed to reflect accurately the present or future condition of the relationship. Hackwood reports that in the Black Country of Staffordshire

> a married woman should never remove her wedding ring from her finger, or it is believed she will be in danger of losing her chastity. If she loses or breaks her wedding ring, it must at once be replaced, and her husband must put it on her finger.

Hole notes that in many parts of the British Isles the loss or breakage of a ring foretells the end of the marriage through death, loss of affection or some other cause. To drop the ring before or during the wedding service was believed to bring death to the clumsy party. Elsewhere omens were bad if the circlet rolled away from the altar, the bride's demise being predicted if it came to rest on a man's tomb, the groom's if it settled on the grave of a woman. [25]

Finally, there was a general belief that a seven-year separation 'broke' the marriage contract and that subsequent remarriage was allowable. In at least one parish, where the death of a former spouse could not be proved, it was believed acceptable to have the bell tolled, as if for the death of the missing person, before the new marriage took place.[26]

Initially, religious 'divorces' seem to have been easy to obtain. A poem dating from the period of Edward II runs:

> If a man have a wyf,
> And he love her nowt,
> Bring her to the constery,
> There trewth schuld be wrowt.
> Bring twei fals wytnes with hym,
> And hymself the thrydde,
> And he shall be deperted,
> As fair as he wold bydde,
> From his wyf. . . .

Such 'divorces' were generally nothing more than annulments. The Roman Catholic Church (and the Anglican Church, for that matter) recognized marriage as an indissoluble contract between husband and wife. When faced with the realities of life, the Church differentiated between 'real' and 'spurious' wedlock; any union falling into the latter category for which dispensation had not been received was no *true* marriage, and the Church not only encouraged but required its 'dissolution'. Therefore it was necessary for those desiring divorce to appear before a bishop's consistory court and to apply for an annulment on one of several grounds. Evidence such as the above poem suggests that on at least some occasions perjury was committed to ensure separations. The Council of Clermont specifically denounced the number of annulments which enabled errant husbands to marry other men's wives. For those whose marriages had broken down, but who could not claim annulment (usually because of adultery by one or both parties), there was only separation *a mensa et thoro*, by which a financial settlement allowed the parties to live apart but not to remarry. The Reformation retained this separation but narrowed the grounds for annulment. In this movement the Anglican Church is noteworthy as the only major Protestant denomination to retain, virtually intact, medieval laws concerning marriage and divorce.[24]

Although it was the religion of a numerically small segment of the population, Judaism provides an interesting period contrast to Catholic and Anglican practices:

> The process for obtaining a *divorce* according to the laws of

England is bothe [sic] tedious and expensive. Matters of this kind
are settled among the Jews in a summary way. The parties go into
the synagogue, each attended by two priests, and having stated
their objection to each other, the woman is asked if she be willing
to part with her husband? and on answering in the affirmative,
They spit in each other's faces; The man throws the bill of
divorcement at his wife, and she receives it; upon which they
jointly exclaim, 'cursed be they who shall bring us together again.'
Thus the business concludes. [28]

As early as the fourteenth century attempts were made to treat
divorce as a secular matter. Sir John de Camoys, whose wife had
eloped with Sir William Paynell, granted his spouse to the latter
with her goods and chattels. This quit-claim was done by charter
and was subsequently cited when the two married after Camoys's
death and claimed dowry out of Sir John's estate. The deed,
however, was considered to be no excuse for their adultery, and
judgment was given against this couple. [29]

Out of the difficulties involved in obtaining an ecclesiastical
divorce that permitted remarriage arose secular divorce by Act of
Parliament. Stone notes that this development was designed to
avoid the problem 'that a nobleman whose wife committed
adultery before producing a son was precluded from marrying
again and begetting a legal heir to carry on the line and inherit the
property'. Initially at least, the injured husband was required to
obtain a decree of separation in an ecclesiastical court and to win
an action for misconduct in a secular court of law before initiating
successful parliamentary proceedings. Later, the Lords Halifax and
Rochester protested a decision in which the Earl of Macclesfield
managed to abbreviate the process:

> Dissentient, — Because we conceive that this is the first bill of that
> nature that hath passed, when there was not a divorce first
> obtained in the Spiritual Court; which we look upon as an ill
> precedent, and may be of dangerous consequence in the future.

Their words were prophetic. Despite the expense involved —
sometimes amounting to thousands of pounds — the number of
private Bills of this sort gradually increased. Stone notes that the
procedure

> was almost entirely confined, especially before 1760, to those who
> had very large properties at stake to be handed on to a male heir by
> a second marriage. Between 1670 and 1799, there were only one

hundred and thirty-one such Acts, virtually all instituted by husbands, and only seventeen passed before 1750 . . . .

This means that between 1750 and 1799 114 Acts were passed, and between 1800 and 1857 203, almost double the number.[30]

By the mid-nineteenth century, however, the unfairness of this approach for the bulk of the population had become apparent. Most people were too poor to avail themselves of an Act of Parliament. The judge hearing the bigamy case of William Hawes at the Oxfordshire Assizes for 1855 noted:

this was one of those cases which showed the present defective state of the law, for although the prisoner's wife had proved unfaithful to him, and cohabited with another man for 16 years, he could not obtain a divorce, or get the marriage annulled, without obtaining from the Ecclesiastical Court a divorce *a mensa et thoro*, getting a bill through the House of Lords, obtaining the assent of the House of Commons to it, and, lastly getting her Majesty's assent to it. It was absurd to suppose that a man in the position of life like the prisoner could avail himself of such proceedings, and the consequence was that, owing to the enormous expense of obtaining a divorce, it amounted to an absolute denial of relief to the mass of society, and, from the circumstance, divorce bills had improperly been called the privilege of the rich . . . .

The prisoner was sentenced to one week's hard labour. Other similar judgments were made at this time, the most famous of which was Justice Maule's address to a bigamous hawker:

I will tell you what you ought to have done under the circumstances, and if you say you did not know, I must tell you that the law conclusively presumes that you did. You should have instructed your attorney to bring an action against the seducer of your wife for damages; that would have cost you about £100. Having proceeded thus far, you should have employed a proctor and instituted a suit in the Ecclesiastical Courts for a divorce *a mensa et thoro*; that would have cost you £200 or £300 more. When you had obtained a divorce *a mensa et thoro*, you had only to obtain a private Act for divorce *a vinculo matrimonii*. The Bill might possibly have been opposed in all its stages in both Houses of Parliament, and altogether these proceedings would cost you £1000. You will probably tell me that you never had a tenth of that sum, but that makes no difference. Sitting here as an English judge it is my duty to tell you that this is not a country in which there is one law for the rich and another for the poor. You will be imprisoned for one day.

A Royal Commission Report in 1853 saw many of the same problems and eventually resulted in the Matrimonial Causes Act of 1857. This Act established a secular Divorce Court, which took over those powers formerly ascribed to the ecclesiastical courts and to Parliament. [31]

A dramatic increase took place in the number of people who took advantage of secular divorce. Nonetheless, this group was probably small when compared to the total number of potential litigants. Again, expense was probably at least partially to blame. Henry Fenn gives the average cost of a suit as £30 and notes that 'many a hard-working man with a small salary has for years saved up the sum rather than support a faithless wife.' Counterbalancing this is his statement that

> people with no money can get a divorce. They can go to the Divorce Registry, Somerset House, and take out proceedings *in forms pauperia*, swearing that their income is something less than £50 a year, the Court fees being dispensed with.

One can only assume, therefore, that the major bar to the use of this method of divorce by all incompatible couples was their ignorance of the proper procedure. [32]

Other actions, although not constituting official divorce or separation, served a similar purpose in the break-up of family units. Bigamy has already been mentioned in the discussion of marriages; in addition to this crime's position as a *de facto* (albeit illegal) form of cohabitation, it represented a method of divorce, as it implied married men's separation from their first wives. Elopement was also popular, to judge by the numerous debt disclaimers published by forsaken husbands and the notices of absconding household heads inserted into newspapers by parish officers. At times this seems to have reached almost epidemic proportions:

> WHOLESALE DESERTION OF WIVES AND FAMILIES —
> On Friday the parochial authorities of St Luke's, and St Leonard's, Shoreditch, issued descriptions and rewards for the apprehension of 54 men, charged with deserting their wives and families, leaving no fewer than 217 individuals a burthen to those parishes, the men are described as good mechanics, and able to earn from 25s to 30s per week.

While many such decampings may have been economically

motivated, there is no doubt that little love was lost between many separated couples.

> A man of the county of Hereford advertises a *mare* that has strayed from him, for the recovery of which he offers a reward of five guineas; in the concluding part of the same advertisement he adds, by way of N.B., that his *wife* eloped from him on the following day, for the discovery of whom he offers a reward of *five shillings*.

Nor was this an extreme; a husband advertising for his eloped wife promised the lucky finder 'so obliging as to bring her back to her husband the first night's lodging with her in his house'. Stone notes:

> In a society without a national police force, it was all too easy simply to run away and never be heard of again. This must have been a not infrequent occurrence among the poor, to judge by the fact that deserted wives comprised over eight per cent of all the women aged between thirty-one and forty listed in the 1570 census of the indigent poor of the city of Norwich.

As late as the nineteenth century it was easy enough to arrange a disappearance. George Herbert has this to say of a Banbury neighbour, George Claridge:

> George got married, but his was a very unhappy life which he led with his wife, and at last he bolted from her and no one knew what had become of him. But some years after, I was on an excursion to Bath, and the train stopped at a small station not far from Bath, and who should walk into the station but George Claridge. I did not speak to him . . . and that was the last I ever heard of him.

However, desertion entailed abandonment of one's community, friends and possessions. If a man left his property at home, he impoverished himself, but any man who removed it could be declared a vagrant by the law and was liable for support payments when found. For a woman the charge for such action could be theft.[33]

As has been indicated, deserted wives and children usually became community charges, often ending up in the parish workhouse. These buildings, along with prisons, often served as agents of informal divorce because of their segregation of inmates by sex. Another *de facto* method of securing separation was through military and naval recruitment and the press gang. Although the army occasionally made provision for transporting some men's wives with the force's baggage to assist in nursing and other chores, the wide range of locales to which troops might be called, and the possibility of immediate transfer, encouraged temporary liaisons and made the armed forces an easy place for an errant husband to hide. Transportation of convicts served the same purpose, as the location (first America and later Australia), the length of sentences and the penalties for illegal return made it unlikely that couples thus separated would reunite. Of course, a more drastic method of *de facto* divorce was murder, and outright gift, although it does not appear to have been too common, is also found. Wright reports that 'In 1919 a woman coolly stated to the Tottenham magistrates that her husband had given her away to another man.' Paynell's quit-claim may also fall into this group. [34]

Diametrically opposed to gift, and embracing the problems of marriage and divorce in wife-selling, was the concept of contract. A contract is now considered to be any agreement concerning goods or services entered into by two or more parties that is enforceable by law. In England there was no general law of contract until the seventeenth century, and even after this date many contractual rules were based on tradition. In general, the two major requirements for validity were considered to be mutual assent by the parties involved and free choice, unhampered by externals. The first of these was judged by objective rather than subjective grounds; hence the preference for 'evidentiary' acts of offering or acceptance for which there could be testamentary proof. Often these actions were ritual in nature. In land law, for instance, symbolic activities, such as livery of seisin or beating the bounds, were used to establish ownership or possession. The same is true of the delivery requirement in a sale of goods, as, for instance, when an animal's halter was exchanged. In contracting for services, hired men or women accepted consideration, a 'fasten- penny', while army recruits took the 'King's shilling'. [35] In these examples free will was implied, fulfilling the other necessary rule for validity. This explains the presence of many mercantile transactions in the marketplace ('market ouvert') which accelerated the granting of title and provided an acceptable proof of ownership. Similarly, sale to the highest bidder represented straight, unrestricted dealing, as the transaction was open to public scrutiny, with witnesses, a receipt or a deed often providing proof of transfer. [36]

While the above proofs of possession and transfer were

primarily community symbols, other practices symbolized the validity of the agreement for the participants themselves. The ratifying drink was one such gesture, reaching beyond economic implications of contract to what Atiyah terms the 'moral factor'. Drinking was a gesture of friendship, a drinking companion traditionally a close friend, a person in whose company one felt comfortable. To accept a drink showed acceptance of the giver — for example, in an eighteenth-century trial involving a prosecution for riot the defence attempted to deride the prosecution's charge by proving that rioters and victim had been seen having a drink together and had shaken hands after the incident. The handshake was also a gesture of greeting, but more than that, it was one of acknowledgement and equality. It showed that there were no hard feelings (as when prize-fighters shook hands after a match), while a refusal to shake hands indicated bitterness or imagined inequality, whether it was social or moral. 'Shaking' was also a traditional form of assent, indicating agreement, as in, 'Here's my hand on it'. Another practice, 'luck money', involved the return of part of the purchase price. This took some of the commercialism out of the transaction; as a gift, 'luck money' had some of the special connotations mentioned by Marcel Mauss in his work *Essai sur le don*. Whatever else it meant, a gift usually implied friendship or good will and signalled that the participants shared more in common than a simple exchange of goods.[37]

More pragmatically, drink and 'luck money' were symbols of compromise and agreement, as they often made the difference between a selling and a buying price. E. P. Thompson notes the importance of this mixture of economic bargaining and tradition to members of the English working class, who: 'saw their wages as regulated by custom or by their own bargaining. They expected to buy their provisions in the open market, and even in times of shortage they expected prices to be regulated by custom also.' Thus most everyday contracts involved an intricate mixing of ritual and realism. While there are many legal methods of classifying contracts, the separation most applicable seems to be a simple one of purpose whether the agreements relate to goods or services. Particularly noteworthy among the former group are slave sales and livestock sales. Service contracts included the rental of husbands, the hiring of servants, military enlistment and indentured servitude, and apprenticeship. There is evidence of at least one contract (declared illegal in court) in which a husband promised to marry a woman upon the death or divorce of his wife, and many legal actions formerly dealt with breach of promise. Marriage itself was a contract, although an agreement ambiguous as to purpose. The relation of these agreements to wife sales will be considered in chapters 9 and 10. [38]

CHAPTER 3
Markets, 'Mops' and Middlemen

The sale of wives by their husbands has a sporadic but worldwide distribution. Instances of the practice are known from Italy and from as far afield as Ethiopia and China. However, there is no concrete evidence that any of these influenced, or were influenced by, the British informal institution. [1]

Within the British Isles, wife-selling has fairly well-defined limits. In the eleventh century ecclesiastical complaints indicate that the practice was found among the Scots. Sixteenth-century examples are found in London, Hertfordshire and Essex, and in the seventeenth century, in Oxfordshire, Warwickshire, Staffordshire and as far north as lowland Scotland. By the later eighteenth century cases spanned England, from Northumberland in the north to Sussex in the south and from the east coast to Cheshire and eastern Ireland. Wales and even western France provide nineteenth-century examples, but by the late 1880s the institution seems to have been confined largely, although not exclusively, to the industrialized north of England. [2]

Early English examples appear to come from urbanized or semi-urbanized areas. This connection may be of importance, but could as easily be the result of more complete records, intensive research or better news coverage. [3] In any case, by the period 1750−1800 wife-selling seems to have been firmly established in the towns and cities of south-eastern, central and northern England.

Contemporary accounts, unfortunately, are often of little use in determining distribution; a statement that the institution is 'rare' cannot always be accepted at face value. Newspapers, then as now, frequently printed what their readers wanted to hear and sources were not as well-informed as they could have been. The Truro Quarter Sessions of 1820, for example, claimed that, 'though the practice [of wife-selling] was not infrequent in other counties, it had but seldom occurred in Cornwall, and that only within the past two years.' In an 1828 petty session held at Five Lanes, Cornwall, however, it appears, that the accused had sold his wife some sixteen years before in about 1812. Another writer notes that the institution is absent from Lancashire, but case evidence totally refutes his testimony.[4]

Any discussion of English wife-sale locations must consider the institution's decline, which commenced in about 1850. This is indicated not so much by a drop in the number of cases as by a contracting range. From about 1880—1900 fewer locales report English cases, with most examples hailing from Yorkshire. Perhaps this was due to the tenacity with which Yorkshiremen are said to cling to old ways, this area and London's East End being noted for their insular societies. Both Smithfield Market in London and the city of Sheffield are particularly associated with the institution.[5]

Few Welsh cases have been reported; pre-industrial Wales differed in many ways from England of the same period. There was a lack of urbanized centres so that individuals wishing a divorce needed to cater only for local opinion. In at least some parts of Wales the old Celtic idea of temporary marriages still prevailed, making divorce the easiest thing in the world and a sale an unnecessary formality. Why, then, did any Welsh sales occur? A manuscript purporting to tell of a sale at Llan-y-bydder fair can be questioned on the ground of internal inconsistencies. All other cases occur in industrialized or urbanized areas located on the Welsh borders, areas susceptible to English influence. Caerleon, for example, abuts on the Usk and is near Newport; Cardiff is a port city; Knighton, near Hereford, is on the Welsh border and Merthyr Tydfil was an industrial complex in Glamorganshire, devoted to the production of iron.[6] In such towns it may have been necessary that divorce be formalized to be respected by the citizenry and by members of the work force. The English-derived wife sale may have provided a suitable method.

Scotland is a region sparse in wife sales, a fact attributable to several causes. In some parts, especially the Highlands, Celtic attitudes towards temporary marriage survived. Then, too, the Scots (at least before the advent of John Knox) were known for their free-and-easy ideas about adultery and cohabitation, which dispensed with one of the rationales for wife-selling. Even after the Act of Union Scotland operated under its own legal system, which

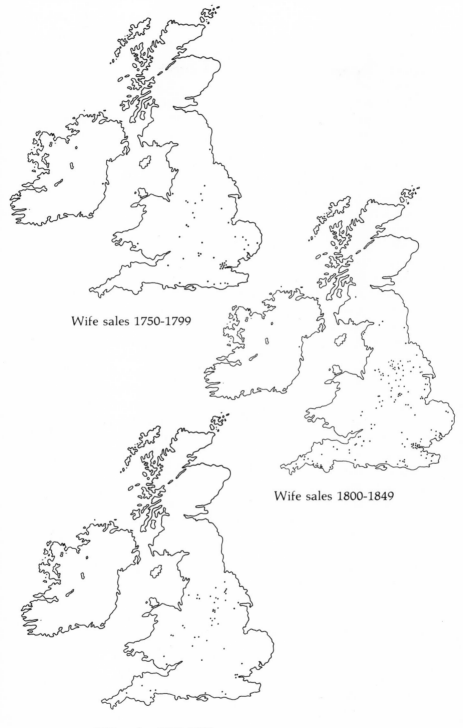

Wife sales 1750-1799

Wife sales 1800-1849

Wife sales 1850-1899

took a more accommodating attitude towards family law. Additionally, a number of Scots, practising Roman Catholics, were members of a Church that tolerated divorce only in very restricted circumstances. The rural examples of wife-selling come from intensively settled parts of lowland Scotland, where Celtic influence was relatively weak. The motive for such sales was apparently straightforward economics, as the prices given appear to have been fairly large. Records indicate that offenders were Anglican or Presbyterian rather than Roman Catholic. Other Scottish cases are found in major urban areas, such as New Sneddon (near Glasgow) and Edinburgh, where English influence might be expected. [7]

Again, Catholicism probably helps to explain why so few Irish examples of wife-selling exist. Despite continuous English hegemony since the Reformation, the bulk of the Irish people remained true to their faith. In 1756 a sale is mentioned in Co. Dublin, while in 1882 another occurred at Belfast in Co. Antrim. Both of these, however, were in urbanized areas adjacent to seaports: the English custom might have been adopted through normal trade contacts, through the return of Irish labourers from England or through other English influence. [8]

Out of place as France might at first seem in a study of a British informal institution, it has relevance because cultural beliefs and institutions do not always respect political boundaries. Despite the influence of Catholicism, scattered records of wife sales in western France do exist. The rural nature of many locations suggests that these sales may be remnants of a French form of the custom, peripherally related to the British institution. That wife-selling was popularly regarded as foreign, however, is evidenced by widespread French commentary on the action as peculiarly English. [9]

Most identifiable locations of wife sales in the eighteenth and early nineteenth centuries seem to have been markets and fairs. Sometimes sales were linked with a market cross, the market house or a nearby inn. Later, particularly from the nineteenth century onwards, wife-selling became closely associated with inns, and eventually inns appear to have replaced markets as preferred locales. All of these locations were used by the general public and served as centres for commercial transactions. [10]

Use of other sites often appears to have been connected with markets and inns. The town hall mentioned in a Knighton sale seems to have been located in the marketplace; the public quay used for a Dartmouth transaction was a nautical mercantile equivalent. Streets are cited as locations for several sales, and in some cases these probably fronted inns. Strategically positioned open spaces were also resorted to. Some records of the institution report homes or lodging houses as sites of sale, while a possible twentieth-century case from Scotland even notes an agreement entered into at a tea shop! Rural locations are almost completely lacking, except where these could guarantee the transaction's public nature. A Norfolk farmer is reported to have led his wife to the highway's verge to be sold, and the tinker who supposedly disposed of his sweetheart on Brough Hill probably did so at the time of the local horse fair. [11]

Dwarfing all other considerations of market use is the economic factor. Markets provided a forum for the exchange of goods and, to a lesser degree, of services. Within each area the market was a focus of commercial activity, particularly for bulky or perishable commodities; this provided the seller with an extended public interested in his or her goods and allowed the buyer to shop competitively. Contract, sale or purchase in open market was usually considered to constitute reasonable proof of title. Often market agreements involved the actual recording of transactions in books kept in some local inn.

Social aspects of markets complemented their economic role. As centres of activity, markets were useful for the transfer of news and ideas; the market cross was a central place used for the reading of banns and proclamations. Here, too, petty criminals were punished publicly. Markets served as a milieu in which urban and rural met, allowing contact between otherwise isolated segments of the population. Additionally, there is some evidence that for some market day may have had sexual connotations. One Wiltshire tradition mentions a town prostitute who numbered farmers come up for market as an important part of her clientele. [12]

Markets were also a centre for sport and ritual. Bull-baiting is said to have been practised at Mottram Cross in Cheshire, while the corn market at Leominster and Beverley marketplace were both connected with this sport. Football was popular in the markets of Barnet, Bolton, Kingston-upon-Thames and Derby. Special ceremonies might also be connected with these areas. In Congleton, on Lammas Day, 'At the Market Cross a travesty of the old religious call to prayer was given. The sweeps urged everyone to drink as much strong ale as they could during the holiday.' In Staffordshire, a mock mayor procession at Newcastle-under-Lyme involved the collection of contributions for an evening celebration held at a similar location. [13]

A large number of sales (at least twenty) were concluded at London's Smithfield Market from the 1790s to the 1830s, which partially explains why this location was so strongly connected with wife-selling. That several markets in a single area or even in a single town were used for conducting such business suggests that any market would do for the transfer of a wife. Livestock markets seem to have been preferred, although this is probably a consequence of the sales' close connections with livestock dealings. Markets are specified as centres for wife sales as early as the 1790s but appear not to have lasted in this role much beyond the early 1870s. During the interim period markets were preferred for a preponderance of wife sales; in one case it was even deemed newsworthy to note that the sale had *not* taken place at such a site. Additionally, markets were often believed to confer legality. One Somerset sale was deemed invalid because it had not taken place in open market, while a Yorkshire woman feared her purchase would not be considered legal for a similar reason. That this legality was not dependent upon the use of traditional locations is demonstrated by sales known to have taken place at new markets. There was a sale at Bristol's Temple Meads market on opening day; another, four months after the start of Islington market; a third, in the 'new' market at Oxford. [14]

Several cases called on the services of butchers or drovers as auctioneers. In others these tradesmen were the sellers or purchasers. Apart from wife-selling's similarity to cattle sales, the market was a logical location for the institution. It was easily accessible to the ordinary husband, who needed only to obey market rules by paying a toll, renting a pen, hiring an auctioneer and so on. As the market was a place of fair and open dealing, claims of irregularity or of collusion could more easily be refuted. Often the toll book was held to provide a duly authenticated record of a transfer's validity. Markets offered a wide clientele, many of whom might have been unaware of a woman's bad qualities or reputation. Further, people who attended markets were in the mood to buy and often had the wherewithal in hand to do so. Transactions could be completed on the spot. Finally, up to a point, the market could provide necessary cover for illegal transactions. Although ostensibly a public place, it could provide cover for someone anxious to avoid authority by losing himself in a sympathetic crowd.[15]

Within the market several points appear to have attracted wife sales. These include market crosses, market houses and inns. Surprisingly, the first two categories appear to have been partially interchangeable, perhaps because of the protection or replacement of some crosses by buildings.

Market crosses appear as wife sale sites as early as 1801 and continue as late as 1862, generally, although not exclusively, in central and northern England. Set on a raised base or a series of steps, such crosses provided a useful location from which to conduct bidding so that seller and lot alike could command the attention of the passer-by, a distinct psychological advantage. That such public display was often part of the sales pitch is suggested by cases in which use was made of chairs, barrels and tables to raise participants above the crowd. The connection of market crosses with speeches and with the reading of banns has already been mentioned. The religious associations of such a location might, in some cases, have provided for these sales authentication as effective in its way as an oath taken on the Bible. Market houses, although less common as sales sites, provided a similar focal point for transactions.[16]

Inns played an important role in many market sales. In addition to providing an easy meeting place for such transactions, some inns housed market books in which sales were duly entered. And, luckily, they could also supply the ratifying drink that many considered necessary to clinch the bargain! While market inns were involved in transactions at an early date, it was not until much later that the inn itself took over as the normal locale for wife sales.[17]

Fairs are closely related to markets and may often have been classified as such. A Horsham sale in 1825, for instance, is reported by two newspapers as having occurred in the market place, but Harry Burstow, a contemporary, adds the fact that the sale took place during the November Fair. In general, fairs were held less frequently than markets but appear to have drawn their goods and clientele from a much larger area and to have been considered important events in the social calendar. Thus the economic and social advantages of a market would have been magnified at fairs. Professor Robert Malcolmson notes:

The majority of these fairs were primarily concerned with commercial functions — there were horse fairs, cattle fairs, sheep or hog fairs, cheese fairs, fairs for hardware, or leather, or general merchandise; but a good many of them were also treated as pleasure fairs, and in a few cases pleasure provided their main rationale. [18]

A very important group of fairs, known as 'mops', served as centres at which servants were hired for the coming year. In addition to the various commercial purposes of these gatherings, many booths or stalls dealt in food and drink, provided variety entertainment or sold trinkets that have come to be known as 'fairings'. Fair advertisements frequently emphasized competitions — smock races were a favourite, but there was also wrestling, singlestick matches and 'girning' for the aspiring participant. [19] Such gatherings were not restricted to a single time of year:

fairs were intimately involved in the seasonal rhythms of agricultural life . . . . In many instances they were fitted into the cycles of agricultural labour at times of convenience, during those intervals between the completion of one set of tasks and the beginning of another.

Particularly popular were late spring, early summer (especially Easter and Whitsuntide) and autumn (Michaelmas). [20]

A large proportion of fair visitors, particularly at the hiring 'mops', were single youths and girls. Their visit to the fair gave them an unusual opportunity to meet or perhaps to renew acquaintance — a fact of some importance because most young people were tied down to their jobs (whether they were hired or apprenticed) and lacked unrestricted free time. It is noteworthy that evidence exists for servants playing truant when a nearby fair or wake was in the offing, a state of affairs that was generally accepted by most masters and resulted only in the docking of pay. Both sexes dressed up for the occasion, which was an opportunity to parade in their best clothes and to indulge in a limited form of conspicuous consumption with whatever money they had saved. Dancing formed a major attraction at such gatherings; John Housman notes in Cumberland that 'It is customary for all the young people in the neighbourhood to assemble and dance at the inns and alehouses,' and goes on:

[as] fiddlers [are] tuning their fiddles in public houses, the girls begin to file off, and gently pace the streets, with a view of gaining

admirers; while the young men . . . follow after, and having eyed the *lasses*, pick up each a sweetheart, whom they conduct to a dancing room, and treat with punch and cake.[21]

A description of a hiring 'mop' suggests much the same pattern of activity:

> When the business of the day is pretty well over, the amusement begins. The public houses, and even some of the better sort of hotels, have laid out their largest rooms with long tables and forms, for the entertainment of the multitude. It becomes the recognized duty of the lads to bring in the lasses from the streets, and give them refreshments at these tables. Great heartiness and mirth prevail. Some gallant youths, having done their duty to one damsel, will plunge down into the street, seize another with little ceremony, and bring her in also. A dance in another apartment concludes the day's enjoyments.

A Birmingham writer in 1827 notes in corroboration that towards evening couples at such fairs met and proceeded together to the public house, while an eighteenth-century account makes passing reference to 'country Beauties and their sweethearts enjoying themselves at the fruit stalls and mountebank's stage' and to fairs 'full of Beaux and Belles before dinner'.[22]

With the mixed crowds and holiday atmosphere, the relaxing of parental or employer restraints, the consumption of liquor and the stimulus of dancing, it is hardly surprising that sexual encounters took place on these occasions and that fairs developed a reputation for licentiousness. This connection is widely celebrated in English literature, as is evidenced by the many ballads that set fairs as the scene for amorous encounters.

> The farmer from Fiddlington, true as my life,
> He's come to the fair to look for a wife.
> O Master John, do you beware!
> And don't go kissing the girls at Bridgewater Fair.[23]

Ben Jonson fixes Bartholomew Fair as a backdrop for his study in lechery and hypocrisy. In *The Country Lasses*, a later comedy, the character Heartwell receives a warning against marrying a country girl: 'ten to one but some Sinewy Thresher . . . has warm'd her brisk Blood at a Mop . . . .' Henry Fielding, in *Joseph Andrews*, notes that Betty, the chambermaid, had been 'long deaf to all the sufferings of her lovers till one day, at a neighbouring fair, the rhetoric of John the hostler, with a new straw hat and a pint of wine, made a second conquest of her'.[24]

Nor was this sexual connection restricted to the minds of the literati; studies at Bromley, Kent, show a yearly bulge in the number of bastard births — nine months after the spring fair. Daniel Defoe reports of the Charlton Horn Fair:

> The mob indeed at that time take all kinds of liberties, and the women are especially impudent for that day; as if it was a day that justify'd the giving of themselves a loose to all manner of indecency and immodesty, without any reproach, or without suffering the censure which such behaviour would deserve at another time.

Hiring fairs were often particularly suspect. The *Gentleman's Magazine* for 1805 noted that at the Axbridge 'mop':

> many of the fair filles-de-chambres, dairymaids, and even fat cooks and greasy scullion wenches, are so civilly greeted by their amorous swains, that this fair is productive of much business for the country justices and their clerks, parish-officers, and mid-wives, for many miles round.

A later writer adds, 'when bastardy cases are being adjudicated, many a poor girl declares that her ruin was effected at the last Martinmas Hireings.' Often, however, the criticism was more general. A newspaper reports of one such hiring fair:

> The King's Norton Saturnalia is growing worse. Hardly a man or women [sic] with any pretension to self-respect could be seen at the Mop last Monday, and the thousands were composed of shouting hobbledehoys, screaming girls, drunken men and shouting women . . . . The public houses were packed and customers had to fight their way in and out, treading on floors wet with slopped beer. Some disgraceful scenes took place in one part or another of the vicinity during the day and night. The general proceedings offered a spectacle of debauchery, drunkenness, noise, and blasphemy. . .[25]

A final aspect linking fairs with wife-selling is the concept of change. Not only is this implicit in 'ex-change', the transfer of goods forming the economic basis of most such celebrations, but it was also explicit in the workings of the hiring 'mop', at which servants transferred (or renewed) their economic allegiance for the coming year.

Fairs, then, served as a point of contact between the sexes and of courtship. They had a reputation for sexual liberality, one also found in connection with wife-selling, and they involved both the exchange of goods and the transfer of places. Without suggesting that men consciously changed their wives as they did their servants, it seems possible that the practice of hirings may also have provided a subconscious parallel to this institution. Those fairs at which wife sales are known to have been concluded took place from 1764 to about 1880 and were scattered over southern and central England. [26]

Market inns have already been considered as foci for wife sales. In addition to these, other public houses, some completely separate from fairs and markets, served as sites for the institution. 'Inn' is really a term of convenience — the buildings were also classified under a number of other headings, such as pot house, beer shop, beer house, tavern, public house or ale house. To some extent, these differed in construction and merchandise, but all served as gathering places for the consumption of alcoholic beverages. It would be wrong, however, to think of this as their only function. As Charles Kindred, a Suffolk farmer, points out:

> you'd get a false impression of the role the pub played if you just listened to tales told of them. They're always about fights, or somebody getting drunk, or something absurd; or somebody taking over — that kind of thing. They're exaggerated, like tales of the Wild West in the United States . . .

In fact, the pub served a number of crucial community roles, changing to suit the clientele and the times. Charles Kindred noted that 'typical directions when I was young were always by the pub', not surprising when one considers its importance to local social life. [27]

In the London of Francis Place's youth:

> It was the custom at this time as it had long been for almost every man who had the means to spend his evenings at some public house or tavern, . . . Almost every public house had a parlour, as some still have, for the better sort of customers. In this room which was often large and well lighted with tallow candles the company drank and smoked and spent their evenings — many constantly supped in these rooms either alone or in parties . . . .

In one pub (which Place's father ran), two punch clubs, two lottery clubs and a 'cutter club' (for rowing enthusiasts) met during the course of the week, in addition to individuals' patronage. In

London, and probably elsewhere as well, inns made frantic attempts to drum up custom. Mary Dorothy George notes:

> There were too many publicans to make a legitimate living and so they were impelled to offer *every sort of inducement* to customers to remain tippling in their houses. Clubs of many kinds ranging from the drinking and gambling club, through various forms of sharing-out club to the benefit society, were promoted . . . .

The result, rather than the cause, is of concern here; inns occupied an important position in the social relationships of the day. Charles Kindred recalls:

> After all the inn had perhaps the only big room in the village available to the public. As its name implied, it was the public house . . . There was nowhere apart from the pub where one could meet or invite the public.

The proprietor of the pub had an important role to play in many of the activities that took place on his premises.

> [He] was in an excellent position to discover what was for sale . . . He would hear the conversation of the workmen; and if he wanted to, he could introduce lots and lots of custom to the people who'd got the stuff to sell. He was in a strong position there; and no doubt he made use of it to the advantage of everybody.
>
> If the publican were a local man and a countryman — I expect he nearly always was — he could get to know lots of things about a district that few other people could have an opportunity of learning. He was an information provider, a news-centre, and quite often a labour-exchange as well.

George notes that publicans of the seventeenth and eighteenth centuries often doubled as constables (perhaps because of the close association of prisons with drunkenness). [28]

Other publicans were contractors or middlemen, as inns often served as hiring centres, transportation terminals and exchanges.

> [For] a large number of trades, the public house was the recognized employment agency. There were houses of call in London for hatters, smiths, carpenters, weavers, boot- and shoe-makers, metal-workers, bakers, tailors, plumbers, painters and glazers, and book-binders, and others. They were probably often kept by members of the trade concerned, retired or otherwise.

This was particularly important for those occupations involving irregular or seasonal employment. The system, however, was one open to abuse:

> The House of Call is an Alehouse where they [workmen] generally use, the Landlord knows where to find them, and Masters go there to enquire when they want Hands. Custom has established it into a Kind of Law that the House of Call gives them Credit for Victuals and Drink, while they are unemployed; this obliges the Journeymen on the other Hand to spend all the Money they earn at this House alone. The Landlord, when once he has got them into his Debt, is sure to keep them so, and by that Means binds the poor Wretch to his House, who slaves only to enrich the Publican.

In the case of the London coal-heavers, for whom the publicans also acted as middlemen, the common wage of £1 a day brought home only 15s a week — each labourer was charged 1s 4d for the right to unload a ship and 12s for his beer. Anyone who refused this drink was not hired for subsequent employment and forfeited all maintenance payments.[29]

In addition to their use as employment centres, workers were often paid off at inns. John Fielding, half-brother of the novelist, complains:

> tradesmen paying their workers at public houses commonly called pay-tables are very injurious, as the men are too often kept out of their money till late on Saturday night, out of indulgence to the publican, by which means the mechanic goes home drunk and empty-handed to his family . . . .

In some cases the publicans came over to clear their customers' old scores; in others, the workmen's wives were also present in the hope of receiving part of the pay packet before it was totally consumed in beer.[30] This connection of pubs with employment suggests that the clientele were well-acquainted and shared a similar lifestyle.

Country or provincial pubs offered other services. In East Anglia they were central locations where stallions often stood for stud. There inquests were held and rights of commonage auctioned. Kindred notes that pubs often possessed the only available public stables — of primary importance in an age when much travel depended on horses and when even churchgoers needed a place to leave their mounts. As travel terminals, public houses were associated with the canal-boat trade, and the 'hundreds of coaches and wagons which plied between London and provincial towns had their headquarters in inns.' These stages for horses and houses of refreshment once closely paralleled the main routes of travel and trade. George Ewart Evans mentions that in old East Anglia inns were found every 3 or 4 miles along any main road. To gain insight into their use, one might read Charles Moritz's account of his perambulations or refer to George Baldry's boyhood memories of his jobs as a hay-trusser and cordwainer's assistant. Inns also served as half-way points to clinch cattle deals, and as Kindred fondly recalls:

> They would prepare a meal for you. Some of the pubs were famous for their farmers' dinners on market-day . . . where a great joint of beef was available there; and you could cut what you wanted, so my father told me. You could keep on; you could have an enormous meal for half-a-crown.

One need only recall Dickens's hymns in praise of pub fare to appreciate the accuracy of his fiction. Additionally, lest it be overlooked, inns offered accommodation to the traveller, and rooms were often rented for longer periods as well. [31]

As a melting pot and place of resort — a London man might well give his address in the form, 'Sir, I am to be found at . . . [his favourite inn]' — the public house attracted all sorts of people. *The Session Papers* of June 1785, describing a highwayman who had lodged in the gallery of the White Bear Inn, notes 'there is all manner of people lays there.' Over a hundred years later, a farmer could still say of inn clientele: 'I met some characters; and when I think of it now, you got to be half a character yourself to get away with some on 'em. Yes, you met all classes o' people.' Criminals certainly used public houses as their headquarters; Francis Place recalled:

> The Dog and Duck . . . I have been there when almost a mere boy and seen the flashy women come out to take leave of the thieves at dusk, and wish them success . . . . In Grays Inn-Lane was the Blue Lion, commonly called the Blue Cat; I have seen the landlord of this place come into the long room with a lump of silver in his hand which he had melted for the thieves, and pay them for it.

George reports that many inns had idlers who specialized in fleecing rustics or in plundering travellers' belongings or other goods. The *London Guide* of 1818 warned:

> most people come up to town by coaches and wagons, a few on foot, and fewer still by water; therefore the inns . . . are places of,

especial resort for thieves and cheats of a better sort. The little public houses on the outskirts, as well as those along shore are frequented by a very ordinary and more desperate set . . . .

Up to 1792 it was often the practice for the proprietor of a brothel to avoid supervision by the justices (under the Disorderly Houses Act of 1752) by obtaining a wine licence. Place, recalling the Charing Cross neighbourhood in which he set up shop, notes: 'No. 24 was a dirty Gin Shop — as was also another house a few doors lower down. Those were frequented by prostitutes and Soldiers.' Nor is it surprising that many pubs, with the characteristic Union Jack hung outside, served as headquarters for press gangs. [32]

Finally, public houses were centres for entertainment. The shape of Elizabethan theatres is said to have reproduced that of the inn yards formerly used for plays; additionally sword matches were often held in these courtyards. Place reports:

Until lately all the amusements of the working people of the metropolis were immediately connected with drinking — chair clubs, chanting clubs, lottery clubs, and every variety of club, intended for amusement were always held at public houses. In these clubs every possible excitement to produce excess was contrived . . . . Then as to games of chance or dexterity, skittles, dutch-pins, bumble-puppy, drafts, dominoes, etc., were all provided by the publicans and as these were the *only* amusements within reach of the working people, drinking was encouraged and promoted to a great extent, and the money staked being always spent on liquor, or rather in the language of these places, the stake was either a pot of beer or a quartern of gin . . . .

Even in the present century Horace White recalls inns as 'places of entertainment, singing and dancing and good fellowship'. Evans, in *The Days That We Have Seen*, gives extensive descriptions of this aspect of pub fellowship, including the practice of 'singing each side of the balk' (a two-group contest), holding all-night 'settin' in's' or just having 'pub talk'. [33]

Many public houses connected with wife sales remain unidentified. This is true for the Southwark ale house at which Higginson sold his wife, although evidence suggests that it may have been frequented by carpenters. In Shearbridge, a beer house seems to have been patronized by factory hands — in fact, several sales may have been at inns used by members of a particular trade. A publican from Shoreditch traded his spouse for a lottery ticket, and it seems probable that the Towcester sale between ostler and coachman took place in the inn at which one of them worked. An innkeeper in Yorkshire sold his wife in 1807, while a Devonshire publican purchased his 'spouse'. At least some of these sales took place at public houses. In addition, the hostler of the Lord Exmouth Inn in Plymouth was asked by a woman who baited her horse there to be her surrogate purchaser, and the publican of a Whitechapel tavern was called upon to serve as auctioneer. A Whitehaven hostess, however, fled from the room to avoid witnessing a wife-sale contract. In some cases location was merely chance — an inn was used by a trio on their way to Bradford market, by a pair of men who 'started talking about women', and by a jealous husband who found himself drinking with his landlord. That the location was chosen in other cases is suggested by the number of notices and oral declarations designating inns as the site of sale.[34]

Inn sales appear to have occurred over a period of about 160 years, from 1730 to 1890. Several examples yield evidence of participation by people involved in the running of the hostelry. Some rural cases come from areas in which pubs may have taken the place of markets as local meeting places; in urban areas there is some suggestion of the use of hostels that catered to specific trade or industrial clienteles. This urban group is related directly to the nineteenth-century transfer of wife sales from the markets, a change that may have been prompted by official or community pressure on the institution, whose practitioners perhaps sought the security of smaller social groupings sharing a similar lifestyle and outlook.

Although wife-selling is mentioned in the eleventh century, the first solid evidence comes from 1553, when a London parson was punished for this crime. Examples came before ecclesiastical courts in 1584, 1585, 1613, 1638, 1646 and 1696. In the 1640s there is a newspaper account of a sale involving a Warwickshire yeoman, while in 1692 John Whitehouse sold his wife to a Mr Bracegirdle in Staffordshire.[35] All this suggests that the institution was probably widespread by this period, ecclesiastical prosecutions representing only a minority of actual cases.

Early eighteenth-century records are sparse; only 1730 and 1735 examples are reported from Inverness and London. By the 1740s, however, accounts were appearing in local newspapers, although there is some question as to whether all such cases were considered newsworthy. From this time on sales seem to have occurred, without a break, well into the early twentieth century. Activitiy is particularly noticeable in the period 1785—1845, with peaks in 1797 (11 sales), 1812 (six sales), 1814 (six sales), 1815 (seven sales), 1818 (six sales), 1823 (seven sales), 1833 (eight sales), and 1837 (eight sales). It is important, however, to keep in mind possible distortions of date by sources and the existence of multiple sales, and to regard these totals as useful indications rather than a final enumeration — which, in any case, would be impossible. In 1797, for example, the interest evoked by several Smithfield sales may have resulted not only in a crop of quips and a topical play but also in more complete, if temporary, newspaper coverage of the institution. Seemingly paradoxically, the 'novelty value' of wife-selling may have caused a disproportionate number of later cases to be reported during a period when the custom had in fact begun to decline. Use of the institution appears to have gradually decreased from the 1840s on. When speaking of twentieth-century examples, it is difficult to assign many to specific years, as they were usually reported secondarily, in connection with court cases on related topics. As recently as 1972, however, one case occurred in Northumberland. [36]

During this period it should be emphasized that the morphology of the institution did not remain static. Certain characteristics like sale by weight and the use of a halter were apparently discarded; others, like the use of private treaties, became more popular. Different social groups made use of the institution, and the sale moved from open market to inns.

Periods of intensive wife-selling seem to have occurred in July, in September and between November and March. This could reflect slack seasons of the agricultural year — after the harvest and during the winter. If such a correlation is significant, it would apply only to those examples whose participants lived or worked in a rural environment (although the sales still could have been urban). Again, sales may have been related to the timing of fairs, which itself would ultimately depend upon the rhythm of the agricultural seasons. Proof of this theory, however, would require a much more intensive analysis than the evidence will bear. What does seem apparent, however, is the lack of positive correlation with those Church feasts during which marriage was traditionally prohibited before the Reformation: Advent, Christmas, Lent and Easter. These prohibitions were carried over into popular tradition ('Marry in Lent, you'll live to repent'), but show no signs of having influenced the scheduling of sales. The only widespread non-religious prejudice is against marrying in May ('Marry in May, rue for aye'), perhaps because of the month's connection with extra-marital relationships and free love. Oddly enough, there are fewer sales at this time, although this seems to be part of a more widespread slump. Positive popular associations are more rewarding; the general monthly occurrence of wife sales neatly parallels the following verse:

> Marry in September's shine,
> Your living will be rich and fine.
> If in October you do marry,
> Love will come but riches tarry.
> If you wed in bleak November,
> Only joy will come remember.
> When December's showers fall fast,
> Marry and true love will last.

In addition, smaller patterns of occurrence may well have existed; the publicity given to London wife sales in July of 1797 may have promoted a rash of such transactions in the subsequent weeks. Harry Burstow, retired bellringer of Horsham, Sussex, recalled several sales that took place at the November Fair but reported none that occurred in the town on other occasions. This suggests a close correlation between the fair and the informal institution, paralleling spatial correlations such as Smithfield Market, and it raises the possibility that further research might isolate other local patterns. [37]

There is an almost complete absence of Sunday sales, despite the child's rhyme, 'Bought a wife on Sunday'. This could well be due to public prejudice against conducting business on the Sabbath, a view supported by the characterization of David Fotheringham (who sold his wife on that day) as 'ane profaner of the Saboth day'. Further evidence may be gleaned from the historical fortunes of the preference for marriage on Sunday. Shakespeare's *Taming of the Shrew* makes several references to Sunday weddings, and Petruchio notes, perhaps in conscious imitation of a song of the times:

> Sunday comes apace:
> We will have rings and things and fine array;
> And kiss me, Kate, we will be married o' Sunday.

By the mid-seventeenth century, however, the authors of the

Directory for Publick Worship (1644) 'advised' that Sunday vows should not take place, a moral view that hardened in the Victorian period. With wife sales there appears to have been an initial tendency to time the bargain for the beginning (Monday) or end (Friday) of the week. (The popular days later became Monday, Tuesday and Friday, Saturday). Beliefs concerning the luck of these days varied widely. The normal marriage rhyme ran:

> Monday for wealth,
> Tuesday for health,
> Wednesday the best day of all;
> Thursday for crosses,
> Friday for losses,
> Saturday no luck at all.

Monday and Tuesday were generally lucky, but Wednesday was shunned in the Midlands as a portent of poverty. Thursdays were lucky in Shropshire and Northamptonshire — elsewhere, they were generally avoided. Friday was inauspicious in all but a few areas, while Saturday weddings were traditionally believed to be followed by the early death of one partner. What seems certain is that the preferred days for wife sales reflect local market days, perhaps traceable to the parallel between wife sales and livestock transactions. In a large number of instances the identification of the date as a market day is made explicit; other sales were similarly tied to local fairs. [38]

While many wife sales presumably took place during market hours, only a few nineteenth-century records specifically state the time of the transaction. Most available information indicates that the sales took place at midday, but the evidence is far too scanty to permit certainty. It can be said, however, that the available evidence does show disregard for the canonical hours long favoured by the Church and adopted into statute law in the eighteenth century. These stated that formal marriages were to be held between 8 a.m. and 12 p.m. unless special dispensation had been granted. (Imagine the chagrin of the Devonshire couple whose marriage was halted when some wag set forward the church clock so that it struck noon during the ceremony!) While marriages outside canonical hours, if properly performed, were still valid, the officiating clergyman could be subjected to punishment as severe as fourteen years' penal servitude. It is known that at least some wife sales took place in the afternoon and some even in the early morning and late evening. [39]

CHAPTER 4
Connoisseurs of the 'Merchandise'

Rough Moey . . . was a stout, burly fellow of about forty-five; his face had once been deeply pitted by smallpox, but the impress of the disease had been literally ploughed out by deep-blue furrows, the result of a pit explosion. He had lost one eye, and the place of one leg was supplied by a wooden stump. Neither in feature nor in figure was he prepossessing.

Interest naturally centres on those involved in wife-selling. Like Rough Moey, most sellers appear to have been older than their wives, usually by a good ten years. Further, there is some reason to believe that certain sales may have coincided with the male 'change of life'.[1] Not surprisingly, perhaps, few of the husbands involved in these dealings are described as beauties. The poor, honest and hard-working labourer at Chipping Ongar, Essex, was certainly the exception; more common are the 'drunkard, non-communicant, [and] contemner of the ministrie', the 'ill-looking diminutive fellow, of apparently low and profligate habits', the labouring man 'of idle and dissolute habits' and the 'wretched-looking fellow' or 'burly rascal'. While it is probable, especially in cases involving adultery, that the husband might have been less physically attractive to the wife than her lover, these descriptions may owe much to the 'jealous cuckold' stereotype of comedy and jest or to the colouring of morality and may have been emphasized when they fitted in with preconceived notions.[2]

No discernible pattern emerges until husbands' employments are compared with purchasers' occupations. It then becomes noticeable that many of the more remunerative, socially prestigious positions were held by purchasers, suggesting that upward social mobility was involved in many sales. This trend may have been responsible for many wives' willing consent to such transactions. A general shift toward more menial male employments seems to be indicated over the course of time; this change, however, is more notable among purchasers' occupations.[3]

Little can be said about educational accomplishments. The speech of Joseph Thompson, a Cumberland farmer, (if it has not been seriously tampered with) may suggest some learning, but another seller (in Worcester) could not even sign his name to the contract. A few minority religions are represented; one seller was a Quaker, while another is described as a Jew from Petticoat Lane in London. Peer acceptance of several of the men is suggested by their nicknames, 'Cupid Hodson', 'Jimmy the Grinder', 'Rough Moey' and 'Duke Farrar', although this appears to have been largely a Staffordshire practice. At least one husband had run afoul of the law, while others were guilty of drunkenness, wife-beating and assault.[4]

Some glimpses are given of the husbands' economic positions in the community. A few were debtors. Others apparently owned their own houses or took lodgers. Joseph Thompson rented a farm of about 42 acres. John Frost, another agriculturalist, gave his second wife £100 to ensure her desirability at market; he subsequently married his housekeeper but supported his former wife with an allowance after her purchaser's death. A London grazier who exhibited his wife was apparently known as a 'person of property' — not surprisingly, as he attired his wife in a silken halter and lace shawl.[5]

Descriptions of the wife are occasionally poetic:

> She can read novels and milk cows . . . She can make butter and scold the maid, she can sing Moore's melodies, and plait her frills and caps; she cannot make rum, gin, or whiskey, but she is a good judge of the quality, from long experience in tasting them.[6]

> she can sow and reap, hold a plow, and drive a team . . . she is damned *hard mouthed* and headstrong . . . She now and then, if not watched, will make a *false step*. Her husband parts with her because she is too much for him.[7]

> Her con carry a hundred and a 'alf o' coals from the pit for three good miles; her con sell it well, and put it down her throat in less ner three minits.[8]

Despite such revealing appraisals, the objects of wife-selling tend to be even more anonymous than their mates. Little firm comparative information is available, as the wives were often dismissed as mere appendages of their husbands. However, careful culling can provide some picture of the women involved in wife sales. With few exceptions, these wives appear to have been in their late teens or twenties, a fact generally corroborated by the absence of any case with a previous marriage lasting over twelve years. In several examples the period between espousal and sale is strikingly short. Specific information that some wives were younger than their husbands is mirrored by the age data available for the men.[9]

Several descriptions of the women involved in sales are available, but most of these accounts concentrate on clothes or are subjective. In many cases the wife was considered a reasonable bargain: a 'smart young woman', a 'pretty black-eyed girl', a woman 'tall, and of a likely form and figure', 'a very pretty and modest-looking young woman' and the like. Occasionally, tags were less complimentary. A London female, reported to be 'a well-looking young woman', was described by her former spouse as 'a troublesome noisy' companion'. A York purchaser's bargain 'appeared to be on the wrong side of 50; has lost one leg, and has a wooden substitute', while a Staffordshire purchaser gained 'a poor little slip of a girl who'd been half starved'. Physical defects were occasionally the butt of auctioneering patter: a tinker at Swaffham Bulbeck offered his wife, replete with red nose, thick lips, bent back, receding chin and eyes of which one 'looks straight at you, the other wanders up to the North'. At Bungay Fair a husband gave this reason for wanting to dispose of his wife:

> Well, that's like this, Sir, when I married her she was straight as a lath, could get my arm round her nice little waist and give her a kiss, and thought she was an angel. Now, dang me, I can't get near her by a yard.[10]

In other cases, however, the wife's failings must have been glossed over; a Warwickshire purchaser in the late nineteenth century attempted to return a wife who, he claimed, had been fraudulently sold to him as child-bearing. While it seems logical that pretty women would predominate statistically among accounts of successful sales, beauty was not the purchaser's only criterion. As one Herefordshire husband ruefully admitted, 'good looks won't put the victuals on the table without willing hands.' (Surprisingly enough, the same woman subsequently helped her purchaser at his weaving.) One woman is described as a former pit wench, another as a potgirl and later chambermaid of a coaching inn, while a third had left service in the Cliffe. Two women had previously acted as housekeepers for their future purchasers. [11]

In addition, as a Carlisle case suggests, accomplishments were occasionally useful selling points. Mrs Thompson was credited with having a literary and musical side, as well as being able to tend to light farmwork and the housewifely duties expected of a reasonably well-off farmer's wife. Another woman, advertised in a 1796 newspaper, was conversant with harder fieldwork, while 'Moll' of Bilston could cook, wash, bake and brew, in addition to her ability to 'swear like a trooper, an' fight like a game cock'. On a few occasions the wife's qualities are implicit — one Worcester wife's education became obvious only when juxtaposed with her husband's inability to sign the sale agreement. [12]

All this raises the question of monetary worth. For the most part, this was inextricably linked with the circumstances of the husband, who might throw in various items with his wife as makeweights. A Devon woman, however, was said to be riding to a town on her own horse, with prospects of £600, which her husband could not touch. Other cases mention legacies subsequently come into by 'wives', but these appear to be variants of a travelling' tale. [13]

The legal position of the wife varied. Some cases give indications of marriage, such as rings or proof in the form of a subsequent prosecution of the husband for bigamy, and several examples go out of their way to mention the legal status of the woman. A Sussex girl was 'married by licence'; a Cumberland daughter was forced into wedlock by her parents; an Epping woman had sworn a child to her husband. Sometimes a woman remarried because of her spouse's protracted absence. A few examples show the woman's position to have been ambiguous — a sweetheart or fiancée. At other times, however, the marriage was common-law. A Yorkshire woman was one of three 'wives', while sales at Woodhead Tunnel, Cheshire, involved 'tally-women'. In other cases 'wives' were already living with their purchasers, had been sold previously or could be married by their purchasers with no resultant problems. [14]

Turning to purchasers, the acquisition of a wife by 'a mulatto, the long drummer belonging to the band of the 4th regiment', shows that the institution was not always limited to individuals of strictly Anglo-Saxon or Celtic antecedents. Too little information is available to permit any definite correlation between age and marital condition. While the absence of cases involving middle-aged men may be significant, it could be argued that only youth or age would be considered important enough to be mentioned specifically in newspaper accounts. There is an interesting statement, however, by Pillet, who notes that the purchaser is 'always a widower or a boy', but the value of this information is called into question by the fact that several sales exist in which the purchaser was already a 'married' man. Mention should also be made of a singular Cornish sale in which a wife was bought by two purchasers, and of the Cheshire man who acquired two wives by purchase.[15]

A study of purchasers' occupations shows an obvious nineteenth-century shift in the social scale of those making use of the institution. No longer were the purchasers artisans or from the independent middle class; the institution was confined almost exclusively to industrial labourers and other members of what was then termed the 'working' or 'lower' class. While this corresponds with findings for husbands, it does not necessarily mean that the institution was restricted to those at the lower levels of society. The practice could simply have been preserved longer among those less susceptible to changes in the moral climate or social structure. Purchasers run the gamut from one who showed a knowledge of good manners to another who could not sign his name. On contemporary standing in the community evidence again is mixed. The purchaser in a Lancashire sale of about 1792 was (or became) 'clerk of Eliel Chapel', suggesting a position of religious trust, and Sir Godfrey Kneller, said to have purchased a Quaker's wife, sat as a Justice of the Peace for Middlesex. Against this may be weighed the following two court records:

> *Millward* is a butcher, and was last week fined before our magistrates, for using uneven balances in his trading transactions.

> Britten Etty . . . only about a week ago returned from Beverley House of Correction, where he had been confined as we are informed, for receiving some flannel from . . . Mrs. Lazenby, which the husband had purchased for clothing for their children.

Other purchasers proved to be unstable individuals, guilty of drunkenness, wife-beating and assault.[16]

Only a few sale prices are of use in determining purchasers' wealth. Purchasers range from individuals notoriously short of cash or those who had to borrow money or to sell their watches to be able to afford the wife to those who could afford prices of 21 guineas, 50 guineas and a fine horse or even 100 guineas. Several purchasers owned or occupied their own houses; others are described as lodgers.[17]

In 1815 Pillet noted that the average purchaser was 'usually a connoisseur of the merchandise for sale', an accusation of adultery that will subsequently be found true of a large number of cases. It is interesting that in a high proportion of those sales for which adultery cannot be proved the purchasers were previously acquainted with husband and wife. In addition to landlords and lodgers, many examples involved neighbours or old sweethearts, the latter purchases sometimes apparently motivated by pity. A large number of examples also involved purchasers who were comrades or shopmates of the sellers, connections that often amounted to much the same thing in the late eighteenth and nineteenth centuries. Opposed to such close associations were those instances in which the purchaser acted as an agent for another party — a practice sometimes claimed in extenuation by purchasers haled into court. One sale (by a parish overseer) was to to an individual specifically residing outside the parish (this removed the woman from the local rates); still other sales were made to chance-met men or to utter strangers. As has been mentioned, in almost all examples there was a tendency for the wife to be upwardly mobile. The Yorkshire auctioneer's patter concerning the spouse of a drunken ne'er-do-well, 'clean, industrious, quiet, and careful . . . attractive in appearance and well-mannered for a woman in her position of life', sounds as though it was pitched at a better class of buyer. Another wife exchanged a coal porter for a man 'of good appearance' who drove off with her in a hackney coach. While many cases involved comparable husbands and purchasers, in no case was the woman left with a partner who was demonstrably socially inferior to the man who sold her.[18]

Those peripherally involved with the institution include children; the auctioneer; bidders; witnesses; the crowd; ecclesiastical, administrative, and judicial officials who became involved with the sales; and miscellaneous individuals. Some wives had children who were either delivered to the purchaser, or remained with the husband, or were divided between the two. Such offspring were often illegitimate and a high proportion of young children appear to have been involved. As a rule of thumb, older, legitimate offspring appear to have had a better chance of staying with the husband, young or illegitimate children, of going with the purchaser. Additionally, the sale affected children born subsequently to the wife and purchaser. An Essex baptismal register lists a baby girl as 'by a bought Wife delivered to him [the father] in a Halter', differentiating the child from normal (legitimate) offspring on the one hand and 'base-born' children on the other.[19]

Although a husband was often responsible for the sale of his spouse, he could resort to professional assistance. On two occasions help was forthcoming from parish officials, the Swadlincote parish officer at Barton-under-Needwood in 1790 and the master of the parochial workhouse at Epping in 1833. In these cases participation seems to have been prompted by a desire to keep the women from becoming (or remaining) a charge on the parish. Contemporary newspapers contained the details of many such conspiracies by parish officials to remove the poor from their rates. In 1767 the deputy overseer of one parish workhouse was carried before the Lord Mayor of London, charged with 'having artfully inveigled a Girl, about 18, from the Workhouse to London, where he had endeavoured to sell her to some Office-Keepers, to send her Abroad'. Some 25 years previously, according to the *Post Boy*:

> the churchwardens from a certain parish in the City, in order to remove a load from their shoulders, gave forty shillings and paid the expenses of a Fleet marriage to a miserable blind youth . . . who plays on the violin in Moorfields, in order to make a settlement on [of?] the wife and future family on Shoreditch parish . . . .

Further examples show that such practices continued into the nineteenth century.[20]

A Sheffield auctioneer in 1803 was a butcher; a Kent cattle salesman refused a similar lot in 1820; and a drover conducted a London sale in 1832. A Suffolk auctioneer was called upon to handle a wife sale in the later nineteenth century, while other professional auctioneers are described as 'itinerant' or as pensioners. The connection between sales and inns could explain why a Whitechapel landlord was called upon to do the honours, but the bystander who attempted to sell a Belper woman simply appears to have been present at the right time.[21]

Several sales involved bidding (in one sale there were as many as nine bidders), but there is little information about unsuccessful contestants. One Yorkshire bidder is described as 'old', while in Devon a small man competed with a worker who appears to have been a stonecutter or a labourer. Two other cases that identify bidders' occupations are suspect, as they derive from broadsides and in neither did any bidder raise his bid. In a Bristol sale a horse dealer, a pig jobber, a publican and a 'rough country wap straw' are supposed to have vied unsuccessfully for the wife, who was carried away by a butcher. A Scottish example is more international in flavour: a Highland drover, a tinker, a half-drunk pig jobber from Killarney, a fully drunk Newry brogue-maker and an elderly naval pensioner slug it out figuratively (and sometimes literally) for the favours of a woman on sale in Edinburgh's Grass Market. Here, too, she went to another, a farmer being the successful purchaser.[22]

Not much is known about witnesses, although they are mentioned in several sales and in many cases names are given. One striking point, however, is their sex. In only a few cases are women cited as witnesses, and even then one was accompanied by her husband. While occupations varied from sale to sale, at least some of the witnesses held prominent, respectable positions in their local communities. Others were obviously connected with the inns at which many of these transactions took place.[23]

Accounts of sales stress the crowds attracted, with estimates ranging from the hundreds to the thousands. Only a few examples, however, are more specific. Prior announcements must have had some effect on a crowd's composition. In Staffordshire a group that followed the bellman 'at last contained nearly all the resident roughs (male and female) of the town'. A Wednesbury announcer had a more respectable audience — shopkeepers and women 'with their arms akimbo'. Such announcements often collected a representative sampling of the town; the first-mentioned Staffordshire auction was watched by men, women and children, while all of a village's inhabitants turned out to see the return of Henry Frise with a haltered wife. A Cheltenham sale commenced when that market was 'crowded with respectable farmers', and in Brighton Thomas Killick, a huckster, and Ellen Head, who kept a market stall, were witnesses to such a transaction. Men, women and boys in Truro chased a woman identified as being up for sale, while hooting boys pursued an absconding purchaser in Newark. Numerous children witnessed the sales — one while with his father, another with a nurse and playfellow, a third when he accompanied his father and father's friends to the fair to sell a pony and cart, a fourth when she was a schoolgirl. Often, certain elements of the crowd are identifiable. The presence of women is noted in several sales, perhaps because of a feminine tendency to take action against the institution and its practitioners. A group of factory workers may have disrupted a sale at Shearbridge; neighbours and friends are mentioned elsewhere. The social composition of crowds varied as well; the recorder of a Halifax sale reports 'a company of fellows of low character who were present', while an 1838 paper claims that in Dulverton, Somerset, 'Several respectable persons, who ought to have known better, were supporting and inciting the principals . . . .' Sales at inns attracted their own crowds, mostly male, and one transaction in Sheffield was overheard by a journalist who was present in the pub. As late as 1863 a correspondent in *Notes and Queries* could say: 'I have conversed with more than one person who has seen a husband offer his wife for sale in a public street, with a halter round her neck.'[24]

Numerous ecclesiastical, administrative and judicial officials are mentioned in connection with wife sales, but little information about individuals is available. Two exceptions to this are William Pecke and John Young of Thame, who signed a presentment against 'Thomas Heath Maulster', accused of buying a wife in 1696. Pecke was a churchwarden in 1683 and was alive in 1703, when his family had a seat reserved· on the north side of the church. Young was churchwarden in 1680 and 1681 and apparently died in 1696. Many town criers and bellringers were involved in announcing wife sales; in Wednesbury they usually doubled as the beadles. Tollkeepers and market and prison officials, however, languish in obscurity. Only a few names are known, and all seem to have been male. Some sales agreements were drawn up by lawyers, variously described as 'an eminent Attorney' or 'a learned clerk'. On plaintiffs and court officials (again, all male) the record is silent.[25]

Then there are 'bit actors' who appeared in only a small number of sales. Guards, used to escort the principals to auction and to hold back the crowd, were always male — one example describes them as 'some young fellows', and others are identified as friends or associates of the husband. Often relatives of one of the principals were present: the mother of a girl sold in Bristol in 1823, the parents of another woman in Sheffield, a 'good-looking young woman, the daughter of the wife' in London. Sarah Deakin, a sweetheart of one purchaser, unsuccessfully opposed a sale, while the buyer's wife in Halifax assaulted him for his actions. A groom to a local landowner, a childhood friend of the wife and the foreman of the granite works where one husband was employed all offered advice about the sale's legality. Other people were involved in the wife's final disposal. Sadler, the Woodward of Bagley, accepted one wife as a gift from her purchaser. Captain Craven, barrack master at Colchester, ordered the return of another woman. A 'respectable family' took responsibility for a Dartmouth girl, while other spouses were restored by disgruntled husbands to their parents. Mr Hambidge of Burford, when only a small boy, was a participant in the rough musicking mob that forced a purchaser to relinquish his acquisition. [26]

The reasons for wife-selling may be divided into the general and the specific. The former refers to those social trends that led to the employment of this social institution, the latter to the individual behaviour from which the practice resulted. The general period in which wife sales are known to have flourished saw a breakdown of religious authority. This is not to indicate that people were not religious, but it suggests that the Church did not intrude to the extent it had formerly into moral matters and their legal ramifications. This is reflected by the general movement of wife-selling prosecutions from ecclesiastical to criminal courts, and possibly by the absence of religious commentary on the institution. The lack of an ecclesiastically approved method of divorce would thus not have bothered many of the participants much, while the rise of commercial, secular interests may have prompted recourse to the marketplace for a solution to marital problems. While it is tempting to see sales as part of a breakdown in public morality, the chronological sweep of the institution does not allow for accurate judgments in this matter. A bulge in the number of cases certainly does coincide with Regency and pre-Victorian licentiousness, but this same period also saw newspaper attacks on the practice, negative crowd reactions and several court actions dealing with wife-selling.

Attributing wife sales to the absence of alternative methods of divorce is also unacceptable. While a certain correspondence does apparently exist between the level of wife sales and the number of divorce cases heard by Parliament, the 1857 Divorce Act does not appear to have caused a falling-off of wife-selling. Sales had declined before this period, and at least one participant used the Act as a justification for the institution. The continuing cost of divorce may have been one incentive to continue with the informal practice.

Wartime dislocation of the population has also been cited as an important general cause of wife-selling. Jannoc suggests:

> After the close of the war in 1815, many soldiers and sailors on their return found their wives married again, with a family to which they had no claim. There can be no doubt that generally all the parties had acted innocently; the wife had received news of her husband's death and in due time had taken a fresh one. What could be done? The law was plain enough . . . but the parties concerned might doubt whether the sin incurred would be made less sinful by these processes, even with the payment of some thousand pounds, and a much easier and quite as effectual a way was found out to set things right. It was declared to be lawful to sell a wife in open market, the first husband being then free to marry again, and the second marriage standing good, *ipso facto*.

Another scholar calls this theory into question, as 'none of the reported cases mentions the husband being an old soldier'. While it appears that Jannoc has exaggerated his claim, examples do exist, spread over a wide time span. The following story shows the extent to which military dislocations could provide conditions suitable for wife-selling:

> in 1800, Sir Ralph Abercrombie, on reaching Malta on the way to Egypt, finding that his expedition was carrying too many soldiers' wives, ordered all those not needed for hospital work to be sent home. Two transports were filled, on which over three hundred women were embarked . . . . [in Minorca] the women fell in with an Irish regiment. When a report reached the island that Abercrombie's expedition had met with disaster and been annihilated, all the wives belonging to the 54th Foot promptly married the Irish soldiers they had found on the island. The latter troops were then dispatched to Egypt, where it was learnt that the

report of a disaster to Abercrombie was utterly unfounded. A truly comic scene then took place when past and present husbands of the ladies met. In the end only one man of the 54th took back his former wife — to become the laughing-stock of his regiment.

Even in times of peace, however, similar mishaps could occur:

> A Sailor who had been abroad about Three Years, coming ashore a few Days since, went to his House, where he had left a young Wife: When he came in, he found her sitting by the Fire with another Man, who said to the Woman, shew the Gentleman a Room. He thereupon ask'd her if she did not know him, and where she had got that Child, for there was one sitting upon her Knee; she reply'd, why dear Jack, I thought you were dead, and I'm marry'd again. Married! Aye, quoth the second Husband. Very well, says John, but I married her first, and by G—d I'll have her while I'm on Shore, and you may be her Husband when I'm at Sea, and I will pay half to maintain the Children. They soon came to an amicable Understanding, and the second Husband is now Drawer to his Wife, hoping John will sail soon, that he may be Landlord again.

In this instance at least a wife sale proved unnecessary. A London newspaperman offered another interpretation of the effect of war on the institution. Speaking of an 1802 sale, he wrote: 'This great advance [in price] must be in consequence of the peace, since which wives have become more scarce.'[27]

To some degree wife sales occurred during a period which saw Britain change from predominantly agricultural and cottage industry to an urban and industrialized economy. A side-effect of this was the population drain on many country districts. The old way of life, in which the community had played a leading role, was disrupted. No longer was the husband-wife relationship part of a web of complex family and community ties; with more and more young couples moving away to the city, the nuclear family became a crucial keystone in personal relationships. One result of this was that it was no longer possible to hold many bad marriages together under community pressure. Industrialization had also caused an economic dislocation in many markets, throwing many into debt, while the break-up of community-help patterns left those who required assistance on their own more than ever before. Although it was possible in some cases for the single wife to support herself, the additional burden of children often placed an unfair weight on her shoulders. The result, as illustrated by the widows who sought refuge in smock weddings, was usually impoverishment. Wife-selling coped with these trends by freeing the husband from an unwanted wife, while assuring the woman of a continuing means of support. [28]

Several reasons are specifically given for wife-selling. Often the cause for the sale was mere incompatibility . A Knaresborough bargain was struck 'Owing to some jealousy or other family difference', while other dealings offer similarly worded generalities. In a few cases difficulties may reasonably be surmised — in the 'family' of the sweep with three wives, for example, or in marriages of very short duration. Sometimes examples provide background to the situation. William Fleming notes:

> A few weeks ago, a younger Daughter of Robert Hendall, Farmer at Whifield was married to a Man named Stable, who was Servant with Mr. Townsend at Furness Abbey, which she was in some Measure compelled to by her Parents, her Choice being fixed upon one Huddleston, a Maker of Slate Pencils at Scalebank.

Not surprisingly, the girl eloped with her lover. Another husband, when questioned in court, 'said, in his defence, that he had been compelled to marry her [his wife] six years ago by the parish officers, in consequence of her having sworn a child to him; that he had never since lived with her. . . .' Other details of incompatibility are often given. Thompson describes his feelings toward his wife in the following manner:

> Gentlemen, it is her wish as well as mine to part for ever. She has been to me only a bosom serpent. I took her for my comfort and the good of my house, but she has become my tormentor, a domestic curse, a night invasion, and a daily devil . . .

A Manchester account records the sort of bickering that must often have led to sales:

> Latterly, times had not gone on so swimmingly as usual — cash was low — the house smoky, and the lady a little irrascible. At length a little domestic bickering ensued — a knotty point was introduced — both were right, and yet, strange to tell, both were wrong: at length came the climax. 'I'll take you to the Market with a halter round your neck, and sell you to the best bidder.' 'Very well — I wish you would,' was the rejoinder: 'I'm heartily tired of you, and I *will* be sold to *a more perfect man.* (Alluding, as was supposed to the [husband's] one arm.)

In a Cornish case the husband had repeatedly threatened to sell his spouse, and she was said to have been agreeable to the idea. Occasionally, sources for this domestic discord are given: one man complained of his wife's physical appearance, while another commented on his spouse's refusal to do the housework. [29]

Seemingly most common as a cause for sales, however, was adultery — often, but not exclusively, by the wife. A Staffordshire husband's wanderings, for example, provoked his mate to retaliate and brought about her subsequent sale. More commonly, the boot was on the other foot. Pillet's observation has already been noted: 'The purchaser, always a widower or a youth, is usually a connoisseur of the merchandise for sale, who knows her; one only presents her at market as a matter of form.' Occasionally adultery is only implicit: a deal made beforehand with a purchaser, a wife sold shortly after the birth of a child or a woman's sale to some connected party — a landlord, lodger, journeyman, fellow workman or companion. In other cases the evidence is geographical; husband and purchaser were neighbours or lived in the same town. A few samples note that the purchaser came to market specifically to buy the wife; or that his identity was known beforehand. Finally, past attachments often suggest similar possibilities. One Kent wife was bought by an old sweetheart; another woman had previously given her husband's goods away to the purchaser. [30] On the other hand, adulterous connections may be explicitly detailed. An Essex woman is described as 'more industrious in a certain way than virtuous', while an advertisement in a country newspaper notes that the wife 'now and then, if not watched, will make a *false step*'. Unexpectedly returning home after missing his coach, a London tradesman found, in his wife's bedchamber, a man who eventually offered to purchase her from the offended spouse. [31]

Background information is sometimes added to these 'bare facts'. Rough Moey, for example,

> had given a sturdy pit wench, about half his own age, a new gown and other articles of dress, with a fortnight's treat, to marry him . . . . . after a time she had transferred her affections to a good looking young collier; upon which the husband naturally became jealous and took to beating her. This, instead of curing her, only awakened thoughts of retaliation; and as Moey often came home at night in a state of helpless intoxication, she would gently unstrap the wooden

leg of the sleeping drunkard and thrash him with it to her heart's content.

At Plymouth, the husband gave the following testimony:

> they had been married about two years and a half, and she brought
> him a child 'three weeks after marriage!' which, until it was born,
> he never knew anything about; that the child soon after died; that
> he got a coffin for it, paid the expenses of the funeral, and put it
> *comfortably* out of the way, without ever reproaching his wife with
> her conduct; but all would not do. She soon after deserted him,
> notwithstanding his kindness, and went to live with another man,
> by whom she had one child since and he was informed she was
> again pregnant with another.

Change of residence is found in several examples. Often the wife
had lived openly with her lover for years. Near Bradford, a
husband

> turned his wife and only child out of doors to shift for themselves.
> The woman placed herself under the protection of a man in the
> same village named Holmes, with whom she had lived since her
> expulsion from her husband's domicile.

In other cases the woman's position was more ambiguous; she
might serve as housekeeper for the purchaser. Or adultery could
be combined with elopement, in which case sales seem to have
taken place only when the wronged husband could track down the
guilty parties. Sometimes adultery was unintentional. A soldier or
sailor was believed dead, and the wife remarried in his absence. If
the former husband returned, the woman was usually sold to her
second spouse. At other times 'trading' may have been more
promiscuous, although it is difficult to tell to what degree such
tales are misinterpretations of the facts. Closely related to
adulterous unions are those examples initiated by the purchaser's
infatuation. While it seems unlikely that Jon Raven's statement, 'in
every documented case of wife-selling in England the purchaser
was previously known by the husband and wife, and the price had
been agreed,' is completely accurate, the anonymous author of
The Laws Respecting Women may be taken as stating a general
causal truth when he noted:

> A purchaser is generally provided before hand on these occasions;
> for it can hardly be supposed, that the *delicate* female would

submit to such public indignity, unless she was sure of being purchased when brought to market.[32]

Barrenness, although less frequent, was another reason for sales. So was cruelty, by the wife or husband. The part played by drink in wife-selling is continually emphasized: sales were located at inns, ratifying pledge cups were quaffed and purchase prices were often in alcohol. In several cases liquor appears to have played an inordinately large role, often serving as the total purchase price. Many husbands are described as drunken, a fault that often went hand in hand with ill-treatment. A Falmouth seller 'stated his only reason for parting with her [his wife] was that he was more fond of the cup of Bacchus than of the society of woman. . . . he wanted to have a good drop of "the crature" that night . . . .' A group of Irthlingborough shoemakers sold a wife to raise money for more drink. Alcoholic stimulants may have temporarily suppressed scruples, releasing subconscious desires which the institution occasionally fulfilled. In many cases sales were subsequently reversed, suggesting that the husband was in liquor at the time of the bargain. Higginson sold his partner 'in a fit of conjugal indifference at the alehouse', while a Manchester couple pleaded drink as an excuse for their conduct. In a few broadsides it was the wife's drunkenness that was cited as a reason for sale.[33]

Scattered cases suggest the influences of gambling, but the evidence is not conclusive. A similar economic fault was extravagance, usually implicitly reflected by the debt disclaimers issued by husbands after such sales.[34]

Occasionally, more unusual causal connections occur. Two Cornish sales, both probably fictitious, turn on the robbing (and murder) of unsuspecting purchasers by a husband-and-wife team. A larcenous intent to swindle the purchaser out of his money may explain other sales. And it seems evident that some examples, at least in their early stages, started as jokes. In York a husband 'in one of his mad freaks . . . had her [his wife] brought into the Market-place' and sold, while a Westmorland man 'was very fond of the girl, and only did it as a bit of fun'. Liverpool and Belper wives were urged on to the act by the attendant spectators. The husband's actual or impending absence was another spur to sales. In some cases this was connected with entrance into the army; in others, with absconding for debt. In such cases sale ensured the wife's continued support. In 1873 a woman specifically told the auctioneer of her husband's effects that 'he must either share the money with her or sell her'.[35]

All causes of sale boil down to a single commonplace: the incompatibility of the wife and husband. Why was the institution resorted to as a form of divorce? As has been indicated, the Church did not recognize divorce *per se*, while parliamentary divorces involved a long and costly process beyond the reach and influence of most of the individuals who practised wife-selling. More informal methods of divorce seem to have been restricted in their distribution, suggesting only local recognition of their validity. Wife sales, however, were tied to market mechanisms, which, although universally recognized, still remained fluid in their application. In particular, wife-selling seems to have been a way in which the husband could avoid his responsibility for maintaining and supporting his wife and children, and the purchaser, by securing proof of the husband's acquiescence in a new relationship, could insure himself against an action for *crim. con.*

The Laws Respecting Women recognized an economic motivation for husbands as early as 1777: 'the husband . . . as he imagines, at once absolves her and himself from all the obligations incident to marriage.' This view, although not frequently expressed explicitly by the parties involved, persisted well into the nineteenth century. The *Manchester Mercury* speaks disapprovingly of husbands who vend their wives 'under the vulgar notion that they thereby get clear of maintaining them'. An Essex man, brought before court, stated to their lordships that 'he had been told that by publicly selling her [his wife] in the market he could get rid of any charge by the parish for the maintenance of her or her children,' a pathetic appeal, considering that the parish authorities had forced him to marry the woman in the first place. Still later, in Staffordshire, a husband was pleased with his deal,

> erroneously imagining that because he had brought her through a turnpike in a halter, and publicly sold her in the market before witnesses, that he is thereby freed from all responsibility and liability with regard to her future maintenance and support.

That this theory was rejected in all court cases in which maintenance was sought does not seem to have disturbed popular belief in its efficacy. To the extent that this view of wife-selling was commonly held in a community, and the purchaser supported his acquisition (or at least that the wife's debts were not charged to her former husband), it made little difference whether the arrangement was strictly legal or only moral in its force. Only when the wife was destitute did the long arm of the parish authorities reach out for laggard husbands.

The benefit to the purchaser of an affirmative defence against any action for *crim. con.* was again perhaps more implicitly than specifically expressed. In a 1775 sale the deal was concluded by a document 'drawn up by Way of a Indemnification from bringing an Action For *Crim. Con.*'. It was not until 1815 that this purpose was again mentioned: 'The intention of these disgusting bargains is to deprive the husband of any right of prosecution for damages.' While court actions were more common in the upper strata of society, they were not unknown at other levels. It could indeed be argued that the very scarcity of such court cases to some extent supports the idea that wife sales could have been used for this purpose. However, first and foremost, wife sales were resorted to as a method of separating incompatible couples and to replace discordant relationships with more harmonious liaisons.[36]

ACCOUNT OF THE

SALE of a WIFE, by J. NASH,

IN THOMAS-STREET MARKET,

On the 29th of May, 1823.

✻✻✻✻✻✻✻:✻✻✻

This day another of those disgraceful scenes which of late have so frequently annoyed the public markets in this country took place in St. Thomas's Market, in this city; a man (if he deserves the name) of the name of John Nash, a drover, residing in Rosemary-street, appeared there leading his wife in a halter, followed by a great concourse of spectators; when arrived opposite the Bell-yard, he publicly announced his intention of disposing of his better half by Public Auction, and stated that the biddings were then open; it was a long while before any one ventured to speak, at length a young man who thought it a pity to let her remain in the hands of her present owner. generously bid 6d. ! In vain did the anxious seller look around for another bidding, no one could be found to advance one penny, and after extolling her qualities, and warranting her sound, and free from vice, he was obliged, rather than keep her, to let her go at that price. The lady appeared quite satisfied, but not so the purchaser, he soon repented of his bargain, and again offered her to sale, when being bid nine-pence, he readily accepted it, and handed the lady to her new purchaser, who, not liking the transfer, made off with her mother, but was soon taken by her purchaser, and claimed as his property, to this she would not consent but by order of a magistrate, who dismissed the case. Nash, the husband, was obliged to make a precipitate retreat from the enraged populace.

✻✻✻✻✻✻✻✻

Copy of Verses written on the Occasion:

COME all you kind husbands who have scolding wives,
Who thro' living together are tired of your lives,
If you cannot persuade her nor good natur'd make her
Place a rope round her neck & to market pray take her

Should any one bid, when she's offer'd for sale,
Let her go for a trifle lest she should get stale,
If six-pence be offer'd, & that's all can be had,
Let her go for the same rather than keep a lot bad.

Come all jolly neighbours, come dance sing & play,
Away to the wedding where we intend to drink tea;
All the world assembles, the young and the old,
For to see this fair beauty, as we have been told.

Here's success to this couple to keep up the fun,
May bumpers go round at the birth of a son;
Long life to them both, and in peace & content
May their days and their nights for ever be spent.

Shepherd, Printer, No. 6, on the Broad Weir, Bristol.

An account of a Bristol wife sale (case 193) printed by Shepherd, Bristol, 1823
(*See page 207*)

CHAPTER 5

'Roll up, and bid spirited'

The procedure in a wife sale may be regarded in two lights: what was supposed to happen and what actually occurred. To understand the institution fully, it is necessary to consider the patterns of procedure and the framework of rules governing wife-selling, as well as to examine actual cases. Such patterns were variously perceived from different vantage points: by participants, by the press and by other observers. Like critics examining a painting from different positions in an art gallery, each of these groups may have been able to see some aspects of the picture very clearly but were perhaps blinded by emotion or prevented by prejudice from comprehending the total work.

Unlike the case of the codified structure supporting formal institutions, there exists an inherent difficulty in determining the rules that are believed to govern an informal practice. Of course, one solution to this problem would be to question a number of practitioners on the subject, trying to cancel out individual emotions or prejudices and noting any areas of agreement that emerged. This option, sadly, is not available in the case of wife-selling; no first-hand evidence can be quoted defining what the participants themselves considered relevant. There are, however, numerous secondary reports of the institution that describe its workings. From these it is possible to sketch a picture that may give an insight into participants' beliefs concerning the rules governing wife sales and into the way in which the institution was perceived by the press and by contemporary society. There is no guarantee, of course, that many reports represent anything other than a straight account of the facts. The paying of a market toll at a public sale, for example, might be considered as incidental rather than a required procedure. Because of this ambiguity, consideration of secondary contemporary sources has concentrated on those statements that specifically suggest stereotypical actions or beliefs. Even so, there always remains the difficulty of separating the views of participants from those superimposed by the press. A third layer of perception is that of authors who have written about wife-selling. Most of these are even further removed from the practice and are subject to the advantages and disadvantages of distance in determining general forms. While not bound by the web of beliefs surrounding participants and their contemporaries, these writers are, of course, themselves susceptible to a different combination of influences. The potential lessening of prejudice and emotion is also accompanied by a potential ignorance concerning the institution. [1]

If probability is taken into account, non-specific sales reports may also suggest something about what was believed to constitute wife-selling. Markets were places at which bargains were struck and money exchanged hands. Wife sales held in markets could hardly be considered out of place, so that evidence of wife-selling at market does not necessarily imply that markets were theoretically required for such sales. The same argument can be used for public sale, minimum prices, written agreements and market tolls. All these may have been desired for a variety of external reasons and may not have been considered a necessary part of the sale proper. [2]

Halters, however, are different. As they were not part of all ordinary commercial dealings but only of those transactions involving livestock, it is possible that halters were believed to be required for the sale. This argument is strengthened by the number of cases mentioning a halter or stating specifically that one was purchased. In an Essex birth register it is noted that the father's wife was 'delivered to him in a Halter', while Moses Maggs noted that his sale was 'all right, accordin' to law, I brought her through the turnpike, and paid the mon the toll for her. I brought her wi' a halter.' An Arundel man was informed that he must put the rope on his wife a mile outside town and lead her into market or the sale could not be considered legal, while in Cheltenham the act of throwing a halter over a wife who had been lured to market indicates that this was considered a necessary element of the sale. A purchaser requested that a Derby woman be delivered 'according to law'; she was subsequently handed over in a halter. In Staffordshire the injured party believed that through a sale with

a halter he was 'thereby freed from all responsibility and liability'.
In Oxfordshire and elsewhere halters were also considered
necessary. Henry Frise argued:

> her's my wife, as sure as if we was spliced at the altar, -for and
> because I paid half a crown, and I never took off the halter till her
> was in my house; lor' bless yer honours, you may ask any one if
> that ain't marriage, good, sound, and Christian, and every one will
> tell you it is.

The practice was well enough established for a lawyer in a Leeds
court case to ask one woman seeking support payments, 'Did he
put a rope round your neck?'[3]
  Several other traditional mechanisms of wife-selling have
already been touched upon. Use of the turnpike is common in
several Staffordshire cases, in one of which the husband compelled
the toll-keeper to take money. Mention is sometimes made of the
necessity for money to pass, but Frise's words offer the only hint of
a minimum price. (Paradoxically, the foreman of a Devon granite
works claimed that in certain circumstances such sales were *illegal*
if money passed.)[4]
  In Scotland one court case suggests that the presentation of the
wife to her purchaser was crucial. James Steill, in response to
questions, admitted that 'he took his wife be the hand to give her
to the other, but the other denys that he receaved her; the woman
also denys that her husband took her by the hand to deliver her . . .'
Others believed that the transfer had to be made at market or on
market day. A 1773 document specifically states that this
condition was fulfilled, while a London attorney advised one
group of participants 'that the sale would not be valid, unless
made in market overt'. This belief persisted through the 1820s,
1830s and 1840s, and one purchase in Somerset was considered
invalid 'because the sale was not held in a public market-place'.
Other examples mention explicitly the necessity for a public sale,
which may explain Moses Maggs's justification that his wife had
been 'cried', 'so everythin's right, accordin' to law'. A Staffordshire man held witnesses to be necessary; a London husband
employed a salesman 'whose certificate of the transfer Crispin
ignorantly considers as a legal divorce'. Patterns may also be
descried in those actions felt to be illegal. In Somerset some said
the purchaser could not have another wife, while in Devon no

money could pass unless the husband held an auctioneer's licence.[5]

Hints of theoretical procedure have been subtly enshrined in newspaper allusions to 'unusual' or 'customary' practice and to previous sales. It is often difficult to determine exactly how accurately a pattern is reflected in a subsequent report, but some generalizations may be made. Again, the overriding image associated with such sales was the halter. The market was also of theoretical importance. Most patterns suggested by the contemporary press occur in cases between about 1790 and 1850, with particular frequency in the first years of the nineteenth century.[6]

Still another group of traits have been deemed characteristic by more distant observers of the institution — foreign travellers, academics and those who have written on the subject of wife-selling. Again, halter and market are commonly emphasized. As these are also represented in the patterns of both participants and the contemporary press, they may be taken as standard in a 'typical' wife sale and form important links in the association of the institution with livestock sales. Evidence shows, however, that both halter and market location were far from universal. Two other points are fairly consistently mentioned by earlier writers: pre-arranged sales and the wife's acquiescence in the bargain. An additional (localized) pattern, occasionally mentioned in connection with the west Midlands, is progression to market through a specific number of turnpike toll gates or villages. This was believed to provide acceptable proof of ownership in much the same way as market toll. Witnesses and a written receipt of the transaction were more widely used precautions that were held to constitute proof of purchase.[7]

The public nature of the sale engendered many of these theoretical practices. Several aspects of procedure ensured that the revised relationship of the participants would become common community knowledge. This protected reputations by preventing subsequent misunderstandings from arising and guaranteed that the public was not imposed upon. Wives, therefore, could be sold only by specific individuals; debts could not be incurred in a former husband's name; subsequent disclaimers of sale or purchase could be rebutted. The stipulations limiting resale and repurchase, while not universally honoured, served to differentiate the institution from prostitution and allowed the participants a measure of respectability. Minimum prices (again not always adhered to) further established each transaction's validity, as did the custom of sale to the highest bidder.[8]

In a 'typical' sale the husband would previously have gained his wife's permission and would have had some idea of a potential purchaser. The woman would be taken to market, where the husband would place a halter or rope around his spouse's neck to sell her to the highest bidder. Reality could often differ, however, as will be seen.

Events that led up to wife sales often stemmed directly from those causes discussed in chapter 4. These events may conveniently be grouped in three general categories: impulse, advertising and pre-sale interviews. One might as well wish to know what song the sirens sang as to fathom the specific origin of most sales. There were, of course, deep-seated causes: drunkenness, adultery and the like. This, however, does not explain why any individual sale took place at a specific point in time.[9]

Some case evidence is as intriguing as it is insubstantial; thus a woman with a black eye was sold at Hythe Market place, and a man at Baylham, Suffolk, 'having a disagreement with his wife', disposed of her to a local farmer. A Barnsley man opted for the institution after being beaten by his spouse. Another story has it that a similar purchase was made when the Duke of Chandos came upon an ostler beating his wife.[10]

Conversation often led to sales. Principals in an East Lothian example explained the origin of their dealings thus:

> they being together in John Wood his house drinking and speaking anent fieing of shearers; in the mean tyme James Steill his wife came in, and they fell in speaking anent her; but they all deponed that they cannot tell how that purpose begane, but grants that in ane idle toy or merriment the one did sell his wife . . . .

Similar descriptions recur: in about 1839 a York husband disposed of his wife in a 'mad freak', while a gypsy in the present century said that his brother had sold a sweetheart on Brough Hill, Westmorland, 'as a bit of fun'. Drink, too, played a part in some sales, as when in 1730 a lieutenant, while drinking with a gentleman, made an offer to buy his wife. The bargain was effected, with guineas given as 'earnest', but the husband subsequently repented and refused to complete the transfer. A

London carpenter sold his fair one 'in a fit of conjugal indifference at the alehouse'; here again, a return was desired. One fair-minded husband consented to keep his wife until morning, the buyer being in liquor and the married man 'wishing to take no unfair advantage of him'. Strange to say, this vendor *also* repented and went to some lengths to buy back his wife. In Renfrewshire

> a party of *drouthy* neighbours met in a house in New Sneddon to enjoy a tankard or two of *reaming swats*, and to decide by which of the rival 'best possible instructors' they were henceforth to be enlightened. In the course of the discussion, one of them announced his intention of setting up a dram shop, and stated there was only one article a wanting. 'What was that?' — 'A wife,' 'A wife,' exclaimed the host . . . 'I will sell you mine for twenty pound scots.'

Northamptonshire shoemakers spent their last coins on beer, and, seeking a further source of finance for the binge in progress, one of them sacrificed for the common good and sold his wife. Another cobbler came home drunk in Lancashire, collected his partner and packed her off to market to sell her.[11]

In other cases sales appear to have been completely due to chance. A man and wife fell 'into Discourse with a Grazier at Parham Fair, the Husband offered him his Wife in Exchange for an Ox . . . .' Often these mad freaks were associated with auctions: at Bungay Fair a man tried to have his wife included as a lot, while a Belper woman demanding either a share of her husband's goods or her inclusion as a lot was taken up on her offer. An enthusiastic bystander offered to serve as auctioneer, much as a spectator might urge on a fight. Perhaps the most unusual case in which a dare was called occurred at an auction room in Liverpool about 1890:

> During the sale of miscellaneous effects a woman of masculine proportions suggested that the next lot should be her old man, as she had been strongly advised to get rid of him. A spectator proposed she might be sold instead, whereupon she mounted the platform and the bidding commenced . . . .

While on the subject of impulse, it should be noted that the view of all sales as pre-arranged is hardly correct. The attention of the Duke of Chandos on one occasion, for example, was only attracted by the hubbub. Some sales were made to total strangers. In Lancashire one story notes that the purchaser had to borrow money from a friendly shopkeeper; a Sussex hopeful pawned his watch to buy 'Nanny pin-toe'.[12]

The idea of a pre-arranged sale is not closely compatible with that of advertising. While there was certainly some compulsion to assure public transactions, it is unlikely that this alone could have prompted the organization and the advertising expense that many examples indicate. In any pre-arranged sale the placing of newspaper advertisements, the posting of notices or the hiring of a bellman would have been a superfluous exercise, as would competitive bidding.

In considering possible sale advertisements, a husband was faced with a variety of options. Rarest, perhaps because of the editors' attitudes and the expense, was use of the newspaper. In addition to initial cost, a tax on each advertisement was levied by the government, and this was often passed on by the proprietors. One advertisement, surviving from 1796, reads as follows:

> To be sold for *five shillings*, my wife, Jane Hebland. She is stout built, stands firm on her posterns, and is sound wind and limb. She can sow and reap, hold a plough, and drive a team, and would answer any stout able men, that can hold a *tight rein*, for she is damned *hard mouthed* and headstrong; but, if properly managed would either lead or drive as tame as a rabbit. She now and then, if not watched, will make a *false step*. Her husband parts with her because she is too much for him. — Enquire of the Printer. N.B. All her body clothes will be given with her.

That such advertisements were rare in this period, however, is shown by the extent to which this offer was picked up and adversely commented upon by other newspapers. Particularly noteworthy is the notice's similarity both to slave sale advertisements and to the auctioneer's patter in actual wife sales. Printers were not only publishers to whom correspondence and literary ventures might be addressed but often sold various items on the side (patent medicines were especially popular). Thus, a newspaper office would have been a logical place to inquire about Jane Hebland.[13]

Another option for publicity was to post a notice of intent to sell. There is evidence of this in at least two cases. Tinkers visiting Swaffham Bulbeck in Cambridgeshire circulated notices of the time for a sale taking place in the local pub. This was done on short ('same-day') notice. In Devon an earlier advance warning was given by a stonecutter, who posted the following handwritten bulletin in several public places:

NOTICE

This here be to hinform the publick as how James Cole be dispozed to sell his wife by Auction. Her be a dacent, clanely woman, and be of age twenty-five ears [sic]. The sale be to take place in the New Inn, Thursday next at seven o'clock.

A written notice was probably preferred to printing because of its ease and the savings in cost rather than because of any negative attitudes shown by printers, to judge by the scurrilous (printed) libels circulating at this period. Certainly, a wife-sale notice would probably have been received with more tolerance than the call to the poor to force down corn prices (by destroying the mills of unco-operative millers) found pinned to the White Lion tavern's inn-sign in 1768.[14]

More widespread was the hiring of a bellman or town crier to announce the sale of a wife. This was common in several areas of England from about 1815 to 1860. The following description gives a good example of what could occur on such an occasion:

It was announced by the bellman that on a Saturday in May, 'Jimmy the Grinder' would put up his wife to auction in the Pig Market to the highest bidder, and that gentlemen in search of a partner were requested to attend, as the said 'Moll' was good-looking, young, and could cook, wash, bake, etc. The announcement, delivered in the broad dialect of the district and embellished with various humourous additions which the fancy of the bellman or the auditors suggested on the spur of the moment, was greeted with laughter from the crowd, which, following the 'crier' from street to street, and receiving fresh accessions of numbers at every stand he made, at last contained nearly all the resident roughs (male and female) of the town, while the comments and criticisms uttered made a perfect babel . . . Having accomplished his mission and 'cried' himself till he could cry no longer without being moistened, the bellman resorted to his favourite pub, where accompanied by a few choice spirits, and plentifully supplied with ditto by the liberality of his attendants, he retailed for their edification as much as he knew (and more) of the causes of the proposed divorce from bed and board of the said Moll. . . .

Announcements were usually delivered after the crier had found a pitch and rung his bell to attract attention. They were made 'in slow deliberate "phrases"':

> a woman —
> and her little baby —
> will be offered —
> for sale —
> in the Market Place —
> this afternoon —
> at four o'clock —
> by her husband —
> Moses Maggs.

In some cases sale followed almost immediately upon the announcement; one in Carlisle occurred less than two hours after the bellman was sent on his rounds.[15]

As municipal employees, bellmen must have lent an aura of respectability to the institution, but in honest truth their voices were for sale. Bellmen would report any local event such as a lost pig or a forthcoming horse race — their talents available for a gallon of beer or a few shillings. That such talents were not always properly employed is suggested by the story of several French sailors who paid a Yarmouth crier to advertise for lost money. Ignorant of the English language, the French missed the force of the resulting message:

> Johnny Crampoo's lost his purse.
> He who's found it's none the worse,
> He who lost it, let him seek it.
> He who's found it, let him keep it![16]

The cheapest form of advertising, however, was rumour. This frequently took up where other advertisements left off. In Bilston, for example, the bellman's information 'was soon after filtered through various channels to the lady gossips of the place, and was soon as common as the air they breathed, and quite as fresh as the beer they usually consumed'. Elsewhere shopkeepers, women and loafers are pictured as remarking on and amplifying the subject. In Plymouth

> The report which accompanied the notice stated that the *lady* was not only young and handsome, but that she had *rode* to town in the morning on her own horse, of her own free will and accord, and with the consent of her husband, who was to act the part of an

auctioneer on the occasion; and that she would, moreover, in the course of a few days, succeed to 600 l., which her . . . husband could not touch.

The noted tendency of rumour to exaggerate would not have harmed such sale prospects! In some cases, there is no sign of a previous announcement. As early as 1815 a local Derbyshire magistrate foresaw that a sale was likely to take place and rumours of sales, founded and unfounded, occur later in the century. In 1859 the information that a wife would be sold on a set night was spread by the husband himself. Truro rowdies beset 'a decently-dressed woman from St Agnes' when 'some mischievous fellow, without any cause, pointed her out as the woman that was about to be sold . . . .'[17]

Sometimes impulse and advertising were both unnecessary. As already mentioned, a large number of cases were associated with the wife's adultery. In these the co-respondent was a natural purchasing party — someone inclined towards the woman in question and (if the pun may be permitted) vice versa. In addition, community pressure to rectify the situation may have been exerted. In such cases sale was a formality that could be dispensed with or reduced to a symbolic transfer. As Pillet puts it, 'one only presents her at market as a matter of form.' The exchange was reduced in importance by the preliminary meeting between husband and purchaser. Often this meeting was brought on by a confrontation, particularly when the husband faced an eloped wife and her lover. A London shopkeeper

On returning home . . . found a stranger in his wife's bed chamber. After some altercation on the subject of this *rencontre*, the gallant proposed to purchase the wife, if she was offered for sale, in due form, in Smithfield market. To this the husband readily agreed . . .

The offer to purchase seems to have been made by the lover on most occasions. A wife to whom 'Neither threats nor soft persuasions . . . were of any avail' was sold 'with view of making the best of a bad bargain' to her despoiler for a 'lucrative offer'. In Derbyshire, a husband tracked down the errant couple and made demands — '£3 for her clothes'. The purchaser agreed, if the husband consented to accompany them to Wirksworth on market day and to deliver the wife 'according to law'. In Cumberland it was the husband who decided upon sale 'after taking Advice on the Subject', when his eloped spouse refused to return home. Elsewhere, too, elopements brought about sales when the husband discovered the whereabouts of wife and lover.[18]

Closely related to elopements were cases in which the woman had become another man's housekeeper, a position in which adultery, if not actually a fact, was commonly suspected. A Huntingdonshire man returned home to find his wife occupying this position with a neighbour: 'On claiming her a quarrel ensued, the result being that an agreement was come to . . . .' At Louth a woman eloped from her spouse to a neighbour's house, where she remained as a housekeeper — 'but as an adulteress', according to the husband.

> a reconciliation being vainly attempted between the wife and her husband, the latter and Sleight, after a good deal of fruitless negotiations owing to the fickleness of the husband's resolution at length decided that the wife should be sold . . . .

In Yorkshire a wife was expelled from the house and was taken in by a neighbour. Again, 'it was mutually agreed upon, that a regular transfer . . . should be effected', as neither man was happy with the *status quo*. In one Plymouth example the wife herself may have arranged the sale. The husband testified in court that he 'had come to Plymouth that morning by her appointment to get the business finished'. His wife even engaged the ostler of the Lord Exmouth Inn (where she kept her horse) to bid for her when the expected purchaser did not arrive. Akin to this situation was one in which an absent soldier or sailor returned home to find his wife remarried. Sometimes it is known only that the husband and purchaser met; in other cases, even this contact must be inferred.[19] The best example of such an interview comes from Spalding, Lincolnshire, in 1786. In the Pied Calf ale house, Thomas Hand

> expressed some words to the company of an intention to sell his wife, if any man would buy her, and without any persuasion went out, and returned with Thomas Hardy, a cordwainer of the same place. They both sat down very friendly, and drank a pint of ale, when they began to talk of a bargain, and soon agreed for Elizabeth, the wife of Hand, to Hardy, for five shillings, to be delivered in an halter, in the presence of the company, provided the contract met the approbation of the wife. Hardy, the purchaser, went out, and soon returned with the woman, and the three parties

retired into a private room, and conversed upon the subject, and very composedly agreed in opinions.

In the 'higgling' at New Sneddon, Renfrewshire, the wife's price was raised and a contract drawn out and signed by three witnesses. This document specified the tabling of the money and required that the sale be completed by noon the next day. A similar initial agreement was drawn up at Stockport in 1831. Often lawyers assisted in the drafting of such a document; several sales are said to have taken place 'agreeably to an engagement drawn up by an attorney for that purpose'. About the same period a sale appeared in which 'the parties had consulted an Attorney, who advised them that the sale would not be valid, unless made in market overt.' Even as late as 1877 one supposed transaction was said to have been based on articles drawn up at a solicitor's office. Such recourse may have been due to instances in which husbands or purchasers repented of their bargains and tried to renege on the terms. [20]

Consultations may have been held prior to other sales. A Plymouth husband had been assured of the institution's legality by 'many people in the country'; a stonecutter's foreman also proffered advice on the matter. In Yorkshire a labourer decided after long and careful thought 'that the act was proper and lawful'.

'Well,' said he to John, groom to — of the Grange, 'I've thought of it and I'm right sure I can buy her, by law.' 'But,' said John, 'our master' (— was at the Bar) 'says you *can't*.' 'Ah,' replied Hodge, 'your master's not seen much law lately; maybe he's never read the new Divorce Act!' John being thus silenced, Hodge went to the old man, and offered him eighteenpence for his wife, who is a good deal younger than her husband. The price was at once accepted; and the woman, who was quite willing to be sold, was handed over . . . . [21]

Interview and sale were often separated by external considerations, chief among which was the necessity to fetch the woman or to await a public occasion for the transfer. At times it was the purchaser who needed the pause. Two Cornishmen in a hotel or inn at Truro

started talking about women and Jan Thomas said to this man I will sell you my wife if you want one The man said what is like he told him what see [sic] was like he said can I buy her next week as I have to go to the Bank to get some money Jan Thomas said that will be alright.

Few participants, however, showed the moderation of the fair-minded husband who sold his wife to a drunken purchaser 'the seller wishing to take no unfair advantage of him, consented to take her to bed and board 'till the next morning . . .'[22]

Many descriptions of sales make use of terms that could (but do not necessarily) apply to dress, describing the woman as 'smart', or 'tidy', the husband as 'ill-looking' or the purchaser as 'of good appearance'. A Nottingham seller was a soldier 'wearing his Majesty's uniform'. In 1836 a London husband is described as of 'shabby-genteel exterior', while twelve years later a man at Mansfield market was dressed as an agricultural labourer. Only one purchaser is accorded a description; he received his purchase at Nottingham in a smock frock. While little more than tentative suggestions are possible, it may be significant that only one case indicates that either husband or purchaser specifically dressed up for the occasion. Market psychology may have been involved in this choice of apparel, as a well-dressed seller or purchaser might have seemed too prosperous to extort a good price. Secure in the knowledge of *his* purchase, a Wiltshire suitor and a group of his friends bucked this trend. They arrived sporting white wedding cockades to demand the purchased wife — the bride *and* her husband, however, were nowhere to be found.[23]

The reverse held true for women when it came to dress. In only one example, a woman sold in her shift, is there a hint of substandard attire. Other cases emphasize clothing: 'respectably dressed' (with a gown *under* which the halter had been placed), 'well-dressed' and 'dashingly attired' are typical descriptions. One Berkshire sale notes the woman was 'decked out in her best'; a London report comments not only on the elegant dress of the woman but also on the fact that the 'silk halter round her shoulders' was 'covered with a rich white lace veil'. In Hereford pig market the wife had a smart hat and a red cloak — the latter, at least, a commonplace of contemporary female dress. A 'black gown and a new white bonnet' attired a Gloucestershire wife sold in about 1841. The following two excerpts are more complete descriptions of women involved in sales. In Wednesbury 'The woman was evidently in her best attire, her face was freshly washed, her hair was gathered behind in a bob and tied by a bit of blue ribbon . . .', while a Cumberland woman

> appeared above the crowd standing on a large oak chair . . . . She
> was dressed in rather a fashionable country style, and appeared to
> some advantage; she wore a leghorn bonnet, trimmed with crimson
> ribbons, her hair in rich ringlets, flowing underneath, a white
> muslin gown neatly flounced and trimmed, a handsome pattern
> thread lace cap, a bosom pin, with a rich silk canton crape shawl.

All this suggests that the wife, as the focal point of the sale, was
usually presented to best effect.[24]

The distance covered to reach a sale location depended to a large
extent upon spontaneity and on whether or not a private contract
was involved. (Often, it was not necessary to move to another
location to complete the bargain.) Only Smithfield market in
London and its Birmingham counterpart are known to have hosted
many sales for which distances covered by the participating parties
can be compiled. To judge by these, it might appear that minor
distances were involved in such transfers because the sales were
urban in nature. When rural markets are included, however, the
picture remains substantially the same. With a few exceptions,
distances involved were under 15 miles. At least initially, this
probably reflected not only the distribution of markets in England
but also the distance of a comfortable day's journey.[25] This
contention is supported by what is known of the location of
purchasers' habitations. The local nature of these sales may also
suggest the prevalence of a sense of continuity and community. In
at least three cases, however, both seller and purchaser went to
another market town, although they lived in the same place. As at
least one of these sales was previously agreed upon, this suggests
that some ulterior reason — perhaps the belief that a sale must
take place on a market day or strong local objections to the sale —
was responsible for this journey.[26]

Something should also be said about the movement of sales.
Some of these had a wide range; one unsuccessful sale in
Bewcastle, Cumberland, was followed by another attempt in
Newcastle, Northumberland, 51 miles away. A disallowed
Somerset sale of 1833 was followed by a successful purchase 3
miles distant, while a Devon woman was offered first at Modbury
and then at Plymouth. In the Cornish story of an oft-sold wife the
sales took place in markets almost equidistant from the couple's

home in Redruth. Finally, movement was possible even within a town. A sale interrupted at Smithfield market in London was concluded at Islington, while a Kent husband made use of an inn when he discovered the local market to be closed.[27]

The sale locale might be approached in a number of ways. Much depended on the type of bargain, the location being of small importance when dealing with spur-of-the-moment sales or with most cases involving private contract. As has already been mentioned, in several cases the husband led his wife caparisoned with a halter about her neck, waist or arm. A Mr Ducksworth, in about 1865, is supposed to have

> told his wife he was going to take her into market to sell her. He had a halter in his hand, and asked her if she was ready. Yes, she was quite ready. She took halter in her mouth, and he led her off to market place.

In sales at Epping and Walsall the lead was round both the woman's neck and waist. Sometimes the positioning of the halter is not specified; in other cases it is entirely absent. To sell a Belper debtor's wife, a halter was borrowed from a neighbour to bring her to market, while husbands in Liskeard and Boston bought their lead ropes on arrival.[28]

At times more intricate approaches were deemed necessary to legalize the sale. In 1824, at Arundel, Sussex,

> A man took his wife a mile out of the town, and then conducted her back with a halter round her neck, he having been told that *he must put a rope on at that distance* or the sale would not be legal; he brought her into the market . . . .

This is the only case collected in which distance was considered a prerequisite for the sale. There is, however, a general parallel from Warwickshire, where J. Harvey Bloom reports that any aspiring seller must take his wife and 'lead her prior to the sale through three turnpike gates or through as many villages, and must pay the toll'. In an early London sale the wife was led thrice around the room by the halter before being turned over to her purchaser. Here the number three is significant and has several parallels in folk belief. It was widely supposed that for a popular protest such as 'rough music' or 'riding the stang' to be legal, it had to be carried out on three nights or at three separate locations. One of Ethel

Rudkin's informants in Lincolnshire noted, 'Ridin' Stang 'ad ter be done three nights runnin', so as the law couldn't get 'em for it,' while an old waggoner added, 'Three 'ousen we used ter visit reg'lar . . . an' we 'ad ter do it for three neets runnin' . . . .' At Hedon, Yorkshire, in 1889 an effigy was carried for three nights in succession. In discussing rough music at Harpenden in the 1860s, Edwin Grey writes:

> I understood the unwritten law concerning these affairs to be that the music makers could, if they wished, perform on three successive nights, that they must keep on the move, that one could make as much noise as one wished, but that the names of the offenders or the nature of the offence must not be shouted out. With these conditions observed, it was affirmed that no police officer could interfere . . . .

In the Wiltshire of the 1830s processions took place during three three-night celebrations, for a grand total of 'nine nights of noise'. In Carmarthenshire, too, processions with effigies took place over a predetermined route for three weeks in a row. Visits on three successive nights *and* to three parishes (Hampton Lucy, Charlecote, and Wasperton) were required by Charlecote inhabitants wishing to protest their neighbours' immorality. At Headington in Oxfordshire processions with effigies and the banging of old tins followed a similar traditionally prescribed routine:

> The rule was that for 'rough music' the procession must march through three parishes, so whenever this form of punishment was considered necessary in Shotover, the men went to Stanton St John, through Forest Hill, and on to the keeper's lodge at Holton.

Repetition may have been used to stress the formal (as opposed to the riotous) aspects of such a protest. Perhaps related to such an idea was the location of many proscribed activities such as prize fights on the boundary of three counties, sites generally said to have been chosen for a practical reason since the activity could easily be moved to another jurisdiction. This use of three, however, may also have been grounded in symbolism. It was popularly believed in Buckinghamshire that a husband could chastise his wife by giving her three blows and no more. One American smock wedding was held at a crossroads where three townships met. Several divinations also involve threes, making use of streams 'where three lands meet'. [29]

Toll gates, when used in wife sales, provided proof of possession in the form of the receipt given for the wife's passage; in addition, perhaps, this gave a touch of 'official' approval. Moses Maggs noted at Wednesbury: 'It's all right, accordin' to law. I brought her through the turnpike, and paid the mon the toll for her.' This practice continued for at least another 30 years in Staffordshire. An account of an 1859 sale at Dudley reports that the husband 'took his wife, with a halter round her neck, through the turnpike gate at Dixon's-green, compelling the tollkeeper to take toll, and lead her about three quarters of a mile down to Hall-street, . . .' Whether this method of approach extended beyond west-central England, however, is uncertain. [30]

Few cases tell of the actual journey to the sale. The following Yorkshire account is an exception:

> The contracting parties, attended by several neighbours . . . left Great Horton for the purpose — the place of sale fixed upon being Bradford market. The whole party stopped at a beer house at Shearlbridge, hoping, we presume . . . to inspire themselves with courage sufficient for the occasion.

In this they failed, and the sale took place at the beer house. Other cases mention entry into market by husband, wife and purchaser-elect *en groupe*. A Mobberley husband 'brought a friend with him, armed with a stout stick' to urge on his wife. Nor is this the only evidence of compulsion or deceit; a 'brute of a fellow dragged his wife to the public quay' in Dartmouth, while in Cheltenham a man named Barnes did the same. Another Cheltenham wife was lured to market under false pretences and a halter thrown over her head; she fled before a sale was arranged. [31]

For each transaction of this kind there was another like that in Boston in which an 'impudent hussey being nothing loth to this public display of her attractions' was 'paraded . . . along the street' before the auction. Rumour in Plymouth noted that the wife 'had *rode* to town in the morning on her own horse', while a coach carried one Smithfield seller and his wife to auction. When the site of a sale was changed from Smithfield market to Islington another seller and spouse hired a hackney coach to reach the latter. All of these people appear to have been fairly well-off, for other cases suggest that transport to the sale was on foot. A Shropshire example varies this; the woman entered town in a cart.[32]

The arrival of the parties was timed to coincide with market activity and took place during normal business hours. John Osborne, coming to Maidstone only to discover that it was not market day, removed his wife to the Coal Barge Inn, Earl Street, to be auctioned. In other cases a delay ensued while crowds, attracted by notices, a bellman or rumour, were given time to assemble, and the parties then appeared to the populace at the agreed hour. When rumour had run before, however, it was unnecessary to wait for onlookers. In Truro 'It was rumoured . . . on Saturday last, that a woman was to be sold on the following Monday, being fair day, by her husband, and consequently the populace were on the *qui vive*, in expectation of some fun.' In Doncaster, Yorkshire, a crowd watched a husband conduct his wife to the Butter Cross. Again, in 1819, at Smithfield, 'An ill-looking diminutive fellow . . . entered the market, leading, by a halter round her neck, his wife, and followed by a numerous crowd of persons.' John Nash, a Bristol drover, appeared in Rosemary Street of that city, leading his wife and 'followed by a great concourse of spectators'. A Derbyshire debtor's wife was 'led into the Market-place, accompanied by a crowd'. From the standpoint of the viewers, these sales were spectacles well worth seeing; for the participants, crowds guaranteed the public nature of the ceremony.[33]

Although in most cases market toll was demanded after a wife was sold, in a few instances it was paid upon entry into market. At Stafford 'Rodney' Hall, 'Having taken . . . [his wife] . . . into the Market Place and paid toll . . . led her twice round the market . . . .' A similar charge was levied at Canterbury in 1820, when James Branchet 'engaged a pen, for which he paid the Tolenger the usual demand of sixpence'. For those who had not already obtained a halter, one was bought or borrowed at this point and placed on the woman. The price of a halter seems usually to have been 6d. If the husband himself did not plan to conduct the sale, it was necessary for him to obtain an auctioneer. In Sheffield in 1803 'The lady was put into the hands of a butcher, who held her by a halter fastened round her waist.' A Kent man attempted to secure a cattle salesman immediately upon arrival in market. When the salesman stated 'that his province was to sell beasts and sheep only', the husband settled the matter by renting a cattle pen. In London a haltered wife was delivered to a drover to be sold to the best bidder, while at Epping, a year later, the master of the parochial workhouse undertook this job. Even as late as the latter part of the nineteenth century a Suffolk husband broached the subject of a wife sale by asking the auctioneer at Bungay Fair if he could put in a lot.[34]

The display of the wife took several forms. The approach has already been alluded to. The woman was led through toll gates and villages, around the market or along the street to attract a crowd and ensure the public nature of the sale. Often the approach merely involved an 'official' entry into the sales room or into the open space where the sale was to take place, the wife having been kept near to hand. At other times the wife was led into the area by a halter and was actually tied to a post or railing. As Pillet makes clear, this was an action that paralleled techniques used with livestock: 'having placed a halter around her neck, he tied her to the railings that serve the same purpose for cattle' and 'The husband leads his wife, tied by the neck with a rope; he ties her up at the place where the cattle are sold.' At other sales as we have seen, it is noted that attempts were made to raise the principals above the surrounding crowd. With market crosses elevation must have been a major consideration. Elsewhere artificial platforms were used. At Bilston in the early nineteenth century a chair and table or two inverted tubs were provided for husband and wife, although anything that came to hand might suffice. A Carlisle woman stood on a large oak chair, her husband elevated nearby. Devonshire and Yorkshire sales in the 1830s and 1840s also made use of tables and chairs. As recently as the late nineteenth century a tinker auctioneer at Swaffham Bulbeck, descanting on a 'most desirable lot', ordered his partner to 'bring in the article and stand her on that footstool, that would-be buyers can get a good look at her.' A more complete description from Wednesbury is worthy of reproduction:

> some sort of order having been obtained, some ale was sent for, two tubs were brought out into the space and up-ended by the four stout fellows, on one of which the woman and her child were mounted, and on the other the man took his stand. While the ale was being consumed by the principals, a fiddler was brought in to enliven the proceedings with a merry tune or two.[35]

The halter used in leading the wife to market or specifically purchased for purposes of the sale was usually, although not always, a characteristic indication of the transaction. The halter or rope might be placed around the neck, the waist or an arm, as has been noted. Occasionally, a double loop was made to secure the wife. In a few instances, the rope was made of silk or ribbon or was decorated with ribbon, perhaps to lessen the humiliation of the symbol. (A rural case from Wales offers the only real anomaly. Here the equipage is translated as a 'saddle', but this may be due to oral substitution or misinterpretation.) In some parts of northern England halters were specifically included as part of the purchase price. Their use appears to have derived from an association with livestock, as a symbolic indication of ownership. Transfer of the halter signified a transfer of control, and at least one folktale deals with this theme. In Scottish versions of 'The Magician and his Pupil' a boy apprenticed to a magician learns how to shift his shape. He allows his father to sell him in a market to raise money but cautions him never to sell the halter. Were this to be done, the son would come under the influence of the magician. (In France when an animal was sold the purchaser took care to take the halter, so that the former master would be forgotten). On a more pragmatic level, the ribbons sometimes mentioned in connection with wife-selling were also used in recruiting and hiring, and Vaughan Williams and A. L. Lloyd report that 'The presenting and wearing of coloured ribbons, once common in Britain, still plays a prominent part in betrothal and marriage in Central and Eastern Europe.' Whatever occurred in the marriage ceremony itself, in England ribbons seem to have denoted subsequent possession, as is shown in the folk song 'The Trees They Are So High':

> We'll send your love to college, all for a year or two,
> And then perhaps in time the boy will do for you.
> I'll buy you white ribbons to tie about his waist,
> To let the ladies know that he's married.

Other versions mention tying 'round his college cap a ribbon of the blue' and binding 'a bunch of ribbons red/About his little waist'. In these cases, of course, it was the *husband* who was so bedecked. [36]

CHAPTER 6

Signed, Sealed and Delivered

Although some husbands sold their own wives and others employed auctioneers, the procedures used appear to have been much the same. Humorous speeches similar to those delivered by political orators are found in several cases and are exemplified by the litany chanted by Rough Moey of Wednesbury:

> Laerdies an' gentlemin, 'ere's all yoar good 'ealths! . . . Laerdies an' gentlemin . . . we all on us know how the matter stands. It caw't be helped, so we needn't be so savige about it. . . . Laerdies an' gentlemin, I ax lafe to oppose to yer notice, a very hondsome young ooman, and a nice little babby wot either belongs to me or to somebody else. . . . Her's a good cratur. . . and goos pritty well in harness, wi' a little flogging. Her can cook a sheep'd yed like a Christian, and mak broth as good as Lord Dartmouth. Her con carry a hundred and a 'alf o' coals from the pit for three good miles; her con sell it well, and put it down her throat in less ner three minits. . . . Now, my lads, roll up, and bid spirted. It's all right, accordin' to law. I brought her through the turnpike and paid the mon the toll for her. I brought her wi' a halter, and had her cried; so everythin's right accordin' to law, and there's nothin' to pay. Come on wi' yer bids, and if yer gies me a good price for the ooman, I'll gie yer the young kid inter the bargain. Now, gentlemin, who bids? Gooin', gooin', gooin'! I cawn't relay — as the octioneer sez, I cawn't dwell on this lot!'

Physical infirmities that could not be glossed over were often emphasized for a laugh. Thus a tinker's wife was characterized as:

> of average height and seems quite normal; her hair is iron grey, not plastered down or waved, but with a wildness like a poet's; her forehead is not one of those high sort, but receding; her hair and eyebrows are not far apart. She has one very good eye, which looks straight at you, the other wanders up to the North; they are both

gravied and watery; the nose is long and narrow, turned up a bit and very red (denoting a tendency to prevarication); the mouth is large with thick sausage lips, denoting that the elbow had often been tilted in raising a mug to the mouth. Her chin is not prominent, but cut off so that she would not be able to poke it in your face, if she was annoyed. Her back is a little bent, but able to carry weight, which she has obviously been accustomed to do; but there is this advantage, she is not likely to bother you with star gazing.

At Bungay Fair, the auctioneer characterized another wife as 'so fat and puffed out she gets wedged in the doorways of Mr. Prinny's house'. That such honesty was not always the case is suggested by a Warwickshire controversy in which the purchaser claimed a woman had been fraudulently sold to him as 'potentially child-bearing'. More formal dialogues are attributed to other husbands. Joseph Thompson of Carlisle referred to several contemporary events when he declaimed:

> Gentlemen, I speak truth from my heart, when I say, may God deliver us from troublesome wives and frolicsome widows . . .! Avoid them the same as you would a mad dog, a roaring lion, a loaded pistol, cholera morbus, mount Etna, or any other pestilential phenomena in nature.

Thompson's address was divided into four parts: an announcement of the sale, listings of the wife's bad and good qualities and a concluding statement. Here, as in broadside ballads, a catchword, 'Gentlemen', at the beginning of paragraphs was used to gain the listeners' attention. The auctioneer's discussion of qualities, like his discourse on physical points, was often of a humorous nature. 'Her con swear like a trooper, an' fight like a game cock', said one. There seems to have been a common tendency to emphasize the woman's capacity for drink. Often only fragments of the patter remain; a York wife was described as 'a clean, industrious, quiet, and careful woman attractive in appearance and well-mannered for a woman in her position of life', while a London woman was characterized as 'a buxom, healthy dame — a frugal, notable housewife; but . . . the owner, having no further occasion for her, wished to dispose of her to the best bidder'. There was some interplay between the crowd and the principals. People exchanged comments not only with the auctioneer but also with the wife. In other examples the husband contented himself with announcing the price for which he

A true and singular Account of
Wife-Selling
EXTRAORDINARY!

ABOUT half past twelve, on Thursday the 12th of December 1822, the public were attracted to Plymouth-*cattle*-market, in consequence of notice which had been previously given, that a man, at that time and place, was to dispose of his wife by public sale! The report which accompanied the notice stated that the *lady* was not only young and handsome, but that she had rode to town in the morning on her own horse, of her own free will and accord, and with consent of her husband, who was to act the part of an auctioneer on the occasion ; and that she would moreover, in the course of a few days, succeed to £600 which her husband could not touch. The concourse of spectators was immense, and they were not kept waiting long, the husband and wife having appeared in the market-place exactly at the appointed time, the latter accompanied by the ostler of the Lord Exmouth Inn, Old Town.—The husband put *the article* up at once, and asked for bidders.—Five shillings was the first offer—ten the next— fifteen the third, and so on, until the ostler aforesaid bade three pounds ; when to the evident disappointment of the auctioneer, as well as of the lady, two constables took possession of the *goods*, and with them the auctioneer, and carried them both directly to the Guildhall, where the chief magistrate was then sitting. The parties were placed before the mayor. The husband named Brooks, and who resides at Ivy Bridge, on being asked why he had committed so illegal an act as to attempt the sale of his wife in the way he had been doing ? very innocently said — They were both willing, and he did not think there was any harm in it—they had not lived together for a considerable time—they had been married about two years and a half, and she brought him a child about three weeks after marriage ! which until after it was born, he never knew any thing about ; that the child soon after died ; that he got a coffin for it, paid the expences of the funeral, and put it *comfortably out of the way*, without ever reproaching his wife with her conduct, but all would not do. She soon after deserted him, notwithstanding his kindness, and went to live with another man, by whom she had one child since, and he was informed she was again pregnant with another.' On being asked who had advised or told him that he could sell his wife, he said ' many people in the country told him he could do it ; and that in consequence of her coming to him, and saying that a person would give him twenty pounds, and take her altogether clean off his hands, (three pounds in hand, and seventeen more at Christmas,) he had had her advertised for sale in Modbury, on three separate market-days, and had come to Plymouth that morning by her appointment to get the business finished.' The lady, a good-looking young woman, stated, ' that she and her husband could not agree, and that in consequence, as she knew of a person that would take her, and give twenty pounds for the bargain, she wished to get separated from him, and she had been told by different persons that the thing could be done by sale in the market-place on a market-day.' On being asked the name of the person who was to buy her, she said ' it was Kane, and that he lived near Plystock : she further said he had disappointed her in not coming forward to bid as he had promised her, and that in consequence of his having deceived her, she engaged with the ostler of the Lord Exmouth Inn, where she was in the habit of putting up her horse when she came to town, to bid for her, if the price did not exceed twenty pounds. She said she had left her own horse by the way, on account of its having a sore back, and borrowed one in lieu of it of a person near Ivy Bridge, with whom she stated herself to be in the habits of intimacy.

After a good deal of consultation it was determined upon, that the parties should be bound over to answer the charge at the ensuing sessions ; but their own recognizances were taken, neither of them being able to find sureties.

W. Stephenson, Printer, Gateshead.

An account of a Plymouth wife sale (case **186**) printed by W. Stephenson, Gateshead, c.1822

was willing to sell his consort. A London male took a stand and repeated: 'At fifteen shillings, my wife! Who wants my wife for fifteen shillings?' A Lincolnshire man sold his woman for '2/- wet and 2/- dry', while a Nottingham husband declared, 'Here is my wife for sale, I shall put her up at two shillings and sixpence.'[1]

Some attention has already been paid to the crowds that greeted many participants upon their arrival at market or gathered in response to advertisements concerning the sale. These varied widely, from vast numbers to only a few people. To an extent, the press of numbers increased the chance of a good sale if the purchaser had not been decided upon beforehand, but it raised its own problems. At the best of times crowds were rowdy and full of chaff; they could also instigate tumults, which disrupted the sale procedure. In Staffordshire special individuals were responsible for crowd control. An early nineteenth-century sale provides one such example:

> Just before the specified time a crowd gathered in the Market Place, in front of the White Lion, a well-frequented tavern, where four tall fellows, armed with cudgels, cleared a space, and kept back the eager sightseers from crushing upon a man, a woman, and an infant — the lions of the day.

In Bilston guards were responsible for clearing a path to an inn selected for the post-sale ratification and drinking.[2]

Several husbands stated a minimum (or asking) price for their wives. At least once a woman was withdrawn when she failed to reach this fixed amount; on other occasions husbands were forced to drop below their stated demand. There appears to have been no single widespread minimum price; this depended either upon local practice or what the market would bear. Many sales offers were initiated by purchasers, and others were, of course, the result of previous agreement or private contracts. But most examples, even those in which a potential purchaser figured, involved bidding for the woman in 'open market'. A London purchaser

> began to examine the wife like he had examined, many times before, a mare that I had seen sold to him; the inspection was favourable, and he offered the price demanded, the husband still repeated his cries to try to draw some bidders, but none appearing, he pocketed the money.

In Yorkshire, dealings were more direct. '"What do you ask for your cow?" said a bystander. "A guinea," replied the husband. "Done!" cried the other.' Several sales involved haggling between seller and purchaser. In one Sheffield case 'The husband demanded £3 for his wife; She herself said it was too much, and her new man said he wouldn't give more than a sovereign. Finally, 30s was the sum agreed upon.' Often more than one individual was involved, several people vying with each other as they bid up the price. In some cases even pre-selected purchasers were forced to run this gamut, and there is a Lancashire example in which the price was definitely bid up in fun. Bids tended to increase in increments of 3d or 2s 6d, but this could reflect available currency as much as customary auctioneering practices. In two instances evidence suggests that the purchaser was acting as an agent. A Lancashire wife appears to have been put up again for auction immediately upon her refusal to accompany the first purchaser. This is reminiscent of a condition of sale stipulated by one Cambridgeshire tinker — 'if there is any dispute, the lot to be put up again'. Finally, an unusual example shows two buyers pooling their resources to purchase the wife between them. [3]

The success of auctions varied. In addition to those wives for whom no acceptable bids were offered, there were cases in which the woman hung on hand for some time. Other transactions were quickly closed, as in 1818, when a Cornish bidder was immediately declared the wife's purchaser. Final prices also varied widely. It may be significant that many of the earliest wife sales appear to have involved significant sums, while the prices paid for later purchases seem to have been only token. Tokenism could explain why such bargains do not appear to follow the rise and fall of wages and commodity prices. Only enough money passed to make the bargain binding by supplying 'consideration' for the contract. This is not to indicate that some sales were not based on financial advantage. For example, there was a 100-guinea offer in Yorkshire, and one canny husband repurchased his wife, only to resell her for a higher price. In London a husband who had secured a purchaser 'still repeated his cries to try to draw some bidders'. A Devon bargain in kind was also based on economics:

> One man offered a coat, but as he was a small man and the seller was stout, when he found that the coat would not fit him, he refused it. Another offered a 'phisgie,' i.e. a pick, but this was also declined as the husband possessed a 'phisgie' of his own.

While many reports indicate surprise at the economic values placed on women, only a few go further to state specifically whether these were believed to be high or low. A Towcester sale in 1797 raised £25 (considered a huge sum), while the contemporary Newcastle price of 10s 6d was considered small. A Smithfield exchange of 7s was (incorrectly) said to have been the highest given in that market. The 'disconsolate' husband at Holme-upon-Spalding Moor went further, declaring the 2s price paid for his wife to be 'quite enough for her, unless she mended her manners'. [4]

Occasionally, prices seem to have been decided upon before actual bidding. An incomplete transaction at Ashby-de-la-Zouch had a rumoured sale price of 5s. Elsewhere purchasers set limits on their expenditure; a Devon wife told an ostler acting as her agent not to bid over £20 for her person. In several cases husbands tried to raise the level of bidding; Rough Moey snorted:

> Eighteenpence . . . on'y eighteenpence for a strong and full-growed young ooman! Why, yo'd ha' to pay the parson seven and six for marryin' yer, an' here's a wife ready made to yer honds — an' on'y eighteenpence bid! . . .
>
> I'll tell thee wot, Jack . . . if thee't mak it up three gallons o' drink, her's thine. I'll ax thee naught fer the babby, an' the halter's worth a quart. Come, say six shillins!

A Cambridgeshire tinker had similar problems with price: 'Two bob I'm bid; it is a disgraceful price, she is dirt cheap.' Such techniques may have been responsible for the increase in price registered in a Nottingham sale with only a single bidder (!), but they did not always sit well with the crowd. The Herefordshire husband who remonstrated that his pretty wife should be valued more highly was greeted with chaffing cries of 'Keep her, master, keep her for her good looks.' In a few cases the purchaser had trouble raising the agreed payment. In Newark a wife was sold for 30s, but the bidding brickmaker could only possess himself of a sovereign; he sloped off with the woman anyhow. At a sale in Horsham the buyer sacrificed his watch to purchase the wife. [5]

Occurring only in earlier cases, sale by weight reinforces similarities with livestock sales and slave sales noted elsewhere. In Massachusetts Hannah Hull, the only daughter of Captain Hull (who produced the Pine Tree Shilling), very appropriately received as a dowry her weight in silver shillings. Such payment in wife sales was occasionally by guess rather than by actual weight. This equation of value with weight may have represented a rule of thumb as to the wife's usefulness based on general health and constitution. Payment might also be partially or totally by barter rather than involving a monetary return. Most commonly cited as commodities for barter are alcoholic beverages, suggesting at least a partial confusion with the traditional post-sale drink. Food, tobacco, livestock or other animals, even lottery tickets were also offered in exchange. Occasionally, these returns were themselves bartered or sold. [6]

Sometimes part of the purchase price was returned to the purchaser. The most common of such sweeteners was 'luck money'. Returns not only kept transactions from degenerating entirely into the commercial but also allowed an area of negotiation between the price stated by the seller and that which the buyer was willing to pay. This practice seems to have been particularly common in northern England, although a few examples are found in London. Such returns ranged from about a tenth to a quarter of the purchase price. Now and again rebates followed a different pattern. A London publican sold his wife for half a guinea but turned over a hefty £20 load of Birmingham halfpennies to her purchaser. In Suffolk Farmer Frost put £100 in his wife's pocket to ensure her purchase. Other cases show money given for a new gown or a coach trip. Additionally, in late eighteenth- and early nineteenth-century sales the woman might be offered with her body clothes, furniture, bed and bedding or other items. There was often a division of children, the split probably determined by both social and economic factors. [7]

In addition to the price given for the wife, 'luck money' and other extras supplied by the husband, several miscellaneous economic transactions might follow sales. Most common was the payment of market toll, a practice touched on earlier. In most of these cases this payment dealt with fees for actual transactions rather than those for the use or rental of market property. In some cases payment was entered in the toll book, often kept at a local inn. Two examples of entries survive at second-hand: 'Aug. 31, 1773. Samuel Whitehouse, of the parish of Willenhall, in the county of Stafford, this day sold his wife Mary Whitehouse, in open Market, to Thomas Griffiths of Birmingham *value, one shilling* . To take her with all faults.' Signatures of the principals and a witness followed. In Brighton, in 1826, entry was thus: 'May 17, 1826, Mr. Hilton, of Lodsworth, publicly sold his wife for 30s., upon which the toll of one shilling was paid.' [8]

Other post-sale payments cover the reimbursement of those

involved peripherally in the transaction. At Fittleworth the auctioneer 'received half a guinea for his trouble'; at Brighton the rate was one shilling. Six years later in London this remuneration was doubled to pacify another auctioneer, a drover who refused to release the wife until he had been paid commission. Even one *witness* in Yorkshire was paid 6d as wages. Another subsidiary transaction involved resale of the halter by the purchaser, an interesting example of thrift in daily life.[9]

In addition to the above market records, written contracts often specified the terms of the transaction. In many cases these were drawn up at inns, but some parties received professional drafting assistance. Several examples of forms follow:

Memorandum.   Oct. 24, 1766

It is this day agreed on between John Parsons, of the parish of Midsummer Norton, in the county of Somerset, cloth-worker, and John Tooker, of the same place, gentleman, that the said John Parsons, for and in consideration of the sum of six pounds and six shillings in hand paid to the said John Parsons, doth sell, assign, and set over unto the said John Tooker; with all right, property, claim, services, and demands whatsoever, that he, the said John Parsons, shall have in or to the said Ann Parsons, for and during the term of the natural life of her, the said Ann Parsons. In witness whereof I, the said John Parsons, have set my hand the day and year first above written.

I, *Booth Millward*, bought of *William Clayton*, his wife, for five shillings, to be delivered on the 25th of March, 1831, to be delivered in a *aliter* at Mr. John Lomases House.

July 3rd, 1857.

Thomas Middleton delivered up his wife Mary Middleton to Philip Rostins, and Sold her for one shilling and one quart of ale, and part wholy and solely for life, not trouble one another for life.

These notices were signed and witnessed. Still other examples are found in late nineteenth-century Yorkshire.

> At the Royal Oak, Sheffield, I, Abraham Boothroyd, agree to sell my wife Clara to William Hall, both of Sheffield, for the sum of 5s.

> Mr. Taylor to have my wife, Elizabeth Smith, free from me for ever, to do as she has a mind, this day, December 11, 1893.

A Belfast example, quoted in court, read: 'I, George Drennan, do hereby agree, to sell to Patrick O'Neill my wife for the sum of 1d. and a dinner.' These documents presumably served as proof of purchase. A Bodmin man used one (unsuccessfully) to justify his forthcoming marriage to a purchased woman, while a wife in a Yorkshire court defended the legality of her sale: 'I have it to show in black and white, with a receipt stamp on it.'[10]

In many of these agreements witnesses played an important role. Because writing skills were not universal, some parties only made their mark, so that recognition of the principals involved was an important consideration. In Whitehaven when an innkeeper was summoned to observe the transaction she ran out of the room, shocked and refusing to have anything to do with the business; 'An impartial friend was then invited off the street to perform the part of witness, and the transaction was closed with every imaginary [imaginable?] formality.' A Nottingham witness has left this reminiscence of his part in a sale:

> beckoning to me one of them said: 'I want you to witness that this man has offered to sell his wife for a shilling and a pint of ale.' The bargain was struck between them. I saw the shilling paid over and we all went to the Bell Inn, where I had a drink out of the two-handled pint measure which was placed before us.

Elsewhere, witnesses also served to testify to the transaction, the delivery of the wife and the husband's non-liability for debt.[11]

Potential liability originating from the wife's debts occasionally formed an important consideration for husbands, especially when sales had been motivated by economic factors. In 1789 the following advertisement was placed in the *Ipswich Journal*:

OCT. 29, SAMUEL BALLS sold his wife to ABRAHAM RADE in

the parish of Blythburgh in this county for 1s. A halter was put round her, and she was resigned up to this Abraham Rade. No person or persons to intrust her with my name, Samuel Balls, for she is no longer my right.

A similar procedure was followed in Yorkshire, where:

Benjamin Brown, of Foxholes, hereby gives notice, that he sold his wife Hannah Brown, to Robt. Turner, shoemaker, of Hull, and delivered her in a halter at the Cross, on Tuesday market. Nov. 24, 1818.

The oral announcement of an Irthlingborough sale may also have been designed to disclaim liability. In any case, it is certain that Lancashire and London husbands sent the bellman round in order to announce that they would no longer be responsible for a former wife's debts.

Yesterday the Common Cryer of St. Clements, made Proclamation, before a great Number of People, in Milford-Lane, Essex street, and Clare-Market, that if any one hereafter should give any Credit to the wife of the Alehouse keeper in Milford-lane, who was sold by her Husband, on Saturday last for Ten Guineas; her Husband would not pay any Debts she should contract. [12]

Other post-sale ceremonies were practised only occasionally. An Oxfordshire case involved the official weighing of the wife — a necessary procedure as her price had been agreed 'per the pound'. In scattered locations mention is made of a bargain being 'struck'. This could be a physical action, with the purchaser attempting to strike the hand of the seller. If he was allowed to do so, the bargain was considered to have been concluded. '[T]he marriage service was afterwards read by a merry fellow of an auctioneer' at Fittleworth, suggesting that the institution was not always considered a proper substitute for the religious rite. The placing or displacing of wedding rings played a part in several transfers. An Oxfordshire woman called for her new circlet, while a wife at Alfreton, Derbyshire, 'readily agreed [to the sale], took off her wedding ring, and from that time considered herself the property of the purchaser.' That the return of the old ring was often expected is suggested by the following anecdote of a Mansfield sale:

After the sale Freeman demanded of the woman the wedding-ring he supposed her to have on her finger. The wily woman, having surmised that such a circumstance might probably occur, had provided herself with a penny brass ring, which she presented to him instead of the gold one, and which the unblushing salesman, with much apparent complacency, deposited carefully in his pocket.

In Staffordshire a different sundering of bonds, reminiscent of Islam's three repetitions, may have been practised. A contemporary newspaper reports that a Dudley husband 'in his ignorance, thinks — this repeated three times — she has actually no claim upon him'. Sometimes it was customary for wife and purchaser to kiss; in one example this courtesy was extended to the former husband by his wife. A Goole waterman offered his wife a parting handshake. Other post-sale actions are slightly more difficult to interpret: a Bristol purchaser took the woman he had acquired to an old clothes shop, 'where he rigged her afresh'. This seems similar to many smock weddings, in which it was felt necessary for the purchaser publicly to assume responsibility for the bride. Providing new clothes showed that she had no assets from her former husband's estate. In Buckinghamshire 'The purchaser accompanied her [the wife] to the house of her husband, who, having seen them within doors, locked them in, and gave them the key of the door through the window.'[13]

The major post-sale proceeding, of course, was the delivery of the wife. This was often according to previous agreement and might depend upon prior payment of the purchase price. At other times it coincided with the transfer of all or part of the purchase money. In Renfrewshire this amount was tabled, with the transfer to be completed the next day, while in Yorkshire delivery was in the presence of a witness. A Rotherham woman surrendered herself after the sale, and a Derbyshire purchaser claimed his bargain on the following Monday — 'on entering the house he made known to Mrs. G. the purport of his visit.'

Several cases have elements of ceremony attached to the transfer. In Scotland a husband confessed that 'he took his wife be the hand to give her to the other, but the other denys that he receaved her;' in Wales the purchaser climbed on to the platform and helped the wife down from her chair before paying the agreed sum to her husband. A Staffordshire case also mentions formal delivery. This may well have taken the form of an exchange of the halter, the most widely accepted method of denoting the transfer. As described by Pillet, the purchaser untied the wife and led her (still haltered) by the cord until he had crossed half the square. Most cases state only that the wife was delivered thus equipped, but a few elaborate upon this. *Jackson's Oxford Journal* describes one transfer thus:

> After a Conversation about the Payment of Five Shillings as the Purchase Money, the old Husband very deliberately pulled out a penny Slip and tied round the Waist of his Wife, the End of which he held fast till he had pocketed Three Shillings in Part, the Purchaser not abounding in Cash. He then put the Cord into the Hands of the new Husband, and took a French Leave.

Transfer of the rope appears to have symbolized the transfer of the woman and often took place only after full payment. Occasionally, transfer was accompanied by a speech or formula. At Spalding, Lincolnshire,

> Hand took [a halter] and put [it] upon her, and delivered her to Hardy, pronouncing the following words: — 'I now, my dear, deliver you into the hands of Thomas Hardy, praying the blessings of God to attend you both, with all happiness.' Hardy replied: 'I now, my dear, receive you with the blessings of God, praying for happiness,' Etc. and took off the halter, saying, 'Come, my dear, I receive you with a kiss; and you, Hand, shall have a kiss at parting.'

A similar statement and response is found in an 1837 Derbyshire case:

> Allen purchased a halter, placed it round his wife, and gave one end of the rope to Taylor, saying, 'I, John Allen, was bereaved of my wife, by James Taylor, of Shottle, on 11th of July last; I have brought her here to sell her for 3s. 6d; will you buy her, James?' James answered, 'I will, here is the money, and you are witness, Thomas Riley,' calling to a potman who was appointed for the purpose.

In another Lincolnshire example a white ribbon was placed around the woman, and the husband completed the transaction by saying, 'There, now, thou wilt either lead or drive.' Perhaps the most involved ritual of all, described in a period newspaper as a 'ludicrous piece of business', involved Jonathan Jowett's transfer of his wife to her purchaser, William Taylor, at Wath Bowling-Green:

a regular Procession was first made, in the following Order: Jowett went first, having his Head ornamented, by his own Desire, with a large Pair of Ram's Horns gilded; on the Front of which the following Sentence was wrote in golden Letters, 'cornuted by William Taylor;' a broad Collar was fixed about his Neck, by which a Ring and a Cord being fastened thereto, one of his Neighbours led him: And the Wife, with a Halter about her Neck, was led by her Husband to the Place appointed . . . .[14]

Other cases indicate that it was necessary for the woman to be led for a certain distance or across a certain area to establish ownership, much as in the initial entrance into market. In Derbyshire and Herefordshire this trek covered the market place; in Suffolk it involved crossing the turnpike. Elsewhere the procession continued on to the purchaser's house, and the distance involved could be fairly long — 12 miles in the case of Henry Frise and approximately 7 miles in that of 'Drummer' Aston. The halter might be removed as soon as the transfer had been signed or might be retained by the husband. In Newark 'a difficulty arose, the lady refusing to be delivered up in a halter', but this seems to have been an exception. The woman was not always led away on foot; some cases mention a horse or other conveyance, and one purchaser 'drove for Blackfriars-bridge, amidst the huzzas of the mob'.[15]

One single tale makes mention of another aspect of post-sale activity. At Blackburn, Lancashire, the wife reacted as follows:

She says as he has bought her she supposes he has bought everything belonging to her. Yes, he says, he supposes he has, but he doesn't care about that. She puts her hand in her bosom and pulls out a bag containing £200 in gold, and gives it to [the] old man.[16]

Many wife sale prices included partial or total alcoholic payment. Beer, particularly ale, appears to have been the most popular commodity, with the spirits used described by taste and tradition. Gin is found from the 1790s through the 1830s, with punch (a mixture of alcoholic beverages) restricted to the late eighteenth or early nineteenth centuries. Brandy, whisky, and cider each received single citations. No mention is made of wine or rum. Mary Dorothy George noted that in London 'Gin was said to be the drink of the more sedentary trades, weavers particularly, and of women. Labouring men and artisans doing heavy work drank strong beer,' but not enough evidence is available to assess this statement in terms of wife-selling. The amount of liquor mentioned is reasonably consistent. Only three examples occur of quantities in excess of 1 gallon; in only one case is an amount more than 3 gallons involved. This could, of course, be a consequence of the tariffs on alcoholic beverages. After the early 1860s there is a concentration of examples in which alcohol formed the total sale price instead of a part. [17]

Drink appears to have become so closely associated with prices that its presence must often be inferred. In 1808 a London husband 'retired to a public-house to celebrate his divorce'. Another case makes it plain that both seller and purchaser continued to celebrate after the sale: 'The weaver got intoxicated on the occasion and fell into the dock [at Billingsgate], where it is probable he would have been drowned, but for the exertions of the tailor.' The mechanics of the post-sale drink are revealed in an account of a Staffordshire sale about 1823:

> 'I'll gie thee half-a-crown, o'd Rough Un,' came from the young man who all knew would be the purchaser.
> 'I'll tell thee wot, Jack,' said Moey, 'if thee't mak it up three gallons o' drink, her's thine . . . . Come, say six shillins!'
> After a little chaffering the young man agreed to pay for three gallons of ale, which it was stipulated should be forthcoming at once, so that his newly-bought wife, himself, and a few chosen 'butties,' not forgetting the obliging fiddler, should participate in the ratifying pledge-cup.

At Bilson in 1819 bodyguards cleared the way to an inn after the sale, where (after the transfer and signing of an agreement) the purchase price was 'spent in spirits and beer, the party drinking together good humouredly as though no such thing as a divorce' had taken place. Several cases mention the presence of the three principal parties at post-sale drinking sessions. In Nottingham a gallon of ale was consumed even before the woman was delivered over, while in Worcester alcohol featured in the sales document, being given 'to moisten the bargain'. Even in cases where drink was not specifically supplied, evidence suggests that most or all of the money was used for this purpose. In London, for instance, 'The parties adjourned to a neighbouring public-house where the late husband spent the greater part of the money in brandy and water.' At Epping the magistrates, roused to action by the shouts of a crowd, dispatched an officer to investigate a wife sale occurring almost under their judicial noses: 'the husband . . . was brought before them in a state of intoxication, having already spent the half-crown [purchase price] in gin.'[18]

The composition of the drinking party varied. In addition to the principals, friends and helpers might be invited. Witnesses were also invited; John R. Riley, who vouched for a Nottingham sale, accompanied the group to the Bell Inn, 'where I had a drink out of the two-handled pint measure which was placed before us'. In other cases the triangle of principals fragmented. Mention is made of the wife and purchaser toasting the bargain, or of the husband drinking alone to celebrate . . . or to forget. Occasionally, post-sale binges ended violently. One London woman was purchased 'for 4s. and the promise of a parting glass', but 'the finish of the bargain was attended with a *row* and breaking the windows of the public house to which they ajourned.' In 1817 the participants adjourned to the Ram 'to wet the bargain' and transfer the purchase price. 'A great mob followed, and several panes of glass were broken in the windows of some of the neighbouring houses.'[19]

What was the purpose of the post-sale drink? The clue lies in such phrases as 'to moisten the bargain' and 'to wet the bargain'. While it is true that alcohol probably helped to cushion the emotional shock arising from the sale, the post-sale drink had several close parallels in contemporary social life. In both Norfolk and Suffolk drink served as a bribe. Here ale was given to the man who rang handbells and fired guns to 'music' newlyweds as an inducement to leave the couple in peace. A similar distribution (including food) was made to the populace during certain mock punishments and at election time as well. Drinks were the perquisite of participants in several feasts and celebrations, such as the Newcastle-under-Lyme mock mayor ceremony and the Black Country toast ale on Mothering Sunday. Much of this alcohol was either a reward for past services and good behaviour or a bribe for their continuance.[20]

Numerous occasions for ritual drinking also occurred during work. Many of these were directly or indirectly associated with the idea of contracts or with the change of state that such agreements might betoken. 'Footings' or 'foot ale' was paid by those who were beginning to learn a new trade, who were visiting the works or handling tools of a craft for the first time or who had completed serving their time as apprentices. In speaking of these practices, a Parliamentary Report notes:

> It is extraordinary the number of drinking usages among the working classes to which custom had given the force of an irresistible law. It is to these usages, more than the temptation of liquor, that the sober and industrious are led, imperceptibly, to form habits of intemperance. Among the chief of these is the usage of exacting entry money, or *footing*, when a new journeyman enters a factory, or when a new apprentice is bound to a trade. The money thus raised is, with a few solitary exceptions, always spent in drink . . . . And besides these footings, fines are exacted from each other on all imaginable occasions that may furnish a fair pretext for raising drink-money . . . .

Additionally, any worker who became a father was liable to stand treat in a celebration known as 'wetting the baby's head'.[21]

Justices, when taking their place on the Middlesex Bench, were required to pay a celebratory fee known as 'colt money'. In 1684 it was ordered that this should be spent on a piece of plate rather than on 'wine or treatment as formerly', but Mary Dorothy George doubts whether this was carried out in practice. In 1722 the judges for Westminster decided that anyone who might

> acquire any title of honour or dignity, or be married, be desired by the Chairman . . . to pay him one guinea each person, which money is to be applied by the Chairman in the same manner as the money called colt money is to be applied.

By 1806 the 'footing' was known as 'spoon money' — 5 guineas, which was to be paid by 'every gentleman who shall qualify himself to act as a justice of the peace for the city and liberty'. With this may be compared contemporary eighteenth or twenty-first birthday celebrations, normally featuring large amounts of drink for friends and acquaintances.[22]

As early as 1725 Benjamin Franklin, when employed at a printer's shop near Lincoln's Inn Fields, was required to pay 'footing', first in the press room and later (an additional 5s) in the composing room. Today in the custom of 'banging out' a newly qualified apprentice is still smeared with printers' ink and led through various departments of the firm, in each of which he has to promise to provide beer money. Alan Smith has noted the variety of payments due within a typical print shop (see table 1).[23]

In the early nineteenth century, among hat makers:

When a young man came up to London and got employment for the first time, the first claim made upon him by his shopmates in his own department was 10s. for a 'maiden garnish'. All the men who partook of this paid their joinings . . . a contribution of 3d. a head . . . . The payment of that 10s. was only the commencement of a series of financial inflictions. . . .

Despite the supposed abolishment of these fines, they survived to the end of the century; any infraction was punished by a levy of 1s 4d (for a gallon of beer), plus 2d each for 'joiners'. A new tailor provided half a gallon of beer as 'footing'. Other fines were paid for births, birthdays and wedding anniversaries. [24]

Francis Place, writing in 1825, summarized the forfeits imposed on coopers (see table 2); in 1780, the period about which Place was writing, it was possible for them to pay out more in fines and forfeits than they took in for a piece of work! By 1795, however, the fines (presumably for release from indenture), were reduced to 2 gallons of beer; in 1821, they were abolished. Building jobs normally began with a preliminary drink, the dregs of which were poured on the site. The placing of the first chimney pot or the completion of the roof tree ('topping off', as it was known) was occasion for another celebration. At Shottesbrook, Berkshire, a fourteenth-century architect is supposed to have been killed by a fall from his recently completed spire, where he had climbed to drink the king's health. For harvest work agricultural labourers appointed one of their group as 'lord', who was responsible for negotiating a contract with the farmer. The satisfactory completion of this bargain was signalled by a handshake, along with a shilling 'handsel' for each man and a pint of 'dew beer' to wet the sickle and drink success to the harvest. In Essex this man was in charge of 'shoeing' new reapers in return for beer; in Suffolk he collected money for 'trailing beer' (due as a fine from any who trampled the corn or made it harder to cut) or by 'crying largesse' (requesting a shilling of every stranger who passed the field. [25]

In such ritual carousals (particularly the agricultural examples) the connection of drinks with a change of state, and especially with contracts, is emphasized. Scattered references to 'colts' and 'shoeing' indicate livestock parallels reminiscent of those found in wife-selling. There seems little doubt, therefore, that wife-selling's post-sale drink was more than an afterthought — it was an integral part of the ceremony.

106

TABLE 1   PRINT-SHOP PAYMENTS

Occasion	Comments	Amount
worker's entry into shop	'bienvenue' or 'entrance money'	2s 6d
worker's return to shop after absence	—	1s 3d
worker's marriage	—	2s 6d
wife's first visit to shop	'welcome drink' (paid by wife)	6d
	'welcome drink' (paid by each journeyman)	2d
birth of a son	—	1s 0d
birth of a daughter	—	6d
apprentice's 'binding'	—	2s 6d
apprentice's release from indentures	—	2s 6d

TABLE 2   FORFEITS PAYABLE BY COOPERS

Occasion	Amount
apprentice's release from indentures	3 gallons of beer (3s 6d)
each piece of work done for the first time	1 gallon of beer (1s 2d)
each different sort of timber used [for the first time?]	1 gallon of beer (1s 2d)

A few wife-sale cases show evidence of festivities connected with post-marital celebrations. In Yorkshire, for example, 'the buyer and his purchased wife were immediately put to bed,' a common north-country wedding practice. A different sort of celebration is found in Lincolnshire:

> A dinner was ordered by the two parties for nine persons then present, and the lady dined with great composure at the head of the table, between Buckram and Wax. After dinner the lady retired, and the remainder of the day was spent with harmony and mirth, agreeable to all parties.

Very occasionally, such celebrations occur elsewhere. At a Shearbridge sale the group of principals and neighbours proceeded to the purchaser's house, where they 'finished the day in drunken revelry'. This practice may have been related to the dinners and feasts associated with many weddings. A faint reflection of the custom may possibly be seen in the dinner specified as partial payment in one nineteenth-century Belfast sale.[126]

On at least three occasions church bells were rung to celebrate wife sales. In 1770 a shepherd at Iver who had sold his wife 'generously gave the Ringers a Crown to ring a merry Peal on the Occasion'. A few years later, in Suffolk, the jubilant husband 'then went to Stowmarket and gave orders for the bells to be rung upon the occasion'. Finally, in the nineteenth century, bells at Buckland, Somerset, rang several peals 'at the joint expense of the parties'. The ringing of bells was associated with many beliefs. It was believed, for example, that this act deflected bolts of lightning and that no evil spirit could hold sway within sound of a church's carillon. Stories were told of benighted travellers on the moors, saved by a peal of bells. Other tales spoke of sunken bells, which mysteriously sounded at midnight or on the anniversary of some great disaster. In actual practice bells were sounded by groups of ringers, some of whom might travel miles to change-ring a particular set. Other ringers were usually paid to ring for various occasions. The funeral bell, often tolled with a muffled peal, gave the sex and condition of the deceased by the number of strokes: nine for a man, usually fewer or a woman or a child. Merry peals were heard after weddings, the charges in this instance usually being borne by the bridegroom. Bells were rung on major holidays such as New Year's Eve, Midsummer Eve and Christmas Eve. The Restoration and royal birthdays were announced in a like manner,

as were military and political victories. Finally, personal
achievements such as ownership of a winning race horse or success
in the lottery might be thus publicized. It seems probable that a
combination of this 'personal' use of the bells and their traditional
association with marriages led to their employment in connection
with wife sales.[27]

A number of sales depart from established norms. Apart from
the questionable evidence of wife-selling songs, two possible
examples of multiple sales exist, both dating from the late
eighteenth century. *The Times* for 2 December 1797 had this to
say: 'At the last sale of wives there was but a poor shew though
there were plenty of bidders. One alone went off well . . . .' In
Macclesfield a man named Twig bought two wives at market in
1799, the implication being that both were for sale at the same time
and place. The increase in popular draw gained by having more
than one woman up for auction is readily apparent. This practice
disappears, however, before the advent of the judicial persecution
that might have been thought to explain its lapse.[28]

Temporary sales included all those transactions in which the
wife was not completely transferred to the purchaser but remained
partly under the control of the husband. In 1768 a Shoreditch
publican 'sold his wife to a butcher for a ticket in the present
lottery, on condition that if the ticket be drawn a blank he is to
have his wife again as soon as the drawing of the lottery is over'.
This custom could be interpreted as a safeguard to ensure the value
of the exchange, but it is obvious that a different motive is at work
in the sale of a wife at Lewes, Sussex, in 1803. In this example the
woman was turned over for a month's trial after payment of
earnest; at the expiration of the time the remainder of the money
was to be paid or the wife returned. A Kent husband expressed his
willingness to resume marital intercourse at any future period,
while a Caerleon woman was to be restored to her spouse after a
three-day trial 'if she did not *please*'. The custom of conditional
sale may have been practised as late as 1845 by the navvies at
Woodhead Tunnel, Cheshire. Henry Pomfret, a surgeon treating
the workers, noted at that time: 'They were utterly drunken and
dissolute — a man . . . would lend his wife for a gallon of beer.'
Although this was denied, it seems likely from the background
shown for this practice that Pomfret was generally correct in his
commentary.[29]

Buying-in occurred for a number of reasons. In 1797 a man

named Carpenter auctioned his wife in Smithfield market. Surprised by the high bids, he figured that 'at this rate she must *be good for something*' and retained her. A Bath report in 1833 neglects to give any reason for the husband's repossession of his spouse — the price offered for her was in fact *greater* than that raised at an 'annulled' sale the previous week. There was a Devon case in which the husband who displayed his spouse for sale at Great Torrington Market had to keep her when bids failed to reach his fixed minimum of eighteen pence. Finally, in many instances the wife appears to have been retained because she did not like her purchaser. Early sale appears to have taken place for other reasons. In one instance the premature disposal of the wife seems to have originated in the husband's and purchaser's desire to avoid the 'public exposure' of Bradford market; elsewhere an impetuous purchaser 'scooped' the lot. [30]

Postponed and interrupted sales can usually be attributed to one of four factors. The first is the lack of a buyer. Three attempts to sell Mrs Brooks at Plymstock on market day were thwarted when her expected bidder did not arrive. Ike Duncan, who was to fill the same role in a Shearbridge sale, was 'detained at his work beyond the time.' An 1810 Bewcastle sale was moved over 50 miles (to Newcastle) when the woman attracted no interest. A second hindrance was the contrary attitude of the wife herself. A Cheltenham woman who had been lured to market 'fled from the scene of degradation', while in Barnsley a wife, adopting the opposite tack with her husband, 'rushed upon him again with her fists, and put him to total route [sic]'. There could also be problems with the general public. As early as 1806 a Hull sale had to be postponed for three hours: 'owing to the crowd which such an extraordinary occurrence had gathered together . . . [the husband] was obliged to defer the sale, and take her away.' In northern England and Scotland it was not unusual for bands of women to interrupt the proceedings: this happened in Manchester in 1824, in Edinburgh in 1828 and in New Sneddon in 1834, and was threatened in an 1830 sale at Ashby-de-la-Zouch, Leicestershire. Or less organized protests might be made. At Dulverton, Somerset, a transaction went ahead after several 'ineffectual' efforts had been made to restrain the parties. A London sale in 1836 was moved from Smithfield to Islington market because of interference, and the 'crowd from a neighbouring factory' that created some disturbance at a Shearbridge auction may have been operating under similar motivation. Most interferences occurred during the 1820s and 1830s, also the heyday of interruptions by the authorities. Several sales were broken up by the police, either because they represented a threat to public order or because of their illegality. In at least one case even this action failed to halt the sale; a Rotherham auctioneer simply assigned the wife to the last bidder.[31] These special cases, while suggesting that wife-selling could adapt itself to outside influences, only serve to underscore the general regularity of the great majority of sales.

CHAPTER 7
The Huzzas of the Mob

How did husbands, wives, purchasers and spectators feels about the institution of wife-selling? How did it affect their lives?

There was a common belief that wife-selling was valid and legal. When brought to the dock, it was normal for a husband to claim that he thought the procedure was allowed, or even supported, by law; when charged with some related fault, such as bigamy, a man was likely to use the sale as his justification. This claim met with only occasional success but fared better than other justifications. Thomas Heath, for instance, who purchased a woman but 'denyes that he has carnall knowledge of her body', offered no convincing reason why he had carried the wife to Benson and visited her in her room there. Other excuses given for sales were drink or jest, and the past behaviour of the wife might also be cited in explanation. To what extent these views were genuinely held or were prompted by court pressure is uncertain.[1]

In some cases belief in the institution's legality was accompanied, seemingly paradoxically, by an acceptance of continuing ties. Several husbands felt free to impose upon the wife and purchaser with further demands for cash. An eighteenth-century Somerset wife complains: 'in three months' time after, he visited me and demanded more money, and abused me, and the man that he sold me to, forcing open the door and swearing he would be the death of us both.' (She apparently wished to have her former mate bound over to keep the peace.) An Exeter woman was similarly annoyed, while in York a ne'er-do-well occasionally pestered his former missus for drinking money. These continuing ties were not always to the husband's advantage; one Suffolk farmer felt obliged to make his wife an allowance after her purchaser's death. Still another husband received his wife back when the purchaser married a new wife nine years after the sale.

111

For whatever reason, a surprising number of couples were reunited, even if one excepts those 'restored' to each other by the courts. The husband was often responsible for this *rapprochement*. Many men left loopholes in the sales agreement for a resumption of co-residence, while others were willing to repurchase their partners at a higher price. In one case the motive was certainly purely economic; a Yorkshire blacksmith bought back his wife, only to sell her again immediately — for a profit. [2]

A number of husbands repented after sales, often causing quarrels and fights with contented purchasers. A Warwickshire yeoman, requesting a return, was spurned by his former wife. In Inverness a purchaser insisted on his bargain and threatened to take action at the Assizes; at Lincoln, when the husband was refused return of his wife, it actually caused a court challenge. One London husband was supposed to have hanged himself when his wife refused to return to him. Finally, in 1904 a Biddulph policeman was summoned to settle a quarrel that had resulted from the remorseful husband's refusal to permit a purchaser to remove the wife. In a few cases retention or 'confiscation' hinged on neglected terms of the purchase agreement. An Essex man, short-changed for his fiancée, avenged himself by forbidding the banns. A Newark husband unsuccessfully approached the police when the wife's reputed lover could only raise partial payment, and 'after a war of words the lady contrived to give her knowing one the slip and started off with the fellow who had purchased her, amidst the yellings and hootings of the husband and a lot of boys.' Non-fulfilment of obligations also seems to have been behind an Irish husband's assault on his wife and her purchaser. [3]

Other circumstances resulted in the retention of the wife or in a reunion with her husband. During the bidding one Carpenter, 'properly conceiving that at this rate she must be *good for something*', actually bought his wife in. Another husband, obliged to go through with a second sale (because the first was considered illegal), also ended by keeping his woman. In a Great Torrington sale a wife who failed to make the minimum price was taken home, and marital life was resumed. Occasionally, husband and wife combined in a confidence game against the purchaser. In Wiltshire and Devon women were not delivered or absconded after the purchaser had paid his money. A Cornish tale of wife sales deals with the murder of purchasers and the theft of their property by a wife sold at Helston and Truro. [4]

Reactions to the sale itself show considerable variation. In a Cornish example, for instance, the husband 'had frequently threatened to sell his wife'. Several cases show positive reactions on the part of the husband to his wife's purchase. A Hadleigh man provided his spouse with £100 to ensure that someone would buy her. An Edinburgh husband, who ended up fighting with members of the crowd attracted by his transaction, insisted that the auction continue after the fighting was quelled. The following quotations exemplify the reactions of husbands satisfied with the day's work.

> [Thompson] with the greatest satisfaction and good humour imaginable, proceeded to put the halter which his wife had taken off, round the neck of his New Foundland dog, and then proceeded to the first public-house, where he spent the remainder of the day, indulging in the effusions of Bacchus, and repeatedly exulting in his happy release from bondage.

> The other man walked home whistling merrily, declaring he had got rid of a troublesome noisy woman, and it was the happiest day of his life.

Such feelings would appear to be only natural, since it was husbands who ostensibly initiated sale proceedings. In other cases, however, many men seemed curiously reluctant to use the institution. James Goyin of Louth was described as vacillating on the topic, while a soldier at Portsmouth required a steadying drink. At Holme-upon-Spalding Moor, the husband 'made his appearance . . . evidently labouring under the greatest agitation of mind . . . the poor disconsolate husband declared it to be quite enough for her, unless she mended her manners.' Though a London husband looked glum, his reaction hardly compares with the dramatic result of a sale at Ansty:

> On Wednesday evening, the husband, fired with jealousy at seeing his frail rib sitting at work in a stocking-frame at the house of her paramour, procured a loaded gun, and was in the act of levelling it at her through the window, where she sat unconscious of her dangerous situation, when a man, unperceived by the husband, suddenly went behind him, and seizing the gun, prevented the fatal catastrophe from taking place.

This is in contrast to the Bath husband who attempted to drown his wife a year after an unsuccesful sale attempt.

Other spouses were annoyed by lost opportunities or attendant mockery. A few left town, although whether departure was based on previous or subsequent plans is not always clear; an Aylesbury example notes that the husband, 'having seen them within doors [of his house], locked them in, and gave them the key of the door through the window. The husband has left the town.'[5]

Now and again, canny husbands issued debt disclaimers in the form of newspaper or cried advertisements; a husband in county court used a sale as an excuse for not paying his wife's debts. Other obligations might also be considered at an end — one man 'turned the children he promised to support out of doors, and told her [his wife] to keep the lot'. This conflicts with the attitude of others. A Hampshire husband gave his (?) small daughter a guinea, while a Blackwood man 'said that he did not sell his baby "because it was my own flesh and blood"'. A St Austell vendor had his future mapped out:

> Trethewey had intended to supply the place of the wife he had so lately disposed of, without delay, and had fixed on a female worthy of his choice, whom he had invited to accompany him home. The woman appeared to be willing, but her departure was opposed by a man who said he had a prior claim to her; this Trethewey disputed, and a violent struggle ensued, which however ended in favor of the wife-seller who marched off triumphantly with his acquisition.

Perhaps the most endearing reaction was that of Ashton, the waterman of Goole. When his wife passed out of his life with her purchaser, the husband held out his hand, saying, 'Give us a wag of your hand, old lass, afore we part.'[6]

The most striking female response to these sales was the wife's acquiescence in the process, which calls into question the oft-expressed claim that there was general resentment among women to the institution. Newspaper accounts abound with wives whose approval of such sales is manifest. A report of one Boston case notes: 'the impudent hussey being nothing loth to this public display of her attractions . . . declared she was quite satisfied with the transfer, for she had "got the lad she loved".' In 1822 a Devonshire woman expressed disappointment when an expected purchaser did not appear. During the course of sale many women displayed their feelings: a Wednesbury girl 'wiped her eyes and smiled cheerfully'; an Edinburgh lass laughed at the fight which had developed; while a Carmarthenshire woman smiled and nodded at the crowd, 'as if to show them that it made no difference to her at all . . . and that the sale was quite all right and nothing which worried her'.[7]

Only in a few cases did the wife show concern for the proceeding's legality. A sale scheduled for Bradford market was completed at a Shearbridge alehouse: 'The only objector to this proceeding was the woman, who feared that the sale would not be legal.' Her doubts were somewhat allayed by the signature of all the party to the deed of sale. A Rotherham wife fled the advent of the constables, but 'understanding that . . . [they] were only there to prevent a disturbance of the peace', she eventually delivered herself to the successful purchaser. Finally, a woman involved in a Ripon court case was questioned about her sale:

> 'Yes, I *was* married to another man,' she said, 'but he sold me to Dunn for twenty-five shillings, and I have it to show in black and white, with a receipt stamp on it, as I did not want people to say I was living in adultery.'[8]

Other examples involved wives who disapproved of the proceedings. One Dartmouth female, 'could scarcely be sustained from fainting as her unworthy husband dragged her along . . . . She was purchased for two guineas by her first sweetheart.' Sometimes unfortunate wives were dragged or driven to market by their spouses. In London a woman 'evinced some shame at this vile exposure'; a Cheltenham wife, marketed unawares, 'fled from the scene of degradation'. Women offered for sale might cry bitterly or entreat on their knees that the transaction should not take place. Or distress could take other forms. A Barnsley Amazon rushed upon her husband and put him to flight with her fists. Another spunky woman lured her husband to Newcastle for the sale; 'this modern Delilah laid her plan so well, that on his arrival, a press-gang conveyed him on board a frigate, preparing to get under way for a long cruize [sic].' A Grassington wife repudiated her sale, while a Devon woman decamped to Exeter with her children, returning only for her husband's funeral. A mob of Scottish females was raised by another wife, nettled that her opinion had not been solicited. In Bristol a woman involved in a sale left with her mother and refused to accompany her purchaser except 'by order of a magistrate'. Often, the woman accepted the sale but reserved her scorn for the former spouse: 'Chris tried to get her back, but she wouldn't come. If he could do what he had done, she said, she had had enough of him. She hoped it would be a lesson to him.' This attitude toward the seller is also reflected in Mrs Ashton's put-down: 'There, good-for-nought, that's more than you would fetch.'[9]

Post-sale actions differed widely. Sometimes wives were left with relatives — siblings or parents. A Horsham woman lived with her purchaser one year and had a child before running away and remarrying. Another woman managed successfully to claim property belonging to her deceased first husband. In Suffolk a wife subsequently removed to an almshouse after her purchaser's demise. Several stories tell of women who were said to have brought their purchasers money, but most of these appear to be fictitious. On other occasions the wife's new lot was quite as hard as the one she had relinquished. One Devon wife discovered that her

> new husband drank, and treated her very roughly, and on one occasion she had a black eye when I was lunching at the inn. I asked her how she had hurt herself. She replied that she had knocked her face against the door, but I was told that this was the result of a domestic brawl.[10]

In court, purchasers' reactions ranged from a full confession to attempts to show only a peripheral connection with the institution. One claimed to be simply an agent in the business! Many defendants maintained the validity of the institution. A Yorkshireman, charged with assaulting a friend of the wife (who had tried to persuade her from taking part in the sale), behaved in court as if *he* were the offended party. Another purchaser was anxious to appeal a lenient verdict.[11]

Commonly, the purchaser is described as delighted with his purchase. In one example from Blackburn, Lancashire, a potential bidder is depicted as thinking: 'Oh! he did wish he had money to buy her. She would just do for him; they'd get on very well together, he was sure they would.' This man's feelings were so intense that he was almost reduced to tears when onlookers bid against him in jest. Other examples cut against this grain. In Coventry one man accused a husband of having fraudulently sold him a wife as potentially childbearing. Another purchaser had swift second thoughts and discreetly disapeared before accepting his 'prize'. A few wives were subsequently resold or even given away; some were deserted; others were returned without apology to their husbands. In London one spouse's joy, was of short duration, for early on Saturday morning [the day after the sale] the wife returned and demanded admittance; her new gallant followed, not to claim her, but to regain his purchase money; Crispin pleaded value received, but that not satisfying the spark, he gave him a hearty drubbing to boot.

Sometimes this restoration was prompted by external forces. Pelted with missiles, one purchaser 'slunk away, leaving the woman to shift for herself'. Another wife was returned after the unlucky bidder was attacked by a body of females — he was forced to pay the husband 2 guineas for the 'privilege' of relinquishing her. The Colchester barrack master ordered another such refund, but the husband refused to give back the purchase money. A man at Burford was obliged to endure rough music for three nights because of his purchase:

This was too much for the sufferer. He burst out of the house with a pitch-fork, flung the flaming straw figure into the river and thrust a good many of the crowd in too. . . . In spite of this spirited demonstration the man felt that he could bear no more and gave the husband £15 to take back his wife again.

The most macabre disposal of a bought wife, however, was carried out by a Brighton man, who 'on reflecting as he bought her, thought he had a right to dispose of her as he pleased; he, in consequence, sold her [corpse] to the resurrection men, and kept the coffin for his sideboard.' The attitude of purchasers towards wife sales must also have been influenced by their families. One wife attacked her husband because of a purchase; in other cases wives were displaced or turned out to make room for the new woman. Moves could and did result from the sales. A Sheffield woman was supposed to be sent to Manchester on the following day, while an Alfreton wife and purchaser subsequently eloped. [12]

When purchasers married these women it may sometimes have been to gain access to property or 'to protect the position of their children against any dispute'. Often, wedlock was obliged to wait upon the death of the first husband, although a few participants later solemnized common-law unions. Varied pressures, economic, legal and moral, often operated on such couples to produce formal unions. A Bodmin pair, refused permission to marry because the wife's husband still lived, 'went away apparently much disappointed'. Subsequent marriages suggest an

understanding of wife-selling's limitations when compared with
the legality conferred by the sacrament of marriage. [13]

The concurrence of individuals participating in the institution is
strongly emphasized. A Bradford sale took place, 'Neither party
being exactly satisfied with the insecurity of the new relation
which had sprung up'. Newspaper accounts often dwell on the
satisfaction shown by those involved in the transaction. (At
Sudbury, however, it was the reunion of husband and wife that
'produced mutual satisfaction'.) A husband and wife in Sussex
appeared 'on very good terms' before the sale, while a reunited
couple at Manchester voluntarily shook hands, 'begging each
other to forget the past' and 'left the dock hand-in-hand, in great
apparent good humour'. The relation of wife and purchaser is
similarly described. Perhaps typical is a Bilston sale in which the
threesome drank together 'as good humouredly as though no such
thing as a divorce [existed]'. [14]

Crowd responses to wife-selling are another matter. The term
'crowd' or 'mob' could mean several things: a general name for the
'lower orders' or working class; a hired gang acting in the interests
of a group or faction; or a group engaged in riots, strikes or
political action. Derek Jarrett notes of the English that 'They were
terrified of the "mob", a word which they were fond of using. . . .'
In his discussion of the London 'Mob', George Rudé has this to
say:

> they shared certain common traditions of behaviour, with their
> ready resort to such activities as house-'breaking', window-
> smashing, burning their victims in effigy, parading under
> recognised 'captains', hallooing, huzzaing, slogan-shouting and so
> forth. Yet they appear as socially identifiable crowds of men and
> women and do not correspond to the static-abstract picture of the
> 'mob' presented by hostile contemporary witnesses or later
> historians.

It is important to remember this individuality within the mass
when dealing with wife-selling. As a sort of 'street theatre', a
public wife sale would normally have attracted crowds and would
occasionally have resulted in group action. [15]

Some background is useful to understand prevalent crowd
attitudes during the late eighteenth and early nineteenth century.
Rudé, speaking of what he terms the '"pre-industrial" crowd',
notes as a distinctive feature 'its attachment to the *traditional* ways

(or believed traditional ways) of the old village community or urban craft and its violent reaction to the sort of changes promoted in the name of "progress"'. More specifically, he notes themes of liberty, 'No Popery' and chauvinism as 'ideas and impulses not limited to the satisfaction of immediate material needs'. Touching on these themes, but more embracing, is the idea of *conformity*. This concept can be used to explain the crowd's dislike of Catholics, foreigners and even of any individual outside the immediate social group. Francis Place reports that his son's foreman, when on the tramp to London, 'was set upon by men, women and children, and hooted through their villages, merely because he was a stranger'. Charles Moritz, a German who visited England in the late eighteenth century, was hounded because he travelled on foot, while the traveller Hans Stanley, seeing a French carriage piled high with luggage and topped with a parrot cage, noted that in England such an equipage would have drawn jeers and catcalls. (In France, it met with no 'animadversion from the populace, so much quieter are they than in England'.) A French scientist with an ear trumpet was made the unfortunate subject of London mockery, and any women in extravagant fashions risked becoming objects of public ridicule. To the extent that wife-selling was unusual, it would have attracted a crowd with attendant cries and comments; to the extent that the institution and its practice did not conform to popular beliefs, wife-selling ran the risk of public action. [16]

As has been mentioned, wife sales commonly attracted crowds of spectators. Their reactions to the institution often began before the sale itself; thus at Bilston a group including the resident male and female 'roughs' of the town greeted the bellman's announcement of a forthcoming sale with laughter and interjected 'humorous additions suggested on the spur of the moment'. A Wednesbury announcement was received with guffaws and hurrahs and became a topic for subsequent discussion. Additional testimony in both of these Staffordshire cases indicates that the background of the sale figured in such crowd conversations. [17]

From the moment that a wife was put up for auction the activity became a public event. There was frequent interaction between the participants and the crowds witnessing the spectacle, reminiscent of the popular theatre and of political hustings. One arrival in market was 'greeted with a tumultuous shout from the assembled crowd, followed by jeers, laughter, coarse wit, and filthy language, such as the humours of the situation either suggested or provoked.' Such reactions do not appear to have been uncommon. A Brighton sale took place 'amid the sneers and laughter of the mob', while a St Albans woman was forced 'to endure endless chaff, none too polite'. An 1823 Bristol sale mentions 'the coarse remarks of the assembled crowd'. In a few cases evidence is specific enough to give some idea of the general run of comments. Thus, the following 1819 exchange:

> 'Her's as sound as a roach in wind an' limb; her con baake, an' wesh, an' brew;' — 'Ah, thee hist reet,' shouted a voice, 'an' her con drink a sup, Jimmy, yo' bet.' 'Ah,' retorted the husband, laughing, 'her con do a tot full as well as the nex'. Her con mak' a suit o' clo's good's any snip.' 'An' con wear the britches,' shouted again a voice from the crowd, a remark which was greeted with uproarious cheers. . . . 'Now, wot shan I say for her; who'll bid?' Somebody humourously offered a penny token, another suggested 'a joey,' a bid which tickled the fancy of the audience immensely, because the intending purchaser was known as 'Joey' among his neighbours.

In Wednesbury the crowd encouraged the women ('Ne'er mind, Sal, keep yer pecker up, and never say die!') and responded with appreciation to the husband's auctioneering sallies. In Carmarthenshire crowd approval was signified by whistling, and the husband 'received some mischievous offers without purpose'. Elsewhere, too, the crowd reacted humorously. In Herefordshire a bystander noted of the woman, 'she has done no good, depend upon it, or else he wouldn't want to sell her.' This was followed by a loud laugh,

> and a man shouted, 'Well done, Jack, that is elevenpence more than I would give; It's too much boy, too much.' But Jack stood firm. 'No,' said he, 'I'll give a shilling, no more, and he ought to be thankful to get rid of her at any price.' 'Well,' said the man, 'I'll take it, though her good looks ought to bring more than that.' 'Keep her, master, keep her for her good looks,' shouted the laughing bystanders.

An auctioneer's fat offering at Bungay met with this response:

> A voice calls out, 'Will you give a guarantee?'
> 'What guarantee would you be wanting, sir?'
> 'That if I buys her she won't be rolling over in the night and overlaying me so I come out as flat as a pancake!' At that they all roars out and starts catcalling and someone else shouts:

'Here be all the Snobs. Best git one o' them to buy her — she'll do well to wax his thread,' and the Auctioneer have to bang down his hammer and call 'Order,' before he can be heard.

A 'company of fellows of low character' were entertained when one Yorkshire purchaser's wife interrupted the negotiations to maul him, and many other accounts mention departure of the new couple 'amidst the huzzas of the mob'. Semi-serious bids were far from unusual: a Cheltenham sweep 'offered sixpence by way of joke', while Blackburn loafers derisively ran up a woman's price 'all in fun' and bid all the more when they saw that there was actually a potential purchaser in their midst. In Liverpool the sale was suggested by a spectator when a woman expressed her disgruntled feelings; a Belper bystander, prompted by 'sympathy — or something else' agreed to act as auctioneer for a deserted wife. [18]

Besides the implicit tolerance towards wife-selling evidenced by the presence of witnesses and the fact that participants were often local residents, testimony shows that in some cases the institution enjoyed active popular support. At Ashburn, Derbyshire, in about 1815

Some constables were sent to secure the seller, the purchaser, and the wife being sold, at the moment at which one presented himself for the formalities of the contract; but the populace covered the constables with mud and quelled them with stones.

While this reaction might be attributed to resentment of interference by an outside authority (the constables had been sent by a magistrate to keep the peace), the support it suggests for the institution is mirrored in other cases. The newspapers, in reporting a sale from Callington, Cornwall, complain: 'We do not learn that either the authorities or the public interfered to prevent so disgraceful a scene.' A Hertfordshire father present at a nineteenth-century sale reassured his son, 'It's all right. She understood,' while in speaking of a Staffordshire sale one individual concluded, 'it is doubtful if one of the number had the least idea that the proceedings were outside the law.' As late as 1865 a sympathetic Blackburn storekeeper is said to have loaned money to a potential purchaser. In Norfolk and Warwickshire sales, if duly carried out, were considered to be legal and 'quite above reproach'. An informant from Devon reports that the practice was not usually considered legal in the south of the country but admits that in the

north 'people were less enlightened.' Finally, the conviction of
Joshua Jackson in Yorkshire for an 1837 wife sale is said to have
'caused widespread surprise and consternation at the time'.[19]

Other wife sales reveal mixed reactions in the attendant crowd.
At a Carmarthenshire sale 'there was a great silence, and there was
a feeling of uneasiness in the gathering and no levity at all could be
sensed among the "quality" which was there, nor in the "stalls"
which were nearby either. . . .' Although some people whistled
their approval of the husband's speech, others muttered 'that the
entire sale was shameful and illegal'. A Canterbury sale was
carried out, but only after the refusal of a cattle dealer to become
involved in the proceedings. In Whitehaven, Cumberland, 'mine
hostess was called to witness the regular transfer of the *goods*, but
she was shocked at the whole business, and ran out of the room
refusing to witness the contract.' (A more amenable acquaintance,
however, was persuaded to ratify the transfer.) London was the
scene of a sale that took place amid 'the disgust of some and the
laughter of others', while at Horsham a few shocked spectators
reported the action to the magistrates. Some twenty years later, in
the same town, a similar incident took place. At that time 'many
people hissed and boo'd, but the majority took the matter good
humouredly'. In 1838 a Dulverton sale was effected '[a]fter many
ineffectual attempts to prevent the demoralizing act'. The
principals were incited and supported by 'several respectable
persons, who ought to have known better'.[20]

Increasingly, during the latter part of the eighteenth and in the
nineteenth century crowds appear to have reacted negatively
toward the institution. At Dartmouth this was translated into aid
for the wife: 'To rescue her from further insult, a respectable
family received her into their house, accommodated her with a
change of dress, a veil, etc. and in this disguise she was conveyed
to a place of safety.' A longtime friend of a woman in Hull was
assaulted by the woman's purchaser for trying to dissuade her
from a sale. Such crowd feelings were often vocalized. One
London 'monster' who attempted to sell his wife 'escaped amid
yells of disgust and abhorrence', and a Bristol drover 'was obliged
to make a precipitate retreat from the enraged populace'. A Boston
party retired 'amid the jeers of the assembled crowd'. Participants
in London, Yorkshire and Nottinghamshire were subjected to
similar abuse, although in some cases this may have been linked to
the wife's adultery. No one would bid for a woman sold at Belper,

and many 'expressed their disgust and annoyance with so debasing a transaction'. A wife and purchaser who attempted to abscond without full payment at Newark did so 'amidst the yellings and hootings of the husband and a lot of boys'. In Blackburn sale resulted in an abusive rhyme concerning the husband:

> Oh, Master Duckworth!
> Oh! you are a cure.
> You sold your wife for beer
> And lived at — Moor.

A Dudley husband was followed, to his annoyance, by a crowd chanting, 'Who sold his wife?'[21]

The above example leads into those cases in which crowds assaulted or attempted to assault wife-sale participants. In Truro in 1858

> It was rumoured . . . that a woman was to be sold . . . and consequently the populace were on the *qui vive*, in expectation of some fun. A decently-dressed woman from St Agnes, being in the High Cross on Monday, some mischievous fellow, without any cause, pointed her out as the woman that was about to be sold; on which a number of boys, men and woman attacked and pursued her by the church and down St Mary's street, where a man seeing the peril she was in, got her into a house by the back door, which having a latch-key the mob was prevented from entering after her. She lost a small basket containing some articles, which have not been recovered. The mob then went to the front of the house which she had entered, and remained some time until policemen were sent to the scene of action.

Similar 'popular justice' was directed against a Lincolnshire trio who, having been released from the Magistrate's Court were chased round Louth church by the mob. They required police protection before they could safely return home.[22]

One common form of assault was pelting. At Pontefract, Yorkshire, a purchaser and wife became targets for snow and mud, retreating 'in more than wedding haste'. Similar punishment in Manchester caused one buyer to sneak away and the woman involved to take refuge in the Shudehill lock-up;

> the female part of the crowd, apprehensive of the dangerous effects of such a precedent and urged on by a proper feeling of the indignity offered them, determined upon a protest against so indecent a proceeding, and in the absence of pen, ink and

parchment, they recorded, with ample heaps of mud upon the faces of the *cattle dealers*, the burden of their indignant sentiments.

Participants in both London and Somerset were subjected to peltings in 1833. Elsewhere this chastisement is closely associated with the stocks, forming by far the most dangerous part of that punishment. Dead dogs, cats, rubbish, and stones were thrown, killing a Stratford prisoner in 1763 and a pinioned coachman in 1780. One Bristol prisoner, who had taken a bribe to screen an individual from justice, avoided this fate by haranguing the crowd to take warning by him. Impressed, 'they were so civil to pelt themselves, and left him to be a Spectator to their dirty Sport.' (Nor does this deflection of purpose appear to have been unique.) Pelting also served as an informal means of expression in other popular protests. The Duke of Wellington emerged covered with dirt from the first trip of the Liverpool and Manchester Railway, and the founders of a Bible Society at Carrick, Co. Tipperary, experienced similar treatment. A suspected bawd was pelted in Middlesex; a newly wedded Suffolk couple — with a combined age of 152 years — was hooted and pelted by the mob; and a 70-year-old man who had married a 17-year-old girl was 'saluted . . . with *sods* and *mud*'.[23]

The Manchester wife sale in which a crowd of women initiated retribution is far from unique. At other times, and particularly during the 1820s and 1830s, organized female groups were responsible for the disruption of several wife sales, an emotional paradox when one recalls most wives' acquiescence in the proceedings. The earliest recorded case appears to be the 1756 'rescue' of a Dublin wife by a party of women. At Sudbury, Suffolk, in 1821 a woman was sold to Robert Whiting,

> but the bargain being offensive to a number of females present, they would have given the new bridegroom a summary chastisement, had he not taken shelter in a cottage, but into which they pursued him, and he was obliged at last to make his escape, by jumping out of the chamber window.

This swashbuckling feat hardly compares with the epic proportions of a supposed Scottish invasion:

> The women of the neighbourhood gathered to the number of 700, and armed themselves with stones, some threw them, and others put them in their stockings and handkerchiefs, and made a general charge through the mob, knocking everyone down that came in

their way, until they got up to the auctioneer, when they scratched and tore his face in a dreadful manner, in consequence of the insult the fair sex had received.

Not surprisingly, this persecuted individual required protection before he would continue with the sale. A similar mêlée involving the daughters of 'little *Ireland*' (called in by the disgruntled wife) was narrowly averted six years later in New Sneddon, while Leicestershire authorities feared disturbances from a similar source. Such feminine activity might appear unusual until one recalls the prominent part played by many women in food riots of the late eighteenth and early nineteenth centuries. In a closer parallel a female disturbance is said to have resulted in the discontinuing of public floggings at Perth:

> the washerwomen . . . with their laps full of stones, and backed by the willing multitude, broke through the line, drove the officers from the circle, and liberated the prisoners. The soldiers had only their side arms with them, except the guard on the prisoners, and appeared more willing to assist, than to resist the people. The moment the prisoner was untied from the halberts, a general attack was made upon the officers. The adjutant was less fortunate than some of the others in escaping. He got a terrible mauling from the women; who laid him down on his belly, in which position he was held by some scores of vigorous hands, till he got a handsome flogging on the bare posteriors, in the presence of thousands. . . .[24]

Scattered references are made to other popular reprisals. A Dublin porter who sold his wife was 'taken into Custody by Order of a Committee of Porters and one of them sitting as Judge, he was tried, found guilty, and sentenced to the stocks, in which he was accordingly put, where he continued till Four next morning'. Stocks were used for both formal and informal punishments in the eighteenth century, and even the court of porters has its parallels. Alan Smith notes:

> Accounts we have from late Victorian workshops still talk of the holdfast being banged to convene a shop meeting or 'court' to settle disputes between workmen. The punishment for an offence against the men's own discipline was usually being 'sent to Coventry' for a period.

Fines involving drink, levied by various groups of artisans, have been discussed (see chapter 6), but informal justice could be of a rougher sort. A footman at the House of Lords who had refused to pay 'footing' to join a club of his comrades was carried on a 'wooden horse' before the 'Head Constable' of that organization. A journeyman hat dyer who worked over hours at cut-rate prices was forced by his fellows to ride through Southwark on an ass, with a placard denoting his offence, to the accompaniment of rough music. A waterman was paraded in effigy at Woolwich for carrying more passengers than he was allowed, while a ribbon maker suffered similar treatment during a Coventry strike. Nor were all the offences trade-related:

> A few days since some workmen engaged in a mine near Plymouth drew up one of their comrads [sic] by a rope in the public thoroughfare, and suspended him in mid-air about thirty feet high, screaming at the top of his voice, for ill-treating his wife.

Elsewhere less homogeneous groups were responsible for physical punishments. It may have been such a gathering that threatened to duck a Cheltenham husband under the pump for the attempted sale of his wife in 1830. [25]

Rough music, a popular protest using a cacophony of sounds, is first found in connection with a 1768 Oxford sale. Here William Pritchard married his old sweetheart after an unsuccessful attempt to purchase his landlord's wife. The landlord was a shoemaker, and upon Pritchard's exit from church, a number of cordwainers 'saluted the Bridegroom with a very Loud Peal upon their Lap-Stones: — a Ceremony never used but on very important Solemnities'. This suggests the interesting possibility that such craft action may have paralleled the informal artisan courts. Several examples of rough music involving butchers' cleavers and marrowbones have been recorded. A Chipping Norton wife sale elicited rough music and a mock punishment in which the offender's effigy was paraded and otherwise degraded. In about 1855 a man had purchased a wife at Chipping Norton market. He returned home to Burford, but

> The town evidently no longer considered this a respectable way of arranging a divorce, so for three nights running they gave him rough music, with horns, trumpets, tin whistles, and cans beaten with sticks. On the third night they burnt the man in effigy outside his door.

Similar practices were adopted by crowds in northern England. Indignant Yorkshire villagers burnt effigies of a wife and her purchaser, while a similar bonfire was held in the 1870s in Bury.

The circumstance [of the sale] was rapidly ventilated, and the scandal created such a sensation in the neighbourhood that on Monday evening an effigy of the woman was burnt in front of her new home. On Tuesday evening a similar event happened, with the difference that on that occasion the effigy represent [sic] P— himself, being stuffed with straw, having a mask for the face, and attired in old clothes. It was fastened to the door latch of his house and then set on fire, the crowd in the meanwhile parading the street and vociferating before P—'s domicile, some of the feminine representatives, who no doubt had waxed considerably warm at his mode of acquiring such a household treasure, asserting that he had better pay a visit to the 'Hatter's Cemetery', which, being properly interpreted, is said to be what is popularly known as — 'Old Charley Lodge,' in which there have been between forty and fifty cases of suicide and 'found drowned' . . . . The indignant neighbours record a promise to make the place unbearably 'hot' so that if the man and his charge desire to abide in peace it will have to be in some less threatening quarter, and not where wife sales are uncountenanied [sic] or contracts and dissolution of marriage at free will unrecognized.

This concentration of popular wrath upon the heads of the wife and her purchaser, with the neglect of the husband's role, establishes a pattern for those cases of rough music and mock punishment known to be connected with wife-selling. It could suggest that such popular protests constituted more a reaction to adultery than criticism of the sales themselves. [26]

Further cases involving crowd reactions are more difficult to define. The men armed with cudgels connected with several Staffordshire sales indicate some need for order, but to what extent their presence resulted from crowd attitudes is unclear. Other records speak of interference or threats of a disturbance of the peace, but the quality of the evidence does not support speculation about accompanying popular attitudes. Still, there must be some reason why a Yorkshire party bound for Bradford market 'shrunk from encountering the public exposure' and completed their transaction at Shearbridge. Two London examples resulted in destruction of property. In 1815 'the finish of the bargain was attended with a *row* and breaking the windows of the public house to which they ajourned.' Two years later a large crowd followed the principals to the Ram Inn, and 'several panes of glass were broken in the windows of some of the neighbouring houses.' In neither example is the crowd held to be specifically responsible for the damage. It is interesting, however, to note that window-smashing appears to have been a notable activity of London political mobs in this period, that windows in a nobleman's residence were broken because of a rumour that card-playing went on there during the Divine Service and that even the schoolboys at Harrow broke all the windows of the school when a favourite teacher was not appointed headmaster. Add to these the case of a widow of 50 whose windows were smashed to punish her for marrying her 17-year-old stepson, and it begins to appear that the practice may well have extended to wife-selling. [27]

Crowd attitudes towards wife-selling apparently changed over a period of time from a humorous, tolerant approach to a negative, and at times violent, reaction against the practice. Many women saw the sale as a threat and an insult to their sex: others equated the practice with adultery. It is more than probable that the change in the public's reaction to wife-selling contributed in part to the institution's gradual decline.

CHAPTER 8

'Where were the Magistrates?'

Newspapers of the seventeenth and eighteenth centuries were avid for saleable news.

> Although news from as far afield as China and Russia was regularly received in London, often there was not enough material of sufficient interest to capture the attention of readers. If, at the same time, there were particularly rigid restrictions as to what items of domestic concerns could be printed, editors were likely to find themselves caught in a tight clamp. . . .
>
> It was these pressures that led some resourceful paper men to discover the appeal of the human interest story. Papers began to feature prominent crimes, omitting not a single one of all the most gruesome details. Matching these in prominence were sex crimes, or an affair that exploited the peccadilloes occurring between husbands and wives, men and women.

In addition to providing the bulk of wife-selling cases, the commentary and presentation of newspaper reports give insight into contemporary reactions toward the institution. Wife sales were considered to be 'events'. This is not to indicate that they were necessarily unusual; births, marriages, death and bankruptcies were also reported in eighteenth- and nineteenth-century newspaper columns. But that the institution was reported at all indicates some interest on the part of either the editor or the readership (probably both). The earliest noted reference occurs in the 1640s, when the account of a Warwickshire sale appeared in *The Kingdome's Weekly Intelligencer*, and even as recently as 1978 popular tabloids have commented in the custom.[1] The British press is said to have developed from propaganda sheets printed in London and Oxford during the English Civil War, but strict licensing procedures and government regulation of the news restricted the range of reporting. Seventeenth-century provincial papers were mostly 'cut-and-paste' editions produced from several London newspapers, as the editors tried to avoid prosecution for their coverage of domestic politics by removing themselves from first-hand reporting. This is not to suggest that there was no provincial coverage; a web of correspondents kept London editors in touch with local events and reactions. Press coverage was, however, removed from actual incidents, and the time that it took for a report to be forwarded to London, printed and returned made some news items quite out of date. The lapsing of the Newspaper Licensing Act in 1695 prompted the appearance of several new papers, including a few in the provinces. While some journals were killed by the Stamp Act of 1712, others survived by exploiting loopholes in the law. The press proliferated, despite continuing increases in this 'Tax on Knowledge' — from ½d per half sheet to 1d per paper (1757), to 1½d (1776), 2d (1789), 3½d (1797) and finally to a peak of 4d in 1815. Reduction of the tax to 1d in 1836 (and its abolishment in 1855) appears to have spurred sales, judging by a circulation graph of the *Lincoln Mercury*. True circulation statistics, however, are difficult to obtain, particularly for earlier years, when one newspaper copy might have passed through several hands. A foreigner, Moritz, writing in 1782, notes:

Near the 'Change is a shop, where, for a penny or even an halfpenny only, you may read as many newspapers as you will. There are always a number of people about these shops, who run over the paper as they stand, pay their halfpenny, and then go on.

The earliest papers were weeklies, the first daily (the *Daily Courant*) being established in 1703. By 1709 London had 17 papers, published three times a week. The provincial press, which saw a period of great expansion in the mid-eighteenth century, generally consisted of weeklies until well into the nineteenth century. Williams notes the occurrence of a major period of 'soft news' (including crime and domestic matters) in the 1720s and claims that such reports were popular and sufficiently well-established to continue when the 1730s brought a period of 'hard news'. This, then, is the background against which newspaper reactions must be judged.[2]

Perhaps the most striking point about early wife-sale reporting is the spectacular nature of most of the sales covered. Only more

PARTICUAR AND MERRY ACCOUNT
OF A MOST ENTERTAINING AND CURIOUS
SALE OF A WIFE!
Of A Pretty Young Woman, who was Sold to a Gallant Young Fellow for £15 and a Doz'n of wine, this morning, together with the Wedding Song.

At an early hour this morning a young couple came into the market; the lady was dressed neat and clean, and so attractive were her rosy cheeks and sparkling eyes that all the folks in the market soon collected about her, she being to be

Well, good folks, says the lady's spouse, here's a rare bargain to be disposed of! ...g's my pre.., sweet wife, who will try all she can to please any man, who's willing to take her for life. What have you got to say, Mr. Butcher? Oh, says the Butcher, she charms my very heart to look at her; here's 17s. for a beginning. That's too little, says Snobby the cobbler, I will run to my uncle's with some of my customer's shoes, to raise the wind, and give 3s. more. Oh, oh, says Frisk the fiddler, and Friz the barber, we will join and buy her between us; 2s. a-piece more, cried they. That won't do, cries Snip the tailor, putting on his spectacles; I have 20s. in my pocket, and I will sell my dandy collar, busk, sheers, thimble, needle and goose, to raise 15s. more. Clear the way, you silly boobies, quoth a miller, or I'll shave you all with a wooden razor, here's 50s. for my duck, so mount upon my old mare

and we'll go home to the mill together.— Botheration, says a farmer, I'll capsize you all: here is £3 for her. Seven shillings more, says a tallow chandler; two shillings more the baker, and ten shillings more the painter. A gallant publican hearing the fun, bounced forward with such hast that he upset the barber and tailor in the , and almost trod the fiddler's toes off. He instantly paid down £15 and took them to an Inn, where they had a capital dinner, and after emptying a dozen of wine, the happy couple mounted a gig and set off in full glee.

THE WEDDING SONG.

Come jolly neighbours, let us dance, sing and pla
And haste to the neighbouring wedding away ;
All the world is assembled, the young and the old,
To see the fair beauty that just has been sold.

So sweet and engaging the Lady did seem,
The market with bidders did presently teem ;
A Tailor sung out that his goose he would sell,
To buy the fair Lady—he loved her so well.

But a gallant young Publican £15 did pay,
And with the young Lady he marched away ;
They drank and caroused and rejoic'd all the day,
The glasses passed round, and the piper did play.

Success to this couple, and to keep up the fun,
May the bumbers fly round at the birth of a son ;
Long life to them both, in peace and content,
May their days and nights in pleasure be spent.

PRATT, Printer.

Wife-selling broadside printed by Wm Pratt, Birmingham, c.1849-56 remarkable sales seem to have been considered worthy of note: wives refusing to return to their husbands, buyers attempting to return their purchases, husbands stubbornly retaining sold wives, buyers refusing to return wives, women being disposed of for unusual prices. Reports of this sort appear to have predominated well into the 1770s. Even beyond this period similar stories were given prominence in local newspapers. [3]

This was followed by a period in which normal wife sales were reported by local newspapers and were occasionally picked up by the national (London) press. During the summer and early autumn of 1797 a strange reaction to the institution developed. Several sales (particularly from London's Smithfield market) were reported, and suddenly wife-selling was all the rage. This is not to indicate that everyone went out and sold his wife, though undoubtedly sales *may* have increased because of the attendant publicity, but the institution became fashionable. Astley's, on Westminster Bridge, produced a comedy called *No Sales at Smithfield*, which (if we are to believe the papers) ran well (as did all of Astley's productions . . . if we are to believe the papers). In addition, the London journals offered many *bon mots* — one frankly hesitates to use the term 'jokes' — on the subject, of which several representative examples follow:

> The encreasing value of the *fair sex* is esteemed by several eminent writers as the certain criterion of encreasing *civilization* [sic]. SMITHFIELD has, on this ground, strong pretensions to refined improvement, as the price of Wives has risen in that market from half a guinea, to three guineas and a half.

> By some mistake or omission in the report of the Smithfield market, we have not learned the average price of Wives for the last week.

> It is quite the *ton* with the *bucks*, as well as the *butchers*, to visit Smithfield market, for the purpose of examining what *cattle* are tied to the *railings*.

> The selling of wives at Smithfield is not, surely, unreasonable: — if a man *buys* he has an equal right to *sell*.

> Several advertisements have appeared in the papers lately of *run-away* wives. It is supposed that the husbands, if they can catch them, mean to bring them to Smithfield while the *market* is *brisk*.

The last state of the *Smithfield Market* informs us, that horned cattle *looked downwards*, and that Wives look upwards.

The Ladies' divorce-notes are now called female *Bills of Exchange.* Some of the fair drawers affect to insert, *'this my Sola Bill.'* But we have not seen any at *single usance*, as all that have yet been in the *market* have been duly *honoured*; it is thought that they will quite supersede the *ready-money business* in Smithfield.

Owing to the briskness of the damand [*sic*] for some time the price of wives at Smithfield rose rather above the proper *level*, in consequence of which the market has been dull of late. To make amends, however, and to *keep up the just value of the fair sex*, it is intended to make this place a *mart* for the *sale of daughters*, where according to *polished* practice they are to be *disposed of by Lottery.*

The *sale* of *wives* in Smithfield is likely to be conducted upon fair principles. No person has yet appeared as a *forestaller* of that article.

An Hostler's wife in the country lately *fetched twenty-five Guineas.* We hear there is to be a sale of wives soon at Christie's. We have no doubt they will *go-off* well.

This vein of humour not only undermined the mechanism and motivation of wife sales but also touched on other period problems, such as gambling, forestalling and currency depreciation. Family social practices, divorce and desertion, arranged marriages and dowries were also quarried. It seems likely that wife-selling achieved this prominence only as one of a number of styles or fads that swept the country at the turn of the eighteenth century. [4]

Jestingly critical witticisms lead to another topic — wife sales as a subject for moralizing. Only some cases were, as William Andrews put it, 'duly reported in the newspapers of the period, without any special comment, as items of every-day news'. Others 'became a popular cause for the regional press, who publicised wife-sales in an attempt to inform the ignorant that the procedure was both illegal and barbaric'. [5]

Any investigation into attitudes towards wife-selling must be seen against the background of current newspaper morality. Attacks were directed against other traditions, institutions and pastimes, including throwing at cocks (tied to stakes), bull-running, boxing, fairs, bear-baiting, bull-baiting, street football and heaving (an Easter custom of lifting men or women for money). Robert Malcolmson notes of such newspaper attacks (on blood sports):

> Many of the criticisms arose from moral and religious considerations which can be easily appreciated: such diversions were 'barbarous', 'inhuman', 'uncivilized', and generally at odds with enlightened morality. They involved 'such scenes as degrade mankind beneath the barbarity of a savage, and which are totally inconsistent with the laws of nature, the laws of religion, and the laws of a civilized nation'.

These crusades appear to have originated in the later eighteenth and early nineteenth centuries. Particularly important for consideration in its application to wife-selling is Malcolmson's comment on the selective nature of such moralizings:

> It is worth noting . . . the extent to which many of the attacks on traditional recreations betrayed a pronounced class bias. The reformers' energies were mobilized largely against popular amusements; few were so indelicate as to storm the citadels of genteel pleasure. The critics were able to discriminate nicely between the fashionable diversions of the rich and the less fashionable of the poor — and to act accordingly.

This is not to indicate that this double standard was not recognized and even commented upon. It was with pragmatic realism, however, that

> the attacks on traditional recreation accommodated themselves to the circumstances of social and political power, concentrated their attention on the culture of the multitude, and fashioned their moral protest in a manner which was consistent with the requirements of social discipline. [6]

Criticisms of wife sales appear in the 1780s and 1790s. They seem to have originated in the major cities but spread throughout the provinces during the following 80 or 90 years. A common (often implicitly critical) comparison was made with upper-class divorces. One advertisement for a wife sale is quoted as a sample of 'how nearly vulgar life approaches to the depravity of the great world. There is not a Lord of them all could manifest more eagerness to turn the infidelity of his wife to profit.' This parallel probably developed from initially favourable comparisons, such as the following:

> Were it fashionable among some of our great folks to adopt a similar mode of separation it would save them abundance of expence and trouble in suing for divorces, and perhaps prove equally satisfactory to all parties.

Nor (as has been previously indicated) was this the only sort of pejorative comparison made with the rich. In reference to the elopement of Sir Henry Hayes with a Miss Pike of Cork, the *Morning Chronicle* had this to say:

> The practice of *selling wives* at Smithfield has, as might have been foreseen, diminished the value of the sex in other places. An Irish Baronet has run away with a lady, and the Government of that country offer no more than *two hundred pounds* for apprehending him.

Whatever grounds may have existed for this class-based differentiation, it was to become firmly established in the minds of the newspaper editors, who frequently referred to wife-selling as a 'vulgar' error.[7]

Most criticism, however, was restricted in scope and resembled the pat denunciations of blood sports. Words such as 'disgusting', 'degrading', 'depraved' and 'disgraceful' were most common, with few traces of praise. This is not to suggest that criticism was universal or consistent. Such attacks were hardly original, and some were in fact borrowed verbatim from other newspapers. Often a paper that has ranted at one sale will print another without comment and, on occasion, sympathy is shown towards the plight of the wife (or even of the husband) involved. Further, the papers *printed* while they criticized. Publishers may have shown due regard for prevailing morality, but they also kept a weather-eye on the tenets of yellow-press journalism (shared by broadside singers and good revival preachers); they were specific and sensational wherever possible. Despite the many cries of 'where are the Magistrates', threats of public whippings or even of the noose, the major (if secondary) effect of such moralizings was to turn *all* wife sales into newsworthy events.[8]

As the self-appointed repositories of local wisdom, newspapers could hardly resist theorizing about the wife sales they reported, even when their statements were wild and, in some cases, demonstrably incorrect. On the origin of the institution much was said. Some connected the practice with historical parallels, notably the Babylonian marriage market, at which *unmarried* women were sold. While the editor responsible for one Norfolk paper appears to have recognised this comparison's essential invalidity, he probably included it as good copy. A similar (implicit) connection may be apparent in the following report:

> At Cairo the slave market still presents a deplorable spectacle. The negroes are huddled together in small pens, *like those at Smithfield*, in a state of the utmost filthiness, awaiting the brutal surveyors, or purchasers, to whom chance may consign them.

A better parallel was made by the *Manchester Mercury* of 1819, which actually quoted William Paynell's fourteenth-century quit-claim as an early example of the institution. Most papers, however, were content to settle for generalities to spin out their reports:

> Our early ancestors used to purchase their wives. During some centuries our fathers received a portion with them; but their enlightened children know their worth better, and sell them.
>
> Corrupt as are our morals, we cannot be reproached with not setting a proper value upon a virtuous wife; we who can fix so accurately the price of a bad one!

A few editors even professed to claim (incorrectly) that wife-selling was a newly established practice![9]

In addition to assuming a knowledge of the origins of wife sales, newspapers prided themselves on familiarity with the proper forms; their pages are full of references to wife-selling 'in the usual manner' or 'as has been lately practised'. Often reference is made to previous sales, and in 1797 the *Morning Chronicle* and other newspapers kept what amounted to a running economic tally, labelling prices 'an advance in the market', a 'poor shew' or 'an indifferent price'. At times, however, especially in reference to the history of sales in a region, newspaper statements can be entirely misleading. A London report, for example, quotes an 1802 price of 7s 'the highest price we believe yet given in that market', which was certainly not the case.[10]

The position of editors as authorities on the subject of wife-selling was occasionally strengthened by queries from their readers. The statement printed in *Jackson's Oxford Journal* of 22 July 1797 gives no easy solution:

Do men sell their wives because there is no law which prohibits such a practice? or, because there is a specific statute which sanctions it? If the former, it is a shame that the Magistrates do not take cognizance of a practice so repugnant to every idea of decency and of morality. If the latter, the Legislature ought surely to take some steps against so gross a violation of the moral ties of the community.

Thirty-five years later, however, many of the same questions were asked by 'an inquirer' in a letter to *The Times*:

> Sir, — The account in *The Times* of to-day of a farmer, named Thompson, in or near Carlisle, publicly selling his wife, induces me to ask, has the Magistrate no power to prevent such disgraceful exhibitions? The act of selling a wife by auction is unlawful, but the question is, ought it not to be prevented or punished as an offence against public decency and morals? Although this crime — (I think it a crime) — is of rare occurrence, is not its prevention a subject worthy a moment's attention from an enlightened Legislature?
> I am, Sir, your constant reader and humble servant,
> London, April 26.
>
> AN INQUIRER
>
> Be so good as to tell your readers what you think on this subject.

This request did not have to be repeated; below the editor added a curt (and informed) note: 'There is no question that the offence is punishable at common law.'

Other commentary was occasionally offered. The *Morning Chronicle* noted that a man could be sent to the House of Correction for the practice and that the custom was adopted to secure an adulterer against action for damages. *The Times* noted that neither party could remarry and that wife and purchaser were open to an action for fornication. A further article adds:

> The lawyers intend to petition against the sale of wives at Smithfield; as the practice is a *contempt of the Courts in Westminster Hall*. The sales there carried on are illegal because they are not sanctioned by the decision of a Jury, and the contracts must be void because they are concluded without the assistance of an Attorney.

Several editors were also aware of the French association of wife-selling with the English. [11]

Consideration should be given to the implicit support afforded the institution. Debt disclaimers based on wife sales, and indeed advertisements of the sales themselves, although rare, do exist. Their presence in newspapers implies acceptance of the practice, suggesting that, at least occasionally, the money obtained from these advertisements overcame any moral scruples that the editors may have had. [12]

In the sixteenth and seventeenth centuries several wife sales were prosecuted in ecclesiastical courts as moral offences. All cases in which sufficient evidence was available resulted in convictions, suggesting the condemnation of such sales by most ecclesiastical authorities. Balanced against this, however, must be the participation of one 'Cheken, parsun of sant Necolas Coldabbay' in a 1553 transaction — the only existing record of an ecclesiastical participant. (In 1804 a purchaser is subsequently described as 'clerk' of Eliel chapel.) Eighteenth-century records of religious connections or commentary are sparse. *Aris' Birmingham Gazette* assures us in 1790 that wife sales were 'considered (a light in which religion must view them) as mere pretence to sanction the crime of adultery'. This, however, is a layman's view. Aside from special mention made in the latter part of the eighteenth century of the sales' offences against decency and morality, no further specifically religious commentary is readily available. [13]

Several cases, however, do indicate a connection between wife-selling and the religious sacrament of marriage. The Duke of Chandos, who reputedly bought a chambermaid from her husband in Newbury, is said to have married her on Christmas Day 1744. A church ceremony of this type would normally have been legitimate only if the woman's husband had died in the interim, or if she had been the man's common-law wife. That such marriages were not uncommon is indicated by R. Pillet, a Frenchman who visited England before 1815 and wrote: 'It sometimes happens that the purchaser of a wife may contract a new marriage in Church, in order to protect the position of their children from any dispute.' (The author alludes to a titled example but omits the exact name.) Other sales indicate further interaction between religious institutions and wife-sale participants. At Halifax in 1805, Rachel Heap, believing her husband to be dead, married a Mr Lumb. The return of her former husband (after children had been born of the new union) resulted in a sale by Heap to Lumb, serving to straighten affairs out on a secular level; Mr Heap's subsequent death allowed the situation to be regularized in the eyes of the Church by another marriage. A York wife married her purchaser after the death of her husband, fully twenty years after the sale itself; a Cockerham wedding took place 12 years after the sale. In these cases the circumstances of wife and purchaser allowed a legitimate church ceremony to confer respectability on their common-law liaison. In contrast to this was the action of a drummer on the Isle of Wight. This man reappeared, after the banns of his wife's remarriage had been twice called in church, to *sell* her to her intended![14]

Religious criticism of the practice occurs in several cases, and the marriage vow is quoted in moral rebuttal. The *Bradford Observer* noted in 1836: 'It is melancholy to think that so much ignorance and vice are to be found in the present day, and it calls loudly on the benevolent to bestir themselves with redoubled energy to promote the spread of knowledge and religion . . . .' Commenting on an 1842 Lincolnshire sale, the writer called the occurrence, 'One of those disgraceful scenes which occasionally violate the laws of God and man . . . .' Much the same view is taken by Quarter Session indictments, which note the practice as being 'to the great Scandall and Subversion of the Holy State of Matrimony and Religion'.[15]

An Essex parish register suggests that the children of purchased wives were neither considered ordinary issue nor classified as illegitimate. In only one other instance is there evidence of the reaction of a churchman involved with the institution. When Henry Frise purchased his wife for half a crown the rector of his Devon parish vainly attempted to convince the purchaser that the institution was not sanctioned by the Bible. Frise replied:

> I don't care . . . her's my wife, as sure as if we was spliced at the altar, for and because I paid half a crown, and I never took off the halter till her was in my house; lor' bless yer honours, you may ask any one if that ain't marriage, good, sound, and Christian, and every one will tell you it is.

The rector, in his turn, refused to be convinced. Upon the woman's death (in about 1843), he refused to enter her in the burial register as Anne Frise, since this was not her legal name. Frise, in high dudgeon, removed the body to another parish for burial.[16]

If one excepts sixteenth- and seventeenth-century ecclesiastical prosecutions, there is a remarkable lack of involvement of the

Church in wife-selling. In a few cases marriage was used to strengthen the bond between wife and purchaser; in others religious arguments were cited (by laymen) against the institution. However, the great majority of cases suggest a tacit 'hands-off' policy. The events of religious and secular life followed their own courses, each without interrupting or impeding the other.

Legal reactions to wife-selling fall into two major groups: theoretical and actual. The former group (although sometimes derived from cases)[17] is concerned with precedents — those laws, case decisions and opinions that were believed to bear on the institution's legal status. The latter group considers the application of such theories by the authorities to actual cases of wife-selling.

Early English law differs from many other legal systems in that it lacked complete codification; the so-called 'codes' that remain are more properly glosses on, or revisions of, popular custom. Without a complete understanding of tribal laws, early Anglo-Saxon royal codes must be treated with extreme caution. A reference to the custom of wife-selling that is often cited is Cnut II, 74: 'And no woman or maiden shall ever be forced to marry a man whom she dislikes, nor shall she be given for money, except the suitor desires of his own free will to give something.' This does not necessarily deal specifically with married women and cannot constitute proof of wife sales at this date. However, the practice may be related to, or may have derived from, such transactions.[18]

The best place to start with legal theory concerning the institution is probably Blackstone. While the first edition of the *Commentaries* does not mention wife-selling, subsequent expanded editions include brief mentions of the practice. The 1836 version, edited by Christian, treats the institution in a footnote to 'Offences Against God and Religion', particularly, 'open and notorious *lewdness* . . . by some grossly scandalous and public indecency'. In considering such crimes, Christian notes cases of indecent exposure in public places, ostensible apprenticing as a cover for prostitution, the assigning of one's wife to another and enticement for the purposes of seduction. He continues:

> It is extraordinary that prosecutions are not instituted against those who publicly sell their wives, and against those who buy them. Such a practice is shameful and scandalous in itself, and encourages other acts of criminality and wickedness. It now prevails to a degree, that the punishment of some, convicted of this offence, by exposure in the pillory would afford a salutary example. All such

acts of indecency and immorality are public misdemeanors, and the offenders may be punished either by an information granted by the court of King's Bench, or by an indictment preferred before a grand jury at the assizes or quarter sessions.

Of Christian's quoted cases, only *R. v. Delaval* is commonly cited as a basis for prosecution of the institution's participants. Perhaps most important is Lord Mansfield's summation:

> I remember a cause in the Court of *Chancery*, wherein it appeared, that a man had *formally assigned his* WIFE *over to another man*: and Lord *Hardwicke* directed a *prosecution* for that transaction, as being notoriously and grossly *against public decency and good manners*. And *so* is the *present* case. . .
>
> It is true that many offences of the *incontinent* kind fall properly under the jurisdiction of the *Ecclesiastical* court, and are *appropriated* to it. But, if you except those *appropriated* cases, THIS court is the *custos morum* of the people, and has the superintendency of offences *contra bonos mores* . . .

Lord Mansfield goes on to state that the conspiracy and confederacy involved further put the dispute under King's Bench jurisdiction. This case, and its incorporated reference (which does not appear to have been published independently), is one of two cited to prove the illegality of wife-selling. [19]

The other case, *R. v. Pardey*, exists only in unpublished manuscript form. It appears to be concerned with an actual case of wife-selling and just might be the example referred to in the footnote to Christian's note 31:

> The offence of buying and selling a wife is unquestionably a misdemeanor at common law, and an indictment against all the parties concerned in a transaction of that nature has been recently prosecuted to conviction at one of our courts of quarter sessions. Either party marrying again, during the life of the other, after a separation thus illegally effected, would, it seems, be guilty of bigamy . . . . [20]

The *Laws Respecting Women* and *The Cabinet Lawyer*, both shortened guides to the law, cite only *R. v. Delaville*. The latter source notes:

> There is no doubt that the vulgar and brutal exhibition, too often tolerated, of a man selling his wife, and delivering her in a halter, is a misdemeanour, both in the buyer and seller, punishable with fine and imprisonment.

The custom is also noted as illegal in *Robinson's Magistrate's Pocket-Book*, which cites *Burn's Justice of the Peace* as a source. By the 26th edition *Burn's* can say, 'many prosecutions against husbands for selling, and others for buying, have recently been sustained, and imprisonent for six months inflicted'. This and later editions include a sample indictment used in prosecutions:

— (venue.) — The jurors For our lady the Queen upon their oath present, that A.B., late of the parish of —, in the county of —, labourer, on the — day of —, in the — year of the reign of our lady the now Queen Victoria, on —, at —, with force and arms, did indecently, immorally, unlawfully, wickedly, deliberately, and wilfully, in and near certain public streets and highways there, publicly and in the presence and hearing of E.F., and divers other liege subjects of our said lady the Queen there then being, expose to sale, and offer to sell and dispose of, for lucre and gain, one C.D., then and there being the lawful wife of the said A.B., and all his, the said A.B.'s, marital rights of and concerning the said C.D., to any person or persons willing to buy and take her, for the purpose and in order that such person and persons might unlawfully cohabit with and have lawful carnal knowledge of the said C.D.; and did then and there unlawfully, publicly, and in the presence and hearing of the said liege subjects, and of the said E.F., endeavour to induce and persuade the said E.F. to purchase and take the said C.D. for the purpose aforesaid, and did then and there sell and dispose of the said C.D., and all his, the said A.B.'s, marital rights of and concerning the said C.D., to the said E.F., for a certain sum of money, to wit, the sum of [2s 6d], for the unlawful purpose aforesaid; and then and there, in pursuance of the sale, unlawfully, publicly, and in the presence and view of the said liege subjects, deliver the said C.D. into the hands and possession of the said E.F., with the intent that the said E.F. might unlawfully cohabit with and have carnal knowledge of the said C.D., and that the said E.F. might commit adultery with the said C.D., *to the great scandal and subversion of the holy state of matrimony and religion, and decency, morality, and good order, to the great corruption of the morals and manners of her majesty's liege subjects, to the great damage of the said C.D., and in contempt of our said lady the Queen and her laws, and to the great damage and common nuisance of all the liege subjects of our lady the Queen then and there residing, inhabiting, being, and passing, to the evil example of all others, and against the peace of our said lady the Queen, her crown and dignity. 2nd Count. — And the jurors aforesaid, on their oath aforesaid, do further present, that the said

A.B., on —, at — aforesaid, contriving and intending to bring into contempt the holy state of matrimony and the duties enjoined thereby, and to vitiate and corrupt the morals of her majesty's liege subjects, with force and arms, did indecently, immorally, unlawfully, wickedly, and wilfully, publicly, in the presence, view, and hearing of the said E.F., and of diverse other liege subjects of our said lady the Queen there then being, expose to sale and offer to sale to the said E.F., for lucre and gain, the said C.D., then and there being the lawful wife of the said A.B., for the purpose and in order that the said E.F. might unlawfully cohabit with and have unlawful carnal knowledge of the said C.D.; and did then and there unlawfully and publicly, in the presence and hearing of the said liege subjects and of the said E.F., sell to the said E.F., for a certain sum of money, to wit, the sum of [2s 6d], for unlawful purpose aforesaid, and did then and there, in pursuance of the said last-mentioned sale, unlawfully, publicly, and in the presence of the said liege subjects, deliver the said C.D., unto the said E.F., with intent that the said E.F. might unlawfully cohabit with and have unlawful carnal knowledge of the said C.D., to the great, &c. [Conclude as in first count, from *] [3rd Count] And the jurors, &c., present, that the said A.B., on &c., at &c., aforesaid, did indecently, immorally, unlawfully, wickedly, deliberately, and wilfully, publicly, in the presence, view, and hearing of diverse liege subjects of our said lady the Queen then and there being, expose and offer to dispose of and deliver for money, to be therefore paid to him, the said A.B., the said C.D., then and there being his lawful wife, to any person, for the purpose of fornication, and in order that the said C.D. might commit adultery with such person; and did then and there publicly and in the presence, view and hearing of the said liege subjects, dispose of and deliver the said C.D. to the said E.F. for a certain other sum of money, to wit, the sum of other [2s 6d], for the purpose last aforesaid, in contempt of our said lady the Queen and her laws, to the great damage and common nuisance of all the liege subjects of our said lady the Queen, to the evil example of all others, and against the peace of our said lady the Queen, her crown and dignity. 4th count. — Stating generally that defendant unlawfully publicly exposed for sale, &c., and did unlawfully publicly, &c., sell the said C.D. to a certain other person to the jurors aforesaid as yet unknown, for a certain other sum of money, &c. 5th count. — Stating that he sold to E.F., in order that C.D. might thenceforth live separate and apart from the said A.B., and be no longer under his control, not be supported or maintained by him, for a certain other sum of money, to wit, &c. 6th count. — Stating generally an exposing to sale.

Burn's Justice of the Peace also served as a basis for the answer given to the following query in *The Justice of the Peace* magazine concerning a wife sale:

> In what manner can these parties be punished for their gross violation of common decency and morality? Can the seller and buyer be indicted; and, if so, by what authority? Is the crier also amenable to law for lending himself to the public announcement of this disgraceful business? The woman, I presume, would be held to have acted under the control of her husband.

Quoting *Burn's* almost word for word, the journal's only addition was: 'We see no reason why an indictment would not lie against the crier also, but can cite no authority upon the subject.'

Finally, passing note should be made of three other cases erroneously cited as being relevant to the topic. *Reg. v. Mears* and *Reg. v. Howell* both concern conspiracy to bring about prostitution (not adultery as Courtney Kenny states) and postdate the bulk of wife-selling cases. *Hall v. Potter* deals not with the sale of a wife but with match-making for profit by an outside party. [21]

One supposes that in the best of all possible worlds the wife would have been sold to a handsome, kindly and rich purchaser, with whom she would live 'happily ever after'. This, however, reckons without legal harassment of the institution and its participants; far from leaving her husband forever, the wife was likely to see him again in court — perhaps sharing the dock with her purchaser. There is no internal clue as to which court (if any) condemned Parson Cheken to be carted around London in 1553 for selling his wife. All other early sales appear to have been considered matters of morality falling under the jurisdiction of the ecclesiastical courts. In no case are all parties to the wife sale charged. Usually husband and purchaser alone appear to have been held accountable for the deal, suggesting that the woman was considered to be an accessory or a chattel. (An alternate, but less likely, interpretation is that husband and wife were counted as a single unit, a legal fiction that was responsible for the rule that wives could not be forced to testify against their husbands.) In other examples emphasis seems to have been placed on the adultery between wife and purchaser. It is possible, of course, that *jurisdiction* may have had something to do with the individuals assembled, but this theory is weakened by the appearance of a stranger before the Stirling court. Reactions varied: some participants confessed guilt; others attempted to explain their actions. In some cases testimony conflicted. It appears to have been customary to examine as many witnesses as possible in addition to those intimately involved in the affair. The difficulties sometimes encountered in this are hinted at in the Humbie case:

> This is all the kirk session can try in the business, either be the depositiones of the parties, or such as were beside that could be found. The shearer who was fied to them both, and who was the speciall witnes and the occasion of their meeting, being ane stranger, is gone from this countrie, and so could not be had.

If the charges were found to be well-grounded, either the case was passed to a higher ecclesiastical body for action, or penance was assigned. In practice, some penances were commuted to monetary fines. [22]

Assize courts were presided over by judges of the King's Bench, who travelled on circuits to the assize town of every county between two and four times a year. They had wide jurisdictional powers but usually dealt with major criminal (and sometimes civil) cases. No assize case dealing directly with wife-selling has been discovered; the major concern seems to be the resulting bigamy. Assize courts, therefore, do not appear to have been a common venue for direct challenges to wife sales, perhaps because the institution was not considered important enough to warrant such attention. [23]

Quarter Sessions, as their name suggests, were held four times a year and could be of either the county or borough type. Peter Walker notes that such courts considered some three-quarters of the total indictable offences in England and were usually ranked in importance below assizes, but above magistrates' courts. Most Quarter Session cases deal specifically with the institution itself, reflecting wife-selling's position as a recognized offence from at least the second decade of the nineteenth century. Quarter Sessions continued to be popular venues for prosecutions until about the middle of the century, but most convictions obtained there seem never to have been cited as specific theoretical authority for the institution's illegality. It may be significant that to date no examples have been found in which more than one wife-selling case came before any single Quarter Session. This may indicate that such trials were 'showpiece' actions to emphasize the law for local citizens — a theory borne out partially by the fairly light sentences often given. One may also recall the explanation that the minister at Clipsham selected Mr Hack for prosecution as 'the most opulent and fittest to make an example of'. [24]

Local magistrates' courts dealt with petty criminal offences and matrimonial cases and served as sites for preliminary hearings on more serious offences. These courts appear to have developed from the magistrates' control of town and parish constables. The term 'petty sessions' was often used in connection with them; in later times they were termed 'police courts'. Wife-selling was fairly frequently associated with magistrates' court proceedings, most of the charges being for the sale itself, for disturbing the peace or for non-support of wife or children. In some cases it *appears* that magistrates' courts provided a preliminary hearing for a wife-selling charge to be pressed at the following Quarter Sessions. A few insights into the workings of the magisterial mind may be gained. One judge, an acquaintance of the French writer Pillet, explained his intervention in a local wife sale thus:

> Although my course in sending some constables, was largely with the aim of preventing the scandalous sale, the apparent motive was that of maintaining the peace which these people, having come to market with a sort of tumult, tended to trouble. As to the action of the sale itself, I do not believe in the right to prevent it, even to put an obstacle in its way, because it was founded on a custom preserved by the people, a custom, perhaps, that it would even be dangerous to pass a law which abolished it.

In this case (and elsewhere) 'disturbing the peace' may have been a dummy charge obscuring the real issue. This is underscored by similar temporal ranges for this charge and for direct prosecutions of wife-selling. In Renfrewshire

> as the Fiscal knew from the paracide [sic] case of old that to prescribe a punishment for a crime, was a powerful means to get the crime introduced, he resolved not to be privy to such a doing, and therefore restricted his charge to a breach of the peace. The magistrate did not find that a breach of the peace could be brought home to the parties, and after animadverting in severe terms on the disgraceful nature of such proceedings and addressing the salesman and purchaser in terms which we dare say they will not soon forget, he dismissed them from the bar.

This reluctance to interfere appears to have been fairly common elsewhere. At Exeter 'The Bench thought it was a most disgraceful case and that she [the wife] did not deserve any protection. If her husband threatened her violently or assaulted her, then they would grant her a summons.' A magistrate at Clerkenwell in London used similar terms in dismissing an action for assault. [25]

Only two detailed court reports on magistrates' court proceedings concerning wife-selling *per se* are available. From these it may be gathered that the magistrates questioned principals and witnesses about the action, the reason and authority given for it and the identity of those involved. Often the magistrates (particularly when they were also mayors) had been responsible for the initial arrest and detention of the parties. Although there was always the possibility of imprisonment or the treadmill, for many no fine or imprisonment seem to have been forthcoming. This suggests a great ability of defendants to convince judges of their honest intent and/or ignorance of the law, or it may indicate that, as in Quarter Session proceedings, many of these trials were for show, serving a social function in warning participants in wife sales to modify their behaviour. There is also the possibility that the involvement of petty local officials in the sale proceedings may often have made a simple reprimand of the principals the easiest way out of a potentially embarrassing dilemma. [26]

In the second half of the nineteenth century a few wife sales are found in non-criminal court contexts. County courts deal largely with support, child care, divorce and contracts. Wife-selling is never of primary importance but usually has some bearing on the case in hand. Action by the police or constables, although to some extent directed by local magistrates, represents yet another layer of legal reaction to wife sales. The predominance of London in such cases and a relatively late date seem to reflect the establishment and spread of local police forces. A few cases even involved attorneys. In 1770 and 1797 sale agreements were supposedly drawn up by practising lawyers. A contemporary squib on the practice assures its readers that the lawyers intended to petition against wife-selling as a *'contempt of the Courts in Westminster Hall'*, claiming that such contracts were void without the assistance of an attorney. Should this have been the case, it suggests the possibility that, despite later evidence to the contrary, at one time a segment of the legal profession might have considered the institution to be valid and binding in some circumstances. [27]

What a strange opinion the world will have of the French society of today! Did all married people, we imagine they will ask, break a certain commandment? They all do in the novels. Was French society composed of . . . disguised princes, who lived in the friendship of amiable cut-throats and spotless prostitutes . . . All these characters are quite common in French novels.

So wrote Thackeray on the French. French views of the British appear to have been similarly coloured; wife-selling was accorded the status of an 'ordinary' unnatural vice. As early as 1789 M. D'Archenholtz, sometime captain in the service of the King of Prussia, wrote of his visit to England. He described a wife sale he had witnessed, quoting it as an example of 'those singular laws which evince the barbarity of remote ages'. Pillet gives the institution more prominence, devoting an entire chapter to 'Divorce chez le Bas Peuple. — Vente de Femmes'. Noting that 'these sales are very common throughout England', Pillet quotes in support not only an example he witnessed in Derbyshire but several other cases as well, one translated into French from the *Statesman*. The Frenchman apparently spoke about the phenomenon to an English judge, who suggested an ancient origin for the custom but found himself unable

> to reconcile with Christian religion, above all with Roman Catholic religion, which was for long dominant in England, the transmission of a similar custom from the centuries of barbarism up to our days .
> . . .

A year later A. J. B. de Fauconpret, yet another French traveller, commented on Smithfield's position as a wife-selling centre. That he was not the last foreigner to emphasize the Englishness of the institution is suggested by the *Worcester Chronicle*'s comment that an 1857 sale

> may very possibly be quoted in the book of the next Frenchman, who treats of English manners and customs as a proof of the very free and easy way in which the matrimonial relation is dealt with amongst us.

Even in 1891 C. A. White wrote:

> French travellers, when describing the moral and social aspects of England, rarely forget to inform their readers that it is customary in this country for men to sell their wives, like any ordinary chattel, in open market . . .

and V. T. Sternberg claims that 'French romancers and dramatists have seized upon it [wife-selling] as a leading trait of English society . . . .' The Reverend Sabine Baring-Gould offers the following anecdote, proving that French ecclesiastics followed suit:

> I heard a country *curé* once preach on marriage and contrast its indissolubility in Catholic France with the laxity in Protestant England, where 'any one, when tired of his wife, puts a halter round her neck, takes her to the next market town and sells her for what she will fetch.' I ventured to call on this *curé* and remonstrate, but he answered me he had seen the fact stated in books of the highest authority, and that my disputing the statement did not prove that his authorities were wrong, but that my experience was limited, and he asked me point blank whether I had never known such cases. There, unhappily, he had me on the hip. And when I was obliged to confess that I *did* know of one such case, 'Mais, voilà, mon Dieu,' said he, and shrugged his shoulders with a triumphant smile.

The English were painfully aware of their association with wife-selling; a *Punch* cartoon of the Frenchman's typical John Bull shows a substantial, florid figure with top-boots, cudgel and bulldog exclaiming, 'Rosbif Godam! I shall sell my wife in Smithfield to-morrow. Godam!' Conan Doyle's French Brigadier, Gerard, confesses: 'it would have interested me to see something of the customs of the English, which differ very much from those of other nations . . . to have seen them eat their raw meat and sell their wives . . . .' Several correspondents who submitted sales to *Notes and Queries* were fretted by this national slur, as the following excerpts prove:

> Has there ever been any foundation in law for the practice of selling of wives, which our neighbours the French persist in believing to be perfectly legal and common at the present day? . . . the custom is introduced as characteristic of English manners, by French and other foreign writers. (1850)

> Can we blame our neighbours across the Channel for thinking us a nation of wife-sellers . . .? (1857)

> The French believe we sell our wives at Smithfield; we call them blockheads for their ignorance of our manners. (1858)

we cannot blame foreigners for thinking that wife-selling is a publicly recognized national custom. (1863)

[The French view of the typical Englishman as a wifeseller] . . . a fact . . . that we one and all repudiate. (1891)

Additionally, writers such as William Chambers and John Ashton mention this bias. It is perhaps understandable that a *Times* foreign correspondent in 1866 (no doubt smarting after many Gallic queries) triumphantly reports a French wife sale in the following manner:

There still exists in remote parts of France, a tradition that in England a husband commonly puts a halter round his wife's neck, leads her to Smithfield, and sells her to the highest bidder. A labourer named Martin, aged 30, at Vire (Calvados), recently went still farther . . . .[28]

CHAPTER 9
Smithfield Bargains

Love Vows are now all lost and Jargon;
And Wedlock's grown a Smithfield Bargain.

Wife sales were sometimes known as 'Smithfield Bargains'. A London newspaper of 1815 uses this term in its report, but the connection is older than that. In 1797 two quips on the institution in the *Morning Chronicle* ran:

> Modern marriages are so frequently and justly compared to *Smithfield bargains*, that a man who wishes to *sell* what he has *bought*, surely has a right to go back to the *old market!*

> A correspondent complains piteously of the late havock made among old proverbial sayings . . . even the vilest of women, when taken to Smithfield, cannot be said to be *worthless*.

'Smithfield Bargain' originated as a proverb, found as early as 1604 in the form: 'That were to buy a horse out of Smithfield.' The phrase signifies 'a roguish bargain; also, a marriage of interest, not love'; consequently, it is not hard to see why it became associated with wife sales. First, only a wife who was deemed inadequate would be put up for auction, making the likelihood of a 'shoddy bargain' fairly high. Second, the 'marriages' effected by these sales ('divorce' was only half the process) were based on love in only *some* cases. At other times the purchaser was a total stranger to the woman and the transaction a matter of whim. Finally, use of the proverb was a punning reference to the frequency of such sales at Smithfield market in London. Some twenty cases have been recorded as having taken place there, and it is probable that it was the site of many others. S. C. Hall noted, 'People have heard of

151

selling and buying a wife at Smithfield . . .,' and both the French and English associated the institution with this market.[1]

At least one French writer described the custom as the 'Horn Market' (*Marché aux Cornes*). Presumably, this was a reference to the number of cases in which the wife's infidelity ended in this form of popular separation and also to the large proportion of women purchased by their lovers. Horns have long been a symbol of cuckoldry, and it is interesting to note that Charlton 'Horn Fair' is popularly believed to have had its origins in such a domestic *contretemps*. Another Horn Fair was held at Ebernoe, Sussex, at which a horned sheep's head was awarded to the highest-scorer of the winning cricket team. At Weyhill Fair, Hampshire, the original of the location of the wife sale in Thomas Hardy's *Mayor of Casterbridge*, a Horn Supper was served. Here newcomers participated in 'Horning the Colt' by drinking a cup of ale with horns affixed to their heads and the then standing treat for another half-gallion for the company. A specific connection between adultery and horn fairs is made by a 1794 ballad, which mentions a husband 'convoy'd to horn fair' by his wife. The connection between fairs and markets and the links between these and wife-selling have already been noted. There is no doubt that a specific association of horns with the sale of wives was prevalent in England; in addition to the staged procession at Wath in 1775, newspaper *bon mots* from 1797 include the following:

> It is very hard upon the *female sex*, that they cannot dispose of their *husbands* at Smithfield as the latter dispose of their *wives*. It ought to be so. Smithfield is a market for *horned cattle*.

> The sale of wives at *Smithfield* is not exactly suited to the *nature* of the market. It would be equally just, and certainly more *à-pro-pos*, were wives to dispose of their husbands in that place. The shew of *horned* cattle would of course be more plentiful.[2]

In addition to many similarities with livestock transactions, the connection of wives with cattle was often directly stated. At Smithfield, the papers noted, 'horned cattle *looked downwards*, and . . . Wives look upwards.' A Sheffield purchaser inquired, 'What do you ask for your cow?' It is interesting that in addition to being popular slang for a woman, 'cow' has had the specific meaning of 'whore' from at least the nineteenth century. It seems possible, therefore, that the term refers not only to the entire livestock analogy, but also to the large number of cases involving infidelity on the part of the woman. While it may be tempting to see the cow as a female counterpart to John Bull, symbol of the ordinary English subject and object of numerous caricatures from the late 1750s onwards, the appeal of this theory is vitiated by the presence of halters in sales as early as 1740. It is just possible, however, that the livestock metaphor may owe something to some such stereotype. Sometimes the wife is compared implicitly with a horse. An advertisement in a country paper makes extended use of this parallel, while a north-country husband exclaimed, 'There, now, thou wilt either lead or drive.' Further etymological parallels crop up from time to time. In the 1790s many London *bon mots* connected wife-selling with financial dealings. A squib from the *London Chronicle* noted that, 'Wives are now transferable like Bank-Stock.' Such comparisons are not surprising, considering the commercial trappings of the transaction.[3]

Parallels have been drawn between wife-selling and marriage ceremonies and customs in other parts of the world. One form of marriage cited as similar to the institution was the Babylonian marriage market, as we have noted. The *Norfolk Chronicle*, after reporting a local wife sale, continues:

'About 500 years before the Christian aera,' says an historian, 'in every district of Babylon, all the virgins of marriageable age, were assembled upon a certain day in every year, the most beautiful was first put up, and the man who paid the largest sum gained possession of her; the second in personal appearance followed; when all the beautiful virgins were sold,' continues the historian, 'all those whom nature had not favored with personal charms were ordered to stand up, and a premium was given with each of them from the money obtained by the sale of those more handsome.'

This practice has only the most superficial connection with wife-selling, however. The Babylonian market involved *unmarried* women and in many cases involved the payment of a dowry rather than a sale price. The temporal and physical distances separating the two practices make it highly unlikely that any real connection between these institutions existed.[4]

Another foreign parallel often cited in connection with wife sales is brideprice or 'bridewealth'. This was a payment or series of payments — livestock, money, objects, food, or services — given by a suitor or his family to the family of his destined bride. (It contrasts with the more familiar dowry, given by a bride's family to the bride or groom.) Brideprice can be assessed in relation to attractiveness, fecundity or status and is found in societies around the world, but particularly in Africa. Lucy Mair has been at pains to point out that such a transfer does not represent the sale of the wife but rather the securing of certain rights over her. A *social* connection is established between the two families involved, which, as S. F. Nadel notes, exists to encourage the survival of the union through the application of external pressure by those with a stake in its success. As Mair remarks, 'cattle are not a general medium of exchange but a means of establishing and maintaining particular social relationships.' Lévi-Strauss emphasizes the association of women with cattle made by some African tribes. When a man divorced he could claim the restitution of varying portions of his 'bridewealth'. Those who see a connection between 'bridewealth' and wife-selling base this tie on the analogy between husband and father. It is true that the dual association with cattle is striking, although it should be noted that this association appears on opposite sides of the matrimonial equation. There is also merit in conceiving of wife sales as the securing of certain rights over a woman rather than as an actual purchase. The fact remains, however, that brideprice is closely connected with the formation of alliances between two groups. Wife sales deals with the dissolution of a union rather than with the addition of a third factor to an already unstable relationship. Again geographic and social diversity suggests no close connections.[5]

Closer to home, attempts have been made to relate wife-selling to early British customs, such as those of 'the ancient *Brises* or Britons, before the Danish dynasties', or to 'Anglo-Saxon law which compelled every freeman seducing another freeman's wife to reimburse the outraged husband for his expenses in obtaining another spouse'. The theory of a Briton background appears to be mere conjecture, with no grounding in fact. The adulterous basis of many wife sales may appear to make Anglo-Saxon fines an attractive parallel, were it not for the fact that in the case of wife sales there is no evidence of formally imposed prices (if one excepts the nominal amounts dictated by custom) that could compare with the Saxon system of fines. No early cases of wife-selling mention pre-sale adultery, although this does not mean that it was absent. Christina Hole suggests that the institution:

may possibly spring from confused memories of the bride-price, or payment commonly made in Anglo-Saxon times by the husband to the father of the bride. This did not, however, represent an actual purchase price for the girl, but rather, a form of compensation to the father for the loss of a daughter's services, nor did the payment confer any supposed right to sell her to someone else should the marriage prove a failure.

The connection of the practice with a law of King Cnut has already been discussed and shown to be improbable. John Udall's and Wilkinson Sherren's suggestions that wife-selling derived from 'Danish barter' or 'Norman serfdom' are offered without accompanying proof. These parallels are unsatisfactory, first in that most do not relate to the wife's husband, and second in that no real evidence of continuity suggesting development from such historical antecedents is offered. [6]

Religious marriages offer several, often surprising, parallels with wife-selling. As we have observed, the pronouncemant of banns was sometimes performed at market crosses, also a place chosen for public sales. Use of this location made the willingness of the parties concerned, and the acquiescence of the general public, plain to all. At marriages, instead of an auctioneer, a priest presided (the 'merry fellow of an auctioneer' who read the marriage service at a Fittleworth sale may be recalled in this context), while phrases from the religious ceremony, such as 'Do you take this woman . . .?' and 'to have and to hold', emphasize the wife's affinity with chattel. Clerical charges may be compared with market tolls or auctioneer fees; signing the register may be taken as 'proof of passage'. Wedding rings played an important part in both institutions. Additional similarities were post-marital drinking and festivities such as the bridal cavalcade, bell-ringing, the post-wedding supper and even bedding the bride and groom. These similarities suggest that at least some people viewed the institution conservatively, as a response to family problems compatible with marriage, rather than as a radical break with that institution. [7]

In addition to such formal ceremonies, there were, of course, secular and informal (irregular) marriages. Handfasting — the joining of hands by the two contracting parties — may be likened to the link formed by the rope and halter between the husband (and later the purchaser) and the woman for sale. A further similarity is the use of witnesses. That secular and informal marriages were sometimes temporary in nature relates them to conditional wife sales. Finally, of course, all these practices involved social recognition of the biological and economic bonds between the two people.

As for divorce, there seems to be no likeness between ecclesiastical annulments and wife-selling. The only possible link with secular (parliamentary) divorce proceedings, the awarding of damages to an outraged husband, was not officially part of the divorce. Debt disclaimers published for absconding wives, however, were similar to those occasionally issued after wife sales. It is in the field of informal and irregular divorce that most similarities with wife-selling occur. Just as any purchaser who accepted his new wife in a halter possessed the right of resale by a similar mechanism, so participants in Welsh broomstick marriages could divorce each other if the dissatisfied partner jumped backwards over the broom and out of the house. Witnesses were required for both ceremonies, and the insistence that the door or doorpost could not be touched during the leap is similar to requirement that the halter should not be removed from a wife until the purchaser had arrived home. In Scotland and Ireland divorce procedure after handfasting ceremonies involved departure through different exits or a requirement that the partners formally turn their backs on each other. This parallels accounts in a few wife sales. In Carlisle in 1832 '[the participants] parted in perfect good temper — Mears and the woman going one way, Thompson and the dog another.' While the resemblance may be fortuitous, a similar symbolic separation may be implied. In Shropshire, and perhaps elsewhere in England, the return of the wedding ring to the husband constituted a valid and proper form of divorce. Hints in several wife sales suggest the same belief: at Oxford in 1789 the woman called for a second ring; at Mansfield market in 1848 the husband demanded the return of his wedding band; and at Alfreton, Derbyshire, the wife: 'readily agreed, took off her wedding ring, and from that time considered herself the property of the purchaser'. [8]

One similarity seems to be lacking. All three of the above-mentioned popular divorce ceremonies involved a *literal reversal* of the matrimonial agreement, but we have little evidence supporting the initial *purchase* of any woman in a halter by her husband. An intriguing, although admittedly less likely, link is suggested by Dr John Smith's passage on handfasting, a custom symbolizing 'an interim tie of mutual fidelity, so strong and sacred that it was generally believed, in the country, *none ever broke it, who did not soon after break his neck, or meet with some other fatal accident'*. Recalling the halter around the wife's neck, one wonders . . . . It may be added that since all these methods were forms of divorce, they presumably resulted from similar causes.[9]

Another obvious parallel with wife-selling would seem to be the slave sales that took place during much the same period. Slavery in Britain was not limited exclusively to the acquisition of blacks imported from Africa or the West Indies. In 1569, for example, 'in the 11th of Elizabeth, one Cartwright bought a slave from Russia, and would scourge him; for this he was questioned, and it was resolved, that England was too pure an air for Slaves to breathe in'. Later on

> The legal status of most Indian [East Indian] domestics corresponded exactly to that of the majority of Africans. They were completely at the disposal of their masters, and, like Africans, they were bought and sold freely on the open market.

By 1555, black slaves were being imported to Britain from West Africa, although others date their introduction to 1553 (or even as early as 1440). Most, if not all, of these slaves appear to have been personal servants, and the indigenous British slave trade (as distinct from the capture or purchase of the slaves in Africa or elsewhere) appears to have remained more or less dormant during the first half of the seventeenth century:

> The English slave trade remained desultory and perfunctory in character until the establishment of British colonies in the Caribbean and the introduction of the sugar industry. . . . by 1660 . . .England was ready to embark wholeheartedly on a branch of commerce whose importance to her sugar and tobacco colonies in the New World was beginning to be fully appreciated.

Indeed, the earliest mention of the employment of Negroes in Britain came in a 1659 newspaper.[10]

After this date accounts of absconded slaves and of slaves for sale occur more and more frequently in newspapers. The belief that blacks could gain their freedom by baptism or by marriage to an English citizen, while popularly accepted, was not recognized legally, and a series of court decisions supported the legality of slavery. The Somerset case tried in 1772 is generally believed to have done away with British slavery, but in fact it only prohibited the *forced* export of slaves from England to the West Indies. Beyond this, the position of such servants remained in a legal limbo, and even the forced exportation of blacks was occasionally practised until the slave trade was officially abolished by Parliament in 1806. This chronology indicates, first of all, that unless the date of 1440 is accepted for the importation of blacks into England, it is unlikely that a widely known slave-sale mechanism existed before the first *specific* case of wife-selling in 1553. Therefore, although these customs may have influenced each other, wife sales probably did not derive from the sale of slaves. Further, the period of the greatest *apparent* slave sale activity only partially coincides with the zenith of wife-selling, and the abolition of the slave trade after 1806 had no apparent effect on the purchase of wives.[11]

Little of the exact mechanism of slave sales has been recorded, but what is known coincides with wife-sale procedure. In slave sales Shyllon reports purchase both by private treaty and by auction on the open market, making mention of multiple sales. The use of a halter is nowhere specified but may perhaps be compared with the collars that many slaves wore. Describing an escaped black belonging to Colonel Kirke, the *London Gazette* notes, in 1685, 'He has a silver collar about his neck, upon which is the colonel's coat of arms and cipher. . . .' The following announcements indicate the commonness of this article:

A black boy, an Indian . . . run away the 8th inst. from Putney, with a collar about his neck with this inscription: 'The Lady Bromfield's black, in Lincoln's Inn Fields. . . .,

Run away, a Tannymoor . . . with a silver collar about his neck, with these directions: 'Captain George Hasting's boy, Brigadier in the King's Horse Guards. . . .,

Run away on Tuesday the 19th instant, from Mr. Thomas Weedon, Merchant in Fenchurch-street, London, a Negro Boy, named Caesar. . . he had a Silver Coller [*sic*] about his Neck. . . .

In fact, these accessories were similar to dogs' collars. This is illustrated by the advertisement in 1756 of Matthew Dyer, working goldsmith, who made 'silver padlocks for Blacks or Dog; collars, &c'. It may be significant, however, that most of these are mentioned in connection with run-away slaves and none with actual slave sales.[12]

Advertisements concerning the sale of slaves are reminiscent of those used to dispose of unwanted wives. The qualities mentioned in the following also have points in common with wife-selling auctioneer patter:

> To be sold, a Negro Boy, about fourteen years old, warranted free from any distemper, and has had those fatal to that colour; has been used two years to all kinds of household work, and to wait at table; his price is £25. . .

> A healthy Negro Girl, age about fifteen years; . . . speaks good English, works at her needle, washes well, does household work, and has had the small-pox.

> TO BE SOLD,
> A FINE NEGROE BOY,

> Of about 4 feet 5 Inches high. Of a sober, tractable, humane Disposition, Eleven or Twelve Years of Age, talks English very well, and can Dress Hair in a tollerable way.

> A Negro Boy, from Africa, supposed to be ten or eleven years of age. He is remarkably stout, well proportioned, speaks tolerably good English, of a mild disposition, friendly, officious, sound, healthy, fond of labour, and for colour, an excellent fine black. [13]

An important difference between slave sales and their domestic counterparts, however, was price. As table 3 shows, prices paid for slaves were substantially higher than those given for wives. Although this is doubtless due to some extent to local and seasonal price fluctuations, the average discrepancy is so great that it indicates an entirely different scale of values. It is interesting to note, however, that judging by a colonial example, slaves, as well as some wives, were sometimes sold by the pound. [14]

Public opinion is a final point of comparison. Newspapers and periodicals found slave sales noteworthy and often deplorable: 'Perhaps the first instance of the kind in a free country', 'a shocking instance in a free country'. This seems close to editorial views about wife-selling, except that such accounts are hardly contemporaneous. While interest in slave sales was aroused by the Somerset case and was evidenced by Parliament in its debates on the slave trade, little corresponding emotionalism can be found in judicial or legislative considerations of wife-selling. [15]

It seems, therefore, that while slave sales offer some interesting

TABLE 3 COMPARISONS OF PRICES PAID FOR SLAVES AND WIVES, 1756—92

Year	Slaves price paid	Slaves estimated worth	Wives price paid
1756	London: £25	—	London: leg of mutton Co. Dublin: 8d and 2 quarts of ale
1763	London £32	—	Staffordshire: £2 2s
1771	Yorkshire: £32	—	—
1772	—	£50	—
1780	Liverpool: £38	—	—
1789	—	£60 — £66 6s 6d	Suffolk: 1s Worcestershire: 1s 1d and a 2s 6d bowl of punch Oxfordshire: 5s; 10s 6d
1792	Bristol: £80 (Jamaica currency)	—	—

parallels with wife-selling, the two were probably never closely connected. Many striking correspondences, such as the collar/halter, the advertisements and the mechanisms of the sales, could be ascribed to general market practices. Slave sales were more strictly economic than their domestic counterparts, and it may well have been this very suppression of the personal and social aspect that was responsible for the early condemnation of the practice.

Occasionally, one discovers references to sales of husbands. An early example, rendered into French by Pillet, is here given in translation:

Saturday evening, a business of an extraordinary nature was brought before his worship, the mayor of *Drogheda*. A woman,

Marguerite Collins, brought a complaint against her husband who
had abandoned her to go live with another woman. In his defence,
the husband said that his wife was extremely violent (which the
conduct of this woman, before the magistrate, fully proved); that
in her anger she had offered him for sale for two *pence* (four *sous*)
to her in the possession of whom he was now; that she had sold and
delivered him for three *half-pence* (six *liards*); that on the payment
of the sum, he had taken by the purchaser; that, many times, his
wife, the *seller*, in her onslaughts of anger, had bitten him so
cruelly, that he still bore terrible scars, although many months had
passed since he belonged to her (and he showed these scars). The
woman *purchaser* having been summoned to give testimony,
corroborated all of these facts, confirmed the purchase, and
declared that every day she was more content with her acquisition;
that she did not believe that there was a law which would order
them separated, because the right of a wife to sell a husband with
whom she was not content, to another woman who agreed with
him, should be equal to the right of a husband whose right to sell
[his wife] was recognized, above all when there was mutual
consent, as in the present case.

This plea, full of good sense and justice, so exasperated the
female plaintiff that, without respect for his worship, she leaped at
the face of her adversaries, and would have torn them with her
teeth and her nails, had she not been separated from them. The
mayor, after having warned all of them to change their conduct,
sent them forth. The crowd was immense, and everyone seemed
very amused by this singular case.

This sale probably took place in a magistrates' court at which the
mayor would have presided and at which he dealt with minor
criminal cases. It is interesting that the purchaser based her right of
purchase on wife-selling, a parallel apparently accepted by the
Frenchman:

> I had thought that the sale of wives by their husbands alone was
> authorized. Sales of husbands by their wives, although very rare,
> are not without example: and although the judges censure
> purchases of men, they no more dare pronounce them void than
> they dare pronounce void the purchase of women.

Some wife sales hint at this parallel. At Goole Ashton's wife
snapped her fingers in his face after the sale, saying, 'There, good
for nought, that's more than you would fetch.' Even as late as 1890
a matron visiting a Liverpool auction room 'suggested that the

next lot should be her old man, as she had been strongly advised to get rid of him'. Instead, *she* was put on the block. [16]

Another oft-noted case took a different twist. In 1853 a Birmingham police-court charge for assault brought to light the following:

> Memorandum of agreement made and entered into this second day of October, in the year of our Lord 1852, between William Charles Capas, of Charles-Henry Street, in the borough of Birmingham, in the county of Warwick, carpenter, of the one part, and Emily Hickson, of Hurst Street, Birmingham aforesaid, spinster, of the other part. Whereas the aforesaid William Charles Capas and Emily Hickson have mutually agreed with each other to live and reside together, and mutually assist in supporting and maintaining each other during the remainder of their lives, and also to sign the agreement hereinafter contained to that effect . . . for the true and faithful performance of this agreement, each of the said parties bindeth himself and herself unto the other finally by this agreement, as witness the hands of the said parties, this day and year first written above.

Somewhat similar to a marriage contract, this document is also reminiscent of the written agreements that accompanied many wife sales. The deed was drawn up by a lawyer, and Mrs Capas referred to the agreement when giving evidence, apparently oblivious of any novelty in the situation. [17]

Some examples fall only peripherally into the category of husband sales because they involve unmarried men or those of an indeterminate status. The following report, while intriguing, raises almost as many questions as it answers:

> On Thursday a man, residing in the vicinity of Deal, of the name of Joseph York, actually agreed to sell himself, body and goods for two sovereigns, which was accepted by a person present, and the money immediately paid. The purchaser has not yet determined upon the most advantageous way of disposing of his bargain.

As to both the cause and the final result, the paper is silent. [18]

Taken as a whole, this group is only fairly similar to wife sales. While many husband sales involve the transfer of a man to a buyer of the opposite sex, the ritualistic trappings of our informal institution appear to be largely absent. While perhaps drawing inspiration from wife sales, the scarcity of purchased husbands should disqualify the practice from being considered a vital tradition in its own right.

In the late seventeenth and early eighteenth centuries many poverty-stricken parents sold their children (actually, their children's services, but to all intents and purposes their persons as well) to chimney sweeps, who needed small and agile assistants for the dirty and dangerous work of cleaning chimneys and putting out fires. Because of the unappealing nature of this work and the fact that the children grew, a constant supply of new assistants was necessary, making this one of the few trades that did not require an apprenticing fee and in which the parents were reimbursed for their children's services.

As there was no specific economic inducement for the employer to protect his assistant, there appears to have been widespread maltreatment of such children. The passing of regulatory Acts by Parliament and the founding of a Society for Improving the Condition of the Infant Chimney-Sweepers only partially alleviated the situation. As early as 1773 some parents were 'ready to dispose of their children under the influence of a glass of gin', a practice similar to that found in some wife sales.

> Orphans, who are in a vagabond state, or the illegitimate children of the poorest kind of people, are said to be sold; that is, their service for seven years is disposed of for twenty or thirty shillings; being a smaller price than the value of a *terrier*: but it is presumed that the children of poor parents, who cannot find bread for a numerous family, make up by much the greater part of the *climbing boys*.

David Porter, a master chimney sweeper, reports that it was common for 'parents to carry about their children to the master-chimney sweepers and dispose of them to the best bidder, as they cannot put them apprentice to any other master at so early an age'. This suggests a parallel to the bidding in wife sales, although no evidence exists that any auction was held. That the sale of children to chimney sweeps was widespread is suggested by a remark by Porter; 'Half of the climbing-boys are now purchased from needy and illiterate parents.' A specific description of the method followed in such sales occurs in a prosecution for ill-treatment brought in 1827:

> the father of the boy had been for weeks hawking the boy about the town, offering him for sale to every chimney-sweep he met; he first

demanded 10£ for him, but that being much above the market-price of the day, he could not get it, and at last he came to 7£ for which he offered the boy to him . . . and after he agreed to take 6£, which sum he . . . paid him for the child, and now that he was worth more, they wanted to get him back again.

In several instances the sale was indirect; in 1827 one Samuel Bennett stole a child and 'pawned' him to a sweep. Table 4 offers a partial comparison of prices offered for such children and for wives in 1785, 1825 and 1827; available evidence on which the comparison is based is inconclusive. [19]

Prostitution provided another rationale for child sales. This was particularly true for girls, some of whom were apparently purchased through baby-farming operations. Despite *exposés* and moralizing, surprisingly few specific instances of sales of this sort are available. Francis Place, however, gives two examples when describing individuals who frequented his father's house:

Duke a Tailor his course of life was the same [he spent money on drink], his business decayed, and being nearly ruined he sold his niece whome he had brought up, to a rich man who came from the East Indies and lodged in his house, he continued to live upon them for some time. His niece was a pretty modest girl, who pined herself to death and Duke became destitute. . . .

Bury he was a gentlemanly sort of man, and held some place in one of the government offices, he kept a shop in the Strand between Arundel and Norfolk Streets which was attended by a very respectable looking woman with whom he lived, it was a bed fringe &c shop. . . . he when his circumstances declined sold his protage's daughter as Duke had sold his niece, before she was fifteen years of

TABLE 4　COMPARISON OF PRICES PAID FOR CHILDREN (BY SWEEPS) AND FOR WIVES, 1785, 1825, 1827

Year	Prices paid for children	Prices paid for wives
1785	—: £1 — £1 10s	Liverpool: £5 5s
1825	London: £6	Yorkshire: 1s 6d and £1 Sussex: £2 5s
1827	Derbyshire: 1s 6d	Yorkshire: 2s Somerset: £5

age. She had a child before she was sixteen and at seventeen was married to a young man who went to the West Indies leaving his wife at home, he gained some money came home and died, she lived on the money as long as she could and then became a common prostitute in the Strand. . .

It is noteworthy that in one of these cases the sale was to a near acquaintance, paralleling many wife sales. Economic motives, however, appear to predominate; the seller was often in reduced circumstances, and to judge from the little data available, the prices appear to have been fairly high.[20]

Now and again it is difficult to determine the exact motive for a child sale. The following agreement, reminiscent of several wife sales, surfaced in Durham in 1894:

> I give my daughter into the care of your hands to feed and clothe her in a proper manner. If not satisfied in one month return my daughter same as she came to work for her living. I give you my daughter, I sell you my daughter for 1s. — Yours truly, B. Shaw.

An Oxfordshire farmer discovered his stolen son at High Wycombe market with a tinker and his wife, who claimed to have bought the child for half a guinea 'from a Company of Gypsies in Maidenhead Thicket'. A Lincolnshire mother parted with her youngest child to a hawker in 1822 for a damask shawl worth £1 but retrieved the child because of the reproaches of her neighbours. As late as 1896 the following case occurred near Sleaford, Lincolnshire:

> a couple of travelling minstrels had been staying in the village, and one evening, accompanied by a little child only a few months old, they were in a public-house when a pig-dealer, well-known to the neighbourhood, offered to purchase the baby. The company regarded the offer as a joke, but the father said he would sell it for a shilling. The pig dealer at once put down the money, expressing a desire to have the 'little stranger'. The musicians visited the dealer's house to see what sort of a home the child would have, and both parties expressed their intention of adhering to the bargain. The matter has given rise to a good deal of talk in the village.[21]

Child sales appear to have been prompted more frequently by economic motives than were wife sales, although the prices vary widely. Many procedures are similar, this may be due to the commonplaces of contractual dealings.

Even the dead were sold. Because of the general respect in which corpses were held, they were traditionally imbued with a symbolic value. That this value was often reckoned in economic terms is indicated by widespread stories of the Grateful Dead, in which the travelling hero is aided by a mysterious helper who eventually turns out to be the spirit of a man whose corpse he saved from abuse. Usually this was accomplished by the purchase of the corpse from creditors of the deceased, which connects the folk tale with the informal institution of arresting a corpse for debt. Such arrests (although eventually judged to be illegal) were fairly common in both Scotland and England. Presumably, the prices paid for corpses reflected the amount of the debt outstanding. [22]

Another form of corpse sale owed its popularity to the difficulty encountered by anatomists in obtaining cadavers for dissection. Attempts to satisfy this need with the bodies of executed felons ran up against popular prejudices (perhaps based as much on residual fears of necromancy as on religious scruples or the popular distrust of surgeons) and often resulted in near-riots following public executions. The lack, however, was remedied by despised and feared opportunists who raided graveyards to exhume newly interred (and thus relatively well preserved) corpses for sale to the anatomists. These 'resurrectionists' (so-called because of their 'anticipation' of the raising of the dead) and 'Burkers' (named after William Burke, who killed and then sold his corpses) almost instantly became bogies in popular folklore. Since these macabre dealings were swathed in secrecy, what little is known about sale procedures stems from court testimony. It is of interest, however, that corpse sales do not seem to have been confined to professionals: *The Times* of 21 October 1791 reports the following:

In Swallow street, the wife of an indecent wretch, who keeps a green-grocer's stall, died a few days ago.

Instantly on her decease, he applied to most of the Anatomical Academies in Westminster, to dispose of the body; the whole tribe of Surgeons repaired to the spot, when the fellow put up his dead rib to auction, where she was knocked down at two guineas and a half.

The populace were so enraged, that on Thursday night they dragged the wretch from his house, and rolled him in the kennel until he almost expired.

In this case the auction suggests a parallel with wife-selling. Table 5 summarizes some instances of corpse sales. Corpse- and wife-sale prices do not appear to have been comparable. That corpse sales were connected with wife-selling in at least one instance, however,

TABLE 5   COMPARISON OF PRICES PAID FOR CORPSES AND FOR WIVES, c. 1750−1831

Year	Seller(s)	Prices paid for corpses	Prices paid for wives
c. 1750	2 women	Edinburgh: 2s + 10d (for a dram of whisky) 6d (carriage)	—
before 1754	husband	Somerset: £3	—
1791	husband	London: £2 12s 6d	London: gallon of beer Leicestershire: 2s 6d
1825	wife	—: £4 4s	Yorkshire: 1s 6d; £1 Sussex: £2 5s
1827	2 men	Edinburgh: £7 10s; £10	Yorkshire: 2s Somerset: £5
1828	2 men	Edinburgh: £10(x 4); £8(x4)	Kent: 1s + pot of beer Edinburgh: £1 15s Hertfordshire: 2s 6d
1831	2 men	Edinburgh: £9 9s	Somerset: £2 2s Cheshire: 5s Lancashire: 3s 6d + gallon of ale

is proved by the following explanation proffered by a Brighton man for the presence of an empty coffin in his house:

> when he first had his wife, he bought her, and she was delivered to him in a halter, and, on reflecting as he bought her, thought he had a right to dispose of her as he pleased; he, in consequence, sold her to the resurrection men, and kept the coffin for his sideboard. . . . [23]

The sale of corpses does not furnish any striking parallels with wife-selling but provides another instance of the transfer of control over a person (albeit a dead one) in return for cash.

CHAPTER 10
Peacock Feathers and the King's Shilling

CHANGE
. . . Here, in promiscuous groups, an anxious band
Along the narrow pathways take their stand: —
These — carters, shepherds, threshers, herdsmen gay,
The various emblems of their art display;
The carter's hat coarse whip-cords now adorn;
The thresher's bears a sheaf of ripen'd corn;
With hair of kine the herdsman's is o'erspread;
And fleecy honors deck the shepherd's head.
All these await the fiat of the train
To whom their various services 'pertain:
While ranks of village maidens, seeking place,
In modest silence throng a distant space,
And, like a show of cattle lent on hire,
Their points display to all who may desire. . . .

Hiring 'mops' have been partially examined in the discussion of
general locales for wife sales (see chapter 3). There they were
linked with courtship and sexual impropriety. Another important
element, however, was the abrogation of old allegiances and the
formation of new ones, suggesting certain parallels with the
mechanisms of wife-selling. [1]

These fairs ('mop fairs' or 'statutes', as they were often called)
appear to have originated with Edward III's Statute of Labourers.
This enactment, occurring as it did in a time when manpower was
in short supply, contained the provision that magistrates were
empowered to determine agricultural wages, and that these rates
would be announced at the Statute Sessions (commonly held at
Michaelmas, Martinmas or at Whitsuntide/Old May Day).
Coming to check the scale of pay, it was natural for workers to
enter into immediate agreements with employers for their services

169

over the coming year. Even when the Statute of Labourers was repealed during the reign of Elizabeth I, these meetings continued, developing into the well-known fairs of the eighteenth, nineteenth and early twentieth centuries.[2]

'Mops' were a popular part of rural life. Parson Woodforde mentions 'a great many Lads and Lasses' going to the 'statute' at Reepham in 1791. In Warwickshire 'farm servants, for several miles around consider themselves as liberated from servitude on this day; and, whether they be already hired, or really want masters, hie away, without leave, perhaps, to the statute.' It was customary to dress in one's best, and great pains were often taken to assure the proper effect. T. E. Kebble, in *The Agricultural Labourer*, notes that in northern England

> The young ladies themselves carry their savings on their backs; and the result of a year's pinching is seen at the 'statty' ball, when a girl, whose ordinary attire is wooden clogs and a serge petticoat, turns out in white muslin, a wreath of flowers, and white kid boots and gloves.

Contemporary ballads also comment on 'attire'. In 'Wrekington Hiring', Bess is told to

> put on that bonny gown,
> Thy mother bought thou at the town,
> That straw hat wi' the ribbons brown,
> They'll a' be buss'd that's comin' — O;
> Put that reed ribbon round thy waist,
> It myeks thou look se full of grace,
> Then up the lonnen come in haste,
> They'll think thou's cum'd frae Lunnen — O.

Upon arrival at the hiring fair, those looking for employ stood at the allotted place in the street or square, with men and women in separate groups. In Cumberland

> Men and women stand in the market place on the appointed day, the former wearing some token in their coats and hats, a straw generally in former times but now commonly an artificial flower, as an indication that they were unhired. The farmers pass among them, and, selecting a likely looking man or woman, the bargaining for wages commence.

William Chambers reports that the unengaged signal was a straw in the individual's mouth, while the Lincolnshire custom of wearing a peacock feather in one's hat when seeking work at a 'statute' may have been based on the same idea. Hole says that the demand for these was such that at some Lincolnshire 'mops' hawkers sold the feathers in the streets.[3]

Gabriel Oak, in Thomas Hardy's *Far From the Madding Crowd*, is forced by circumstances to seek a situation at such a mop:

> At one end of the street stood from two to three hundred blithe and hearty labourers waiting upon Chance . . . Among these, carters and waggoners were distinguished by having a piece of whip-cord twisted round their hats; thatchers wore a fragment of woven straw; shepherds held their sheep-crooks in their hands; and thus the situation required was known to hirers at a glance.

As this description suggests, clothing at several hiring fairs provided detailed indications of the skills possessed by each labourer. Some of the symbolic equivalents associated with various trades are strikingly reminiscent of the halter of the wife sale. Once a farmer discovered the type of worker he wished to employ, the bargaining commenced. The broadside 'Country Statutes' offers the following advice to potential employees:

> The master that a servant wants will now stand in a wonder;
> You all must ask ten pounds a year and none of you go under.
> It's you that must do all the work and what they do require,
> So now stand up for wages, lads, before that you do hire.
>
> So to the hirings we have come, all for to look for places,
> If with the master we agree and he will give good wages.

A correspondent reporting on Warwickshire mops notes:

> Where a master or mistress was engaged in conversation with a servant they were usually surrounded by a group . . . this in some, perhaps, was mere idle curiosity, in others, from desire to know the wages asked and given, as a guide for themselves.

The *Preston Guardian* of 1845 records a number of conversations between employer and labourer, supposedly occurring at Kendal hiring fair. These indicate a considerable amount of familiar give and take — girls who wished to know about the house and work, farmers who could not afford the terms and were not afraid to say so ('Ah, that's above my cut') and hard-driven bargains — with the principals urged on by interested outsiders. Margaret Baker, writing of her mother's girlhood in Victorian Canterbury, recalls:

she always enjoyed going to the Michaelmas Hiring Fair, where she liked to listen to the farmers re-engaging their labourers for another spell of work. They would walk up to particular workers who had satisfied them during past service and say, 'Pawk agin, er 'ow?' Her father explained that this was 'Pork again or how?', i.e. 'Will you have pork again with me, or what will you do?'

All this supports Chambers' claim that it 'gives occasion for some coquetry and badinage, and an air of good-humour generally prevails throughout'.[4]

Successful bargains were concluded by the payment of earnest, a sum of money which bound the labourer to his employer for half a year or a year, until the time of the next major hiring fair. In the Lake District this earnest was known as a 'yearl' or 'arl'; elsewhere the coin was a 'fasten penny' or 'fastening penny'. A few areas granted a week's grace, during which the bargain might be successfully repudiated. If the employer changed his mind, the servant kept the earnest; if the servant annulled the contract, he was required to return the coin. A Warwickshire labourer, hired as a boy in 1917, recalls:

> The farmer used to come up to us and say, 'Oh, will you come and work for me?' If you said, 'yes', he gave you the shillin' and you'd start next morning. You had to be there twelve months. You had to go twelve months without any wages. . . . I had my shillin' but I got talking to some people afterwards and they said: 'The farmer ent worth tuppence.' So, next day, I got the shillin' off my father and I sent it back to the farmer, so I didn't go.

Similar returns were made by dissatisfied employees in Shropshire, where earnest was not considered part of the regular wages. Near Oswestry 2s 6d earnest was given rather than the normal shilling, but three months' advance notice (rather than one) of quitting was expected. For those who did break their bargains one or more 'runaway mops' were held, at which further job placement was possible. Some considered it unlucky not to spend one's earnest immediately, a fact which (along with reference to 'the shillin') suggests parallels with army recruitment. In Hertfordshire labourers who had been hired sported a common symbol — a streamer or cockade, suggesting one explanation for the statement that after Warwickshire hirings 'the emblems in the hats are exchanged for ribbons of almost every hue.' This, too, parallels military enlistment.[5]

The last four lines of the poem on the Henley 'mop',

> While ranks of village maidens, seeking place,
> In modest silence throng a distant space,
> And, like a show of cattle lent on hire,
> Their points display to all who may desire.

are of interest, in that they suggest that a simile common in wife-selling was also applied to this institution. Nor is this the only sample of such a connection. John Clare, in his *Village Minstrel*, speaks of

> Milkmaids and clowns that statute joys pursue
> And rattle off like hogs to London mart
> Weary of old they seek for places new

Finally, Francis Heath, in his attack on hiring 'mops', uses a similar comparison:

> These fairs, annually held to enable servants of both sexes to be hired, were, oftentimes, the occasion of the greatest drunkenness and profligacy. Young girls dressed in their finest clothes were exhibited like cattle to be hired by the would-be employers, who came to the fair to seek their services; and the scenes which frequently took place at the close of the day were too disgraceful for description.

These, along with aforementioned links with courtship and sexual impropriety and symbolic parallels with the halter, all suggest a similarity between hiring fairs and wife sales. In both the element of change was strong, and both provided 'fail-safe' mechanisms to ensure the support of the people involved.[6]

No more I'll work in the harvest fields or go and reap the corn
For I've been and took the shilling, boys, and I'm off tomorrow morn.

To 'take the shilling' or 'collar a shiner' were cant phrases for enlisting in the army, the money received being equivalent to the earnest paid in a normal bargain or to the 'fasten penny' received at hiring fairs. Although a further bonus was often paid to recruits, the shilling remained a constant symbol of enlistment, having much the same significance as the wife sale's halter.[7]

Siting of enlistment in the armed forces at markets, fairs and inns paralleled siting of wife sales. Thomas Jackson, for instance, who served in the army during the early nineteenth century, filling a stint as a recruiting sergeant, visited 'all the wakes, races and revels within twenty miles of London'. The approach might be as direct as that adopted in *The Recruiting Officer*:

> If any gentlemen Soldiers, or others, have a mind to serve her Majesty, and pull down the *French* King, if any Prentices have severe Masters, any Children have undutiful Parents, if any Servants have too little Wages, or any Husband too much Wife, let them repair to the noble Serjeant *Kite*, at the Sign of the *Raven*, in this good town of *Shrewsbury*, and they shall receive present Relief and Entertainment —.
>
> Gentlemen, I don't beat my Drums here to insnare or inveigle any man; for you must know, Gentlemen, that I am a Man of Honour: Besides, I don't beat up for common Soldiers; no, I list only Granadeers, *Granadeers*, Gentlemen—.

This bears some resemblance to the auctioneer's patter that inspired wife-sellers. Regrettably, it appears that some recruiters were not above trickery. At Winchester Fair two soldiers, dressed as countrymen,

> went strutting about, playing all manner of pranks. Having attracted some rustics they offered to treat them and retired to a tent where, after a few pots of beer, they declared their intentions of enlisting, Peters spinning out 'a long rigmarole of how his eldest brother who enlisted that day three years ago, was now a captain in India, as rich as a nabob'. The moment seemed propitious, so one man slipped out for the sergeant, who dropped in as if by accident. Andrews then offered a drink to the sergeant, and shook hands with him, and they all sat down to beer. Andrews formally volunteered to enlist; Peters rose in a jolly, offhand way and offered to go with him. 'The shilling was put into each of our hands in the king's name and we gave three cheers.' Ten to one but two or three of the company followed suit. If not, the sergeant sat down and pulled out a fistful of money and a couple of watches. Then he presented the watches to the new 'king's men' on behalf of their company, while advancing a part of their bounty, adding that there were eight vacancies for sergeants which such smart men could well hope to fill soon. The watches usually had an astonishing effect and secured three or more fish. One man hung back. 'Oi, tell you what, Mr Sergeant! You'll not have me unless you makes me the same as yourself now. So if you loiks to do that, why here's your man!' Sergeant Brown then cut three pieces of tape in the shape of three v's and pinned them on the yokel's sleeve. He then drew his sword, made the fellow kneel down, and in a tone of martial command cried out: 'Rise, Sergeant Turner, in the name of St George and the Dragon!' Another recruit was caught! When they asked for watches

the sergeant said he had just given away twenty-two, but had sent to the barracks for twenty-six more and two hundred pounds in cash.

As the anti-war song 'The Young Recruit; or, Thirteen Pence a Day' bitterly puts it:

> When you are a soldier lad, if you do not limp,
> You shall go recruiting, and then you'll be a crimp.
> A lad may take your shilling when in drink he's fresh,
> But you know it's quite respectable to kidnap human flesh.

The contribution of drink to enlistment, as to wife-selling, is well substantiated. Even as late as 1863, Edwin Mole, tempted but not ensnared by recruitment talk of handsome uniforms, easy money and pretty girls, spent an evening out with several 'friendly' sergeants.

> Next morning, when I awoke, my head was very lumpy. The first thing I saw was Sergeant Gibbs, sitting up in bed, smoking. . . .
> '. . . . you'll have to go before the doctor this morning, and as it's rather late I think you had better get up at once.'
> 'What have I to go before the doctor for?'
> 'Why, because you 'listed last night of course; and there's the medical to pass. You're a soldier now. If you feel in your pocket you'll find the bob, and if you want any luck you'd better come down'stairs and break it, for that's the custom and according to the Articles of War.'
> This information staggered me, for I had no recollection of taking any shilling. Thinking Sergeant Gibbs was only joking, I said: 'Don't talk silly. If I had 'listed last night I should have remembered it.'
> 'Not by the way you looked when you went to bed,' he replied. 'Why, you drink me and Hudson blind, toasting your new regiment, and it was as much as we could do to carry you upstairs and sling you on to your cot. But just look in your pocket.'
> I had my trousers on, and I slipped my hand into my pocket and pulled out what was there. All my money, I found, was gone, except a few coppers and —
> 'The Queen's Shilling,' put in Sergeant Gibbs, with a knowing nod of his head . . .

Given such tricks, it was not surprising that many were wary of recruiters' blandishments:

> It's now, my brave fellows, if you want to enlist
> It's five golden guineas I'll clap in your fist;

Besides, there's five shillings to kick up a dust
As you go to the fair in the morning.

It's then you will also go decent and clean
While all other fellows go dirty and mean. . . .

Och, you need not be talking about your fine pay,
For all you have got is one shilling a day. . . .

And you need not be talking about your fine clothes,
For you've just got the loan of them, as I do suppose;
And you dare not sell them in spite of your nose,
Or you would get flogged in the morning. . . .

Nonetheless, it is true that incentives were often offered to potential recruits. About 1778 in Perth

The trades' deacons were converted into recruiting sergeants, and paraded the streets at night with flambeaux, offering high bounties, and the freedom of the trade to all who would come forward. Amongst these, the deacon of the Glovers was most conspicuous; in his train the trades' officer, in the fantastic garb of a morris dancer, with jingling bells, performed a variety of antics. [8]

One report of a recruitment with striking similarities to wife sales comes from *Jackson's Oxford Journal* of 1795:

A singular circumstance, in the recruiting way, happened a few weeks since, which for its oddity deserves to be recorded. A stout young man went into the Market-Place, and mounting a stool in the midst of the recruiting Sarjeants, addressed himself to them and said, he had two girls with child, and as he could not marry them both, he would offer himself to the best bidder. One bid twelve guineas, another fifteen, a third eighteen, and a fourth twenty; a Captain's lady then stepped up, and bid twenty-five, saying, she admired his spirit, and would not lose the man; at which price he knocked himself off.

Many elements of wife-selling — the auction, the display of the 'merchandise' even sale by weight — are paralleled here. Nor did the institutions' reputations differ markedly. 'Chelsea Pensioner', writing in *Jottings from my Sabretache*, noted in 1805: 'Whoever "listed for a soldier" was at once set down among the catalogue of persons who had turned out ill,' and J. MacMullen reported some thirty years later that 'the British Army, as is well known, is the *dernier ressort* of the idle, the depraved, and the destitute.'[9]

A connection in the popular mind between apprenticeship and wife-selling is suggested by the case of *R. v. Delaval*, which dealt with the apprenticing of a girl ostensibly to learn music, but actually for immoral purposes. The custom of apprenticing youths (and girls) to masters in different trades or crafts, sometimes across normal sex boundaries, was of ancient origin. An Act of 1601 allowed the binding of parish children by the parish officers (with the consent of two justices) until the age of 24 for boys and 21 (or marriage) for girls. Acceptance of these apprentices was compulsory, but because of an Act of 1691 (which stated that anyone serving 40 days' apprenticeship in a parish could become resident), many children were sent to *other* parishes to serve their articles, in the hope that they would cease to be a drain on local rates. In such cases (reminiscent of one Staffordshire wife sale), it became customary to pay fees as an inducement to tradesmen who took on such apprentices. Once apprenticed, it was necessary for the young man or girl to appear before a Quarter Sessions in order to revoke the articles. Mary Dorothy George notes that parish apprenticing differed from the regular form both in its longer terms of service and in the use of compulsion.[10]

Until attacks on the institution in the late eighteenth and early nineteenth century eventually resulted in the repeal of the Statute of Apprentices in 1814, apprenticeship was the gateway to social advancement. Through apprenticeship one could acquire a skilled trade, gain the freedom of the city and avoid prosecution for practising a craft without the required seven-year preliminary. In some areas the use of apprentices helped to keep journeymen's wages down, but in others the system worked as a union 'closed shop', increasing prosperity by restricting trade practice. Normally, apprentices were given food, training and lodging; in return, they were required to complete a period of service, during which all the money they earned became their master's or mistress's property. Articles could be transferred from one master to another, and it is clear that matrimony, if not actually forbidden, was at least frowned upon. In connection with female apprenticeship, testimony by a Mrs Cappe concerning the Gray Coat School in York in about 1785 suggests that many girls, when serving apprenticeships, were seduced by their masters and so entered into prostitution. It was not unknown for masters to have their apprentices impressed or kidnapped and taken to the colonies as indentured servants in order to save payment of the remainder due on their fee. Later, 'outdoor' apprenticeships became fashionable, and those learning a trade no longer boarded in. With 'clubbing' a fraction of normal wages was paid to an aspiring craftsman by contract for three years, rather than having him serve full seven-year indentures. Some parishes allowed trial apprenticeships, while Jonas Hanway eventually succeeded in reducing the term of service to the age of 21 for the parish poor. [11]

Francis Place records that his father apprenticed him by going to the parlour of the inn he managed 'and [offering] me to any one who would take me'. After a three-week trial period 'I was bound apprentice and my father gave his parlour guests a feast on the occasion.' Both inn locale and post-transactional feasting are, of course, reminiscent of wife sales. [12]

Indentured servitude was a process by which the impecunious, desirous of transportation to Britain's American colonies, bartered their services for a span of time in return for the price of the passage. (Clifford Alderman notes the similarity of this to apprenticeship.) Indentured servitude may also be regarded as a form of 'temporary slavery'. The basis of the institution was the colonies' need for manpower. Until the advent of black slavery indentured servants provided much of the economic backbone of the colonies in the seventeenth and early eighteenth centuries. The cultivation of tobacco in Maryland and Virginia was of such crucial economic importance that there are records of women indenturees being impressed for fieldwork. Elsewhere the need for help was less pressing but still present. In a few areas the institution lasted beyond 1800. [13]

The liberty of indentured servants was subject to restrictions of various kinds. At least initially, they could not vote or marry without the permission of their master. Those who disobeyed might receive an extra term of servitude, a punishment extending to free men or women who married indenturees. Servants were not allowed to trade. They could not sell their indentures but could be sold by their masters. Later, however, conditions became more liberal. Limits were set for periods of service, although these were often evaded by means of a 'custom of the country' clause inserted in the agreement. Servants, however, gained the right to take complaints to court and could adjust the terms of their contract, serving longer terms to escape fieldwork or shorter terms in return for practising particular skills. [14]

While the Irish provided most of the indentured labour from the

British Isles, Scots were normally preferred and commanded higher prices. Few English men and women appear to have availed themselves of the institution. In some cases, as has been noted, servants were kidnapped, resulting in London and Bristol ordinances requiring the registration of all indentures, with the date of signing and the servant's destination. Debtors in the Colonies could sell themselves into service to avoid prison, or could even be sold against their will by the courts. Parish overseers often sold work-house inmates; in Pennsylvania in 1740 some 40 vagrants were jailed and advertised for sale with the explanation 'Thought to be runaway servants'.[15]

London served as headquarters for the English indentured-servant trade. Agents known as 'spirits' were responsible for recruiting cargoes of servants. These 'spirits' often congregated at the Royal Exchange or in the middle aisle of St Paul's, while others prowled the slums of provincial seaports. As disliked as his counterpart, the recruiting sergeant, it was said that 'All that was necessary to start a riot in a crowd was to point out some person as a spirit and he would instantly be set upon by angry citizens.' These agents, too, often resorted to tricks. Some used doxies to bait potential prey; others relied on a meal and liquor. In Aberdeen one recruiter hired a drummer to announce a forthcoming voyage; elsewhere he found pipers just as effective. Once an indenture was signed, the prospective colonist was lodged in a 'safe house' until he could be conveyed on board his ship. Formal indentures were in use as early as 1624; by 1636 they were printed with blanks to be filled in by the participants. Those unlucky enough to make *verbal* agreements in Britain often found that their terms of servitude had 'lengthened' during passage across the Atlantic.[16]

How, then, does this institution relate to wife-selling? The period of indentured servitude overlaps with that of the informal institution but does not appear to parallel it. Restrictions in servants' rights might be compared to those faced by a wife but show no close correlation. The influence of drink and the presence of written agreements are minor similarities, but purchase prices appear to have been economic rather than token amounts to ensure legality. The overwhelming impression is that, despite certain similarities, the connection between indentured servitude and wife-selling was a minor one.[17]

Etymological parallels between sales of wives and of livestock have already been noted, in which the woman involved in a wife sale was equated with a horse or cow. Livestock dealings themselves may now be considered in more detail. The sale of cattle, sheep, horses and other animals was commonly associated with fairs and markets. Anne Wilson notes:

> The long-distance trade in meat animals between upland and lowland Britain, already a feature of medieval marketing, continued and grew. . . . By the Georgian period the system had developed into an industry. Graziers in the counties around London devoted themselves entirely to improving their pastures, so that they could buy the beasts that had been raised far away, feed them up and resell them to the town butchers. . . . The droving of sheep and cattle for the meat market (they were often sold at fairs on the way, and rested for a time before continuing their long journeys) was a part of the country's economic life until the middle of the nineteenth century.

The renting of pens, found occasionally in wife-selling, was a necessity for many livestock transactions. In other areas cattle were sold in the open streets, often tied to rings driven into nearby walls. (One broadside print of the institution shows both cattle and a woman tied to a wooden fence.) The wife-selling role of butchers and of auctioneers drawn from the ranks of professional practitioners suggests other connections. Butchers were of great importance to the cattle trade. The memorandum book of John Howell, a Shropshire farmer in the 1770s, mentions receipt of 'earnest money' from a butcher in return for a contract for all of his calves during the coming year. One newspaper account of Smithfield market reports purchases made by butchers from herds driven into town (strongly indicating that they were forestalling); another notes a petition from the cutting butchers requesting that the market day be changed. One of the best descriptions of Smithfield livestock dealings is provided by Andrew Blaikie, a 65-year-old Scottish farmer who went to London (to see the king) in 1802:

> Attended Smithfield back and forward from five in the morning till four in the afternoon. . . . [Cattle] mostly stand tied to strong railings made on purpose. The heavy cattle stand in droves; they cannot move much, the holders-up have prods in the end of a stick to goad their legs with to keep them on foot; after 100 miles, or perhaps double, were they to allow them to stand still a minute or

two they would lie down, and could not easily rise again. So soon as the cattle are sold, the holder-up takes out his knife, cuts off all the hair, of which he makes money by selling it to the upholstrers. Being acquainted with the value and weight, I now and then risked my opinion as to weight and price; told the salesman I was a farmer; they saw this, and gave me every information I wished. I offered to treat them with a glass of wine or so, which they all declined; no drinking there, either buying or selling. The butchers that came to purchase are very civil also. The business is done at one word or two at most, or no bargain; very unlike our Scotch butchers in every respect. Both salesmen and butchers all wore light-blue aprons, which meet behind the back. Every kind of cattle have their own corner in the market place; different kinds of sheep have their own corner or place also; calves stand tied to stakes by themselves. The Market Place, I think, may be about two acres or thereabouts. When the market is full two clerks take up the list or number, which the salesman gives; as also when the market is over merely the average prices both of beef and mutton. I saw the market on Friday also, which was by far a better market; no persons sell their own cattle or sheep; it is all done by salesmen, who are either paid so much a head or so much a cwt.[18]

A closer glimpse into livestock marketing methods is given by the case of *Lees v. Weaver*, tried at the Chester summer Assizes. The case, reported with humour and gusto, is described as 'an action of trover for a female, of the designation of Miss Rachael':

It appeared that a person, by the name of Woodcock, claimed the exclusive rights to this young creature. He had two other females, over whom he professed an absolute dominion, that it extended even to the right of selling them by auction, or by private contract, just as an African merchant would sell his slaves. Besides Rachael, he had a Miss Tidy, and no less personage than Lady Williams. Rachael, Miss Tidy, and Lady Williams, had all seen their best days; but the two latter, particularly, were declining into the vale of life and had manifested unequivocal symptoms of fertility. Mr Woodcock therefore determined to get rid of them all; and with that in view, agreeably to the custom of this country, he put halters round their necks, and carried them to the public market, *just as the lower orders of people in London carry their wives for sale to Smithfield Market*. They were put up to auction, by Mr Prince, an auctioneer. . . . Lady Williams was first offered for sale, but no one would have anything to say to her; and even Rachael and Miss Tidy were bought in. The auctioneer, finding the bidders had no spirit, bethought him of a very excellent expedient; he gave them a dinner and plied them afterwards with a bottle of wine apiece. He then remounted the *rostrum* and Lady Williams, Miss Tidy, and Rachael, all sold at very high prices. The plaintiff purchased Rachael, the defendant had Lady Williams, and somebody else got Miss Tidy. The parties were conveying their respective purchases home, but, elated by the libations with which the auction had been accompanied, they stopped by the way, and renewed their devotions at the shrine of Bacchus, so devoutly, that they, neither of them, knew Rachael from Miss Tidy, or either, from Lady Williams. . . .

The owners inadvertently switched cows; the resulting court case was brought to force Rachael's return. In addition to the presence of an auctioneer, a halter was used, and the sale proceedings were influenced by drink; all are practices found in connection with wife-selling. Both institutions shared the assessment of price per pound, and the price paid for animals was similar to that paid for women. [19]

With livestock sales, at least occasionally, the offer was made by the purchaser; in one case a buyer severely underestimated the animal's weight and wished to forfeit a guinea and be quit of his 'bargain'. Common to some transactions was the idea of 'luck money', a portion of the beast's price returned to the purchaser. In Cheshire a cow's horn was supposed to be 'tipped with silver', a shilling being given to the buyer or allowed off the price. (Experienced buyers often attempted to have both horns so treated.) Elsewhere in the county, a 'luck penny' was given after being ceremoniously spat upon. For the bargain to be legal it had to be concluded with a shaking of hands. Christina Hole describes the procedure thus:

> The buyer, after the necessary preliminaries were over, would say: 'Well, now, I'll fasten you. Hold your hand.' He would then make his final offer and try to strike the seller's hand. If the price was acceptable, his hand would be taken and the matter was settled. It could not afterwards be altered.

Several wife sales feature a final handclasp, and one Yorkshire case makes reference to 'striking a bargain'. The ratifying drink was a commonplace, and the payment of market toll was also shared by both institutions. Wife sales thus display many close parallels to cattle sales, even allowing for normal contractual similarities. [20]

Several punishments made use of halters. A 1784 Act passed in Connecticut dealt with the crime of adultery:

> Be it enacted by the Governor, Council and Representatives in general court assembled, and by the authority of the same, that whosoever shall commit adultery with a married woman, & be thereof convicted before the superior court, both of them shall be severely punished, by whipping on the naked body, and stigmatized, or burnt on the forehead with the letter A on a hot iron; *and each shall wear an halter about their necks on the outside of their garments during their abode in this state, that it may be visible. . .*

This is particularly interesting in view of the number of wife sales involving adulterous women, but a halter was used in punishment for other crimes as well. Sarah Hales, censored for her miscarriage (presumably an abortion) was 'to be carried to the gallows with a rope about her neck, and to sit upon the ladder, the rope end flung over the gallows, and after to be banished'. Court records from Ipswich, Salem and Boston, Massachusetts, show that a similar punishment — sitting on the gallows for an hour with a rope round the neck — was meted out to numerous thieves. At Gibraltar in 1738 Margaret Dove was sentenced to 300 lashes for the murder of Alexander Stuart, the punishment to be administered in three places, while the prisoner wore a rope around her neck. A soldier of the Monmouth militia was drummed out of his regiment for desertion, with a label on his chest detailing his offence and 'a halter about his neck'.[21]

The halter was also used for more informal punishments. Mention has been made of the rope with which a miner was suspended above a Plymouth street for ill-treating his wife. At Tutbury, Staffordshire, the following rough musicking was made for a runaway wife who had returned home:

> Proceedings commenced by a mob assembling in front of the house of the returned fugitive, and demanding that she be given up to its tender mercies. The husband wished the ceremony to be postponed until the morning, but the mob would not be denied, and he then unlocked the door, and delivered her up to the mob, *who placed a rope round her waist, and trailed her around the village*, blowing cows' horns, ringing bells, shouting, and making other noisy accompaniments. On arriving at a place called the Little Dove, they dragged the woman into the water, and committed all kinds of barbarities. . .

In such cases the rope appears to be a not so subtle reminder of a more severe alternative. This leads us to the subject of actual executions. . . and a surprising parallel. [22]

'The Maid Freed From the Gallows', Child ballad no. 95, deals with a theme long popular in the British Isles. Over 250 variants have sprung from the version apparently sung by gypsies in the seventeenth century. Even recently the song was current in an amended (and very loud) version by Led Zeppelin. The plot, as developed by Child, is as follows. A girl facing death by hanging, awaits deliverance from the hangman by means of a ransom. She sees her father coming:

> 'It's hold your hand, dear judge,' she says,
>   'O, hold your hand for a while!
> For yonder I see my father a coming,
>   Riding many's the mile.'

> 'Have you any gold, father?' she says,
>   'Or have you any fee?
> Or did you come to see your own daughter a hanging,
>   Like a dog, upon a tree?'

Unfortunately, the father refuses to help, and the girl now pins all her hopes on her mother. This matron comes riding into view, but the girl is told her ransom will not be paid:

> 'I have no gold, daughter,' she says,
>   'Neither have I any fee;
> But I am come to see my own daughter hanged,
>   And hanged she shall be.'

Father, mother, sister and brother all say no. Fortunately, at this point, the lover comes into sight. *He* has the required gold, so —

> 'Some of my gold now you shall have,
>   And likewise of my fee,
> For I am come to see you saved,
>   And saved you shall be.'

This little scenario is remarkably close to that of a wife sale if one substitutes the husband for the judge or the hangman: the halter symbolizes a power of life and death over the wife; the lover, by paying the symbolic price for his beloved, frees her from her husband's sway. [23]

It is interesting to remember in this context the traditional belief that a maiden or prostitute could beg a felon's life from the gallows were she willing to marry him. In 1602 John Manningham noted in his diary: 'In England it hath bin used that yf a woman will beg a condemned person for hir husband shee must come in hir smocke onely, with a white rod in hir hand. . . .' This was tried (unsuccessfully, it may be noted) in 1686 and in 1722. Gustavus Vassa, however, a former slave and a widely travelled man of the world, reports that this practice *did* work on at least one occasion.

> In the spring of 1784 . . . I embarked as steward on board a fine new ship called the *London*, commanded by Martin Hopkins, and sailed for New-York. . . . While we lay here a circumstance happened which I thought extremely singular: — One day a malefactor was to be executed on a gallows; but with a condition that if any woman, having nothing on but her shift, married the man under the gallows, his life was to be saved. This extraordinary privilege was claimed; a woman presented herself; and the Marriage ceremony was performed.

Peter Linebaugh, in his article on the Tyburn Riots, has noted further parallels between hanging and marrying, centring on the festive dress and attitude of many of the condemned. This dress was similar to the clothes normally worn for a wedding. M. Mission, a Swiss visitor to Tyburn, noted: 'He that is to be hang'd or otherwise executed . . . first takes Care to get himself shav'd, and handsomely drest either in Mourning or in the Dress of a Bridegroom.' Philip Thomas, hanged for horse-stealing, was granted permission to ride to the gallows on his own horse, wearing his shroud, with a pair of white gloves, a crêpe hatband with a white favour and a nosegay in one hand and a book in the other. John Weskett, hanged for theft in 1764, wore a white ribbon in his hat and declared, 'I look upon this as my Wedding-Day.' Even 'Wicked Lord Ferrers' wore wedding clothes to his execution. It is no wonder, then, that hanging and marrying were linked in popular tradition, or that executions should have been known popularly as the 'hanging-match'. As popular representations of a change of state, it seems possible that at least a *symbolic* connection existed between public executions and wife-selling.[24]

SALE OF A WIFE.

Livsey, Printer 12 Whittle street Manchester.

Come all you lads and lasses gay,
And banish care and strife
A spinner in Smithfield Market,
Did by auction sell his wife,
Thirteen shillings and a penny
For the lady was the sum
And for to see this funny spree
Some lots of folks did run.

In Smithfield market I declare It's true upon my life,
A cotton spinner the other day by auction sold his wife

This man and wife good lack-a-day
They never could agree
For she often pawn'd her husbands clothes
and went upon the spree,
So he led her to the market,
With an halter I am told,
And there she was so help me bob
By public auction sold.

when the auctioneer commenc'd the sale
a jolly farmer cried,
Here's five and fourpence halfpenny
For the cotton spinner's bride
A tailor cried out seven and six
and then a butcher said,
I'll give you ten and sevenpence,
Besides a bullock's head.

She is going cried the auctioneer, she's going pon my life,
Tinkers, cobblers, tailors, will you buy a charming wife

Such fighting, scratching, tearing too
Before no one did see,
Such roaring, bawling, swearing,
O, blow me, 'twas a spree,
At length a rum old cobbler
He gave a dreadful bawl
Here's thirteen and a penny
With my lapstone on my knee.

Thirteen shillings & a penny bid when down the hammer drop
With whiskers, apron, bustle, shawl, stays, petticoat and smock.

A cotton spinner's lady was
This blooming damsel gay,
She was sold in Smithfield market,
Upon a market day,
Bakers, Butchers. Tailors,
they did bid for her we hear,
While a lot of rum old women,
Pitch'd into the auctioneer.

Young men & maids did hollo while married folks did sneer.
They frighten'd the old cobbler & knock'd down the auctioneer,

The cobbler took the lady up
Just like a Scotchman's pack
And the cotton spinner's lady rode
Upon the cobbler's back
Some laughed till they bursted
While others was perplex'd.
But the cobbler bristled up his wife
With two big balls of wax
The cobbler sat her on his knee and joyfully did bawl
While the lady knock'd about his seat the lapston & his awl,

Then the cotton spinner sold his wife
As you shall understand
And thirteen shillings and a penny
Popp'd into his hand ;
He whistled, danced, and capered
For to banish care and strife,
He went to the Casino
Singing. I have sold my wife
So the cotton spinner he may go and banish care and strife
And go to Smithfield market for to buy another wife

Now the cobbler and the lady
Are both happy in a stall
While the cobbler works his bristle
Why the lady works the awl
And they upon the lapstone
So merry play together
Singing heel and toe gee up gee wo
Big balls of wax and leather.
And day & night in sweet delight they banish care and strife
The merry little cobbler and his thirteen shilling wife.

An example of a widely used wife-selling song. This version is printed
by Livsey, Manchester

CHAPTER 11

'Pay heed to my ditty'

As might be expected, wife-selling, by its very notoriety, influenced contemporary society in a number of secondary ways. These include folklore, verse, music, drama, literature and even popular art.

At first glance, the great majority of wife-sale cases appear to be genuine, although the general sparseness of evidence often makes it difficult to assess a sale's validity. More intensive analysis, however, reveals several instances in which separate accounts show striking similarities, giving rise to the possibility that they represent versions of floating folk traditions. The dividing line between fact and fiction is often blurred, so that no firm criteria can be offered to separate such stories from accounts of actual wife sales. As most newspaper stories were based on oral accounts, folklore often appeared as truth in the journal columns. This is evidenced by tales of the discovery of animals inside stones, of sheep thieves hanged in the course of their thefts, of divine judgments or treasure uncovered by adhering to romantic directions — even an example of the well-known folk legend in which a raven leads a man to safety moments before some natural disaster. [1]

In general, fictional wife-sale reports offer a suspicious paucity of concrete detail (personal names are cited remarkably rarely); conversely, they are often connected with well-known personalities. Some wife-sale traditions, notably those connected with the Duke of Chandos and an ostler and the purchase made by an unnamed English Lord from his lackey, deal with transactions involving an aristocratic purchaser. The Chandos story, marred by uncertainty about the reputed sale's location, offers only circumstantial evidence in the form of a manuscript notation in a peerage to support the claim. Indeed, one *Notes and Queries* author dismisses the story as 'apocryphal'. The second tradition is too incomplete to permit checking. Few other sales show any signs of aristocratic involvement. [2]

If such transactions were not founded on fact, why did these stories emerge? One answer is suggested by the critic Louis James, who makes mention of 'the theme of the innocent country girl pursued by the member of the upper classes'. This, he demonstrates, is found in such penny fiction as *The Farmer of Inglewood Forest* (1825), *Eliza Grimwood; A Domestic Legend of the Waterloo Road* (c. 1838); *Gideon Giles* (1841); *Adeline; or the Grave of the Forsaken* (1842); *The Maniac Father* (1844) and *Jane Brightwell* (1846). The theme occurs still earlier, however, in eighteenth- and nineteenth-century ballads and in newspaper accounts of suicides. Explaining a similar theme, James adds: 'An interest in unrecognized heiresses would be natural to lower-class girls, particularly if they were doing drab and insignificant jobs. . .' The divination tradition of 'Master and Servant' also enshrines a longing for advancement. In this tale a servant practises divination to discover the identity of her future spouse. Her sick mistress asks who has appeared to her. 'Only Master,' replies the artless girl. Her mistress conveniently dies, and the servant marries her master. 'The Aristocratic Purchaser' appears to be similar to this and other traditions, a 'class dream' expressing the desires of a particular segment of the general population. This particular wife-selling tale may have resulted from a daydream about an undesired and neglected wife who is purchased by an ardent aristocrat. Twisted in transit, such traditions might have been the basis for V. T. Sternberg's statement that in some French novels and dramas based on English domestic life 'it is not unusual to find the blue-beard *milord Anglais* carting milady to Smithfield, and enlarging upon her points in the cheap-jack style to the admiring drovers'. [3]

Another tradition, which appears to have no factual basis, involves the discovery that a wife who has been sold has or will come into a substantial legacy. Three very similar versions of this story, all of which are sited in London, occur in newspapers between 1767 and 1814. From Plymouth, in 1822, comes evidence that the tale may have been associated with actual sales as unsubstantiated rumour:

a man, at that time and place, was to dispose of his wife by public sale! *The report which accompanied the notice stated that . . . she would moreover, in the course of a few days, succeed to £600 which her husband could not touch . . . .*

Finally, a gypsy tale, recorded at the turn of the century, concerns an old man who bought a wife at Blackburn for 2s 6d, only to discover that she had brought £200 in gold with her. None of the London examples names the individuals involved, nor is there any evidence that the marriages mentioned in these accounts ever took place. While this alone might not be deemed sufficient to call the newspaper evidence into question, the similarities shared by these cases do appear to require an explanation, and they in their turn suggest a connection with the seemingly fictitious Blackburn example. Only an 1840 Suffolk case offers any substantial parallel; John Frost of Friars Farm sold his wife, Harriet, at Hadleigh Market, putting £100 in her pocket to ensure a purchase. In this example, however, silence concerning the money would have proved counter-productive, and in all of the questioned cases discovery of the legacy or gift comes as some surprise.[4]

Several folk parallels occur, notably in stories of the 'Loathly Lady' type, in which a hideous supernatural bride is turned into a beautiful woman through her husband's love or by his submission to her whims. On a more removed plane, 'useless' fairy gifts often became valuables at dawn. Following a dream spurned by more sensible men, the Swaffham Peddler recovers a rich treasure. In these and in other traditions, it is the hero's 'correct action' that is rewarded; in 'The Fortunate Purchase' the wise move of choosing the discarded woman secures the legacy. It may be that such stories encouraged potential purchasers to 'speculate' on women spurned by their former partners. The legacy could be considered emblematic of the woman herself. 'Try me,' the story suggests, 'and *you* may be the lucky one.' On a more practical level, *any* legacy made *any* woman more desirable. Although a large proportion of wife sales were based on the woman's infidelity (her lover being the purchaser), buyers had few compelling reasons besides morality to marry their purchases — even when this was possible. Property, however, was an important consideration. Although the hope of a legacy rarely appears to have been fulfilled, it is possible that this tradition benefited both the seller (who was ridding himself of an unwanted dependent) and the wife (whose status was enhanced) by working on a potential purchaser's cupidity. This, then, was a folklore belief with a social purpose beyond mere entertainment value. [5]

Implicit in many versions of 'The Fortunate Purchase' is the husband's late repentance when he discovers that he has allowed a fortune to slip away. Other cases show this in a possible folklore belief, 'The 'Spurned Husband', which emphasizes the sale's finality. In eighteenth-century London, for example, one despairing spouse was driven to suicide when the wife he had sold to a 'brother workman in a fit of conjugal indifference at the alehouse' refused to return home to him; 'A sale was a sale and not a joke,' she said. This story would be completely believable, were it not for a strikingly similar tale recorded from Johnny Smith, brother of a man who had reputedly sold his sweetheart on Brough Hill: 'Chris tried to get her back, but she wouldn't come. If he could do what he had done, she said, she had had enough of him. She hoped it would be a lesson to him.' Perhaps this woman's reaction was natural, although in another case the repentant husband was able to repurchase his wife. The similarity of such repudiation accounts, however, leaves open the possibility that they represent a moralistic travelling tale of the 'act in haste, repent at leisure' type. As cautionary examples, such stories may have served to prevent unnecessary sales. [6]

Each of these travelling stories connected with wife-selling would be believable were it not for the fact that similar versions occur over a wide spatial and chronological span. 'The Wife Sale Murders', however, is not only localized in Cornwall but is demonstrably fictitious on internal evidence. There is no logical way that the facts of the matter could have become known. Told as a 'true story', it was part of the repertoire of humorous and gruesome tales passed down to 'an Old Ex-Cornish Rabbit Trapper and horse-braker' by his mother. The sequence of the tale — murder and robbery of the purchaser by the wife, the innocent victim's execution and the subsequent killing of the wife by another purchaser's daughter (the husband was presumably aware of foul play but unable to prove anything) — contains melodramatic elements common to ballads, popular fiction and folk tales. 'Marrowbones', for instance, tells the story of a woman who attempted to murder her blind husband but ended by drowning herself when he stepped aside as she tried to push him into a river; similarly, the youngest of 'The Twa Sisters' is drowned by her jealous sibling. *The String of Pearls*, which introduced the person of Sweeney Todd, demon barber of Fleet Street, to popular lore, was based on multiple murders, the victims of which were consigned to meat pies. It is perhaps with the Scottish tales of Burkers (murderers of travellers), with stories of the 'Long Pack' (containing a diminutive accomplice, whose duty it was to slay and rob the inhabitants of isolated farmsteads) or with traditions of hospitable hosts who murdered and robbed their guests that we come closest to the theme of 'The Wife Sale Murders'. 'Mr Fox,' a widespread English folk tale, offers a similar Bluebeard-like story, in which the villain, caught in his own toils, can only sit helplessly as his bride-to-be recounts her gruesome adventure to the assembled wedding guests. In all such tales, as in 'The Wife Sale Murders', villainy rebounds on itself.[7]

Another story in which wife-selling occurs is 'Misfortune Early or Late', an example of which was recorded in 1930 from an inhabitant of Clear Island, Co. Cork. A farmer met Misfortune while driving his cattle from one field to another and was soon left with nothing. He decided to become a sailor, and his wife went with him to the harbour.

> They were standing near a ship that was at the quayside, when the captain asked him would he sell his wife. The man and his wife discussed this.
>
> 'Tis better for me to sell you to him,' said the husband. 'We may meet each other somewhere again.'
>
> He made a bargain with the captain to sell the wife for a hundred pounds. The captain went down to his cabin and handed him the money into his cap, but no sooner was the money in the cap than the cap fell down between the ship and the quayside. Misfortune was well on top of him now. . .

Happily, the farmer eventually met with good luck and recovered his spouse. Here, and in other folk tales in which it occurs, wife-selling is mentioned, according to Dr Kevin Danaher, as 'something extraordinary and reprehensible'. While Misfortune may have come upon the husband of its own accord, his actions presumably made him deserving of it.[8]

The above folk-tale types reflect conscious or subconscious dreams and fears and are of great importance in understanding wife-selling as an institution. Thus in 'The Aristocratic Purchaser' and 'The Fortunate Purchase' the sale represented a change for the better for the wife or buyer. Husbands contemplating the sale of a spouse may have been deterred by the latter story or by traditions of 'The Spurned Husband' (if this was a valid folk belief), and potential purchasers may have seen their fears of a continuing husband — wife attachment reflected in 'The Wife Sale Murders'. Stories such as 'Misfortune Early or Late', by treating wife-selling as 'inconceivable', may have strengthened the bonds of marriage or countered the practice in certain areas. Each of these tales thus produced some sort of pay-off. Additionally, assuming an ability to isolate the elements that characterize each story as fiction, popular perceptions of the institution remain that anchor the story to reality. Thus all details not dependent upon an aristocratic purchaser in versions of 'The Aristocratic Purchaser', such as the inn (to some extent), the social position of the husband and wife and the husband's drinking problem, may be taken as accepted components of a wife sale. Using these versions is one method of reconstructing a popular impression of what went on at such sales. We see, for instance, accuracy in the identification of seller and purchaser as members of the 'lower' or 'middle' class, the influence of drink in bringing some sales about, the use of the halter, the jocular bidding and comments by spectators, location of the sale at an inn, hotel or market, the relatively low purchase prices received, the role of alcohol and the sexual motivation of many purchasers. All of these are paralleled by details of actual sales. [9]

A few popular rhymes are also associated with wife-selling. One often quoted in connection with the bells of Hatfield Church —

> Lend me your wife today,
> I'll lend you mine tomorrow.
> No, I'll be like the chimes of Ware,
> I'll neither lend nor borrow.

does not appear to be totally germane. There does seem to be a veiled reference to the institution in the Warwickshire children's rhyme:

> Nebuchadnezzar, the King of the Jews,
> Sold his wife for a pair of shoes,
> When the shoes began to wear, good lack,
> Nebuchadnezzar wished her back.

In Staffordshire and the east, a variant ending occurs:

> When the shoes began to wear,
> Nebuchadnezzar began to swear.

The king thus immortalized was of course not King of the Jews, but the ruler of Babylonia, who captured and sacked Jerusalem. He is mentioned in several books of the Bible, and his proverbial madness may have been partially responsible for this connection with wife-selling. (It is interesting to recall in this context the nineteenth-century association of wife-selling with the Babylonian 'marriage market', where the prices paid for pretty women supposedly served as dowries for their uglier sisters.) On the other hand, many rhymes utilize Babylon, the Queen of Sheba, and other exotic biblical names. Worcestershire children did a ring dance to their ditty:

> Thomas-a-Didymus hard of belief,
> Sold his wife for a pound of beef.
> When the beef was eaten, good lack,
> Thomas-a-Didymus wished her back.

(Thomas-à-Didymus was the disciple Thomas, who is occasionally referred to by this more formal appellation.) These biblical associations might suggest an indistinct popular theory about the origins of wife-selling, although no such sales occur in the Bible. The bartering of a wife for goods is supported by actual cases in which women were exchanged for bread, a leg of mutton or an ox and by other instances in which actual objects formed part of the purchase price. Even the second thoughts evinced in the rhyme are paralleled by actual examples (and perhaps floating traditions) of husbands regretting, and sometimes rescinding, their sales. The wife is also sold in a version of 'Dicky, Dicky Dilver':

> Little Dicky Dilver
> Had a wife of silver;
> He took a stock and broke her back
> And sold her to the miller;
> The miller wouldn't have her
> So he threw her in the river.

Lest this appear excessively bloodthirsty, it should be noted that the Opies believe the rhyme 'to relate to the fortunes of a grain of wheat, personified as the wife of the farmer' — a sort of female John Barleycorn. Not so easily explained, however, is:

> Bought a wife on Sunday,
> Brought her home on Monday,
> Beat her well on Tuesday,
> Sick she was on Wednesday,

> Dead she was on Thursday,
> Buried she was on Friday,
> Glad I was on Saturday,
> And now I'll buy another. [10]

In addition to popular rhymes, the institution appears to have been treated by at least one minor poet, William Hutton. Hutton, who lived from 1723 to 1815, was a local historian of Birmingham, Derby, and other areas and published verses in several magazines. In his 'Pleasures of Matrimony', composed in 1793, Hutton tells the story of a binge in a public house. The young wife of one drinker attempted to persuade her husband to return home, but he reacted violently.

> 'To rid his hand he would not fail,
> He'd sell her for a quart of ale.'
> 'Your bargain I'll not disappoint,'
> Cried Martin, 'I'll give you a pint.'
> The husband in his price won't sink,
> Nor Martin rise one drop of drink.
> Hannah's *in equilibrio*,
> Not knowing how the sale will go
> But, like a wife of prudent cast,
> Show'd strict obedience to the last.
> The husband tried to raise the buyer,
> Martin declared he'd go no higher.
> The pint was ordered, bargain struck
> And nothing back returned for luck.
> The parties of a halter thought,
> But this they found would cost a groat,
> The halter scheme was instant lost
> As being twice what Hannah cost.
> For that same reason neither would
> Pay fourpence that she might be toll'd.
> While they consume the pint in strife —
> The purchase of a prudent wife —
> 'Twas thought a deed would best avail
> To ensure the bargain and the sale;
> For when a treaty is to last
> 'Tis needful we should make it fast.
> An article they jointly drew
> Declaring rights in terms of law.

In the poem further problems arise over the division of the wife's children. Eventually, the father keeps the elder, while the wife retains her baby. She leaves with the purchaser to live happily until the husband, regretting his impulsive action, causes the parish overseers to intervene, and the woman, despite her protests, is returned. Hutton ends the poem with a question:

> What would the ancients think he said
> To wives being sold two pence a head?

This poem is particularly interesting because of its detailed nature and the mention of components of many wife sales, such as the purchase for drink at an inn, the mention of a halter, tollage and luck money, the use of a written agreement and the division of the children between husband and purchaser. The purchaser is specifically identified as William Martin; the wife's first name is given as Hannah. While these could be merely enlivening details, there is a chance that Hutton, known for his poetry on local subjects, may have set an actual wife sale to rhyme. That this effort may not have been unique is indicated by a similar topic chosen by Councillor Samuel Cox, whose lines were worn on the breast of a young widow at a masquerade in Bath.

> To be let on a *Lease* for the term of my life,
> I Sylvia J--n, in the shape of a wife;
> I am young, though not handsome, good-natured, though thin,
> For further particulars pray enquire within. [11]

The earliest datable evidence for songs dealing with the institution of wife-selling comes from eighteenth- and nineteenth-century song books. 'The Hopeful Bargain', for example, is found in Thomas D'Urfey's *Wit and Mirth: or Pills to Purge Melancholy*, published in 1719. Located in London, it is apparently the first surviving song to emphasize the adulterous aspect of wife sales. Its importance lies in the fact that it dates from a time when we have little firm evidence of specific sales, so it is a valuable indication that the institution was well enough known to feature in period music. Details such as price and occupation are probably fairly accurate. [12]

Another song may date from the 1790s, a period in which wife-selling was popularly associated with Smithfield market and sales made a splash in newspapers and in at least one play. Called 'The Smithfield Bargain, or, Love in a Halter', this comic song was the stock-in-trade of a Mr Emery and was based on the ever-popular theme of conflict between the sexes. The Irish purchaser, dominated by his new acquisition, eventually comes to the conclusion that it might be best to resell her at Smithfield. A similar song, 'John Hobbs', is found in songbooks and in oral forms as well. Here, interest again centres on the antagonism between the sexes, and we have specific names. This humorous song was known at least as early as 1812 and was collected from oral tradition as late as the early part of this century. It apparently originated in a play and involves the 'miraculous recovery', found in other period songs. 'Poor Will Putty' and 'Easter Monday', both dating from a similar period, are the earliest songs emphasizing trade similes — Putty, appropriately, was a glazier, and Dick Awl, a shoemaker. In both songs infidelity forms the basis for the sale, while the latter makes use of the 'knock-down' pun often associated with wife-selling in period newspapers. A similar chestnut involving a pun on 'spare ribs' seems to serve as the rationale for 'Peg Briggs and her Pigs', confidently reported as having been sung 'with unbounded Applause' by Mr Sloman, who appeared at Sadler's Wells in the comic interlude, 'Mrs Mullins'. On a more romantic note there is the undated ditty performed by Mr Fawcett: 'If wives in the market were to be sold'. Still other songs and fragments have been recorded from Staffordshire. [13]

By far the best source for wife-selling songs, however, are nineteenth-century broadsides, which offer variants of at least three songs. Unfortunately, most of these sheets lack dates, but evidence allows us to attribute several to a fairly restricted time period. 'Account of the Sale of a Wife', for instance, is associated with a Bristol wife sale that occurred on 29 May 1823; the song must have been current at this time. Another version was published by James Catnach, perhaps the best-known broadside publisher of the period. Catnach issued a *Catalogue of Songs and Song Books, Sheets, Half-Sheets, Christmas Carols, Children's Books*, etc., in 1832 from his press at Seven Dials. As 'Sale of a Wife' is listed under 'Addenda', this indicates that the version must have been printed in about the same period, as this was one of his newer offerings. William Pratt who, in addition to publishing a third version of this song, was responsible for a different 'Sale of a Wife', published broadsides in Birmingham from about 1848 to 1856. Walker, another printer of this second song, did not start work at Otley until 1810. A third broadside on the topic appeared in London, and, according to Mr James N. Healy, appears to have crossed the Channel to Ireland. (Table 6 offers a summary of wife-

TABLE 6 NINETEENTH-CENTURY WIFE-SELLING BROADSIDES

Location	Printer	Year
Birmingham	Wm Pratt	c. 1849–56
Birmingham	Wm Pratt	c. 1849–56
Bristol	Shepherd	1823
Glasgow (?)	—	—
London	J. Catnach	c. 1832
London	H. Such	—
Manchester	Livsey	—
Manchester	Pearson	—
Otley, (Yorks)	Walker	after 1810

selling broadsides.) It is obvious that the songs were fairly widespread. London, Bristol and Birmingham all offered sheets of 'Account of the Sale of a Wife', while versions of 'Sale of a Wife' occur in Birmingham, Manchester, Otley and probably Sheffield. It seems likely that similar songs were found in all large nineteenth-century urban centres. [14]

To a degree, this standardization limits the usefulness of such material as a source of evidence. No names are mentioned, and in many cases there has been an obvious attempt to stretch the ballad's suitability to its ultimate limits. In 'Sale of a Wife' the subheading 'IN THIS NEIGHBOURHOOD — MRS. YOU-KNOW-WHO' suggests that the printer was supplying metaphorical blanks to be filled in by the potential purchaser. 'Wife for Sale' also varies the location of the transaction, presumably according to the provenance of the broadsides consulted. Adherence to the dictates of rhyme and metre would have made accurate reporting — had it been attempted — extremely difficult. Attention was often attracted by a catch phrase and retained by repetitions, which also served to inform latecomers. Additionally, several broadsides (particularly 'Sale of a Wife') attempt to evoke a sexual response from their readers by couching many aspects of the sale in Freudian terms. Passages such as 'the lady knocked about the seat the lapstone and the awl' leave little to the imagination and suggest that all parts of these texts cannot be approached literally. Several of the speeches in these broadsides appear to have been sensationalized, and it seems likely that the appearance and emphasis on stock types in the sales described may have been attempts to relate a single broadside to as many potential purchasing groups as possible. Further, such statements as 'some thousands soon did run' may be taken as exaggeration for effect. [15]

Despite these facts, the number of surviving broadsides suggests that the topic must have appealed to the man in the street. To a certain extent, therefore, wife sales must have been accurately depicted, and indeed, the portrayal of occupations, motivations, procedure and prices all accord with what is known about the institution. While songs demonstrate no pattern in the raising of bids, mention wives as being sold from carts and contain enigmatic references to the women being carried off on their purchasers' backs, such details as multiple sales, female intervention and collective purchase can be confirmed from actual accounts. [16]

Wife-selling songs, therefore, accurately reflect *some* aspects of the institution, closely paralleling the views of the man in the street. [17] Most share a humorous approach to the subject, and it seems significant that no songs exist that deal in a serious way with the potential heartbreak, shame and misery involved in such sales. The ale draper's wife returns in the end; the hoyden is resold; John Hobbs is miraculously cut down from his tangle and revived to begin anew. . . .

'Nay, if there be no remedy for it, but that you will needs buy and sell men and women like beasts, we shall have all the world drink brown and white bastard.' [18] This speech by Elbow in *Measure for Measure* is as close as Shakespeare ever comes to a direct reference to the custom of wife-selling. The first dramatic depiction of a sale seems to have occurred in Thomas Middleton's *The Phoenix*. This play deals with the travels through his kingdom of a disguised prince (Phoenix) and his faithful retainer to discover the abuses that thrive there. Produced early in the seventeenth century and set in Italy (a common convention), many of the play's details are in line with contemporary English life. When Castiza is sold by her husband, the Captain, Phoenix claims never to have heard of the practice. He is asked: 'didst ne'er hear of that trick? Why Pistor, a baker, sold his wife t'other day to a cheese-monger that made cake and cheese; another to a cofferer; a third to a common player; why, you see, 'tis common.' A written agreement is produced by a notary, which reads:

> To all good and honest Christian people to whom this present writing shall come: know you for a certain, that I captain, for and in the consideration of the sum of five hundred crowns, have clearly bargained, sold, given, granted, assigned, and set over, and by these presents do clearly bargain, sell, give, grant, assign and set over, all the right, estate, title, interest, demand, possession, and terms of years to come, which I the said captain have, or ought to have . . . in and to Madonna Castiza, my most virtuous, modest, loving, and obedient wife . . . together with all and singular those admirable qualities, with which her noble breast is furnished . . . in primis, the beauties of her mind, chastity, temperance, and above all, patience . . . excellent in the best of music, in voice delicious, in conference wise and pleasing, of age contentful, neither too young to be apish, nor too old to be sottish . . . and which is the best of a wife, a most comfortable sweet companion. . . . Which said Madonna Castiza lying and yet being in the occupation of the said captain. . . to have and to hold, use, and . . . to be acquitted of and from all former bargains, former sales . . . gifts, grants, surrenders, re-entries. . . . And furthermore, I the said, of and for the consideration of the sum of five hundred crowns to send me abroad, before these presents, utterly disclaim for ever any title, estate, right, interest, demand or possession, in or to the said Madonna Castiza, my late virtuous and unfortunate wife . . . As also neither to touch, attempt, molest or incumber any part or parts whatsoever, either to be named or not to be named, either hidden or unhidden, either those that boldly look abroad, or those that dare not show their face(s). . . . In witness whereof, I the said captain have interchangeably set to my hand and seal, in presence of all these, the day and date above written.

In the event, this sale does not go through; Phoenix and his servant reveal themselves and manhandle the Captain.[19]

While bigamous marriages were certainly not uncommon, no records survive of a husband selling two women at one time, much less three. Although sales for this period are scanty, the occupations of seller and purchaser (baker, cheesemonger, cofferer and actor) appear to be consistent with real transactions, as does the written agreement and use of a notary. The price, however, seems far more than that found in actual sales. Finally, the agreement contains bawdy passages that might have been considered extraneous in a real document of this type. Although *The Phoenix* is promising evidence that wife-selling was known and practised at the time, it offers little reliable information about the institution. [20]

Other seemingly promising plays are even more disappointing. *Love the Leveller: or, The Pretty Purchase* was produced at Drury Lane in January of 1704 and seems to have been reasonably successful. 'G.B.', the author, has been panned, however, by critics who note 'the foolish anachronism of placing chocolate-houses, as well as persons such Sir Thomas and Lord Pickrup, in ancient Egyptian realms'. Nonetheless, the work seems to have provided a basis for the plot of Mrs Eliza Haygood's more popular *A Wife To be Lett*. This drama, published in 1723, follows the fortunes of Sir Henry Beaumont, who loves Mrs Graspall. As one might guess by the name, her husband is eager and willing to sell his wife for £2000, but when it comes to the crunch Sir Harry is confronted by a former flame, and his repentance ensues. Any connection with wife-selling is superficial at best. [21]

As far as is known, this topic as a central dramatic theme lay dormant for almost three-quarters of a century, until *Times* readers on Monday, 31 July 1797, picked up their papers to be greeted by the following advertisement:

> FIFTEENTH WEEK'S CHANGE OF AMUSEMENTS
> AMPHITHEATRE OF ARTS,
> ASTLEY'S, WESTMINSTER-BRIDGE
> Royal Highnesses the PRINCE of WALES and Duke
> of YORK'S Servants.
>
> THIS, and every EVENING this Week only, will be presented (1st Time), a New Comic Musical Piece, with its Grand and dependent Spectacle, called, NO SALES at SMITHFIELD: or, The Reasonable Wife.
> . . . . to begin at half past Six o'clock precisely.

For those who further perused their papers, the entertainment was explained on page 3:

> The sale of Wives at Smithfield is the chief topic of conversation; as such, *Astley* has taken it up, and to-night brings out a new

Entertainment founded on this curious event. The Public naturally look up to the old soldier for something whimsical; and if report can be relied on, they will not be deceived. The Amphitheatre, Westminster Bridge, with such an Entertainment, cannot fail to be crouded on the occasion, and at an early hour.

Or, turning to the *Morning Chronicle*, they could read:

The new method of disposing of Wives by sale, as practised at Smithfield, has given rise to a new Spectacle, prepared by Astley, and intended for representation This Evening at Westminster Bridge. — Full of whimsical occurrences as this Piece is, according to report, the Old Manager may rely on having an excellent and overflowing house, and the Town on receiving much amusement and information.

With this sort of coverage one might be led to expect a smash hit. In fact, the drama did rather well for a production of the period; if one may accept the evidence of advertisements, it ran for slightly over a week. The glowing reports were paid for by the theatre (true fifth-column advertisements), as may be seen by comparing other puffs. While this might incline one towards dismissal of the piece's pretensions, Astley's was considered to be one of the prime theatres of the period. Even well into the nineteenth century, Dickens selected this playhouse as that to which Kit in *The Old Curiosity Shop* brings his mother on his first real holiday. Many of the newspaper blurbs have phrases that indicate why wife-selling might have been considered an appropriate topic by the theatre management: 'Astley. . . . suits his entertainments to times and seasons'; 'with ASTLEY, *novelty* is the order of the day'; 'The Pieces and Performances . . . are happily adapted to the times.' With changes in the programme every Monday, it was advantageous to capitalize on any event of the moment, and even if wife sales were not the talk of the town, the institution was ready to hand and fitted in well with the generally romantic and comic plot lines. Unfortunately, it has not proved possible to trace a text of this production. The only quote that remains comes from a song at the end of Act II:

Learn then, ye Fair, if ye wou'd conquer man,
To act like women, as in truth ye can;
And you, ye husbands, who with happy lives,
Act too like men, nor think of selling Wives.

To judge by this snippet, it seems unlikely that a more complete text would add significantly to our knowledge of wife sales. Another play, entitled *Wife to be Sold* and written by A. McLaren, was produced in 1807, and mention has already been made of the humorous wife-selling songs associated with operatic farces of the period. The statement by V. T. Sternberg quoted above (p.188) suggests that wife sales were depicted in at least some French dramas concerned with English life. Specific examples of these are not given, however. [22]

While hardly accurate, plays do illustrate the general public attitude (conceptions and misconceptions alike) towards wife sales. Taking the contemporary institution, each playwright appears to have portrayed it in such a way as to fulfil the requirements of his work. Itself a form of street theatre, wife-selling offered an emotional mixture of humour and melodrama, a combination readily apparent in many contemporary newspaper, periodical and broadside accounts. With such a background, *The Times*'s correspondent of 2 August 1797 could confidently write:

> the new Musical Piece taken from the practice of carrying Wives to Smithfield Market, certainly ranks the highest in point of stage effect, and is the best calculated, of any piece we ever saw, to create laughter, the principal object of the Manager of a Comic Theatre. [23]

Wife-selling also found a place in literature. George Borrow's jockey (whom the Romany Rye meets during his horse trading) tells of a sale in which he bought his wife, a childhood acquaintance, from a drunken basketmaker. Dale saw this woman, Mary Fulcher,

> in the — market on a Saturday . . . with a halter round her neck, led about by a man, who offered to sell her for eighteen-pence. I took out the money forthwith and bought her; the man was her husband, a basket-maker, with whom she had lived several years without having any children; he was a drunken, quarrelsome fellow, and having had a dispute with her the day before, he determined to get rid of her, by putting a halter round her neck and leading her to the cattle-market, as if she were a mare, which he had, it seems, a right to do; all women being considered mares by old English law, and, indeed, still called mares in certain counties, where genuine old English is still preserved.

Fortunately, her husband was killed in a tavern brawl that afternoon, allowing a proper marriage with banns to take place.

Dale further noted, 'I am told she was legally my property by virtue of my having bought her with a halter round her neck', but felt that he should do right by the parson. It is interesting that Borrow not only introduces the halter into his account, but also incorporates the necessity for a subsequent marriage.[24]

By far the best-known fictional account of a wife sale is Thomas Hardy's *Mayor of Casterbridge*. Based in part on actual examples, this sale creates a subsequent confusion and a split between Henchard and his step-daughter that has repercussions in the decline of the Mayor's fortunes. Most of the sale's incidents, in fact, occur in three examples found in Hardy's commonplace book and copied from the *Dorset County Chronicle* of the late 1820s. Although at a later date Hardy became vague about his source and states in his preface that the sales formed part of the history of the real-life Casterbridge (Dorchester), the correspondences noted by Christine Winfield in her article seem to settle the matter. She finds similarities in the description of the husband and wife and the crowd's reaction and shows additionally that the price and the division of children closely corresponded with Hardy's first draft.[25]

In Hardy's novel the sale takes place at Weydon-Priors Fair, when Henchard becomes drunk. Both the location and drink have numerous parallels, but one exchange between husband and wife suggests a more specific source:

> She turned to her husband and murmured, 'Michael, you have talked this nonsense in public places before. A joke is a joke, but you may make it once too often mind!'
> 'I know I've said it before; I meant it. All I want is a buyer.'

This is instantly reminiscent of a London wife's statement, 'A sale was a sale and not a joke,' reprinted in an 1861 edition of *Chamber's Journal*, which would have been available to Hardy. In addition, Hardy's reference to both gypsies and the disposing of horses in connection with this wife sale suggests a debt to Borrow's *Romany Rye*, which had been in print for over twenty-five years. The minimum price, the auctioneer, the wife's consent and the disposal of the child are all paralleled in actual sales. Even the return of Henchard's wedding ring can be matched by an 1882 newspaper account. It seems probable that in addition to the sources quoted in his commonplace book, Hardy was familiar with more recent (if sometimes secondary) accounts of the institution and used these in his work. Although no relationship can be substantiated, a 1786 Lincolnshire sale involved a Mr Hand and a Mr Hardy, both family names of the author. It is ironic that Hardy's well-known account occurs in an area sparsely represented in the corpus of sales and that the institution's existence was actually challenged by many Victorian readers.[26]

Lady Catherine Milnes Gaskell produced a short story, 'T' Wife Bazaar', which appeared in her *Prose Idylls of the West Riding*. It dealt with a custom of the villagers at Holgate, where colliers were allowed to 'sworp wives month o' May' (during the first fortnight of the month). Under this 'miner's law', the wives and their children were exchanged for a period of one year, according to an agreement signed by all parties at one of the town's inns. (The ceremony was usually accompanied by a dinner and drink; the women afterwards received bouquets and trinkets from their new 'masters'.) In the story Bob Bolton, a miner, wishes to exchange his wife for Rose Farrar and does so, despite the protests of the former. Doris, Bob's wife, pines away after her exchange. Her husband refuses to visit her, and cannot be forced to do so, because of his prowess as a fighter. Fate, however, takes a hand; the 'boy Parson', Lord Mirfield's eldest son (and an ex-soldier), who has entered the Church, comes to Holgate. He fights and conquers Bolton, forcing a reconciliation with the collier's wife on her death bed. It is difficult to tell to what degree this practice was related to wife-selling. The story is so overladen with Victorian morality, pathos and character stereotypes that it cannot be considered an accurate portrayal of any popular custom.[27]

The 'Chinese' fair of Walpole's *Rogue Herries* is the scene of a wife sale seemingly based on Hardy's *Mayor of Casterbridge*. In it the narrator's father divests himself of a common-law partner (who lives in his household in addition to his recognized wife). Beatrice Tunstall has her sexton in *The Shiny Night* recall: 'I had a wife myself in days agone, afore I was sexton. But I sold her to a Welshman at Kettlewych Wakes for a load of turf and a bit of kindling throwed in. Howsomever, I kept her daughter . . .' In the same year, 1931, Alison Uttley introduced the story of a wife sale into *The Country Child*. The woman is a scold and dominates her husband. He vents his frustrations at the Pig with Two Faces at Leadington, and a Frenchman there offers to buy the woman. The price is 6d, and the purchaser goes to collect his bargain. After a few weeks, however, the wife runs away, and her husband receives her back. Such reactions find their parallel in actual sales. In more recent fiction, Rosalind Laker's boxer hero outbids his brother and buys a wife at Brighton market to impress his uncle with his 'respectability', and in *Desolation Island* Captain Jack Aubrey's steward, Killick, makes a similar purchase on market day:

> He bought one, legal. It seems her husband and she did not agree, so he brought her to market in a halter; and Killick, he bought her, legal — laid down the pewter in sight of one and all, and shook hands on it. There were three to choose on.[28]

As has been noted in the discussion of French reactions to the institution, Conan Doyle's comical French hero, Brigadier Gerard, makes passing mention of wife-selling. Here the institution serves to emphasize typical French misconceptions of the English, accepted by the Brigadier in much the same way that he misinterprets fox hunting. In addition, there appear to be other late nineteenth-century references. Sternberg states that the subject was exploited by 'French romancers'. Maupassant uses a French sale as a basis for his short story, 'Une Vente', in which the woman is sold by the cubic metre, paralleling British examples of payment by the pound.[29]

In all these novels or stories an attempt is made to place wife-selling in its cultural and social context. Borrow and Hardy are most successful, although the latter's work suffers from the melodramatic trap of stressing the husband's unreasonableness and cruelty, contrary to significant case evidence that points to the wife's infidelity as an important motive for selling. Gaskell is guilty of over-sentimentality; Walpole may have been guilty of borrowing. In general, authors of fiction appear to have succeeded best when dealing with socially and temporally familiar events. Borrow benefited from his travels and his (at times) semi-autobiographical approach; Hardy, from his research and his familiarity with local customs and history.

Despite the popularity of the theme in music, drama and literature, wife sales do not appear to have been depicted in high art. James Gillray, whose print of Justice Kenyon whipping the 'daughter of Faro' followed close on the heels of the popular press's interest in that game, produced nothing dealing specifically with wife sales. Neither, apparently, did William Hogarth or (perhaps more surprisingly) Thomas Rowlandson. Later, although the

A Modern Market Scene.

CRISPIN in his GLORY,

THE

Butcher's bad BARGAIN,

Or a Ready way to get rid of a

BAD WIFE.

ON Thursday the 28th of November, 1822, a very novel transaction took place in our market ; about half past eleven o'clock, by which time many live beasts had changed masters, into the market popp'd a jolly son of crispin with his better half genteelly led by him in a halter, for the purpose of disposing of her in the same manner as other gentlemen dispose of live stock when they have no farther occasion for them. It appeared that they had lived a most uncomfortable life for a length of time, the husband ruling her, (not with a rod of iron) but with a strap of leather, with which he used to alter the colour of her beautiful hide, till it displayed as many glowing colours as the rainbow. By her drunkenness and extravagance he was at length reduced to his Last, as he had absolutely spent his all, and he declared upon his sole (soul) that he could no longer vamp up his credit, and therefore, he having a heart as hard as his lap-stone, he declared, that although they were united as close as sole and upper-leather yet that they were entirely out of welt ; and that a seperation must immediately take place ; fully aware that he could not dispose of her by private contract, she agreed to be exposed to public sale in the market, with a halter about her neck ; Crispin, nothing loth, took her at his word, and brought her to market, where the first bidding was made by a horse-dealer, who offered half-a-crown ; 5s. said a pig jobber, 10s. says a publican, 15s. says a rough country wap straw ; £1. said a butcher, who it is supposed had trespassed upon the premises before. No one seemed anxious to advance on this price, and they adjourned to a public-house, where the money was paid, the bargain delivered to the purchaser, who took her to an old clothes shop, not a hundred miles from Temple church, where he rigged her afresh and took her home, leaving Crispin to the enjoyment of his pot and pipe.

Shepherd, Printer, No. 6, Broad Weir, Bristol.

An apparently fictitious wife sale (case 184) printed by Shepherd, Bristol, 1822 institution was a suitable subject for the covers of sensational tabloids, it does not appear to have been used. [30]

Nineteenth-century broadside ballads do provide pictorial documentation of wife-selling, however. The one opposite issued by a Bristol printer (supposedly for an 1822 sale) has a woodcut depicting the institution. On the left a man, presumably the potential purchaser, inspects the merchandise. He wears a long coat and a hat that can best be described as a turban, and stands with his hands in his pockets. The husband or auctioneer is shown in the centre, wearing a scarf, waistcoat and long coat. His hat is wide-brimmed, and he holds the wife by a rope fastened around her neck. The woman, standing to the right in the print, is depicted in a dress with a long apron and seems to be wearing a blouse and a very low-cut bodice. The woodcut also features on an 1823 broadside, 'Sale of a Wife, by J. Nash', issued by the same printer (p.68). John Ashton's Modern Street Ballads shows a variant of this illustration from an unidentified source. Here the turban has been changed, possibly through misinterpretation, into a pointed cap. The husband's scarf becomes a ruffled shirt, and there are other slight modifications of facial feature and expression and of the posture of the potential purchaser. [31]

A different picture appears on the Catnach broadside, 'Particular and merry Account' (see the Frontispiece). In it the woman, dressed in a skirt and long apron and wearing what appears to be a fancy hat, is secured to a railing by a halter, which encircles her neck. She stands in the centre, with cattle (and sheep?) behind her. To the right are three figures, one presumably the purchaser, who holds a bag of money outstretched in his hand. He is dressed in a long coat and waistcoat, is booted and has what appear to be garters round his legs. The other onlookers may be butchers; they wear long smocks and scarves around their necks. To the left of the purchaser is a more mature individual. Since he holds the end of the wife's tether in his hand, he is presumably the husband. This man is attired like the purchaser, carries a walking stick (or goad?) and wears a scarf. Behind him stand two other onlookers with a calf. (One has a badge with the numeral '1' on his arm, and might represent a porter or a market official.) The husband has a winsome leer on his face; the onlookers appear amused; the purchaser's and the wife's expressions are more serious. All the men wear wide-brimmed hats. [32]

Both of these pictures appear to represent contemporary

portrayals of wife-selling, but neither can be associated with a specific sale. In both cases a halter is visible, secured around the wife's neck, the lead retained by her husband. In one example the purchase appears to be only contemplated; in the other the transaction is actually being effected. Cattle (and possibly sheep), the presence of men dressed like butchers and the badge denoting a porter or official, all combine to suggest a market locale. Although these were (at least initially) personal artistic statements, they must to some degree conform to popular stereotypes of wife-selling.

CHAPTER 12

A Custom Observed by the People

Francis Place isolated a problem when he noted:

> I am not aware of any book which contains descriptive accounts of any class of people which will enable any one to judge accurately of the manners of our ancestors; strong features are occasionally shewn, from which we may calculate some of the great changes and infer the moral condition of the people, but we have very little of correctly detailed domestic history, the most valuable of all as it would enable us to make comparisons [that] shew clearly the progress of civilization. . . .[1]

This study of wife-selling attempts to go some way towards addressing Place's problem. As a descriptive ethnography of an informal institution in British society, it is intended to contribute to anthropological knowledge of unofficial, quasi-legal practices in advanced communities.

Wives for Sale has considered three major factors that bear on the informal custom of wife-selling: marriage, divorce and contract. It has reviewed the locations and procedures associated with the custom, the causes and consequences of wife sales, and the people who took part in them. It has examined reactions of the courts, the press and the public. It has drawn parallels between wife-selling and other contemporaneous social practices and beliefs, and it has considered the effects of the institution on popular culture.

Although many anthropological questions must remain unanswered, both because the details of wife-selling have been obscured by the passage of time and because of the characteristic informality of the institution, it is clear that wife sales alleviated friction in social life, providing one solution to intersecting problems of marriage, divorce and support. Based on well-known market mechanisms, with numerous symbolic parallels, wife-selling represented a conservative and traditional social solution to the dilemmas faced by individuals, relieving stress on the social fabric with a minimal strain on the communal *status quo*.

This study demonstrates the rewards of an anthropological examination of a single informal institution in an advanced community. The very nature of social relations makes many such topics ill-suited to intensive localized treatment. [2] The unevenness of surviving records, the mobility of the population, the arbitrariness of many geographical and social stratifications and the danger of perceiving regional variations as controlling definitions — all these militate against restrictive approaches. The book has attempted an historical sweep by offering a temporal and geographical overview while at the same time avoiding the perils of unjustified cross-cultural comparisons (a major criticism of Frazer and other early anthropologists). [3]

For social historians it is hoped that this work will illustrate the strengths of an anthropological approach. Wife sales are emphasized as the centre of a network of social interchanges rather than as broken links in an incomplete and unsatisfactory chain of evolution. The informality of the institution makes comparative treatment particularly apt, as the amorphous nature of the practice allowed it to shape itself to the contingencies of the moment. The importance of wife-selling lies primarily in its meaning to the individual and to his contemporary society.

Now that historians are at long last concerning themselves with the minutiae of cultures, it may be hoped that they will turn increasingly to anthropology for guidance in describing the *individual's* place within his society. Anthropologists, for their part, may advantageously make use of the historian's familiarity with sources and with temporal development to scrutinize 'advanced' European cultures with the same zeal that they have shown in studying and exposing the 'primitive'.

Future research might start with some of the unanswered questions posed by this book. Are all points of social stress covered by informal institutions? Are such practices always conservative and traditional in their approach? If so, when and how does change occur? And at what point does the formality of the legal process, or some similar substitute, supersede informal practice? It is only through further studies that solutions to these and similar problems may be found.

APPENDIX

Wife-Sale Cases and References

Bibliographical details of works and journals cited in abbreviated form will be found in the Select Bibliography.

1 Scotland or Ireland
c. July – November 1073
(a) complaint by Pope Gregory VII to Lanfranc, cited in A. O. Anderson, *Early Sources of Scottish History*, vol. 2 (Edinburgh, 1922), note on p. 74

2 London
before 24 November 1553
(a) ms. diary of Henry Machyn, 24 November 1553, quoted in Henry Machyn, *The Diary of Henry Machyn, Citizen and Merchant Taylor of London, From A.D. 1550 to A.D. 1563*, John Gough Nichols (ed.), Camden Society, vol. 42 (London: J. B. Nichols and Son, 1848), p.48

3 Rickmansworth, Hertfordshire
before 3 November 1584
(a) ms. act book entry concerning Thomas Griffys. ASA 7/11 (Hertfordshire Record Office)
(b) ms. act book entry concerning Richard Baldwyn. ASA 7/11 (Hertfordshire Record Office)
(c) ms. act book entry concerning Thomam Gryffys, p. 68. ASA 7/11 (Hertfordshire Record Office)
(d) ms. act book entry concerning Richardum Baldwyn. ASA 7/11 (Hertfordshire Record Office)
(e) ms. churchwardens' presentment of a penance completed by Thomas Griffen, 3 November 1584 ASA 5/5 (Hertfordshire Record Office)
(f) ms. churchwardens' presentment of a penance completed by Richard Baldwin, 14 November 1584. ASA 5/5 (Hertfordshire Record Office)

4 Great Warley, Essex
1585

(a)   act book of an ecclesiastical court, 1585, quoted in W. Hale Hale, *A series of precedents and proceedings in criminal causes, extending from the year 1475 to 1640; extracted from Act-books of ecclesiastical courts in the diocese of London, illustrative of the discipline of the Church of England* (London, Francis & John Rivington, 1847), p. 186

Note: this sale does not appear in the Act Book of the Archdeacon of Essex (letter of Mr John Booker, Senior Assistant Archivist, Essex Record Office, April 1978).

5   Murroes (?), Angus (source gives 'Murhous'. Suggested by Mr W. C. Brown, Senior Reference Librarian, Dunfermline Central Library, letter of April 1978)
Sunday, 15 August 1613)

(a)   act book of an ecclesiastical court, September 1613, quoted in Charles Baxter, *Selections from the Minutes of the Synod of Fife, 1611 — 1678* (Edinburgh: Abbotsford Club, 1837), p. 68

Note: the original is not in the Scottish Record Office (letter of Mr James D. Galbraith, Assistant Keeper, November 1979).

6   Stirling, Stirlingshire
before 31 December 1638

(a)   ms. register of the Kirk Session of Stirling, 31 December 1638. Ch 2/1026/3 (Scottish Record Office)

7   near Warwick, Warwickshire
c. December 1642 — January 1643

(a)   *The Kingdomes Weekly Intelligencer* (London), in existence c. December 1642 — January 1643 according to *Tercentenary Handlist of English and Welsh Newspapers* (London: The Times, 1920), quoted in K. Williams (1977), p. 11

8   Humbie, East Lothian
before 25 October 1646

(a)   ms. register of the Kirk Session of Humbie, 25 October 1646. Ch 2/389/1, p. 33a/b (Scottish Record Office)

(b)   ms. register of the Kirk Session of Humbie, 22 November 1646. Ch 2/389/1, p. 34a (Scottish Record Office)

9   Cawood area, West Riding, Yorkshire
c. Monday, 14 April 1690

(a)   John Aubrey, *Miscellanies* [1695], printed in *Three Prose Works*, John Buchanan-Brown ed. (Fontwell, Sus.: Centaur Press, 1972), p.62

Note: alibi of wife sale used by a man who had murdered his spouse.

10   Bilston, Staffordshire
        November 1692
        (a)   ms. document from Bilston, Staffordshire, quoted in
                Hackwood (1974), p. 70
        (b)   Jon Raven, ms. notes for television interview on wife-
                selling (letter from Mr Jon Raven, April 1978)
        Note: for information which may relate to the participants in this
        sale, see H. Sidney Grazebrook, 'Junior Branches of the Family of
        Sutton, Alias Dudley', *Collections for a History of Staffordshire*,
        William Salt Archaeological Society, vol. 10 (London: Harrison
        and Sons, 1889), pp. 87, 136.

11   Chinnor, Oxfordshire
        before 6 January 1696
        (a)   ms. churchwardens' presentment against Thomas Heath, 6
                July 1696. *Oxon.*, c. 162(?), p.195, quoted in Peyton (1928),
                pp. 184 — 5
        (b)   ms. oaths of witnesses, 6 July 1696. *Oxon.*, c. 162, p. 107,
                quoted in Peyton (1928), pp. 184 — 5
        (c)   ms. reply of Thomas Heath to the presentment of 6 July.
                Oxon., c. 162, p. 108, quoted in Peyton (1928), pp. 184 — 5
        (d)   ms. churchwardens' presentment of a penance completed
                by Thomas Heath, 6 August 1697 (1696?). *Oxon.*, c. 162, p.
                115, quoted in Peyton (1928), pp. 184 — 5 (text partially in
                Latin)

12   London
        c. 1674 — 1723 (based on the years Kneller spent in England before
        his death)
        (a)   Horace Walpole, *Anecdotes of Painting in England*, etc., 3
                vols. (London: Strawberry Hill, 1765), vol. 3, p. 113
        (b)   James Everard, Baron Arundell and Sir Richard Colt
                Hoare, Bart., *The History of Modern Wiltshire. Hundred
                of Dunworth and Vale of Noddre* (London: John Bowyer
                Nichols and Son, 1829), p. 32
        Note: for more information on the participants in this possible
        sale, see Lionel Cust, 'Kneller, Sir Godfrey', *Dictionary of
        National Biography*, vol. 31 (London: Smith, Elder & Co., 1892),
        pp. 240 — 9 and (b), pp. 30 — 2.

13   Inverness, Inverness-shire
        before 31 March 1730
        (a)   *Oedipus: or the Postman Remounted* (London) 31 March
                1730, p.2
        (b)   *The Whitehall Evening Post* (London) 31 March 1730, p.3
        (c)   *IJ* 4 April 1730, p.3
        Note: the Burgh Court Records, held at Inverness Town House,
        do not include cases for 1730 (letter of Miss Carol A. Goodfellow,

Branch Librarian, Inverness Branch Library, April 1978).

14   St Clements, London
      Saturday, 12 March 1735
      (a)   *GEP*, 18 March 1735, p.2
      (b)   *Weekly Register:*or *Universal Journal* (London) 22 March
            1735, p.2
      (c)   *London Journal* (London) 22 March 1734/5, p.3
      (d)   *Applebee's Original Weekly-Journal* (London) 22 March
            1735, p.3
      (e)   *Weekly Oracle:*or *Universal Library* (London) 22 March
            1735, p.4
      (f)   *LP, GSJ,* (London) 27 March 1735, p.2
      Note: information on events following the sale is found in *GEP*,
      25 March 1735, p.3

15   Newbury, Berkshire (or Marlborough, Wiltshire)
      before 1736 (or before 1744) (the dates given in the accounts for
      the Duke's marriage with his purchase)
      (a)   recorded from an old woman of Newbury, Berkshire, who
            was 10 at the time of the sale and had heard the story from
            her mother. E. W— (1870), p. 179
      (b)   unidentified crimson-velvet-bound volume in the British
            Library, cited in Money (1895), pp. 13—14
      (c)   Money, *A Popular History of Newbury in the County of
            Berks. from Early to Modern Times* (London: Simpkin,
            Marshall, Hamilton, Kent, 1905), note p. 182
      (d)   P.T.A—(1938), p. 314
      Note: for further information concerning the participants, see the
      ms. notation (by Shaw, according to E.W—, 1870, p. 179) in A.
      Collins, *The Peerage of England*, 4th edn. (London: H. Woodfall
      et al., 1768), vol. 2, p. 258 (identified in a letter from Dr J. S. C.
      Riley-Smith, April 1978). For the marriage entry in the register at
      Mr Keith's proprietary chapel, Mayfair, see George Clinch,
      *Mayfair and Belgravia, Being an Historical Account of the Parish
      of St. George, Hanover Square* (London: Truslove & Shirley,
      1892), p.60. For information and anecdotes about the wife, see
      Money (1895), p. 14. It is possible that this sale or its details are
      fictitious.

16   London
      before 20 April 1740
      (a)   *Ch*, 29 April 1740, p.3
      Note: a 'Trader in Wives' committed to the Gate House for
      bigamy.

17   St Anne's Lane, Westminster, London (?) (home of husband)
      Saturday, 3 September 1740
      (a)   *Ch*, 9 September 1740, p. 3

18 near Birmingham, Staffordshire (?) (possibly Warwickshire)
before 11 March 1745
(a) *ABG*, 11 March 1745, p.3

19 Rowley, Staffordshire
Wednesday, 13 March 1745
(a) *ABG*, 18 March 1745, p.3

20 Oxford Road, London (?) (this report appears in the text under the heading 'London')
before 17 April 1756
(a) *J Ox J*, 17 April 1756, p.2

21 Dublin, Co. Dublin, Eire
Thursday, 19 October 1756
(a) *London Evening Post* (London), 28 October 1756 quoted in H. A. Thorpe, correspondence, *Hertfordshire Countryside*, vol. 12 (Letchworth, Herts: Autumn, 1957), p. 71

22 Bitton (?), Gloucestershire (location of the couple's marriage)
c. 1760 (date given in J.L. (1887), p. 675)
(a) ms. deposition for support by Ruth Beard, sworn to Henry Creswicke, c. 1760, quoted in J.L. (1887), p.675

23 Coton (?), Staffordshire (home of the wife's 'second husband' and purchaser)
13 June 1763
(a) ms. agreement between Thomas Moss and John Keeting, 13 June 1763. D. 917/11/1. (Staffordshire Record Office)

24 Parham, Suffolk
c. 10—17 November 1764
(a) *IJ*, 24 November 1764, p. 3
(b) *GM*, vol. 34, November 1764, p. 542
(c) [A.M.B.], *The Parlour Portfolio or Post-Chaise Companion: Being a Selection of the Most Amusing and Interesting Articles That Have Appeared in the Magazines, Newspapers, and other Daily and Periodical Journals, from the Year 1700 to the Present Times*, 2 vols. (London: Matthew Iley, 1820), vol. 1, pp. 230—1
Note: (b) incorrectly gives the location of the sale as Norfolk.

25 Southwark, London
c. 2—8 March 1766
(a) *AR 1766*, p. 75
Note: 'The Sale of Wives', *Chamber's Journal of Popular Literature* (London), n.s. vol. 16 (12 October 1861), pp. 238—9 appears to be a recorded account.

26 John's Street, Westminster, London
Monday, 8 March 1766
(a) *Lloyd's Evening Post* (London), 15 March 1766, p.1

27   Bredon, Worcestershire
       c. 24 March 1766
       (a)   extract of a letter from Tewkesbury, 24 May 1766, quoted
              in *StJC*, 29 May 1766, p. 3
28   Birtley, Northumberland
       before 31 March 1776
       (a)   extract of a letter from Newcastle, 31 March 1766, quoted
              in *StJC*, 5 April 1766, p. 1
29   Midsomer Norton, Somerset
       Friday, 24 October 1766
       (a)   ms. petition to a Somerset Justice of the Peace by Ann
              Parsons, 1768. Additional mss. 32, 084 (British Library),
              quoted in Kenney (1929), p. 496
30   Marylebone, London
       c. May 1767
       (a)   *LC*, 4 June 1767, p. 534
       (b)   *JOxJ*, 6 June 1767, p.2
       (c)   *AR 1767*, p. 99
       Note: it is possible that this sale is fictitious; see 68 and 145.
31   Shoreditch, London
       Thursday, 14 September 1768
       (a)   *PA*, 19 September 1768, quoted in O—, 'Wife-Selling', *NQ*,
              series 5, vol. 10, 16 November 1878, p.387
       (b)   *JOxJ* 24 September 1768, p.1
32   Oxford, Oxfordshire
       Friday, 14 (?) October 1768 (given as 'Last Friday')
       (a)   *JOxJ*, 15 October 1768, p.3
       (b)   *JOxJ*, 22 October 1768, p.3
       Note: for further information on one of the participants, see ms.
       entry in the marriage register, St Ebbe's parish church, Oxford,
       Oxfordshire, 22 June 1754 – 2 May 1805 (20 October 1768) (St
       Ebbe's, Oxford, Oxfordshire).
33   Newmarket, Suffolk (?) (there are other Newmarkets, in
       Cornwall and Co. Kilkenny)
       Tuesday, 6 March 1770
       (a)   *LC*, 10 March 1770, p. 240
       Note: the *Ipswich Journal* makes no reference to this sale (letter
       from Dr W. R. Serjent, Suffolk Record Office, April 1978).
34   Iver, Buckinghamshire
       Friday, 27 July 1770
       (a)   *JOxJ*, 4 August 1770, p. 1
35   Birmingham, Warwickshire
       Friday, 31 August 1773
       (a)   newspaper 1773, quoted in H. S. G., 'Wife Sale at

Birmingham', *NQ*, series 3, vol. 2, 6 September 1862, p. 186

(b) *The Annual Register, or a View of the History, Politics, and Literature for the Year 1773*, vol. 16, 5th edn. (London: J. Dodsley, 1793), p. 130

Note: Brown (1951), p. 460, incorrectly gives the date as 8 August and the seller's name as 'Whitehorn'. Hackwood (1974), p. 70, incorrectly gives the date as 1733 and the amount paid as one guinea and the voucher, as 'T. Buckley'. Briffault (1927), vol. 2, note p. 222, gives the seller's name as 'Whitehom'.

36 Spa, Rosoman's Row, London
Monday, 15 November 1773
(a) *PA*, 17 November 1773, p. 2

37 Windsor Forest, Berkshire
before 25 February 1775
(a) *StJC*, 25 February 1775, p. 3

38 Wath, North Riding, Yorkshire
Thursday, 3 August 1775
(a) *StJc*, 17 August 1775, p. 4., quoted in Herbert Hughes, *Chronicle of Chester 1775-1975* (1975), p. 170

39 Farnham (?), Surrey (source gives 'Fareham')
Saturday, 16 September 1775
(a) *PA*, 19 September 1775, p. 4
(b) *JOxJ*, 23 September 1775, p. 3

Note: there is no mention of this case in the *Hampshire Chronicle* (letter of Mr R. R. Lawson, County Librarian, Hampshire County Library, October 1979). Surrey had no newspaper at this date (letter of Mrs S. J. Himsworth, Surrey Record Offices, October 1979).

40 Swindon, Wiltshire
before 23 December 1775
(a) *JOxJ*, 23 December 1775, p. 3

41 Pontefract, West Riding, Yorkshire
Tuesday, 12 November 1776
(a) *LM* 19 November 1776, quoted in *Thoresby Society*, vol.38, 1939, p. 187

42 Penistone area (?), West Riding, Yorkshire (husband worked at Flashhouse Coal Pit, near Penistone)
Monday, 27 January 1777
(a) *YCh*, 7 February 1777, p. 2

43 Llan-y-bydder, Carmarthenshire (?) (possibly Cardiganshire)
c. 1777 (story from individual who was a farmer and sexton 'about two hundred years ago', subtracted from the date, April 1977, when the story was received from the Welsh Folk Museum)
(a) ms. from an informant, who had heard the story from his

father (born 1843). This account was said to have come from the informant's maternal grandfather, a sexton of Henfynyw Church, who farmed at Sychpant, Cardiganshire, c. 1777. 1654/11, Welsh Folk Museum (text in Welsh)
Note: likenesses to the speech reported in 234 suggest that at least part of the details of this case were based on the newspaper reports or broadside of the Carlisle sale. It is possible that the entire example is fictitious.

44 Seven Dials (?), London (home of husband)
before 17 February 1778
(a)   *LC*, 17 February 1778, pp. 166–7

45 Blackfriars, London
Thursday, 9 July 1778
(a)   *PA*, 11 July 1778, p. 2

46 Chesterfield, Derbyshire
1781
(a)   *ChC*, 1781, quoted in Herbert Hughes, *Chronicle of Chester 1775-1975* (1975), pp. 170-1

47 Purleigh parish (?), Essex (location of couple after sale)
before 27 September 1782
(a)   ms. entry in baptismal register, Purleigh Parish, Essex, c. 15–27 September 1782 (Essex Record Offices)

48 Ossett(?), West Riding, Yorkshire (home of the husband)
Friday, 31 May 1782
(a)   J. W. Walker (1939), p. 495

49 Baylham, Suffolk
June 1783
(a)   *IJ*, 21 June 1783, p. 2

50 Liverpool
before 20 August 1785
(a)   *JOxJ*, 20 August 1785, p. 3
Note: there appears to be no reference to this sale or case in either *Gore's Advertiser* or *Williamson's Liverpool Advertiser* (letters of Ms Naomi Evette, Liverpool Record Office, October 1979 and January 1980).

51 Stowupland, Suffolk
c. January 1786
(a)   *IJ*, 28 January 1786, p. 2
Note: the date is incorrectly given as 1787 in Andrews (1892), p. 199; *East Anglian Miscellany*, no. 10,882 (1942), p. 31; W. H. Howse, 'Wife-Selling in 19th Century', *NQ*, vol. 196, 31 March 1951, p. 152; and Porter (1974), p. 29.

52 Lincoln (?), Lincolnshire (location of court case)
before 17 March 1786
(a)   *LSM*, 17 March 1786, p. 3
(b)   *JOxJ*, 25 March 1786, p. 3

53 Spalding, Lincolnshire
Monday, 12 June 1786
(a)   *LSM*, 23 June 1786, p. 3
(b)   *WFP*, 3 July 1786, p. 3

54 Kennington (?), Oxfordshire (home of husband)
Tuesday, 1 August 1786
(a)   *JOxJ*, 5 August 1786, p. 3

55 Thame area, Oxfordshire
c. 1787—8
(a)   *NM*, 2 January 1790, p. 3

56 Worcester, Worcestershire
before 1788
(a)   D'Archenholtz (1789), vol. 2, p. 33

57 General (?)
before 12 September 1789
(a)   *NM*, 12 September 1789, p.1
Note: a general query about 'the Sale of Wives, of which continual Instances occur among the lower class of People'.

58 Blythburgh, Suffolk
Thursday, 29 October 1789
(a)   *IJ* 7 November 1789, p. 3 (advertisement)
Note: for further information concerning the participants, see mss. entries in the marriage (6 August 1782), baptismal (11 April 1789) and burial (28 December, 1799) registers of Blythburgh. FC 198/D1/2 (Ipswich and East Suffolk Record Office) (notes of Mrs Roger Walker).

59 Worcester, Worcestershire
Wednesday, 18 November 1789
(a)   *JOxJ*, 21 November 1789, p. 3

60 Oxford, Oxfordshire
Wednesday, 9 December 1789, p. 3
(a)   *JOxJ*, 12 December 1789, p. 3
(b)   *NM*, 19 December 1789, p. 1

61 General (?)
c. 1789—90
(a)   *NM*, 27 February 1790, p. 3
(b)   *ABG*, 1 March 1790, p.3
Note: these are *general* admonitions against wife-selling. Hackwood (1974), p. 70, gives a version similar to (b).

62 Derbyshire (?) (this report appears in the text under the heading 'Derby')
c. November 1789 — January 1790
(a)   *WFP*, 15 February 1790, p. 1
Note: in a discussion of 66 it is noted: 'the woman was delivered in the usual way, which has been lately practiced.'

63   Thame, Oxfordshire
      Tuesday, 29 December 1789
      (a)   *NM*, 2 January 1790, p. 3
64   Chorley Wood, Hertfordshire
      c. January—February, 1790
      (a)   *LC*, 6 February 1790, p. 122
65   Barton-under-Needwood, Staffordshire
      Tuesday, 2 February 1790
      (a)   *NM*, 13 February 1790, p. 3
      (b)   *WFP*, 15 February 1790, p. 1
66   Wolverhampton, Staffordshire
      Wednesday, 3 February 1790
      (a)   *NM*, 13 Feburary 1790, p. 3
67   Bow (London ?)
      before 8 February 1790
      (a)   *NM*, 13 February 1790, p. 3
      (b)   *LC*, 15 February 1790, p. 150
68   Southwark, London
      before 25 June 1790
      (a)   *LC*, 26 June 1790, p. 603
      (b)   *The Exeter Flying Post, or, Plymouth and Cornish
             Advertiser* (Exeter, Devon) 1 July 1790, p. 2
      Note: it is possible that this sale is fictitious; see 30 and 145.
69   Ninfield, East Sussex
      Friday 29 October 1790
      (a)   *SWA*, 8 November 1790, p. 3
      (b)   *T*, 19 November 1790, p. 4 (*apparent* reference to sale)
      Note: for information on events following the sale, see 70a.
70   Ninfield, East Sussex
      c. 8—14 November 1790
      (a)   *SWA*, 15 November 1790, p. 3
      (b)   *T*, 19 November 1790, p. 4 (*apparent* reference to sale)
      Note: for information on events preceding the sale, see 69a.
71   Liverpool
      Wednesday, 6 April 1791
      (a)   Liverpool newspaper before 6 April 1791 cited in *LNJ*, 15
             April 1791, p. 4
      (b)   *Liverpool Herald*, before 6 April 1791, cited in *NM*, 16
             April 1791, p. 1
72   Red Lion Street, Whitechapel, London
      before 25 June 1791
      (a)   *PA*, 25 June 1791, p. 3
73   Bitteswell, Leicestershire
      Thursday, 4 August 1791
      (a)   *LNJ*, 12 August 1791

(b)   *NM*, 13 August 1791, p. 3

74   Downham Market, Norfolk

c. 1791 (sale took place 'About 30 years ago')

(a)   *NC*, 22 September 1821, p. 3, quoted in Charles Mackie, *Norfolk Annuals* (Norwich, Norfolk: Norfolk Chronicle, 1901), p. 199

75   Cockerham (?), Lancashire (location of couple after sale)

c. 1792 ('he had bought her about 12 years ago')

(a)   *LG*, 2 June 1804, p. 3

76   Hereford, Herefordshire

c. 1777 — 1806 (as 'nonagenarian' was presumably between 90 and 99, and could hardly have called herself a 'playfellow' past the age of 20)

Note: Baker (1977), p. 134 mistakenly gives the date of the sale as 1876.

77   Anon

before 1793

(a)   William Hutton, *Pleasures of Matrimony* (1793), quoted in Lawley (A)

Note: the poem *may* have been based on an actual sale.

78   Sheffield, West Riding, Yorkshire

Saturday, 26 March 1796

(a)   *Sheffield Courant* (Sheffield, Yorks), 26 March 1796, p. 3 (cited in a letter of Mr R. F. Atkins, Director, Sheffield City Library, April 1978)

(b)   *Sheffield Register* (Sheffield, Yorks), c. 26 — 30 March 1796, quoted in *T*, 30 March 1796, p. 2. Mr R. F. Atkins, Sheffield City Library, states that the *Sheffield Register* did not exist in 1796 (letter of April 1978); (c) and (d) also quote this as the source, however.

(c)   *GEP*, 31 March 1796, p. 3

(d)   *MH*, March 1796, quoted in Crawford J. Pocock, 'Selling a Wife', *NQ*, series 5, vol. 4, 27 November 1875, pp. 425 — 6

79   Anon

before 9 August 1976

(a)   country newspaper, before 9 August 1796, cited in *LNJ*, 12 August 1796, p. 2

(b)   country newspaper, before 12 August 1796, cited in *DSJ*, 12 August 1796, p. 4

(c)   country newspaper, before 13 August 1796, cited in *JOxJ*, 13 August 1796, p. 2

80   Smithfield Market, London

Monday, 12 June 1797

(a)   *MC*, 13 June 1797, p. 3

(b)   *LC*, 15 June 1797, p. 564

(c)	*MC*, 15 June 1797, p. 3
(d)	*GEP*, 15 June 1797, p. 4
(e)	*MC*, 16 June 1797, p. 2
(f)	*LNJ*, 16 June 1797, p. 2
(g)	*GEP*, 29 June 1797, p. 4
(h)	*MC*, 11 July 1797, p. 3
(i)	*MC*, 11 July 1797, p. 3
(j)	*MC*, 19 July 1797, p. 2
(k)	*T*, 22 July 1797, p. 2

Note: (c)−(k) are secondary commentary.

81   Bury, Lancashire
before 23 June 1797
(a)   *MC*, 23 June 1797, p. 2

82   Lewes, East Sussex
c. 8−15 July 1797
(a)   *SWA*, 17 July 1797 p. 3
(b)   *RM*, 24 July 1797, p. 4
(c)   *LNJ*, 28 July 1797, p. 3
Note: see 85.

83   Smithfield Market, London
Friday, 14 July 1797

(a)	*LC*, 15 July 1797, p. 56
(b)	*S*, 17 July 1797, p. 3
(c)	*T*, 18 July 1797, p. 3
(d)	*MC*, 20 July 1797, p. 3
(e)	*MC*, 20 July 1797, p. 3
(f)	*MC*, 24 July 1797, p. 3
(g)	*RM*, 24 July 1797, p. 4
(h)	*MC*, 25 July 1797, p. 2
(i)	*MC*, 26 July 1797, p. 2
(j)	*MC*, 27 July 1797, p. 2
(k)	*LNJ*, 28 July 1797, p. 3
(l)	*T*, 31 July 1797, p. 1 (advertisement)
(m)	*T*, 31 July 1797, p. 3 (puff).
(n)	*MC*, 31 July 1797, p. 1 (advertisement)
(o)	*MC*, 31 July 1797, p. 4 (puff)
(p)	*T*, 2 August 1797, p. 1 (advertisement)
(q)	*T*, 2 August 1797, p. 3 (puff)
(r)	*MC*, 2 August 1797, p. 1 (advertisement)
(s)	*MC*, 2 August 1797, p. 3 (puff)
(t)	*MC*, 4 August 1797, p. 1 (advertisement)
(u)	*MC*, 5 August 1797, p. 3
(v)	*MC*, 5 August 1797, p. 3
(w)	*T*, 7 August 1797, p. 1 (advertisement)
(x)	*MC*, 7 August 1797, p. 1 (advertisement)

(y)   *MC*, 9 August 1797, p. 3
(z)   *T*, 10 August 1797, p. 3
(aa) *T*, 11 August 1797, p. 2
(bb) *JOxJ*, 12 August 1797, p. 2
(cc) *MC*, 14 August 1797, p. 3
(dd) *MC*, 14 August 1797, p. 3
(ee) *T*, 17 August 1797, p. 2
(ff) *T*, 17 August 1797, p. 3
(gg) *MC*, 17 August 1797, p. 3

Note: (d)−(f) and (h)−(gg) are secondary commentary. For other such comments which may apply to this sale, see 84 (d), (e), and 86 (g)−(o).

84   Smithfield Market, London
     Monday, 17 July 1797
(a)   *MC*, 19 July 1797, p. 2
(b)   *MC*, 19 July 1797, p. 2
(c)   *T*, 22 July 1797, p. 2
(d)   *T*, 22 July 1797, p. 2
(e)   *MC* 24 July 1797, p. 3

Note: (b)−(e) are secondary commentary. For other such comments which may apply to this sale, see 83 (d)−(f) and (h)−(gg), and 86 (g)−(o).

85   Leeds, West Riding, Yorkshire
     before 20 July 1797
(a)   *MC*, 20 July 1797, p. 3
(b)   *S*, 20 July 1797, p. 3
(c)   *JOxJ*, 22 July 1797, p. 2

Note: there is a strong possibility that this is a confused reference to case 82, due to the similarity between the Cliffe, Leeds, and Cliff, Lewes.

86   Smithfield Market, London
     Monday, 24 July 1797
(a)   *S*, 26 July 1797, p. 3
(b)   *LC*, 27 July 1797, p. 94
(c)   *MC*, 27 July 1797, p. 2 (*apparent* reference to sale)
(d)   *LNJ*, 28 July 1797, p. 3
(e)   *MC*, 29 July 1797, p. 3
(f)   *MC*, 4 September 1797, p. 3
(g)   *T*, 14 September 1797, p. 2
(h)   *MC*, 15 September 1797, p. 4
(i)   *MC*, 18 September 1797, p. 2
(j)   *MC*, 18 September 1797, p. 3
(k)   *T*, 4 October 1797, p. 2
(l)   *T*, 24 October 1797, p. 2
(m)   *MC*, 28 October 1797, p. 2

(n)   *MC*, 15 November 1797, p. 3

(o)   *MC*, 20 November 1797, p. 3

Note: (f)—(o) are secondary commentary. For other such comments which may apply to this sale, see 83 (h)—(gg).

87   Fittleworth, West Sussex

c. 30 July — 5 August 1797

(a)   *SWA*, 7 August 1797, p. 3

(b)   *S*, 10 August 1797, p. 3

Note: (b) incorrectly gives the site of the sale as Suffolk.

88   Towcester, Northamptonshire

c. 26 August — 2 September 1797

(a)   *T*, 8 September 1797, p. 3

(b)   *LNJ*, 8 September 1797, p. 3

(c)   *LC*, 9 September 1797, p. 245

(d)   *GEP*, 9 September 1797, p. 1

(e)   *T*, 19 September 1797, p. 2 (*apparent* reference to sale)

Note: (f) is secondary commentary. There is no reference to this sale in the *Northampton Mercury*, the only local newspaper at the time (letters from Mr P. I. King, Chief Archivist, Northamptonshire Record Office, April 1978, and from Mr J. B. Stafford, Deputy District Librarian, Northampton Central Library, May 1978). Textual evidence, however, suggests the existence of at least one more London newspaper source pre-dating 9 September.

89   Newcastle, Northumberland

Monday, 6 November 1797

(a)   *MC*, 13 November 1797, p. 3

90   Covent Garden Market, London

Friday, 24 November 1797

(a)   *LC*, 30 November 1797, p. 523

91   Smithfield Market, London (?) (this report appears in the text under the heading 'London')

before 2 December 1797

(a)   *T*, 2 December 1797, p. 2

(b)   *MC*, 22 December 1797, p. 3

92   Queensborough, Kent

Monday, 3 September 1798

(a)   *GEP*, 13 September 1798, p. 1.

93   Brighton, East Sussex

Friday, 22 February 1799

(a)   *SWA*, 25 February 1799, p. 3

94   Macclesfield, Cheshire

before 24 April 1799

(a)   *ChC*, 24 April 1799, quoted in Landwor (1880), pp. 245—6

95   Stafford, Staffordshire
Tuesday, 25 February 1800
(a)   *Staffordshire Advertiser* (Stafford, Staffs), 1 March 1800, quoted in Lawley (A)
(b)   *LM*, 15 March 1800, p. 3
Note: there is evidence that (b) may derive from a London newspaper account. Hackwood (1974), pp. 70−1 gives a version of (a) which suggests a misprint in Lawley.

96   Smithfield Market (?), London (transaction referred to as 'a fair Smithfield bargain')
before 18 July 1800
(a)   *MH*, 18 July 1800, p. 3

97   New Malton, North Riding, Yorkshire
Saturday, 10 January 1801
(a)   *YH*, 17 January 1801, p. 3
(b)   *GEP*, 22 January 1801

98   Beverley, East Riding, Yorkshire
before 6 July 1801
(a)   *T*, 6 July 1801, p. 3

99   Colchester, Essex
c. 26 October − 1 November 1801
(a)   *EC*, 13 November 1801
(b)   *T*, 17 November 1801, p. 3
Note: the incorrect date given in (b) suggests that this derived from some intermediate newspaper source.

100   Smithfield Market, London
Friday, 20 November 1801
(a)   *T*, 23 November 1801, p. 3
(b)   *Cambridge Independent Press and Chronicle* (Cambridge, Cambs), 30 November 1801, quoted in P.D.M−, 'Wife Selling in 19th Century', *NQ*, vol. 197, 19 January 1952, p. 42. But Fitzwilliam Library, Cambridge, states that there is no 30 November 1801 edition of the *Cambridge Independent Press* or the *Cambridge Chronicle* (letter of April 1978).

101   Walton, Shropshire (?) (subsequent home of purchaser)
c. 1762−1841 (assuming the purchaser, who died aged 94, would not have bought a wife before he was 15)
(a)   *Shrewsbury Chronicle* (Shrewsbury, Salop), c. 13 September 1841, cited in *OCC*, 18 September 1841, p. 2.

102   Plymouth, Devon
Tuesday, 5 January 1802
(a)   *T*, 9 January 1802, p. 3

103   Chapel-en-le-Frith, Derbyshire
Thursday, 11 February 1802

    (a)   *MH*, 11 March 1802, p. 3

104   Hereford, Herefordshire
before 16 April 1802
    (a)   *MH*, 16 April 1802, p. 3

105   Wrentham, Suffolk
Wednesday, 2 June 1802
    (a)   *IJ*, 5 June 1802, p. 2

106   Smithfield Market, London
Monday, 9 August 1802
    (a)   *GEP*, 12 August 1802, p. 4

107   Smithfield Market, London
Friday, 17 September 1802
    (a)   *T*, 21 September 1802, p. 3

108   Sheffield, West Riding, Yorkshire
before 25 March 1803
    (a)   *DG*, 25 March 1803, quoted in Roberts (1957), p. 146
    (b)   K.P.D.E.— (1856), p. 420
Note: 'Daily Magazine. The Trade in Wives', *Daily Mail* (London), 1 March 1899, p. 7, adds information without supporting evidence.

109   Lewes, East Sussex
Tuesday, 6 September 1803
    (a)   *SWA*, 12 September 1803, p. 3
    (b)   *JOxJ*, 17 September 1803, p. 2

110   depot, Isle of Wight
Sunday, 6 May 1804
    (a)   *Hampshire Telegraph* (Portsmouth), 7 May 1804, p. 3
        (letter of Mrs M. J. Guy, District Librarian, Portsmouth Central Library, June 1978)

111   London and Smithfield Market, London
c. 8—14 July 1804
    (a)   *T*, 19 July 1804, p. 3

112   Norwich, Norfolk
before 9 February 1805
    (a)   *NC*, 9 February 1805, p. 2

113   Hythe, Kent
c. 3—9 March 1805
    (a)   *KG*, 15 March 1805, p. 4
    (b)   *O*, 17 March 1805, p. 3

114   Tuxford, Nottinghamshire
before 8 July 1805
    (a)   *DSJ*, 2 August 1805, p. 1
    (b)   *The Annual Register, or a View of the History, Politics and Literature for the Year 1805*, vol. 47 (London: W. Otridge and Son, 1807), p. 405

115 Halifax, West Riding, Yorkshire
c. 1805 ('about 25 years before', and allowing three years for the wife's three children)
(a)   newspaper (?), 1 October 1827, quoted in William Andrews, *Curiosities of the Church: Studies of Curious Customs, Services and Records* (London: Methuen, 1890), p. 159
116 Hull, East Riding, Yorkshire
Tuesday, 4 February 1806
(a)   *HA*, 8 February 1806, p. 3
(b)   *DSJ*, 21 February 1806, p. 2
(c)   *The Annual Register, or a View of the History, Politics, and Literature for the Year 1806*, vol. 48 (London: W. Otridge and Son, 1808), p. 370
(d)   *The Annual Register, or a View of the History, Politics, and Literature for the Year 1806*, vol. 48 (London: F. C. and J. Rivington, 1815), p. 21
Note: Rayner (1881), p. 135, gives Gowthorpe's name as 'George Gowthorp'. Andrews (1892), p. 202 gives 'Gosthorpe'.
117 Smithfield Market, London
Friday, 2 May 1806
(a)   *T*, 5 May 1806, p. 4
118 Pontefract, West Riding, Yorkshire
Monday, 8 September 1806
(a)   *York Courant* (York, Yorks) 15 September 1806, p. 2
119 Horse Shoe Corner, Lancaster, Lancashire
Wednesday, 3 December 1806
(a)   *LG*, 6 December 1806, p. 3 (letter of Miss U. B. Murphy, District Librarian, Lancaster Central Library, August 1978)
120 Grassington, West Riding, Yorkshire
c. 20 February 1807
(a)   *The Annual Register, or a View of the History, Politics, and Literature for the Year 1807*, vol. 49 (London: W. Otridge and Son, 1809), p. 378
Note: incorrectly identified as occurring in Cambridgeshire in Brown (1951), p. 460. Brown, and Briffault (1927), vol. 2, note pp. 222−3, give the name 'Grassington' as 'Grossington'.
121 Minchinhampton, Gloucestershire
before 8 June 1807
(a)   *T*, 8 June 1807, p. 3
(b)   *JOxJ*, 13 June 1807, p. 1
Note: this sale is *not* mentioned in the *Gloucester Journal* (letter of Mr G. R. Hiatt, Divisional Librarian, Gloucester Central Library, June 1978).

122 Knaresborough, West Riding, Yorkshire
Friday, 2 September 1807
(a) *Morning Post* (London), 10 October 1807, p. 3
(b) *Satirist*, November 1807, quoted in S. H. Ward, 'Wife Selling in the Eighteenth Century', *NQ*, vol. 196, 21 July 1951, p. 327

123 Smithfield Market, London
Friday, 8 April 1808
(a) *JOxJ*, 16 April 1808, p. 1

124 Smithfield Market, London
c. 3—9 July 1808
(a) *JOxJ*, 16 July 1808, p. 4

125 Smithfield Market, London
Friday, 8 July 1808
(a) *JOxJ*, 16 July 1808, p. 4

126 Billingsgate Market, London
Friday, 8 July 1808
(a) *JOxJ*, 16 July 1808, p. 4

127 Bewcastle, Cumberland, and Newcastle, Northumberland
before 22 April 1810
(a) *JOxJ*, 28 April 1810, p. 4
(b) *Evans and Ruffey's Farmer's Journal and Manufacturer's and Trader's Register* (London), 28 April 1810, p. 15
Note: K.P.D.E— (1863), p. 486, incorrectly gives the date of (b) as 5 May 1810.

128 Plymouth (?), Devon (location of court case)
Wednesday, 17 October 1810
(a) Hewett (1973), pp. 128—9
Note: *presumably* derived from newspaper reports.

129 Sittingbourne, Kent
before 2 March 1811
(a) *G*, 2 March 1811, p. 4
(b) *MJ*, 5 March 1811, p. 4
Note: this sale involving a woman named Coveney appears to be the sale 'at Coventry' involving the same price and extras reported in P.T.A— (1939), p. 96.

130 Skipton, West Riding, Yorkshire
before 3 January 1812
(a) *LivM*, 3 January 1812, p. 214

131 Whitehaven, Cumberland
Tuesday, 28 January 1812
(a) William Fleming, ms. diary and commonplace book, 27 January 1812 (Fleming, 1812)
(b) William Fleming, ms. diary and commonplace book, 28 January 1812 (Fleming, 1812)

132 Smithfield Market, London
Friday, 14 February 1812
(a)   *T*, 17 February 1812, p. 3
(b)   *JOxJ*, 22 Feburary 1812, p. 4
133 Hearne, Kent
Monday, 2 March 1812
(a)   *LivM*, 13 March 1812, p. 295
134 Smithfield Market, London
Monday, 8 June 1812
(a)   *JOxJ*, 13 June 1812, p. 2
135 Sheffield, West Riding, Yorkshire
before 19 June 1812
(a)   *LivM*, 19 June 1812, p. 406
136 Camelford, Cornwall
c. 1812 ('about 16 years since')
(a)   *WB*, 8 February 1828, p. 2
137 Hull, East Riding, Yorkshire
Tuesday, 11 May 1813
(a)   *HA*, 15 May 1813, p. 3
(b)   *JOxJ*, 22 May 1813, p. 4
(c)   *LivM*, 28 May 1813, p. 283
138 Lincoln, Lincolnshire
before 9 July 1813
(a)   *LSM*, 9 July 1813, p. 3
(b)   *JOxJ*, 17 July 1813, p. 4
139 Canterbury, Kent
Wednesday, 16 February 1814
(a)   newspaper, 18 February 1814, quoted in Pillet (1815), pp. 302−3 (text in French)
(b)   *MJ*, 22 February 1814, p. 4
140 Nottingham, Nottinghamshire
before 26 February 1814
(a)   *Stm*, 26 February 1814, quoted in Pillet (1815), pp. 303−4 (text in French)
141 Cirencester, Gloucestershire
Monday, 23 May 1814
(a)   *G*, 31 May 1814, p. 4
142 Portsmouth, Hampshire
July 1814
(a)   de Watteville (1954), pp. 135−6
Note: melodramaticized. This sale does not appear in the *Hampshire Telegraph*, according to Mrs M. J. Guy, District Librarian, Portsmouth Central Library (letter of September 1979)
143 Wakefield, West Riding, Yorkshire
Thursday, 15 September 1814

(a)   *T*, 26 September 1814, p. 3
(b)   J. W. Walker (1939), pp. 495−6
Note: (b) incorrectly gives the date as 13 September.

144   Hailsham, East Sussex
c. 23−9 October 1814
(a)   *Hampshire Courier* (Portsmouth, Hants), 31 October 1814, quoted in Clifford Morsley, *News from the English Countryside 1750−1850* (London: Harrap, 1979), p. 196

145   Kent Road, London
c. December 1814
(a)   *MC*, 16 January 1815, p. 3
(b)   *JOxJ*, 21 January 1815, p. 4
Note: it is possible that this sale is fictitious; see 30 and 68.

146   Anon
before 1815
(a)   Pillet (1815), p. 300 (text in French)
Note: it is possible that this sale is fictitious.

147   Ashburn, Derbyshire
before 1815
(a)   witnessed by R. Pillet before 1815 and quoted in Pillet (1815), pp. 299−300, 301−2 (text in French)

148   Maidstone, Kent
Tuesday, 3 January 1815
(a)   *MJ*, 10 January 1815, p. 4
(b)   *Maid. Gaz.*, c. 3−14 January 1815, quoted in *G*, 14 January 1815, p. 4
(c)   *MC*, 14 January 1815, p. 3
(d)   newspaper (1815), quoted in Ashton (1899), pp. 216−17

149   Pontefract, West Riding, Yorkshire
Wednesday, 1 February 1815
(a)   *DG*, 3 Feburary 1815, quoted in K.P.D.E— (1856), pp. 420−1

150   Manchester, Lancashire
before 4 February 1815
(a)   *LG*, 4 February 1815, p. 3 (letter of Miss U. B. Murphy, District Librarian, Lancaster Central Library, January 1980)

151   Wigan, Lancashire
Saturday, 18 February 1815
(a)   *LivM*, 3 March 1815, p. 287

152   Smithfield Market, London
Friday, 21 April 1815
(a)   *JOxJ*, 29 April 1815, p. 4

153   Croydon, Surrey
Saturday, 17 June 1815
(a)   J. W. Walker (1939), p. 496

154   Smithfield Market, London
      Friday, 14 July 1815
      (a)   *MC*, 17 July 1815, p. 3
      (b)   *JOxJ*, 22 July 1815, p. 4
      (c)   *Ladies Magazine*, 1816, quoted in White (1891), pp. 24—5
      Note: P.T.A.— (1939), p. 96 incorrectly dates the sale to 1816.
155   Manchester, Lancashire
      Saturday, 5 August 1815
      (a)   *JOxJ*, 12 August 1815, p. 4
      (b)   *LivM*, 25 August 1815, p. 62
      (c)   *MM*, 12 October 1819, p. 3 (*apparent* reference to sale)
      Note: Mr D. Taylor, Local History Librarian, Manchester Central
      Library, notes that 'a cursory examination of the Sessions Order
      books does not reveal any details of the . . . case' (letter of April
      1978).
156   Staines, Surrey
      Friday, 15 September 1815
      (a)   *Windsor and Eton Express and General Advertiser*
            (Windsor, Berks), 17 September 1815, quoted in W.G.B.—,
            'Wife Selling in 19th Century', *NQ*, vol. 196, 17 February
            1951, p. 82
      (b)   *G*, 19 September 1815, p. 3
      (c)   newspaper (1815), quoted in Ashton (1899), p. 217
      Note: there is no copy of (a) at the Croydon Public Library or at
      the Berkshire County Library.
157   Doncaster, West Riding, Yorkshire
      Monday, 9 December 1816
      (a)   county newspaper (Yorkshire), c. 9—16 December 1816,
            quoted in *T*, 16 December 1816, p. 2
158   Smithfield Market, London
      1816
      (a)   de Fauconpret *Six Mois à Londres en 1816* (Paris:Alexis
            Eymery, 1817), ch. 17, pp. 131-3
159   Stockton, Durham
      Friday, 21 March 1817
      (a)   *Durham Advertiser*, (Durham, Dur.), 29 March 1817, p. 2
            (letter of the District Librarian, Durham Central Library,
            May 1978)
160   Dartmouth, Devon
      Friday, 4 April 1817
      (a)   *T*, 12 April 1817, p. 3
      (b)   *JOxJ*, 12 April 1817, p. 4
161   Smithfield Market, London
      Friday, 18 April 1817
      (a)   *JOxJ*, 19 April 1817, p. 4

162   Macclesfield, Cheshire
before 11 November 1817
(a)   *T*, 11 November 1817, p. 3
(b)   JOxJ, 15 November 1817, p. 2
Note: Mr Brian C. Redwood, County Archivist, Cheshire Record Office, writes: 'The reference to wife-selling is one that I have met, but have never found substantiated in court proceedings. The records of the County Quarter Sessions, January 1818, have been searched without result' (letter of April 1978).

163   Anon
before 27 July 1818
(a)   J. Chitty, *Burn's Justice of the Peace and Parish Officer*, 6 vols., 26th edn. (London: S. Sweet, 1831), vol. 5, note p. 1025
(b)   G— (1847), p. 223
Note: mention of a conviction for wife-selling in *King v. Pardey* (or *R. v. Padley*). This manuscript case is not available through the Bodleian Law Library, Oxford, or the Institute of Advanced Legal Studies, London (letter of April 1978).

164   Leominster, Herefordshire
Friday, 18 September 1818
(a)   newspaper (Hereford, Herefordshire), c. 18 September — 30 October 1818, quoted in *T*, 30 October 1818, p. 3
Note: the *Hereford Journal* of October 1818 appears to make no reference to this sale (letter of Mr C. J. Pickford, Hereford Record Office, April 1977).

165   Clipsham, Rutland
Tuesday, 29 September 1818
(a)   ms. entry in Rutland Quarter Session Minute Book, 14 January 1819, pp. 192—5 (Leicestershire Record Office)
(b)   *T*, 2 Feburary 1819, p. 3
(c)   *JOxJ*, 6 February 1819, p. 4
(d)   ms. entry in Rutland Quarter Session Minute Book, 22 April 1819, p. 211 (Leicestershire Record Office)
Note: Mr Aubrey W. Stevenson, Leicestershire Studies Librarian, Leicester Central Library, reports that the *Leicester Chronicle* and the *Leicester Journal* have nothing on this case (letter of May 1979).

166   Bodmin, Cornwall
Saturday, 7 November 1818
(a)   *WB*, 13 November 1818, p. 2
(b)   *WFP*, 16 November 1818
(c)   P.T.A— (1939), pp. 95—6 (*apparent* reference to sale)

167   Grimsby, Lincolnshire
Friday, 20 November 1818

(a)   *LivM*, 18 December 1818, p. 194

Note: Mr R. G. Roberts, Director of the Grimsby Central Library, reports that there is no reference to this sale in the *Lincoln, Rutland and Stamford Mercury* for this period (letter of January 1980).

168   Hull, East Riding, Yorkshire
Tuesday, 24 November 1818
(a)   *HA*, 26 December 1818, p. 2 (advertisement)
(b)   *HA*, 2 January 1819, p. 3
(c)   *T*, 2 January 1819, p. 2

169   Clipsham, Rutland
before 14 January 1819
(a)   *T*, 2 February 1819, p. 3
(b)   *JOxJ*, 6 February 1819, p. 4
Note: in a discussion of 165 the papers add: 'The purchaser was selected for punishment, as the most opulent, and fittest to make an example of', suggesting the existence of other sales.

170   Bilston, Staffordshire
Saturday, — May 1819
(a)   'Sale of a wife in Bilston in 1819', quoted in Lawley (B)
Note: possibly a reworked account of an actual sale.

171   Smithfield Market, London
Monday, 27 September 1819
(a)   *T*, 28 September 1819, p. 3

172   Manchester, Lancashire
before 12 October 1819
(a)   *MM*, 12 October 1819, p. 3
Note: this is a *general* admonition against wife-selling, which 'has of late years been punished with laudable severity'.

173   Redruth, Cornwall
before 11 April 1820
(a)   ms. entry in Truro Quarter Session Minute Book, 11 April 1820, p. 61, Q.S.M. (Cornwall Record Office)
(b)   Whitfeld (1900), pp. 296−7
(c)   P.T.A— (1939), pp. 95−6

174   Canterbury, Kent
Tuesday, 9 May 1820
(a)   *KG*, 12 May 1820, p. 4
Note: Andrews (1892), p. 203, gives 'Boughton Blean, as 'Broughton', incorrectly gives the seller's name as 'Brouchet' and states that the sale was to 'a resident in the city', suggesting the possible existence of an intermediate newspaper source.

175   Bedminster, Gloucestershire
before 12 September 1820
(a)   *K*, 12 September 1820, p. 83

176 Southern Staffordshire
c. 1820
(a) *Lloyd's* (1820), quoted in Lawley (A)
Note: Hackwood (1974), p. 70 incorrectly gives the date as 1720.

177 Horsham, West Sussex
c. 1820
(a) Burstow (1911), p. 73
Note: for information on events following the sale, see 189.

178 Tunbridge, Kent
Tuesday, 17 April 1821
(a) *WFP*, 30 April 1821, p. 1

179 Sudbury, Suffolk
c. 6–12 May 1821
(a) *IJ*, 19 May 1821, p. 3
Note: for information on events following the sale, see *IJ*, 26 May 1821, p. 3.

180 Liverpool
Friday, 18 May 1821
(a) newspaper (Liverpool), c. 18 May – 12 June 1821, quoted in *K*, 12 June 1821, p. 398
Note: this does not occur in the *Liverpool Mercury* (letter of Ms Naomi Evette, Liverpool Record Office, January 1980)

181 Huntingdon, Huntingdonshire
Saturday, 29 December 1821 (?) (date of husband's return)
(a) W. H. Bernard Saunders, *Legends and Traditions of Huntingdonshire* (London: Simpkins, Marshall, 1888), p. 277

182 Caerleon, Monmouthshire
Tuesday, 17 September 1822
(a) *BM*, 23 September 1822, p. 3 (cited in a letter from Mr G. Langley, County Reference Librarian, Avon County Library, April 1977)
(b) *T*, 25 September 1822, p. 3
(c) *JOxJ*, 5 October 1822, p. 2

183 Nottingham, Nottinghamshire
Saturday, 16 November 1822
(a) *T*, 23 November 1822, p. 2

184 Bristol (?) (the town in which the broadside – reproduced on p.206 – was issued)
Thursday, 28 November 1822
(a) 'A Modern Market Scene./Crispin in his GLORY,/THE/Butcher's bad BARGAIN,/Or a Ready way to get rid of a BAD WIFE'/, broadside, (Bristol:Shepherd) (Avon County Library, Miscellaneous Broadsides)
Note: it is possible that this sale was fictitious and was localized

temporally and spatially only in order to sell the broadside. Mr G. Langley, County Reference Librarian, Avon County Library, says that there is no mention of this sale in the *Bristol Mercury* for 2 December 1822 (letter of April 1977).

185 Brighton, East Sussex (?) (location of couple after sale)
before 1 December 1822
(a) *Brighton Chronicle* (Brighton, Sussex), before 1 December 1822 quoted in *ST*, 1 December 1822, p. 4. (According to a letter from Mr C. Batt, Brighton Area Library, of May 1977, the *Brighton Chronicle* did not exist at this time.)
Note: Mr E. M. Watkins, Area Librarian, Brighton Area Library, reports no report of the sale in either the *Brighton Gazette* or the *Sussex Weekly Advertiser* for this period (letter of September 1979).

186 Modbury, Devon (three times), and Plymouth, Devon
before 12 December 1822 ('on three separate market days'), and Thursday, 12 December 1822
(a) *S*, before 23 December 1822, quoted in *T*, 23 December 1822, p. 3
(b) 'A true and singular Account of **Wife-Selling/ EXTRAORDINARY!**', broadside — reproduced on p.91 — Gateshead:W. Stephenson, (n.d.) (John Rylands University Library, Manchester)

187 Smithfield Market, London
1822
(a) Chateaubriand, cited in J. W. Walker (1939), p. 496

188 Sheffield, West Riding, Yorkshire
1822
(a) Leader (1901), p. 42

189 Billingshurt (?), West Sussex (location of 'husband')
c. 1822 (allowing two years after her c. 1820 sale for her two children by the purchaser)
(a) Burstow (1911), p. 73
Note: for information on events preceding the sale, see 177.

190 Wednesbury, Staffordshire
before 1823 (Hackwood, 1974, p. 71, says that the sale took place 'upwards of a century' before 1923, the date of publication of his book)
(a) R.B— (before 1923), quoted in Hackwood (1974), pp. 71–3. (R.B— is given as the author in Hackwood's *Notes and Queries*, vol. 2, no. 319, according to a letter from Mr R. B. Ludgate, Borough Librarian, West Bromwich Central Library, Staffs, April 1978.)
Note: possibly a reworked account of an actual sale.

191   Norwich, Norfolk
       c. 27 – 30 April 1823
       (a)   *NC*, 3 May 1823, p. 2
       Note: Miss J. Kennedy, County Archivist, Norfolk Record Office,
       notes that 'the minute book of the Norwich Court of Guardians
       contains no reference to Mrs Turner applying for relief', and that
       'no account of this case is to be found in the Mayor's Court Book,
       April-May 1823' (letter of April 1978).

192   Halifax, West Riding, Yorkshire
       before 10 May 1823, and Saturday, 10 May 1823
       (a)   newspaper (York, Yorks), c. 10 – 20 May 1823, quoted in
              T, 20 May 1823, p. 3
       (b)   *JOxJ*, 24 May 1823, p. 4
       Note: the accounts note that '5s has hitherto been the average
       price'.

193   Bristol
       Thursday, 29 May 1823
       (a)   *BM*, 2 June 1823, p. 3
       (b)   Shepherd (1823) (broadside) reproduced on p.68)
       Note: Mr G. Langley, County Reference Librarian, Avon County
       Library, reports that the Record Office holds only Quarter
       Sessions records for this date and that these make no mention of
       the sale (letter of April 1978).

194   Warwick (?) Warwickshire (location of the trial)
       before 7 August 1823
       (a)   *WB*, 7 August 1823, p. 4 (letter from Mr Max Hodnett,
              editor of the *West Briton Newspaper*, Truro, April 1978)

195   Chipping Ongar, Essex
       Saturday, 27 December 1823
       (a)   EC, 2 January 1824, quoted in J. B. Wainewright, 'Wife-
              sales', *NQ*, series 13, vol. 151, 16 October 1926, p. 286. Mr
              K. C. Newton, County Archivist, Essex Records Office,
              however, says that no *Essex Chronicle* was published on
              this date, and that no reference to the sale is to be found in
              issues of the *Chelmsford (Essex) Chronicle* (letter of April
              1977).
       (b)   *JOxJ*, 3 January 1824, p. 2
       (c)   newspaper (1824), quoted in *NOW*, (1924)
       (d)   evening newspaper (1824), quoted in *NOW*, (1924)
              (*apparent* reference to sale)

196   Altrincham, Cheshire
       1823
       (a)   C. Nickson, *Bygone Altrincham Traditions and History*
              [1935], reprint edn., 1971 (Manchester; E. J. Morten), pp.
              64 – 5

(b)   Hole (1970), p. 7

197   Liskeard, Cornwall
1823
(a)   Whitfeld (1900), pp. 296−7

198   Aylesbury, Buckinghamshire
Tuesday, 22 June 1824
(a)   *T*, 29 June 1824, p. 2
Note: R. Gibbs, *Buckinghamshire, A Record of Local Occurrences*, vol. 3 (Aylesbury, Bucks:1880), p. 128, incorrectly gives the date of sale as 31 July.

199   Shudehill Market, Manchester, Lancashire
Friday, 25 June 1824
(a)   *Manchester Gazette* (Manchester, Lancs), 26 June 1824, p. 4
(b)   *Exchange Herald* (Manchester, Lancs), 29 June 1824, p. 5
(c)   *T*, 29 June 1824, p. 2

200   Arundel, West Sussex
Monday, 21 December 1824
(a)   *BrG*, 23 December 1824, p. 3
(b)   *T*, 25 December 1824, p. 2
Note: (b) incorrectly gives the sale date as Tuesday, suggesting a possible intermediate source.

201   Sheffield, West Riding, Yorkshire
Tuesday, 1 March 1825
(a)   *Leeds Intelligencer* (Leeds, Yorks), before 12 March 1825, cited in *BCh*, 12 March 1825, p. 4

202   Cheltenham, Gloucestershire
Thursday, 3 March 1825
(a)   *JOxJ*, 12 March 1825, p. 3
Note: Mr G. R. Hiatt, Divisional Librarian, Gloucester Central Library, says that there is no mention of this sale in the *Gloucester Journal* (letter of June 1979).

203   Wakefield, West Riding, Yorkshire
before 7 June 1825
(a)   *CoC*, 7 June 1825, p. 4
(b)   *JOxJ*, 11 June 1825, p. 4

204   Horsham, West Sussex
Saturday, 19 November 1825
(a)   *BrG*, 28 November 1825, p. 3
(b)   *T*, 29 November 1825, p. 2
(c)   *CoC*, 29 November 1825, p. 4
(d)   Burstow (1911), p. 73

205   Brighton, East Sussex
Tuesday, 16 May 1826
(a)   *BrG*, 18 May 1826, p. 3

(b) *DCC*, 25 May 1826, p. 4

(c) *JOxJ*, 27 May 1826, p. 4

(d) *Brighton Herald, or Sussex, Surrey, Hampshire and Kent Advertiser* (Brighton, Sussex) 27 May 1826, p. 3

Note: the whereabouts of the Market Book in which the sale was recorded is unknown (letter of Mr E. M. Watkins, Area Librarian, Brighton Area Library, May 1978). There is no mention of a Hilton in the Quarter Session reports for Lewes on 15 July or 21 October 1826 (*BrH*, 22 July 1826, p. 3, and 25 October 1826, p. 3). This is probably the sale which P.T.A— (1939), p. 96, lists with a *purchase price* of 1s.

206   Windsor, Berkshire
Wednesday, 6 December 1826

(a) *CoC*, 12 December 1826, p. 4

(b) *JOxJ*, 16 December 1826, p. 4

Note: there appears to be no reference to this sale in the *Windsor and Eton Express* (letter of Ms Cathy Millar-Smith, staff reporter of the *Windsor, Slough and Eton Express*, Windsor, Berks, December 1979).

207   Nottingham, Nottinghamshire
c. 3–9 December 1826

(a) *CoC*, 12 December 1826, p. 4

(b) *JOxJ*, 16 December 1826, p. 4

(c) *O*, 24 December 1826, quoted in *O*, 26 December 1926, and secondarily in *NWG*, 15 January 1927, p. 2 (?)

208   Great Grimsby, Lincolnshire
1826

(a) reminiscence of an old inhabitant of Grimsby who had seen the sale, c. 1892, quoted in Anderson Bates, *A Gossip About Old Grimsby* (Great Grimsby, Lincs: Albert Gait, 1893), p. 68

209   York, Yorkshire
Thursday, 5 July 1827

(a) *YG*, 7 July 1827, p. 2

210   Buckland, Somerset
Thursday, 29 November 1827

(a) *DCC*, 6 December 1827, p. 4

(b) *T*, 8 December 1827, p. 2

211   Smithfield Market, London
1827

(a) P.T.A— (1939), p. 96

Note: *general* statement that Smithfield was a recognized centre for sales until 1827 or later, suggesting the existence of a sale in that year.

212 Hereford, Herefordshire
c. 1777—1876 (after case 76 and before the date of publication of the source)
(a) Nonagenarian [pseud.] (1876), p. 16
Note: this may be identical to case 104.

213 Somerset
c. 1823—31 (marriage 'some eight or ten years ago')
(a) *KBJ*, 14 February 1831, p. 3

214 Tunbridge, Kent
Monday, 2 June 1828
(a) *MJ*, 10 June 1828, p. 4
(b) ms. entry in West Kent Quarter Sessions Records, Midsummer, 1828. Cat. Mk. Q/SI W550 (Kent Archives Office) (extracts supplied by Mr Felix Hull, County Archivist, Kent Archives Office, April 1978)
(c) ms. addition to *pre-trial Calendar of Prisoners*, West Kent Quarter Sessions, Midsummer, 1828 (Kent Archives Office)
(d) *post-trial Calendar of Prisoners*, West Kent Quarter Sessions, Midsummer, 1828 (Kent Archives Office)
(e) *CoC*, 29 July 1828, p. 4

215 Edinburgh
Wednesday, 16 July 1828
(a) 'SALE OF A WIFE/A **full and particular Account of the Sale of a Woman, named Mary Mackintosh which took Place on Wednesday Evening,** the 16th of July, 1828, in the Grass Market of Edinburgh, accused by her Husband of being a notorious Drunkard; with the Particulars of the bloody Battle which took place afterwards', broadside, (Newcastle: W. Boag n.d.) (John Rylands University Library, Manchester)
Note: it is possible that this sale was fictitious and was localized temporally and spatially only in order to sell the broadside. The sale is not mentioned in either the *Scotsman* or the *Edinburgh Evening Courant* (letter of Mr Antony P. Shearman, City Librarian, Edinburgh Central Library, May 1978).

216 St Albans, Hertfordshire
c. 1828
(a) interview with Mr William Mileman, who witnessed the occurrence when aged about 7. *Hertfordshire Advertiser & Times* (St Albans, Herts), 3 September 1898, n.p. (letter of Mr D. W. Smith, editor, *Hertfordshire Advertiser*, St Albans, Herts, September 1979)

217 Ansty, Leicestershire
before 9 February 1829

(a)   *Stamford News* (Stamford, Lincs), before 9 February 1829, quoted in *T*, 9 February 1829, p. 4. (There is no reference to this in the *Stamford News*, according to Mr John Chambers, Stamford Central Library (letter of November 1979.)

Note: there also appears to be no reference to the sale in the *Lincoln, Rutland and Stamford Mercury* (letter of Miss J. Tasker, Lincoln Central Library, January 1980)

218   Boston, Lincolnshire
Saturday, 20 June 1829
(a)   *BG*, 23 June 1829, p. 3
(b)   *T*, 26 June 1829, p. 2
(c)   *LSM*, 26 June 1829, p. 3

219   general
before 25 September 1829
(a)   *LSM*, 25 September 1829 (cited in a letter from Mr K. Williams, April 1978)

220   Stamford, Lincolnshire
before 16 October 1829
(a)   summary by Thomas Hardy in his commonplace book, 'Facts: From Newspapers, Histories, Biographies and other chronicles — (mainly local)', from *DCC*, 16 October 1829, quoted in Winfield (1970), pp. 225–6

Note: there is no reference to this in the *Stamford News*, according to Mr John Chambers, Stamford Central Library (letter of November 1979). There also *appears* to be no reference in the *Lincoln, Rutland and Stamford Mercury* (letter of Miss J. Tasker, Lincoln Central Library, January 1980).

221   Hereford, Herefordshire
c. 1797–1876 ('a few years' after case 212 and before the date of publication of the source)
(a)   Nonagenarian (1876), p. 16
Note: this *may* be identical with case 104

222   Temple Meads Market, Bristol
Thursday, 4 February 1830
(a)   *BM*, 9 February 1830, p. 3 (letter of Mr G. Langley, County Reference Librarian, Avon Central Library, April 1978)

223   Cheltenham, Gloucestershire
Thursday, 18 March 1830
(a)   *Cheltenham Chronicle and Gloucestershire Advertiser* (Cheltenham, Glos), 25 March 1830), p. 3
(b)   *T*, 30 March 1830, p. 3

224   Ashby-de-la-Zouch, Leicestershire
Saturday, 12 June 1830

(a) *Leicester Chronicle, or Commercial and Agricultural Advertiser* (Leicester, Leics), 19 June 1830, p. 3
(b) *BG*, 29 June 1830, p. 3
225 Sheffield, West Riding, Yorkshire
Wednesday, 8 September 1830
(a) *Sheffield Independent and Yorkshire and Derbyshire Advertiser* (Sheffield, Yorks), 11 September 1830, p. 3
226 Horse Shoe Corner, Lancaster, Lancashire
c. 1823−6 (the author, born c. 1821, who witnessed the scene, describes himself as 'a little puny fellow', suggesting he was not under 2 or over 15 years old)
(a) Bond (1891), p. 4
227 O−,−
after 1830 (date of daughter's birth)
(a) W. N. R. Baron, 'Wife-Sales', *NQ*, series 13, vol. 151, 13 November 1926, p. 356
228 Curry Rivel, Somerset
Tuesday, 15 February 1831
(a) *KBJ*, 28 February 1831, p. 2
(b) *T*, 1 March 1831, p. 3
229 Stockport, Cheshire
c. Friday, 25 March 1831 (date of delivery specified in agreement)
(a) *Stockport Advertiser* (Stockport, Cheshire), 1 April 1831, p. 3
(b) *T*, 6 April 1831, p. 3
230 Bolton, Lancashire
Tuesday, 7 June 1831
(a) *Manchester Guardian* (Manchester, Lancs), 11 June 1831, p. 3
(b) *T*, 15 June 1831, p. 5
231 Smithfield Market, London
Monday, 20 February 1832
(a) evening newspaper (London), c. 20−25 February 1832, quoted in *T*, 25 February 1832, p. 6
Note: this piece incorporates a reference to the subject in *The Cabinet Lawyer.*
232 Cranbrook, Kent
Wednesday, 7 March 1832
(a) *Maid. Gaz.* 13 March 1832, p. 4
(b) *Kent Herald* (Canterbury, Kent), 15 March 1832, p. 3
(c) *G*, 17 March 1832, p. 4
233 Horncastle, Lincolnshire
c. 25−31 March 1832
(a) *LSM*, 6 April 1832, p. 3

234 Carlisle, Cumberland
Saturday, 7 April 1832
(a) broadside quoted in *Lancaster Herald* (Lancaster, Lancs),
21 April 1832, p. 117
(b) *T*, 26 April 1832, p. 4
(c) *T*, 27 April 1832, p. 4 (letter to the editor)
(d) *The Annual Register, or a View of the History, Politics, and
Literature, for the Year 1832*, vol. 74 (London: F.C. and J.
Rivington, 1833), pp. 58 − 9
(e) newspaper cited in Andrews (1892), pp. 203 − 5
Note: the broadside is said to have been 'hawked about the streets
of Lancaster', but the Lancaster Central Library has no copy
(letter of Mr E. H. Lowe, District Librarian, April 1978).

235 Stafford, Staffordshire
Saturday, — —1832
(a) newspaper (Wolverhampton, Staffs), 1832, quoted in
Hackwood (1974), p. 71

236 Norfolk
c. 1832
(a) told to Mr Cloudesley Brereton, Briningham House,
Melton Constable, Norfolk, by a friend of his father's, who
was a partial eyewitness to the proceeding. *NOW* (1924)
(b) J. W. Walker (1939), p. 496

237 Dorchester, Dorset
before 1833 (the date of the repeal of the Corn Laws, which was a
terminus post quem for some of the action of Hardy's plot)
(a) Hardy (1912b), pp. 7 − 13
Note: Hardy notes in his preface that the sale in *The Mayor of
Casterbridge* was based on an actual event in the history of the
real-life Casterbridge (Dorchester). See, however, Winfield's
(1970) discussion of his sources, which casts doubt on this
assertion.

238 Stockport, Cheshire
Monday, 11 March 1833
(a) *Blackburn Gazette and Lancashire and Yorkshire General
Advertiser* (Blackburn, Lancs), 20 March 1833, p. 5
(b) *T*, 25 March 1833, p. 2

239 Epping, Essex
Friday, 15 March 1833
(a) *O*, 18 March 1833, p. 4
(b) *T*, 18 March 1833, p. 4
(c) *EC*, 22 March 1833, p. 3
Note: (c) gives the husband's name as 'Stace' rather than 'Bruce'.
Mr John Booker, Senior Assistant Archivist, Essex Record Office,
reports: 'no petty sessions records for the Epping Division survive

for the date in question' (letter of April 1978).
240 Portman Market, London
Tuesday, 2 July 1833
(a)   *T*, 4 July 1833, p. 3
241 Lansdown and Bath, Somerset
Monday, 12 August and Friday 16 August 1833
(a)   *T*, 27 August 1833, p. 6
(b)   *BH*, 1833, quoted in K. Williams (1977), p. 50
242 Melksham, Wiltshire
Monday, 19 August 1833
(a)   *T*, 27 August 1833, p. 6
(b)   *BH*, 1833, quoted in K. Williams (1977), p. 50
(c)   ms. addition to *Calendar of Prisoners from the Marlborough Quarter Sessions, 'II/SUPPLEMENT for the Sessions'*, 15 October 1833 (letter of Mr Maurice G. Rathbone, Wiltshire Record Office, May 1978)
243 Falmouth, Cornwall
Thursday, 22 August 1833
(a)   *Falmouth Packet* (Falmouth, Corn.), c. 22−9 August 1833, quoted in *T*, 29 August 1833, p. 3
Note: there is no reference to this sale in the *West Briton* (letter of Mr Max Hodnett, editor of the *West Briton*, September 1979)
244 Glastonbury, Somerset
Wednesday, 16 October 1833
(a)   *Sherborne Mercury or Weekly Advertiser* (Sherborne, Dorset), c. 16−23 October 1833, quoted in *T*, 23 October 1833, p. 6
245 Whitechapel, London
c. 1833 ('such transfers of conjugal rights were frequent fifty years ago')
(a)   Samuel Carter Hall, *Retrospect of a Long Life: From 1815 to 1883*, 2 vols. (London: Richard Bentley & Son, 1883), vol. 1, pp. 43−4
246 Newark, Nottinghamshire
Wednesday, 12 February 1834
(a)   *LinC*, 14 February 1834, p. 3
(b)   *T*, 19 February 1834, p. 6
247 Birmingham
March, 1834
(a)   *Monthly Argus and Public Censor*, vol. 7, no. 3 (Birmingham), March 1834, p. 194
248 New Sneddon, Renfrewshire
Monday, 12 May 1834
(a)   *Paisley Advertiser* (Paisley Renf.), 17 May 1834, p. 4
(b)   *T*, 24 May 1834, p. 6

249 Holme-upon-Spalding Moor, East Riding, Yorkshire
Wednesday, 9 July 1834
(a)   *YCh*, 16 July 1834, p. 3
(b)   *T*, 18 July 1834, p. 4

250 Nottingham, Nottinghamshire
Saturday, 13 September 1834
(a)   *Nottingham and Newark Mercury: A Political, Commercial, Agricultural and Literary Journal* (Nottingham, Notts), 20 September 1834, p. 301.
(b)   *T*, 23 September 1834, p. 2

251 Birmingham
1834 (?) ((a) gives the date as 'about eighteen years ago', while (b) gives it as 1835)
(a)   Sc. [pseud.], 'Selling a Wife', *NQ*, series 1, vol. 8, 9 July 1853, p. 43
(b)   Chambers (1869), vol. 1, p. 487
(c)   Ann Monsarrat, *And the Bride wore . . .* (London: Gentry Books, 1973), p. 146

252 Much Wenlock, Shropshire
c. 1834 (case took place 'some sixty years ago')
(a)   Lady Catherine Milnes Gaskell, 'Old Wenlock and its Folklore', *The Nineteenth Century*, vol. 35, February 1894, p. 260

253 Bolton, Lancashire
Monday, 2 February 1835
(a)   *Bolton Chronicle* (Bolton, Lancs.), before 9 February 1835, cited in *O*, 9 February 1835, p. 3

254 St Austell, Cornwall
Friday, 20 March 1835
(a)   *WB*, 27 March 1835, p. 2
Note: there is no copy of the St Austell tollbook in the Cornwall Record Office, nor is the case mentioned in the Quarter Session Minute Book for June or October 1835 (letter of Mr Stephen Hobbs, Assistant Archivist, April, 1978).

255 Chinnock, Somerset
January 1836
(a)   *Sherborne, Dorchester and Taunton Journal* (Sherborne, Dorset), January 1836, quoted in *T*, 1 February 1836, p. 3

256 Barnsley, West Riding, Yorkshire
Wednesday, 30 March 1836
(a)   *HE*, 31 March 1836, p. 4
(b)   *T*, 4 April 1836, p. 5

257 Smithfield Market and Islington Market, London
Monday, 1 August 1836
(a)   *T*, 2 August 1836, p. 6

258 Bradford, West Riding, Yorkshire
 Saturday, 15 October 1836
 (a) *Bradford Observer* (Bradford, Yorks), 20 October 1836, p. 301
 (b) *HE*, 26 October 1836, p. 4
 (c) *T*, 2 November 1836, p. 5
 Note: (c) gives the name as 'Jogger' not 'Jeggar'.
259 Bradford, West Riding, Yorkshire
 Saturday, 28 January 1837
 (a) *HE*, c. 4–9 February 1837, quoted in *T*, 3 February 1837, p. 6
 (b) *T*, 9 February 1837, p. 5
260 Halifax (?), West Riding, Yorkshire
 Monday, 1 May 1837
 (a) *HE*, c. 1–8 May 1837, quoted in *T*, 8 May 1837, p. 3
261 ——, West Riding, Yorkshire
 c. 3 April – 28 June 1837 (the part of the year covered by the June Quarter Sessions)
 (a) S.R— (1853), p. 209
 (b) Roberts (1957), p. 146
 Note: (b) follows Andrews (1892), p. 206 in giving the prison sentence as *two* months. For another version, see Chambers (1869), vol. 1, pp. 487-8.
262 Whitehaven, Cumberland
 c. June – 8 July 1837
 (a) *Whitehaven Herald, and Cumberland, Westmorland, and Lancashire Advertiser* (Whitehaven, Cumb.), 8 July 1837, p. 3
 (b) *T*, 15 July 1837, p. 6
263 Wirksworth, Derbyshire
 Tuesday, 15 August 1837
 (a) *Derbyshire Courier; Chesterfield Gazette; and Derby, Ashborne etc. General County Advertiser* (Chesterfield, Derby), 19 August 1837, p. 3
 (b) *T*, 22 August 1837, p. 4
264 Walsall, Staffordshire
 Tuesday, 17 October 1837
 (a) *Wolverhampton Chronicle and General Advertiser for the Midland Counties* (Wolverhampton, Staffs) 25 October 1837, p. 3
 (b) *G*, 26 October 1837, p. 8
 (c) *T*, 28 October 1837, p. 7
 Note: Lawley (B), Hackwood (1974), p. 71, and Raven (1978), p. 62, give (a) as occurring in a newspaper of November 1837.

265   Bakewell, Derbyshire
       Monday, 18 June 1838
       (a)   *DeC* c. 18—22 June 1838, quoted in *T*, 22 June 1838, p. 7
266   Dulverton, Somerset
       before 10 November 1838
       (a)   *Plymouth and Devonport Weekly Journal and General
              Advertiser for Devon, Cornwall, Somerset*, etc.
              (Plymouth, Devon), before 10 November 1838, quoted in
              T, 10 November 1838, p. 3
       Note: this paper is unavailable from the Devon Record Office
       (letter of Mr P. A. Kennedy, County Archivist, April 1977) and
       from the West Devon Central Library. Mr J. R. Elliott, Area
       Librarian, reports no mention of the case in the *Plymouth,
       Devonport and Stonehouse Herald* (letter of September 1979).
267   Stourport, Worcestershire
       before 23 March 1839
       (a)   newspaper (Worcester, Worcs), before 23 March 1839,
              quoted in *OCC*, 23 March 1839, p. 4
268   Witney, Oxfordshire
       Thursday, 2 May 1839
       (a)   *JOxJ*, 4 May 1839, p. 3
269   Bradford, West Riding, Yorkshire
       Monday, 27 May 1839
       (a)   Rayner (1881), p. 87, supposedly citing *LM*, 1 June 1839
270   Rotherham, West Riding, Yorkshire
       Monday 7 October (?) 1839
       (a)   *Rotherham Independent* (Rotherham, Yorks), before 9
              October 1839, quoted in *T*, 9 October 1839, p. 7
       (b)   *JOxJ*, 12 October 1839
271   Boston, Lincolnshire
       c. 1832—46 (as Mary Anne Townsley, born c. 1826, who
       witnessed the sale, is described as a 'schoolgirl', it seems unlikely
       that she was younger than 6 or older than 20)
       (a)   *NWG*, 13 November 1926, p. 2
272   York, Yorkshire
       c. 1839 (the sale took place 'about fifty-four years ago')
       (a)   William Camidge, *Ye Old Streets of Pavemente* (York,
              Yorks: *Yorkshire Gazette* c. 1893), p. 18
273   Hadleigh, Suffolk
       before 1840
       (a)   ms. entry in diary of Rev. Henry Bary Knox, 1841 (Ipswich
              and Suffolk Record Office), quoted in a letter of Mr W. A.
              B. Jones, February 1980
       (b)   ms. entry in diary of Rev. H. B. Knox, 7 October 1842

(Ipswich and Suffolk Record Office), quoted in a letter of Mr W. A. B. Jones, February 1980

Note: the diary also notes (13 October 1842): 'called on Frost at Friars — found only a middle aged woman of the name of Gardiner who keeps house for Mr. Frost — There appeared to be something suspicious about her. They seldom come to Ch. Mr. F is at times out of His mind' and (15 July, 1843): 'Married John Frost of Friars to Miss Margaret Gardiner' (Ipswich and Suffolk Record Office), quoted in a letter of Mr W. A. B. Jones, February 1980. Mr Jones adds: 'I have seen the Register of Burials in Hadleigh Cemetery, and found that Frost was buried there on 21 December 1877, and Margaret joined him in the same grave on 1 March 1878. He was aged 81 and she was 77 . . . . The Church accounts show that Knox occasionally helped the wife who had been sold from the Communion alms given in Church, and some time after Secker had died, she was admitted to an alms house, and ended her days in peace.' The Bury St Edmunds Record Office, however, gives the date of a John Frost's burial as 7 January 1852 (aged 82) (notes of Mrs Roger Walker).

274   Stourbridge, Worcestershire
      Saturday, 5 December 1840
      (a)   *HJ*, 9 December 1840, p. 3
      (b)   *T*, 11 December 1840, p. 7

275   Gloucester, Gloucestershire
      Saturday, —, c. 1841
      (a)   F.G.B—, 'Wife Sale', *NQ*, series 3, vol. 4, 24 October 1863, p. 324
      Note: Mr G. R. Hiatt, Divisional Librarian, Gloucester Central Library, reports that the *Gloucester Journal* apparently has no reference to this sale (letter of June 1978).

276   Prussia Gardens, Norwich, Norfolk
      Saturday, 7 May 1842
      (a)   *NC*, 14 May 1842, p. 2

277   Louth, Lincolnshire
      Wednesday, 9 November 1842
      (a)   *LSM*, 11 November 1842, p. 2
      Note: P. Smith (1957), p. 548, incorrectly gives the date of the report as October.

278   Boston, Lincolnshire
      Wednesday, 16 November 1842
      (a)   *LSM*, 18 November 1842, p. 3

279   Louth, Lincolnshire
      Wednesday, 30 November 1842
      (a)   *LSM*, 9 December 1842, p. 4

Note: P. Smith (1957), p. 548, gives the magistrate's name as 'Frought' and identifies him as mayor. As Smith's version of the quote differs slightly in wording, the possible existence of another source is suggested.

280   Okehampton, Devon
      before 1843 (date of wife's death)
      (a)   Baring-Gould (1926), pp. 59—60

281   Nottingham, Nottinghamshire
      Saturday, 23 December 1843
      (a)   *Nottingham Journal* (Nottingham, Notts) 29 December 1843, p. 3
      (b)   *T*, 30 December 1843, p. 7

282   Charlbury, Oxfordshire
      1843
      (a)   newspaper (Charlbury, Oxon.), August 1900, n.p. (Miller Library, Colby College, Waterville, Maine, USA)

283   Horsham, Sussex
      c. 1844
      (a)   Burstow (1911), pp. 73—4

284   encampment, Woodhead Tunnel, Cheshire
      June—July 1845
      (a)   Coleman (1968), pp. 119—20
      (b)   Coleman (1968), pp. 119—20
      (c)   Thomas Nicholson, *Strictures on a Pamphlet published at the request of the Manchester Statistical Society*, quoted in Coleman (1968), p. 188
      Note: some confusion in the accounts as to whether lending or selling was involved.

285   Anon
      c. 1845
      (a)   *Birmingham Daily Mail* (Birmingham), 29 April 1871, p. 4

286   Callington, Cornwall
      Wednesday, 7 January 1846
      (a)   *WB*, 16 January 1846, p. 2

287   Horse Shoe Corner, Lancaster, Lancashire
      c. 1839—53 ('some sixteen years' after case 226)
      (a)   Bond (1891), p. 4

288   B—, —
      before 20 March 1847
      (a)   G— (1847), p. 223

289   Sheffield, West Riding, Yorkshire
      1847
      (a)   S. H. Ward, correspondence, *Hertfordshire Countryside*, (Letchworth, Herts), vol. 12, Summer 1957, p. 32

290 Mansfield, Nottinghamshire
before 7 October 1848
(a) *Nottingham Review and General Advertiser for the Midland Counties* (Nottingham, Notts), before 7 October 1848, quoted in *T*, 7 October 1848, p. 8

291 Truro, Cornwall
Monday, 20 November 1848
(a) *WB*, 24 November 1848, quoted in R. M. Barton, *Life in Cornwall in the Mid Nineteenth Century* (Truro: D. Bradford Barton, 1971), pp. 165−6

292 Bilston, Staffordshire
1848
(a) lady correspondent who had witnessed the scene, Antiquarian Column, cited in Lawley (B)

293 Horton, West Riding, Yorkshire
before 8 November 1849
(a) *Evening Standard* (London), 8 November 1849, cited in William Kent, 'Wife-Selling in 19th Century', *NQ*, vol. 196, 31 March 1951, p. 152

294 Goole, West Riding, Yorkshire
Wednesday, 15 December 1849
(a) *DeC*, (c. 5−15 December 1849), quoted in *T*, 15 December 1849, p. 7
(b) *Manx Sun* (Douglas, Isle of Man), 22 December 1849, p. 6

295 Kingston, Somerset
c. 1840−58 (Mrs J. C. Dening, born 1838, who witnessed the sale 'in her childhood days' could not have been under 2 or over 20 years old at the time)
(a) *Somerset Gazette*, 30 January 1937, p. 11 (obituary)

296 Horwich End, Derbyshire
before 22 December 1850
(a) *Stockport Mercury* (Stockport, Cheshire), before 22 December 1850, quoted in *ST*, 22 December 1850, p. 5

297 Knighton, Radnorshire
Thursday, 29 April 1851
(a) *HT*, 1 March 1851, p. 8

298 Yorkshire
c. 1851 ('about thirty years ago')
(a) A.J.M— (1881), p. 133

299 Nottingham, Nottinghamshire
Sunday, 18 April 1852
(a) John B. Riley, 'Wife Sold in Nottingham Market', Local Notes and Queries, *NWG*, 12 January 1924, p. 2

300 Nottingham, Nottinghamshire
Wednesday, 28 April 1852

(a)   *NDB*, (1884), p. 483

(b)   *NWG*, 11 September 1926 (?), quoted in A. L. Cox, 'Wife-Sales', *NQ*, series 13, vol. 151, 27 November 1926, p. 393

Note: Mr Stephen J. Best, Nottinghamshire County Library, notes: 'The Nottingham press of 1852 seems to have ignored the incident altogether' (letter of April 1978).

301   Burton-on-Trent, Staffordshire
1852
(a)   J. W. Walker (1939), p. 496

302   Bodmin, Cornwall
before 27 July 1853
(a)   *WB*, 5 August 1853, p. 5

303   Tipton, Staffordshire
1853
(a)   interview of Mr Roy Palmer with Mr Tom Langley (aged 63; his grandfather had seen the sale) on 17 April 1970; R. Palmer (1974), p. 198

304   Knighton, Radnorshire
Saturday, 29 April 1854
(a)   *HT*, 6 May 1854, p. 9

305   Nottingham, Nottinghamshire
Saturday, 25 August 1855
(a)   *NDB* (1884), p. 494
Note: Mr Stephen J. Best, Nottinghamshire County Library, notes that the Nottingham press seems to have ignored this sale (letter of April 1978).

306   Derby, Derbyshire
1855
(a)   *DM* (1899)

307   Chipping Norton, Oxfordshire
1855
(a)   information from Mr Hambidge, a partial eyewitness; told by Mrs Groves (his daughter) to Dr Katharine M. Briggs, Briggs (1974), pp. 116–17
(b)   information from Mrs Groves (presumably related by Mr Hambidge), Shipton-under-Wychwood, Oxon; *ODFS* (1951), p. 14

308   general
c. 1855–June/July 1856
(a)   *Daily Telegraph and Courier*, c. 29 June 1855 – July 1856 (cited in a letter from Mr Keith Williams, April 1978)

309   Worcester, Worcestershire
Friday, 3 July 1857
(a)   *Worcester Chronicle* (Worcester, Worcs), 22 July 1857, p. 2
(b)   *HJ*, 29 July 1857, p. 3

310   Shearbridge/Little Horton, West Riding, Yorkshire
      Monday, 22 November 1858
      (a)   *LSM*, 26 November 1858, p. 3
      (b)   *Manchester Guardian*, 23 November 1858, p. 2
      (c)   newspaper cited by Rayner (1881), p. 135
      (d)   *Punch*, 4 December 1858, p. 225 (tongue-in-cheek account)
311   Dudley, Staffordshire
      Tuesday, 23 August 1859
      (a)   *DT*, 25 August 1859, p. 3
      (b)   *The Record* (London), 26 August 1859, p. 4
      (c)   newspaper cited by K.P.D.E—, 'Wife Selling', *NQ*, series 2,
             vol. 8, 24 September 1859, p. 258
312   Leeds, West Riding, Yorkshire
      before 10 September 1859
      (a)   based on an article by J. R. Green in *OCC*, 10 September
             1859, p. 7 Green (1901), p. 119
313   North Riding, Yorkshire
      January—February 1860
      (a)   account taken down about a fortnight after the events by
             A.J.M— February 1860. A.J.M—, 'Wife-Selling', *NQ*,
             series 6, vol. 5, 4 February 1882, p. 98
314   Selby, West Riding, Yorkshire
      December 1862
      (a)   Andrews (1880), p. 4
315   Cardiff, Glamorganshire
      Monday, 16 February 1863
      (a)   *Cardiff and Merthyr Guardian* (Cardiff, Glam.), 28
             February 1863, p. 5 (letter of Mr G. A. C. Dart, County
             Librarian, South Glamorgan County Library, October
             1979)
316   Merthyr Tydfil, Glamorganshire
      c. 8—14 March 1863
      (a)   *LM*, 16 March 1863, p. 3
      (b)   *LSM*, 27 March 1863, p. 7
317   General
      before 20 June 1863
      (a)   K.P.D.E— (1863), p. 486
      Note: general reference: 'I have conversed with more than one
      person who has seen a husband offer his wife for sale in a public
      street, with a halter round her neck.'
318   Blackburn, Lancashire
      c. 1865
      (a)   recorded by Mr T. W. Thompson from Taimi Boswell
             (probably a gypsy) of Oswaldtwistle, Lancashire, 1

October 1915. T. W. Thompson (1915)

Note: possibly fictitious.

319 Manchester, Lancashire
before 14 July 1866
(a)   *The Athenaeum* (London), before 14 July 1866, quoted in
Jannoc (1866), p. 29

Note: general reference.

320 Chagford, Devon
before 1868 (the date at which the Rev. W. H. Thornton became
the incumbent of the living)
(a)   Thornton (1906), pp. 54–5

321 Blackburn, Lancashire
Saturday, 11 January 1868
(a)   *Blackburn Standard* (Blackburn, Lancs), c. 11–18 January
1868, quoted in *DT* 18 January 1868, and secondarily in W.
Carew Hazlitt, *Faiths and Folklore of the British Isles*, 2
vols., rpt. of 2nd edn. (New York: Benjamin Blom, 1965
[1905]), vol. 2, p. 635

322 Dittisham (?), Devon (home of the husband and wife)
before 3 March 1869
(a)   *T*, 3 March 1869, p. 11

323 Tipton, Staffordshire
Tuesday, 1 June 1869
(a)   *Birmingham Daily Gazette* (Birmingham), 5 June 1869, p. 5

324 Coventry, Warwickshire
c. 1866–73
(a)   Rev. F. J. Odell, 'Wife-Sales', *NQ*, series 13, vol. 151, 6
November 1926, p. 340

325 Bury, Lancashire
c. 5–11 November 1870
(a)   *Bury Times* (Bury, Lancs), 12 November 1870, p. 5 (letter
of Reference Librarian, Department of Leisure Services,
Bury, Lancs, October 1979)

Note: the editorial note in the *East Anglian Miscellany*, no. 10,874
(1942), p. 29, saying that the husband was burned in effigy
appears to be incorrect.

326 Preston, Lancashire
Monday, 21 November 1870
(a)   *LG*, 26 November 1870, p. 8

327 Witney, Oxfordshire
c. 1840–1900
(a)   recorded by Angeline Parker from an old man in the Long
Hanborough/Barnard Gate area of Oxon., before 1913.
Angeline Parker, 'Oxfordshire Village Folklore (1840–
1900)', *Folklore*, vol. 24, March 1913, p. 76

328   Exeter, Devon
       before 6 July 1872
       (a)   newspaper, 6 July 1872, quoted in H. J. Fennell, 'Selling a
              Wife', *NQ*, series 4, vol. 10, 5 October 1872, p. 271
329   Hull, East Riding, Yorkshire
       before 15 March 1872
       (a)   *Eastern Morning News* (Hull, Yorks), 16 March 1872, p. 4
       (b)   *LSM*, 22 March 1872, p. 4
       Note: K.P.D.E—, 'Selling a Wife', *NQ*, series 4, vol. 9, 13 April
       1872, p. 297, incorrectly gives (b)'s date as 21 March.
330   London
       before 20 May 1872
       (a)   *DT*, 20 May 1872, p. 2
       Note: Bates (1872), p. 469, appears to quote this incorrectly.
331   General
       before 1873
       (a)   Harland (1973), p. 177
332   Haslington, Lancashire
       before 1873
       (a)   Harland (1973), p. 177
333   Belper, Derbyshire
       Saturday, 23 August 1873
       (a)   newspaper (Derbyshire), 29 August 1873, quoted in
              Andrews (1880), pp. 4—5
       Note: see case 334.
334   Devon
       September 1873
       (a)   *Western Morning Star*, 9 March 1894, quoted in Hewett
              (1973), pp. 129—30
       Note: there is a strong possibility that this is a confused reference
       to case 333, as the occurrences are strikingly similar. It seems less
       likely that 333 derived from this case.
335   Much or Little Wenlock (?), Shropshire (bought at 'Wenlock Fair')
       before 1875
       (a)   Charles F. Peskin, 'Memories of Old Coalbrookdale',
              Transactions of the Caradoc and Severn Valley Field Club,
              vol. 11, no. 3 1941, p. 218
336   Swaffham Bulbeck, Cambridgeshire
       before 1876, November (derived from Porter (1974), p. 28 — i.e.,
       in the middle of the last century)
       (a)   Dr Charles Lucas, 'A Wife Sold by Auction', ms. 1933, UL
              MS. Add 7515, Cambridge University Library
337   Crowle, Lincolnshire
       before 15 January 1877

(a)   *SDT*, 15 January 1877, p.3
(b)   *LinC*, 19 January 1887, p. 7
(c)   *SDT*, 23 January 1877, p. 3 (letter?)
(d)   *T*, 24 January 1877, p. 5
Note: husband denied a sale, claiming the money was a settlement for not taking legal action.

338   Bungay, Suffolk
c. 1877—81, 14 May (the former, the date of the flood in Waveney Valley (Baldry, 1976, p. 113), the latter, that of the sharp winter in which Old Bill died (Baldry, 1976, p. 226); the book is a chronological reminiscence)
(a)   Baldry (1976), pp. 146—8

339   Near Wrexham, Cheshire
before June 1879
(a)   Landwor (1880), p. 245

340   Dunmow, Essex
1880
(a)   Wright (1928), pp. 26—7

341   Much Wenlock (?), Shropshire (subsequent home of the wife)
before 1881
(a)   Burne (1973—74), vol. 1, p. 295

342   Sheffield, West Riding, Yorkshire
January 1881
(a)   Anon., 'Wife selling', *NQ*, series 6, vol. 3, 18 June 1881, p. 487 supposedly quoting *LM*, 26 May 1881
Note: this may be identical with case 344: Mr L. J. Feiweles, Chief Librarian, Wakefield Central Library, reports that he could find no reference to wife-selling in the relevant issue (letter of May 1977).

343   Ripon, West Riding, Yorkshire
before 7 July 1881
(a)   newspaper, 7 July 1881, cited in A.J.M— (1881), p. 133
Note: this appears to be the case mentioned in Hole (1970), p. 8. However, Miss Hole has written that she thinks the case was in London and that she heard of it from Beatrice Tunstall, who gave a course of lectures (letter of April 1977). Miss Hole also notes that later writers on Cheshire have mistakenly quoted her as saying the County Court case took place there. This case appears to be the Ripon sale mentioned in P.T.A— (1939), p. 96, where the purchase price is incorrectly given as £25.

344   General
before 1882
(a)   Briffault (1927), vol. 2, note p. 223
Note: this may be identical with case 342.

345 Alfreton, Derbyshire
Saturday, 29 April 1882
(a)   *South Wales Daily News* (Cardiff, Glam.), 2 May 1882, p. 3
Note: this appears to be the 1882 'Alfreton' sale at which a wife was sold for 4d. P.T.A— (1939), p. 96

346 Belfast, Co. Antrim
before 20 October 1882
(a)   *Pall Mall Gazette* (London), 20 October 1882, p. 11

347 Merrivale Bridge, Devon
Thursday, before 1882 — 85
(a)   S. Baring-Gould, *Further Reminiscences: 1864 — 1894* (New York: E. P. Dutton, 1925), p. 145
(b)   Baring-Gould (1926), pp. 60 — 1

348 York, Yorkshire
April—May ('within a few weeks') and Thursday, 8 May 1884
(a)   *YH*, 9 May 1884, p. 3
(b)   *YG*, 10 May 1884, p. 6
Note: (a) appears to be the case quoted in A.J.M—, 'Wife-Selling', *NQ*, series 6, vol. 9, 7 June 1884, p. 446.

349 Sheffield, West Riding, Yorkshire
before 13 July 1887
(a)   Andrews (1892), p. 207
Note: *GT* (1903), p. 1, apparently misquotes the agreement.

350 Wakefield, West Riding, Yorkshire
June 1887
(a)   *Wellington Journal and Shrewsbury News* (Wellington, Salop), 6 June 1891, p. 3
Note: this is probably the 1887 Wakefield case in which a wife was sold for 10s. P.T.A— (1939), p. 96. This may be the 1887 case mentioned in Ashton (1888), p. 1.

351 Paddock (?), West Riding, Yorkshire (home of wife and purchaser)
before 1888
(a)   T. Harrison, 'Wife sales', *Yorkshire Folk-Lore Journal* (Bingley, Yorks), p. 87

352 Barnsley, West Riding, Yorkshire
before 1888 (date of court case)
(a)   J. W. Walker (1939), p. 496

353 Liverpool
Friday, 31 October 1890
(a)   newspaper, 6 November 1890, n.p. (Miller Library, Colby College, Waterville, Maine, USA)

354 Sheffield, West Riding, Yorkshire

Monday, 11 December 1893
(a)   *DM* (1899)
(b)   *GT* (1903), p. 1

355   Croydon, Surrey
        Sunday, 11 March 1894
        (a)   *HJ*, 17 March 1894, p. 6
        Note: there is no report of this sale in the *Croydon Chronicle* or the *Croydon Advertiser*, according to Mr A. O. Meakin, Chief Librarian, Croydon Central Library (letter of May 1978).

356   Morcombelake (?), Dorset (subsequent home of wife)
        before 1896
        (a)   Sherren (1902), p. 20
        Note: Udal suggests that this might be the same as case 375.

357   Leeds, West Riding, Yorkshire
        before 1896
        (a)   P.T.A— (1939), p. 96

358   Sheffield, West Riding, Yorkshire
        before 1896
        (a)   P.T.A.— (1939), p. 96

359   New Conisborough, West Riding, Yorkshire
        Saturday, 28 March 1896
        (a)   *DM* (1899)
        Note: the element of purchase may be lacking here. This appears to be the 1896 sale of a wife and four children at Doncaster referred to by P.T.A— (1939), p. 96. *GT*, (1903), p. 1, misspells Child's name.

360   Chichester, West Sussex
        spring 1898
        (a)   Thornton (1906), p. 55

361   Yapton, West Sussex
        autumn, 1898
        (a)   newspaper, quoted in *Sussex County Magazine* (Lewes, Sussex) June 1927, p. 336

362   Irthlingborough, Northamptonshire
        c. 5—11 March 1899
        (a)   *Worcester Journal* (Worcester, Worcs), 13 March 1899 (Miller Library, Colby College, Waterville, Maine, USA)
        (b)   *GT* (1903), pp. 1—2
        Note: neither the *Northampton Chronicle* nor the *Herald* makes reference to this sale (letter of Mr P. I. King, Chief Archivist, Northamptonshire Record Office, April 1978).

363   Leeds, West Riding, Yorkshire
        before 1900
        (a)   *GT* (1903), p. 1

364 Cradley, Staffordshire (?) (follows a description of the female chain-workers of this area)
before 25 April 1901
(a)   *Chronicle*, 25 April 1901 (Miller Library, Colby College, Waterville, Maine, USA)

365 Stockport, Cheshire
before 1900−3 (after case 363 and before the article's date of publication)
(a)   *GT* (1903), p. 1

366 Devonport, Devon (?) (either the heading or the end to a previous report)
1901
(a)   newspaper (1901) (Miller Library, Colby College, Waterville, Maine, USA)

367 London
before 16 November 1903
(a)   *GT* (1903), p. 1

368 anon
before 1904
(a)   reminiscence by 'Veritas', the granddaughter of the wife sold. 'Veritas' [pseud.], 'In Former Days', *Mothers' Union Journal*, no. 65, January 1904, p. 10 (letter of Mrs Faye Roberts, November 1978)

369 Biddulph, Staffordshire
before 11 January 1904
(a)   newspaper, 12 January 1904, n.p. (Miller Library, Colby College, Waterville, Maine, USA)

370 Great Torrington, Devon
before March 1906
(a)   recorded by Rev. W. H. Thornton from John Badger (an old poacher and fisherman), March 1906. Thornton (1906), p. 54

371 North Devon
before 1906
(a)   statement by Mr Roberts (clerk) of Wolborough, Devon, who had it from his father. Thornton (1906), p. 55
Note: general reference to several sales.

372 Brough, Westmorland
before 1915 (?) (date of the recording of case 318, which directly precedes this)
(a)   recorded by Mr T. W. Thompson from Johnny Smith, brother of the seller, after September 1915 (?); T. W. Thompson (1915)
Note: possibly fictitious.

373   Winster (?), Derbyshire (subsequent home of wife and purchaser)
       before 1918
       (a)   personal communication to author from Mrs Roger Walker
              (24 July 1976), who had it from Mr Laurence Bentall
374   Southend, Argyll
       before 1921
       (a)   Wright (1928), pp. 26−7
       Note: husband persuaded man to sign document agreeing to take
       over wife and look after her.
375   West Dorset
       before 1922 (original date of publication of Udal's book)
       (a)   Udal (1970), p. 197
       Note: Udal suggests that this might be the same as case 356.
376   Rothamsted (?), near Harpenden, Hertfordshire (site where
       husband worked)
       before 1922
       (a)   information gathered from a co-worker of the husband's,
              cited in Edwin Grey, *Rothamstead Experimental Station:
              Reminiscences, Tales, and Anecdotes of the Laboratories,
              Staff and Experimental Fields, 1872−1922* pp. 143−4
377   Newcastle, Northumberland
       before 1925
       (a)   Wright (1928), pp. 26−7
       Note: man signed an agreement to take over 'with all appur-
       tenances' the wife of another man.
378   Devon
       before 1927
       (a)   Wright (1928), pp. 26−7
379   Leeds, West Riding, Yorkshire
       before 1927
       (a)   Wright (1928), pp. 26−7
380   Blackwood, Monmouthshire
       before May 1928
       (a)   Wright (1928), pp. 26−7
       Note: there is no reference to the proceedings in the 'relevant
       Petty Division [records] for 1928' (letter of Mr W. H. Baker,
       County Archivist, Gwent Record Office, April 1978).
381   Northumberland
       September 1972
       (a)   Porter (1974), p. 29
382   Mottram, Cheshire
       n.d.
       (a)   Haworth (1952), p. 92
       Note: general mention of the practice here.

383 Helston and Truro, Cornwall
n.d.
(a) letter to Mr Tony Deane from a correspondent (aged 79) signing himself 'old Ex-Cornish Rabbit Trapper and horse-braker [*sic*]', who said that he had heard stories going back to the time of his great-grandmother from his mother, December 1967, pp. 5 — 9 (photocopy supplied by Mr Tony Deane, May 1977)
Note: almost certainly fictitious, due to internal inconsistencies. Mr Deane noted: 'The 'Rabbit-Trapper' wrote to me . . . replying to my appeal in the *Western Morning News* for Cornish folklore survivals; at first I feared a hoax, but exhaustive enquiries failed to confirm the suspicion and I am now quite satisfied of its validity' (letter of May 1977).

384 Spalding, Lincolnshire
n.d.
(a) *Lincolnshire Free Press* (Spalding, Lincs), 4 September 1956

385 Bilston, Staffordshire (?) (identified as 'A Bilston Ballad')
n.d.
(a) 'Sally Lett, or, A Wife For Sale', quoted in Lawley (B)
Note: the song may have been based on an actual sale.

386 Warwickshire
n.d.
(a) Bloom (1921), p. 47
(b) Bloom (1930), pp. 53 — 4
Note: general accounts.

387 Sheffield, West Riding, Yorkshire
n.d.
(a) Leader (1901), p. 42

Notes

Bibliographical details of all works and journals cited in abbreviated form will be found in the Select Bibliography.

Numbers in bold type denote cases listed in the Appendix.

CHAPTER 1: A POPULAR INSTITUTION

1   Hardy (1912b), pp. 9–10; ibid., p. 8.
2   *Africa*: in addition to the widespread practice of brideprice, wives were sold in Ethiopia – Wood (1869), vol. 1, p. 174; *China*: ibid., vol. 1, p. 106; *Hungary*: M. Kowalewsky. 'Marriage Among the Early Slavs', *Folk-Lore*, vol. 1, Kraus reprint (Neudelen, Liechtenstein: Kraus Reprint, 1969 [1890]), p. 478.
3   D'Archenholtz (1789), vol. 2, p. 33; Pillet (1815), p. 300.
4   D'Archenholtz (1789), vol. 2, p. 33; Pillet (1815), p. 299.
5   P.T.A— (1939), p. 96.
6   Hole (1961), p. 363; Sherren (1902), p. 20 (see also Udal, 1970, pp. 197–8); Jannoc (1866), p. 29; P.T.A— (1939), p. 95; A. R. Wright (1928), pp. 26–7.
7   Hackwood (1974), p. 73; Palmer and Raven (1976), p. 26; Raven (1978), pp. 64–5.
8   Kenny (1929), p. 495.
9   *navvies*: Coleman (1968), p. 188. *knife-grinders*: DM (1899), p. 7.
10 G. Williams (1897), p. 474, relates this to slave sales.
11 Raven (1978), p. 62.
12 *JOx*], 31 December 1808, p. 1.
13 *attacking Hardy*: Winfield (1970), p. 224 and note; *correspondent*: G.L.B— (1850), p. 217. *questions*: G.L.B— (1850), p. 217; P.T.A— (1938), p. 314, and (1939), p. 96. *claims as Hardy's source*: Winfield (1970), p. 225, and note 4; H. L. Scudder, 'Selling a Wife', *NQ*, ser. 15, vol. 188, 24 March 1945, pp. 123–4; J. R. Moore, 'Two Notes on Thomas Hardy', *Nineteenth Century Fiction* (Berkeley, Calif.) vol. 5, no. 2, September 1950, pp. 159–63; J. T. McCullen, Jr, 'Henchard's Sale of Susan in *The Mayor of Casterbridge*', *English Language Notes* (Boulder, Colo.: University of Colorado), vol. 2, no. 3, March 1965, pp. 217–18.

14 Place (1972), p. 15. [William Thackeray], 'Half a Crown's Worth of Cheap Knowledge', *Fraser's Magazine for Town and Country* (London), vol. 17, no. 99, March 1838, p. 280 (the author of this piece is identified as Thackeray in James (1974), p. 1).

15 *historians*: E. P. Thompson (1972); Thomas (1971); *folklorists*: Judge (1979); Cawte (1978); Trefor M. Owen, 'A Breconshire Marriage Custom', *Folklore* (London), vol. 72, June 1961, pp. 372−84. *anthropologists*: (witchcraft) Macfarlane (1971); (land tenure) Macfarlane (1977); (domestic relations) Macfarlane (1970).

16 Brand (1890−93), vol. 2, pp. 70−2; E. M. Wright (1913), pp. 267−9; Hole (1961), pp. 174−5.

17 Tongue (1965), pp. 148−9; *cf.* legitimization of children 'under the apron string' at the time of marriage, F. H. Brett, 'Smock Marriages', *NQ* series 1, vol. 7, 19 February 1853, pp. 191−2, and 'Scotus' [pseud.], 'Smock Marriages', *NQ*, series 1, vol. 7, 30 April 1853, p. 349.

18 Keith Thomas, 'Rule and Misrule in the Schools of Early Modern England', the Stenton Lecture, 1975 (Reading, Berks: University of Reading, 1976); Brand (1890−93), vol. 1, pp. 441−54; Hole (1941), p. 39, (1975), pp. 34−5, and (1976), pp. 25−6.

19 *rough music*: Menefee (1977), pp. 797−888; E. P. Thompson (1972); Hole (1961), pp. 287−9. *mock punishments*: Menefee (1977), pp. 889−1012; E. P. Thompson (1972); Hole (1961), p. 288. *chaffing*: Menefee (1977), pp. 767−96.

20 *mummers*: Brand (1890−93), vol. 1, pp. 461−6; Hole (1975), p. 45; Sir E. K. Chambers, *The English Folk-Play* (Oxford: Oxford University Press, 1969 [1933]). *plough-jaggers*: Rudkin (1973), pp. 42−3, 49; Hole (1975), p. 23, and (1976), pp. 157−8. *soulers*: Brand (1890−93), vol. 1, pp. 392−5; Hole (1975), pp. 98−9, and (1976), pp. 187−8. *carollers*: Brand (1890−93), vol. 1, p. 474; Hole (1976), pp. 46−7, and 100−2. See generally Cawte (1978).

21 *winding yarn*: Menefee (1974), pp. 289−326; Banks (1941), pp. 141−3. *'sowing' hempseed*: Menefee (1974), pp. 64−140; A. R. Wright and T. E. Lones, *British Calendar Customs*, vol. 3, *England* (London: William Glaisher, 1940), pp. 12−16; Banks (1941), pp. 128−39; Hole (1961), p. 189. *baking a 'dumb cake'*: Hole (1961), pp. 143−4. *washing the sark*: Menefee (1974), pp. 204−77; Banks (1941), pp. 139−41.

22 *barring the way*: Baker (1977), pp. 105−6; Hole (1961), pp. 32−3. *flinging the stocking*: Brand (1890−93), vol. 2, pp. 170−3; Hole (1961), p. 323; Baker (1977), p. 125. *racing for the garter*: Hole (1961), p. 170; Baker (1974), pp. 142−3, and (1977), pp. 107−10.

23 Menefee (1977), pp. 586−686; Jeaffreson (1872), vol. 2, pp. 93−4; Andrews (1975), pp. 186−90; G. S. Tyack, *Lore and Legend of the English Church* (London: William Andrews, 1899), pp. 186−7; Earle (1898), pp. 53−60; Hole (1961), pp. 311−12; Baker (1977), pp. 46−7. This is similar to the custom of marrying a felon to save his life; see Andrews (1975), pp. 191−4.

24 Tongue (1965), pp. 178−9; R. W. Patten, 'Tatworth Candle Auction', *Folklore* (London), vol. 81, Summer 1970, pp. 132−5, and 'Chedzoy Candle Auction', ibid., vol. 82, Spring, 1971, pp. 60−1; *WFP*, 4 December 1780, p. 3; ibid., 25 February 1787, p. 1; *JOxJ*, 2 February 1754, p. 4.

25 Menefee (1977), pp. 687−766; R. U. Sayce, 'The One-Night House, and Its Distribution', *Folklore* (London), vol. 53, September 1942, pp. 161−3, and 'Popular Enclosures and the One-Night House', *Montgomeryshire Collection*

(Welshpool, Mont.), vol. 47, part 2, 1942, pp. 109−20; Ann R. Everton, 'Built in a Night . . .', *The Conveyancer and Property Lawyer* (London), n.s. vol. 35, 1971, pp. 249−54; 'Ty un Nos', ibid., n.s. vol. 36, 1972, pp. 241−4, and 'With Smoke Ascending . . .', ibid., n.s. vol. 39, 1975, pp. 426−9.

26 Hole (1940), p. 54, and (1961), pp. 83−5; Puckle (1926), pp. 122−3; 'Establishing a Right of Way by Carrying a Corpse over Ground', *Oxfordshire and District Folklore Society Annual Record* (Oxford), no. 2, 1950, p. 13.

27 Macfarlane (1971), pp. 103−9; C. L'Estrange Ewen, *Witchcraft and Demonianism* (London: Frederick Muller, 1970 [1933]), pp. 105−7; Thomas (1971), pp. 543−4; Hole (1940), pp. 167−8, and (1977), pp. 133−4; Briggs (1971), part B, vol. 2, pp. 720, 723−5 and 737−40.

28 'Crossing the Line': Hone (1878a), vol. 2, pp. 697−8; Horace Beck, *Folklore and the Sea* (Middletown, Conn.: Wesleyan Univ. Press, 1973), pp. 116−19; Harry Miller Lyndenberg, *Crossing the Line: Tales of the Ceremony During Four Centuries* (New York: New York Public Library, 1957); Henning Henningsen, *Crossing the Equator: Sailors' Baptisms and Other Initiation Rites* (Copenhagen: Munksgaard, 1961). *agricultural labourers*: George Ewart Evans, *The Horse in the Furrow* (London: Faber and Faber, 1960), pp. 238−71; Hole (1961), pp. 168, 195−8, 342−3. This power is similar to that said to be exercised over animals by witches; see Burne (1973−74), vol. 1, pp. 152−3; Ella Mary Leather, *The Folklore of Herefordshire* (East Ardsley, Wakefield, Yorks: S. R. Publishers, 1970 [1912]), p. 55; Briggs (1971), part B, vol. 2, pp. 618, 634−6, 740−1; Hole (1977), pp. 56, 178−80.

29 *wakes*: Brand (1890−93), vol. 2, pp. 237−45; E. M. Wright (1913), pp. 278−81; and Puckle (1926), pp. 61−4. *bleeding of corpse*: Hone (1878c), pp. 590−1, 592; Brand (1890−93), vol. 3, pp. 229−32; Hole (1961), pp. 343−4, and (1977), pp. 104−5; Thomas (1971), p. 220. *sin-eating*: Brand (1890−93), vol. 2, pp. 246−8; Puckle (1926), pp. 69−70; Hole (1961), pp. 309−11; Burne (1973−74), vol. 1, pp. 306−8.

CHAPTER 2: JUMPING THE BROOM − AND BACK

1 Stone (1977), p. 54. *property control*: *JOxJ*, 14 March, 1812, p. 2; Jones-Baker (1977), p. 72. *vagrancy*: Chitty (1845), vol. 6, pp. 431−2.

2 *previous marriages*: *WFP*, 21 June 1790, p. 3; *LNJ*, 20 May 1796, p. 3; *T*, 11 July 1797, p. 2; *JOxJ*, 12 August 1797, p. 4. *soldiers*: de Watteville (1954), p. 133; R. Palmer (1977), pp. 134−5, 154−6. *sailors*: *WFP*, 21 June 1790, p. 3 (bargeman); *T*, 7 July 1797, p. 3. *criminals*: ibid., 27 July 1797, p. 3 (thieves); ibid., 23 September 1797, p. 3 (coiners); *MC*, 27 September 1797, p. 3 (thieves); ibid., 13 November 1797, p. 3 (rapist); Tobias (1972), p. 104. *mobile individuals*: Coleman (1968), pp. 32, 187, 188−9, 191−2 (navvies).

3 Hole (1961), p. 45. *north Wales*: ibid. 'Broomstick Marriage Act': *YG*, quoted in *JOxJ*, 12 September 1840, p. 1 ('We always expected that the Broomstick Marriage Act would be treated as a dead letter by the people of this country'). In Leicestershire few marriages under the Act took place initially, 'the inhabitants preferring the ceremonies of the Church to the vaulting levity of the *broomstick*', *Leicester Herald*, cited in *JOxJ*, 8 September 1838, p. 4. *widespread*: see the song 'Jumping Over the Broom' in

Pop. Voc., p. 22. *Woodhead Tunnel*: Coleman (1968), p. 22. *gypsies*: in the latter case, a rush ring was placed on the wife's finger; Hole (1961), p. 45. *soldier: Oliver's* (18—), p. 184. *Negro slaves*: Norman R. Yetman, *Life under the 'Peculiar Institution': Selections from the Slave Narrative Collection* (New York: Holt, Rinehart and Winston, 1970), pp. 269, 298, 304. *Virginia*: Hubert J. Davis, *The Silver Bullet and Other American Witch Stories* (Middle Village, NY: Jonathan David Publishers, 1975), p. 21 and note.

4 *chimney*: Hole (1961), p. 44; Cambridgeshire, Porter (1969), pp. 391—2. *mocking husband*: the 'mommet' or effigy indicated that he needed a new housekeeper; K. Palmer (1976), p. 32. *immorality*: Addy (1973), p. 102 and note. *Yorkshire*: ibid. *gypsy*: Baker (1977), pp. 50—1 *stepping over broomstick*: Addy (1973), p. 102. *Mabinogion*: Gwyn Jones and Thomas Jones (trans.), 'Math Son of Mathonwy', *The Mabinogion*, reprint edn. (London: J. M. Dent & Sons, 1963 [1949], p. 63. This may also be responsible for a number of related beliefs. Thus in West Virginia people who step over a broom will never be married, and to be touched by a broom means bad luck; Gainer (1975), pp. 124, 123. Stepping over a broom dooms one to be an old maid; Fanny D. Bergen, *Current Superstitions*, Memoirs of the American Folk-Lore Society, vol. 4 (Boston, Mass., American Folk-Lore Society, 1896), p. 62. In Labrador if a girl steps over a broom she will be a bad housewife; ibid., p. 59. The same belief is found in the Ozarks. Vance Randolph, *Ozark Magic and Folklore*, reprint edn. (New York: Dover Publications, 1964 [1947]), p. 74. For a Derbyshire tale connected with this belief, see Addy (1973), p. 13. An American plantation owner had two slaves involved in a wedding jump backwards over a broom to determine which would have the mastery. Norman R. Yetman (ed.), *Life Under the 'Peculiar Institution': Selections from the Slave Narrative Collection* (New York: 1970), p. 164.

5 Stone (1977), p. 31. *'The Blacksmith'*: Williams and Lloyd (1969), pp. 22, 11.

6 *Ring of Brodgar*: Hole (1961), p. 191; paper given by Dr Henry before the Society of Antiquaries of Scotland in 1784, cited in Tudor (1883), pp. 307—8; Ernest W. Marwick, *The Folklore of Orkney and Shetland* (London: B. T. Batsford, 1975), p. 59. *Kintyre*: Dr John Smith in Sir John Sinclair, *The Statistical Account of Scotland* (Edinburgh: William Creech, 1793), vol. 10, pp. 537—8, quoted in A. D. Hope (1970), p. 157. *Teltown*: it would appear that a man could have judged a hand not only by its age and beauty but also by the familiarity with work which it showed. John O'Donovan (1836), quoted in MacNeill (1962), p. 316, and secondarily in A. D. Hope (1970), p. 154.

7 *Gretna Green location*: Baker (1977), p. 49; Jeaffreson (1872), vol. 2, pp. 205—8. *prints*: 'Gretna Green', engraved by Thomas Rowlandson in 1815; Robert W. Wark, *Drawings by Thomas Rowlandson in the Huntington Collection* (San Marino, Calif.: Huntington Library, 1975), p. 92 and plate 308. *laymen*: these included a former soldier, a tobacconist, and a peddler. The popular conception that a blacksmith usually performed the ceremonies is erroneous; Jeaffreson (1872), vol. 2, pp. 208—12; Hone (1878b), p. 477. *number of marriages*: Baker (1977), p. 49. *certificates*: under Lancaster, Trial of the Wakefields, dateline 23 March, *JOx]*, 31 March 1827, p. 4. Claverhouse (1905), citing Rev. J. Roddick in the *Statistical Account of Scotland* (1834), says that 300—400 marriages were performed annually at a normal fee of 2s 6d. *quotation*: ibid. *Liverpool: Liverpool Daily Courier*

(Liverpool), 1867, cited in Baker (1977), p. 22. *symbolism of union*: Mair (1977), p. 121.

8   Stone (1977), p. 31. *breakdown*: ibid., pp. 31−2. *spousals binding*: ibid., p. 31. *written agreements*: ibid. *banns*: Jeaffreson (1872), vol. 1, pp. 104−5, 130−1. *forbidding the banns*: ibid., vol. 1, pp. 104−5, 124−33; Baker (1977), pp. 45−6; Stone (1977), p. 31. *special licence*: Jeaffreson (1872), vol. 1, pp. 133−7; Baker (1977), pp. 45−6. *no banns or licences*: Jeaffreson (1872), vol. 2, pp. 115−21; George (1976), p. 305. *canons*: the canons stipulated that the service must have been preceded by a triple reading of the banns, must take place between 8 a.m. and noon and must be held in the local church of bride or groom; Stone (1977), p. 32.

9   *abuses*: Stone (1977), p. 33. *fortune-hunters*: George (1976), p. 305; Jarrett (1976), p. 118. *bigamy/seduction*: George (1976), p. 305. *back-dating ceremonies*: a husband by law assumed his wife's indebtedness and was responsible for her issue subsequent to the union; Stone (1977), p. 33. *debt*: George (1976), p. 305. *pregnancy*: Stone (1977), p. 33. Place (1972), p. 85. *Leaver*: Baker (1977), p. 47; Thomas Pennant, *Some Account of London* (London: Robert Faulder, 1791 [1790]), pp. 224-5. *taverns*: Jeaffreson (1972), vol. 2, pp. 133−4. *'Virtuous'*: vol. 5, February 1735. This quote is also found in *GSJ*, 27 February 1735, pp. 1−2. *lawyers*: Jeaffreson (1872), vol. 2, p. 146. *swearing a child*: Jarrett (1976), p. 65. *handcuffs*: Stone (1977), p. 631.

10 *Lord Hardwicke's Act*: Jeaffreson (1872), vol. 2, pp. 167−91; Stone (1977), pp. 34−5. *substance*: ibid., p. 35; Jeaffreson (1872), vol. 2, pp. 187−9.

11 *statistics*: Stone (1977), pp. 42−62. *scope*: ibid., p. 44. *marriage age*: ibid., p. 50. *accumulation of capital*: Stone (1977), pp. 50−1. *length of marriage*: ibid., p. 55. It seems to have been fairly common for a person to marry several times if his or her spouse died, to judge by the (newsworthy) extremes. Thus a Gornal (Staffs) sailor had been married eight times (*JOxJ*, 20 October 1838, p. 4); and a Somerset woman, seven (*The Nonsense of Commonsense*, London, 10 January 1738, p. 2). Defoe reports that in the Essex marshes 'it was very frequent to meet with men that have had from five or six, to fourteen or fifteen wives; nay, and some more; and I was inform'd that . . . there was a farmer who was then living with the five and twentieth wife, and that his son who was but about 35 years old, had already had about fourteen . . .' (Defoe, 1974, p. 13). Even allowing for much exaggeration, it can be seen that at least in some areas mortality must have shortened many cohabitations. *equivalent to divorce*: Stone (1977), pp. 55−6. *endogamy*: based on data for Kent in the early seventeenth century; ibid., p. 61. *remarriage*: ibid., p. 56.

12 *Bryant*: MC, 13 November 1797, p. 3. Parallel cases, however, suggest that this relationship might have been claimed in order to gain custody of the body for sale to surgeons. *bigamous wife*: *JOxJ*, 28 July 1832, p. 4. Robert Morley, a butler by trade, was convicted of polygamy at the Warwickshire Assizes, having married four ladies' maids in the several families he worked for; *JOxJ*, 22 August 1840, p. 4. Walsh, a cordwainer, married four wives at the Fleet within the space of 14 months; George (1976), pp. 305−6. *Penson*: *JOxJ*, 3 November 1832, p. 4. *civil offence*: Stone (1977), p. 519. *desertion*: ibid., pp. 40, 519.

13 Stone (1977), pp. 615−20; Pearsall (1972), pp. 307−66. See also Place (1972), pp. 73, 75−6.

14 *Wales*: there were several Welsh codes, with custom and outside contact

influencing their interpretation. Ellis's study is itself a *survey* of the available mss. evidence; Ellis (1926), vol. 1, pp. 4—12, 418—20. *Ireland*: ibid., pp. 3, 422. *Ethelred*: ibid., p. 421. *Church*: Jeaffreson (1872), vol. 2, pp. 307—9, *post-Reformation*: Stone notes that the Anglican Church, unlike other Protestant denominations, 'failed to provide for remarriage by the innocent party in cases of separation for extreme cruelty or adultery'; Stone (1977), pp. 37—8. *seven-year absence*: the *Globe* quotes the idea of remarriage after a seven-year absence as a 'popular error'; *GT* (1903), p. 1.

15 *Parliamentary divorce*: Stone (1977), p. 38. *Divorce Act*: Pearsall (1972), p. 219. *Acts of 1878 and 1886*: ibid., p. 226.

16 *class-conscious*: note the treatment of strangers as a class in Welsh law; Ellis (1926), vol. 1, p. 19. Additionally, many of the religious divorce rules presume the existence of an influence which would have been lacking in the 'lower classes'. *Acts of Parliament*: Jeaffreson (1872), vol. 2, pp. 340—1; Pearsall (1972), pp. 215—16; Stone (1977), p. 38. *1857 Divorce Act*: Fenn (n.d.), pp. 106—7; A. R. Wright (1928), pp. 26—7. *Waugh*: Evelyn Waugh, *A Handful of Dust* (Harmondsworth, Middx: Penguin Books, 1973 [1934]), pp. 126—52. *first female divorce suit*: Stone (1977), p. 38; Westermarck (1921), vol. 3, p. 337.

17 *Farrant (Som)*: *WFP*, 22 March 1790, p. 3. Phyllis Dimery (Oxford) also claims to have parted from her husband by mutual consent; *JOxJ*, 1 December 1781, p. 3. *French (Plymouth, Devon)*: John French served on His Majesty's sloop of war *King Fisher*; *WFP*, 26 June 1786, p. 1. Fridiswed Rew (Stringston, Som.) had left her husband six years previously to go into 'gentlemen's service' and 'is against my consent eloped with one John Pole, by whom she declares herself to be with child', ibid., 15 January 1787, p. 3. *Gifford*: ibid., 13 November 1786, p. 3. An earlier issue (2 October 1786, p. 1) notes that this was done 'in a state of insanity'. Joseph Townsend (Aston, Oxon.) charges his wife with 'having absconded from her husband and family and obtained goods from several shopkeepers on his credit'; *JOxJ*, 19 October 1822, p. 2. Many of the disclaimers involve abandonment. Not all, however, deal with wives; Luvina Norris of Berkshire states that her husband 'has eloped from my bed and board, without any just cause; this is therefore to caution all persons against harbouring the said Jesse Norris, as I am determined not to liquidate any debts of his contracting'; *BCh* 5 February 1825, p.4.

18 *Wiltshire*: the case came before the County Quarter Sessions, ms. x56.18/168, in Wiltshire Record Office, quoted in B. Howard Cunningham, '"A Skimmington" in 1618', *Folklore* (London), vol. 41, no. 3, 30 September 1930, pp. 288—90. *Bermondsey*: eyewitness report c. 1843. Done to the accompaniment of rough music; N—, 'Skimmington', *NQ*, series 4, vol. 11 31 May 1873, p. 455. *Bladon Feast*: this included parading and burning the offender's effigy; *ODFS* (1951), p. 13. *Coombe*: ibid., p. 14. *Wooset Hunt*: 1830. Four participants carried 'spunkies' (hollowed out turnips with candles inside) on long sticks, while the horse skull itself surmounted a skirt; F. A. Carrington, 'Of Certain Wiltshire Customs', *Wiltshire Archaeological Magazine*, vol. 1, 1854, pp. 88—9, *Somerset*: Muchelney, c. 1883—93; K. Palmer (1976), p. 32. *Yorkshire*: Northallerton, 1882; W.G—, 'Riding the Stang', *NQ*, series 6, vol. 6, 25 November 1882, pp. 425—6. *ecclesiastical courts*: Hair (1972), especially pp. 235—8, 244—5.

19 *non-consummation*: Hair (1972). *aphrodisiacs*: walking or sitting on the

Cerne Abbas Giant (Dorset), Baker (1977), p. 98; sleeping with therapeutic object under the pillow (Cambs), ibid., p. 99; drinking 'still liquors' (brewed from wheat and herbs) or 'matched cider' (produced by burning a brimstone taper within the half-full barrel) in Devon, ibid., pp. 100 – 1; drinking tansy tea in the Fens, ibid., p. 103; eating powdered briony root (Lincs), Hole (1961), p. 69; eating a specially treated orange (Norfolk), ibid., p. 256; eating stout and oysters, Harrison (1971), p. 39. *barrenness*: working in flax fields was said to bring this on. *bewitchments*: Thomas (1971), p. 437.

20 *Tenby*: an effigy of the offender, carried on a ladder, was accompanied by rough music; *Tales and Traditions of Tenby* (1858), pp. 95 – 6, quoted in Owen (1968), p. 168. *Rudkin*: a ceremony, known as 'rantanning', which occurred if a man 'ad been yuckin' [jerking] 'is ole woman, or owt'. The music was made on three nights, and the effigy was burned on the third. Rhymes differing from those in Pembroke were used; Rudkin (1973), pp. 52 – 4. *Barrett*: eyewitness report by a participant, quoted in Porter (1969), pp. 9 – 10. *Cambridgeshire woman*: ibid., p. 9. *Shotover*: ODFS (1951), p. 14.

21 *debt disclaimers*: *JOx]*, 15 June 1754, p. 2 ('Supposed to be gone to Service in Buckinghamshire' – husband a glover); ibid, 6 March 1756, p. 3; *WFP* 6 March 1786, p. 3; ibid., 10 April 1786, p. 1; ibid., 17 April 1786, p. 3; ibid., 1 May 1786, p. 1 (husband a carpenter); ibid., 2 October 1786, p. 1; *RM* 31 March 1788, p. 2 (father a breeches-maker); *YCh* 18 May 1797, p. 1 (husband a 'yeoman'); *WFP* 14 January 1799, p. 3; *JOx]*, 19 October 1822, p. 2; *BCh* 5 February 1825, p. 4 (*husband* deserted); ibid. 19 March 1825, p. 1 (absconded, 'leaving her Infant from the breast'). Numerous other examples could be added. *Somerton*: *WFP*, 17 April 1786, p. 3. *Stimson*: c. 1793 – 95; Place (1972), p. 135. *Powell*: c. 1797 – 99; Powell's wife appears to have been a prostitute, but Place indicates that this was not unusual (ibid., note p. 179). *seven years' absence*: *GT* (1903), p. 1; W. Wells Bladen, 'Folklore of North Staffordshire Chiefly Collected at Stone', *North Staffordshire Field Club Transactions*, vol. 35 (1899 – 1901), p. 155, quoted in Raven (1978), p. 61. See also 1 Jacob. 1 c. xi, 'An Act to restrain all persons from marriage until their former wives and former husbands be dead', which exempts from bigamy those whose spouses have been abroad or presumed dead for seven years; Jeaffreson (1872), vol. 2, note p. 327.

22 *Wales*: Hole (1961), p. 45. *song*: P.T— 'Jumping over the Broom', *Pop. Voc.*, p. 22.

23 *Orkneys*: Tudor (1883), pp. 307 – 8. Tudor repeats the story of a Miss Gordon who, about 1725, had taken the 'Odin oath' with John Gow, clasping hands through the holed stone. She travelled to London after he was hung in chains for piracy (in 1729) to retract her promise while holding his dead hand; ibid., p. 295. *Gretna Green*: Claverhouse (1905), pp. 72 – 3. *Teltown quotation*: A. D. Hope (1970), p. 155. *'deed of separation'*: MacNeill (1962), p. 316, quoted in A. D. Hope (1970), p. 154. *Kintyre*: Dr John Smith, in Sir John Sinclair, *The Statistical Account of Scotland*, vol. 10 (Edinburgh; 1793), pp. 537 – 8, quoted in A. D. Hope (1970), p. 157. *Paul Jones*: personal observation, Oxford, November 1977, 'Sadie Hawkins Day': personal observation, at a high school in Baton Rouge, Louisiana, USA, spring 1966.

24 *Eskdalemuir*: see A. D. Hope (1970), pp. 158—9. *Skye*: written c. 1695; Donald Macleod (editor) *A Description of the Western Islands of Scotland*,

p. 175, quoted in A. D. Hope (1970), p. 159. For two examples of this practice (one involving a two-year trial and the other an indeterminate time span), in both of which the offspring were considered to be illegitimate or were deprived of their inheritance, see J.M.G—, 'Taking a Wife on Trial', *NQ*, series 1, vol. 2, 3 August 1850, p. 151. *McDonalds*: Nicholson, *History of Skye*, p. 104, cited in A. D. Hope (1970), p. 160. Mr Robert E. Wilson of Dallas, Texas, reports that former Justice of the Peace W. J. Richburg granted symbolic divorces as late as 1969 by sundering the partners' hands; oral communication, November 1979.

25 *removal and return*: Burne (1973—74), vol. 1, p. 295; Wright (1928), pp. 26—7. *Exeter*: *Exeter Alfred* (Exeter, Devon), quoted in *JOxJ*, 31 October 1829, p. 2. *divinations*: Addy (1973), pp. 78, 85; Hole (1961), p. 357; Baker (1977), p. 76. *cures*: Hole (1961), p. 357. *Staffordshire*: Hackwood (1974), p. 61. *loss or breakage*: Hole (1961), p. 357. In West Virginia a loss means separation, a breakage means widowhood; Gainer (1975), p. 129. In Digby (Lincs) removal of the ring brought seven years' bad luck; Rudkin (1973), p. 17. *dropping ring*: Hole (1961), p. 358. *omens*: ibid.

26 *tolling of bell*: *JOxJ*, 30 March 1850, p. 4.

27 *poem*: 'A Poem on the times of Edward II'. Percy Society Publications, quoted in Jeaffreson (1872), vol. 2, note p. 310. *annulment*: ibid., vol. 2, pp. 307, 308, 310. *Council of Clermont*: ibid., vol. 2, pp. 309, 310. *separation*: ibid., vol. 2, p. 339; Stone (1977), p. 37. *Anglican Church*: Stone (1977), pp. 32, 37, 38.

28 *Jewish divorces*: *JOxJ*, 6 April 1799, p. 3.

29 Kenny (1929), p. 494 and note.

30 *rationale*: Stone (1977), p. 38. *initial process*: the Duke of Norfolk was twice refused a parliamentary divorce before he initiated an action in the Court of King's Bench to prove his wife's adultery. Subsequently, he was granted his Act; Jeaffreson (1872), vol. 2, p. 341; Westermarck (1921), vol. 3, p. 337. *protest*: *Books of the House of Lords*, quoted in Jeaffreson (1872), vol. 2, p. 342. Stone (1977), p. 38. *number of acts*: Westermarck gives the total number of bills passed as 317; Westermarck (1921), vol. 3, p. 337. I have assumed that both Westermarck and Stone (1977, p. 38), are correct in their figures.

31 *unfairness*: Fenn (n. 2), p. 9. *Oxford Assizes*: Hawes is identified as a 'labourer'; *JOxJ*, 10 March 1855, p. 2. *Maule's address*: Thomas Arthur Nash, *The Life of Richard Lord Westbury Formerly Lord High Chancellor, with Selections from his Correspondence* (London: Richard Bentley and Son, 1888), vol. 1, p. 211. For another version, see *Law Magazine*, quoted in Jeaffreson (1872), vol. 2, note pp. 343—4. That the problems involved in such situations were recognized before this date is suggested by the sentencing of Thomas Higgs to only 24 hours' imprisonment upon his conviction for bigamy in 1807; *JOxJ*, 11 July 1807, p. 3. *Act of 1857*: Pearsall (1972), pp. 216—17.

32 *numbers*: 326 people divorced in 1858 alone, as compared with a total of 203 in the previous 57 years. However, the 708 British divorces in 1886 are hardly equivalent to the 25,000 that took place in the United States in the same year (even allowing for double the population); Pearsall (1972), p. 218 and note. Fenn (n.d.), pp. 106—7. *ignorance*: Wright (1928), pp. 26—7.

33 *notices*: this was due to the fact that forsaken wives and children often became a parish liability; *JOxJ*, 27 December 1791, p. 3; ibid., 26 January

1799, p. 3 (shepherd); ibid., 6 July 1799, p. 3; ibid., 5 October 1799, p. 3 (bricklayer); ibid., 7 June 1800, p. 3; ibid., 26 August 1815, p. 1 (gardener). *'WHOLESALE DESERTION'*: *JOx]*, 1 January 1848, p. 2. *Herefordshire*: *WFP*, 18 March 1796, p. 3; *LNJ*, 18 March 1796, p. 1. *reward*: Green (1901), p. 119 J. F. Pound, *The Norwich Census of the Poor 1570* (Norfolk Record Society, 1971), p. 95. George Herbert, *Shoemaker's Window, Recollections of a Midland Town before the Railway Age* (Oxford: B. H. Blackwell, 1948), p. 10. *support payments*: Chitty (1845), vol. 6, pp. 431 — 2. Punishments of husbands convicted of desertion appear to have ranged from one to six months' imprisonment; (Oxon.), *JOx]*, 13 March 1824, p. 3 (1 month); (Flints) ibid., 22 May 1824, p. 4 (6 months, hard labour: eloped with a publican's wife); (Berks) ibid., 26 April 1828, p. 3 (2 months; had deserted wife because of her incontinence — she subsequently had two or three children for whom he was held legally responsible).

34 *press gang*: many stories and ballads hinge on the separation of lovers by third parties. However, as the aftermath to one attempted wife sale in 1810 (**127**) shows, women could upon occasion betray their husbands. *army*: de Watteville (1954), pp. 129 — 32, 133; R. Palmer (1977), p. 135. *murder*: *GSJ*, 6 June 1734, p. 2 (journeyman gardener killed his wife after having words with her — 'he said she provoked him, and that he would rather be hanged than live with such a woman'); *Portsmouth and Gosport Gazette and Salisbury Journal* (Salisbury, Wilts), 20 April 1752, p. 3 (wife hired four men to kill husband 'that she might marry a poor deformed Cobler [sic]'); ibid., 20 April 1752, p. 1 (husband killed wife for fear she would interrupt his cohabitation with another woman); *JOx]*, 21 July 1753, p. 3 (sailor seriously wounded wife after 'having some Words'); ibid., 8 August 1767, p. 1 (master bricklayer seriously wounded wife for infidelity with his journeyman); *StJC*, 12 January 1775, p. 4 (jealous butcher killed wife). *gift*: Wright (1928), pp. 26 — 7.

35 *contract*: Atiyah (1971), pp. 1 — 2; interview with Professor John H. Langbein (University of Chicago and All Souls, Oxford), March 1977. *major requirements*: Atiyah (1971), pp. 4 — 10. *'evidentiary' acts*: ibid., p. 4, and interview with Professor John H. Langbein. *livery of seisin*: interview with Professor John H. Langbein. *beating the bounds*: Hole (1941), pp. 57 — 60, (1975), pp. 72 — 3, (1976), pp. 167 — 8, 179. Popular methods also existed by which it was believed title could be gained to commonage, such as by building a house in one night, circling or lighting fires on the property and so on.

36 Interview with Professor John H. Langbein

37 *'moral factor'*: Atiyah (1971), p. 1. *trial for riot*: R. v. Skerving (Court of King's Bench, 10 July 1797); *LC* 13 July 1797, p. 42. *gift*: Mauss (1969).

38 E. P. Thompson (1976), p. 68.

CHAPTER 3: MARKETS, 'MOPS' AND MIDDLEMEN

1 *Italy*: Italian newspaper, October 1926, quoted in H. Heldmann, 'Wife-Sales', *NQ*, series 13, vol. 151, 27 November 1926, p. 393. *Ethiopia*: Wood (1869), vol. 1, p. 174. *China*: ibid., vol. 1, p. 106. One of the New Zealand wife sales reported in S. E. Gregory, 'Wife-Selling in the 19th

Century', *NQ*, vol. 196, 4 August 1951, pp. 348—9, shows possible Chinese derivation or influence (although Dr Raewyn Dalziel, Senior Lecturer in History at Auckland University, notes in a letter of June 1978 that few of the Chinese in New Zealand at this time were married).

2   Eleventh century: Scotland or Ireland (see 1). Sixteenth century: London (2); Hertfordshire (3); Essex (4). Seventeenth century: Angus (5); Stirlingshire (6); Warwickshire (7); East Lothian (8); Yorkshire (9); Staffordshire (10); Oxfordshire (11). The latter half of the eighteenth century: Northumberland (89); Sussex (69, 70, 82 and 87); Essex (47); Lincolnshire (52 and 53); Norfolk (74); Suffolk (24, 33?, 49, 51 and 58); Yorkshire (38, 41, 42, 78 and 85); Cheshire (94); Co. Dublin (21). Nineteenth century: Glamorgan (315 and 316); Monmouthshire (182); Radnorshire (297 and 304); Calvados, France (*T*, 27 November 1866, p. 10); Loire, France (*Gazette des Tribunaux*, before 9 November 1846, translated and quoted in *T*, 9 November 1846, p. 3); Nièvre, France (*T*, 5 February 1829, p. 4); Nord, France (*BJ*, 25 March 1865, p. 3). The late 1880s: Essex (340); Yorkshire (342, 343, 347, 349, 350, 351, 354, 357, 358, 359, 363 and 379); Derbyshire (345); Co. Antrim (346); Liverpool (353); Surrey (355); Sussex (360 and 361); Northants (362); Devon (366 and 378); London (367); Staffordshire (369); Argyll (374); Northumberland (377 and 381); Monmouthshire (380).

3   *records*: two-thirds of the surviving sixteenth- and seventeenth-century sale examples, for instance, are preserved in the records of ecclesiastical courts. *research*: indices that exist for *The Times* and for several local newspapers, such as those of York (York Central Library), Hull (Department of Adult Education, University of Hull) and Liverpool (Liverpool Record Office), may make for more complete coverage of wife sales from these locations. (Often, however, these ignore non-local sales, which were nonetheless reported, or may not be completely accurate.) Previous researchers seem have concentrated on the *Ipswich Journal* (Suffolk), the *Sussex Week Advertiser* (Sussex), the *West Briton* (Cornwall), the *Lincoln, Rutland and Stanford Mercury* (Lincolnshire), and the *Globe* (London). *news coverage*: London, with more extensive coverage and older dailies, probably received more intensive coverage than many rural locations. The distribution of local cases should be weighed against the number and frequency of newspapers covering an area (and their survival). For some of the problems encountered in using British historical data, see Macfarlane (1977), pp. 33—4, 202—7.

4   *Truro*: 173c (this may be a reference to 166). *Five Lanes*: 136. *absence in Lancashire*: GT (1903), p. 1. *refuting case evidence*: 75, 119, 155, 172, 226, 230, 287, 318, 319, 325, 326, 332.

5   *Sheffield*: 78, 108, 135, 201, 225, 289, 342, 349, 354, 358.

6   *Llan-y-bydder fair*: the speech given by the husband is similar to one connected with an 1832 Carlisle sale (234). This latter case was not only fully reported in several contemporary newspapers (234a, b) and books (234d) but also appeared in broadside form in Lancaster (234a), from where it could have reached Wales; see 43 (note). *Caerleon*: 182. *Cardiff*: 315. *Knighton*: 297 and 304. *Merthyr Tydfil*: 316. *iron*: M. W. Flinn, *An Economic and Social History of Britain: 1066—1939* (London: Macmillan, 1961), p. 137.

7   *adultery and cohabitation*: A. D. Hope (1970), esp. pp. 129—97. *family law*: Andrew Dewar Gibb, 'Scots law', *Encyclopaedia Britannica* (1964), vol. 20, p. 178A and *LM* 27 October 1810, p. 4. *rural example*: 6. *New Sneddon*: 248. *Edinburgh*: 215.

8 *Catholicism*: corroborated by Dr Kevin Danaher (University College, Dublin) in a letter of May 1978. *Co. Dublin*: **21**. *Co. Antrim*: **346**. *trade contacts*: compare the occurrence of the Spanish custom of 'burning Judas' on Good Friday in the Liverpool dock area; Hole (1975), pp. 40—1. *Irish labourers*: see George (1976), pp. 120—31, for a discussion of the lives of these labourers in London. Irish agricultural labourers often migrated to the countryside around London for the summer season; Jarrett (1974), p. 78. In July 1808 a London wife was bought by an Irish labourer at Smithfield (**125**). See T. Jones, *Vauxhall Songster* (c. 1790—99), British Library, no. 9.B1 1876 e 20, p. 71, in which another Irish labourer makes such a purchase (copy supplied by Mr Roy Palmer, May 1978).

9 *crossing of political boundaries*: see, for example, E. P. Thompson (1972), and S. P. Menefee, 'The "Merry Maidens" and "Noce de Pierre"', *Folklore* (London), vol. 85, Spring 1974, pp. 23—42.

10 Menefee (1978), p. 539, and S. P. Menefee, "A Halter Round her Neck', *New Society* (London), vol. 43, no. 799, 26 January 1978, p. 182.

11 *Knighton*: **297**. *Dartmouth*: **160**. *streets*: **210** and **311**. *open spaces*: **295**. *homes*: **142** and **248**. *lodging houses*: **355**. *tea shop*: **374**. *Norfolk*: **236**. *Brough Hill*: **372**. *fair*: Rowling (1976), p. 102, and Hole (1975), p. 166.

12 *banns*: this was done during the Commonwealth period; J. S. Udal, 'Called Home', *NQ*, series 5, vol. 1, 31 January 1874, p. 87. *proclamations*: war and peace were announced from Alnwick Cross (Northumb.), and John Wesley preached from its steps; J. W. Thompson and D. Bond, *Victorian and Edwardian Northumbria from Old Photographs* (London: B. T. Batsford, 1976), plate 68. Lord Pomfret addressed his tenants on a political question at Richmond Cross (Yorks); *AR 1770*, p. 138. *prostitution*: Kathleen Wiltshire, *Ghosts and Legends of the Wiltshire Countryside* (Compton Chamberlayne, Salisbury, Wilts: Compton Russell, 1973), pp. 84—5.

13 *Mottram Cross*: Haworth (1952), p. 92. *Leominster*: Malcolmson (1973), p. 46. *Beverley*: ibid., p. 67. *Barnet*: Malcolmson (1973), plate 2. *Bolton*: ibid., p. 139. *Kingston-upon-Thames*: ibid., pp. 139—40. *Derby*: ibid., pp. 141—2; Hole (1976), p. 182. In Chester the football was presented at the Cross on the Roodee; Hole (1949), p. 52, (1975), p. 30, and (1976), pp. 181—2. In a Shrovetide game similar to hurling at Scone (Perthshire) the ball was thrown up at the Cross: Hole (1949), pp. 52—3. *Congleton*: Hole (1970), pp. 101—2. *Staffordshire*: Raven (1978), pp. 120—2.

14 *multiple markets*: London — Covent Garden (**90**), Smithfield (**91**), Billingsgate (**126**), Portman Market (**240**) and Islington Market (**257**); Plymouth — Dock market (**102**) and cattle market (**186**); Nottingham — hog market (**140**) and cattle market (**250**); Bristol — St Thomas's market (**184?**, **193**) and Temple Meads market (**222**). *livestock dealings*: Worcester market (**56** and **59** — 'beasts'); Hereford market (**76** and **104?** — pigs); Smithfield, London (livestock); Islington, London (cattle); Bilston market (**170** and **292** — pigs, cattle, horses); Ashburn market (?) (**147** — cattle); Plymouth cattle market; Canterbury market (**139** and **174** — cattle); Nottingham hog market; Nottingham cattle market; Nottingham market (**183**, **281** and **299** — sheep, cattle; Helston market (**383** — horses, cattle, pigs); Shudehill, Manchester, market (**199** — cattle); St Thomas, Bristol market (cattle); Temple Meads, Bristol, market (cattle); Temple Meads, Bristol, market (cattle); Horsham market (**204** and **283** — colts); Hadleigh market (**273** — cattle and corn). Other commodity markets used include the Hereford butter market (**212**);

London's Covent Garden (fruit and vegetables) and Billingsgate (fish and coal); Bradford market (**258** and **259** — butter); Mansfield market (**290** — corn); Cheltenham market (**202** and **223** — corn); Hadleigh market (corn and cattle). Many of these probably sold some livestock, while other markets should not be deemed to have been devoted exclusively to cattle, horses, hogs, and sheep. *1790s (Hereford)*: **76**. *1870s (Belper)*: **333**. It is not obvious that an 1887 sale at the Borough Market Hotel, Wakefield, Yorks, took place in the market (**350**). *absence of sale noted*: **262**. *Somerset*: **241**. *Yorkshire*: **258**. *Temple Meads market*: **222**. *Islington market*: **257**. *new Oxford market*: **60**.

15 *sellers*: **33** (butcher sold wife to tanner), **83a**—**c**, **f** (butcher sold wife to hog-driver), **104**, **171**, **337a** (pork butcher may have sold wife to publican). *purchasers*: **31**, **117**, **184**, **229** (butcher who had been fined previously for using uneven balances in his trading transactions). *avoiding authority*: **171** and **270**.

16 *1801*: Yorks, **314**. One sale took price at the market cross at Liskeard, Cornwall (**197**). *market houses*: **195**.

17 *market inns*: **282** (Bull Inn), **83a**—**c**, **f**, and **171** (Ram Inn), **231** (Half Moon Public House), **382** (Bull's Head Inn), **235** (Blue Posts Inn), **190** (White Lion), **299** (Bell Inn), **300** (Spread Eagle), **383** (hotel/inn), **156** (King's Head), **266** (White Hart).

18 *Horsham*: **204a**—**c**; Malcolmson (1973), p. 20.

19 *mops*: Malcolmson (1973), pp. 23—4; Hole (1975), pp. 166—7; (1976), p. 97. Entertainments included puppet shows, giants, dwarfs, monsters ('the Pig Faced Lady'), wild animals, trained animals, buffoons, magicians and tightrope walkers. Among 'fairings' were numbered china, buttons, buckles, notions and cheap jewellery; Malcolmson (1973), pp. 20—3. *competitions*: ibid., p. 22. Other amusements included climbing a greasy pole, ducking for sixpences, and catching a greased pig; R. Palmer (1976), p. 124. *smock races*: Malcolmson notes that these races could have sexual connotations, as women competitors were urged to come lightly clad; Malcolmson (1973), pp. 21, 31, 77. *wrestling*: ibid., pp. 22, 43. *singlestick*: played with one cudgel and the left hand tied down. ibid., pp. 22, 43—4. *'girning'*: making faces through a horse collar; R. Palmer (1976), p. 124.

20 Malcolmson (1973), p. 24. *late spring and early summer*: ibid., pp. 24—5. *Easter and Whitsuntide*: ibid., pp. 29, 31—3; Hole (1976), p. 97; Burne (1974), vol. 2, pp. 461—2 and note p. 462. *autumn*: Malcolmson (1973), p. 25. *Michaelmas*: ibid., p. 25; Hole (1976), p. 97; Burne (1973—74), vol. 2, pp. 461—2 and note p. 462.

21 *single individuals*: Malcolmson (1973), pp. 53—4. *opportunity to meet*: Jude and Richard Wandsworth, for example, met when they were about 18 at Heptonstall Fair, near Halifax, Yorks, and married shortly thereafter; *S*, 29 July 1797, p. 3; *YCh*, 3 August 1797, p. 1. *'truancy'*: memorandum book of John Howell, a farmer living near Oswestry, Salop, c. 1770, quoted in Burne (1973—74), vol. 2, note p. 463. Elsewhere servants were often given time off to visit a 'pleasure fair'; Burne (1973—74), vol. 2, p. 464. Amy Robsart, Lord Robert Dudley's wife, was found dead in her house (in 1560) after all the household servants had gone to Abingdon Fair; J. E. Neale, *Queen Elizabeth* (London: Jonathan Cape, 1934), p. 87. *clothes*: Malcolmson (1973), pp. 86—8. *Cumberland*: John Housman, *A Topographical Description of Cumberland, Westmoreland, Lancashire, and a Part of the West Riding of Yorkshire* (Carlisle, Cumb.: Francis Jollie, 1800), p. 71.

22	*hiring 'mops'*: Chambers (1869), vol. 1, p. 645. *Birmingham*: eyewitness account of Warwickshire statutes, quoted in Hone (1878b), p. 88. *eighteenth century*: Silas Neville, *The Diary of Silas Neville, 1767–1788*, Basil Cozens-Hardy (ed.), (Oxford: Oxford University Press, 1950), pp. 279, 316.

23	*relaxing restraints*: Malcolmson (1973), pp. 78–9. *liquor*:

> Drink was a basic component of this temporary culture of licentiousness; and drunkenness was a regular and more or less tolerated feature of a large number of festive occasions. Heavy drinking was often reserved for holidays, and it was indulged in by many men who were ordinarily temperate. The liberating powers of drink at fairs and festivities were commonly celebrated in popular stories and songs . . . (ibid., p. 76)

See also Brian Harrison, *Drink and the Victorians: The Temperance Question in England, 1815–1872* (London: Faber and Faber, 1971), pp. 40–4. *dancing*: Hope (1970), pp. 187–8. *Fiddlington*: traditional, published in *Country Fair* (London), vol. 6, no. 4, April 1954, p. vi. 'Wickington Hiring', another song, includes the lines:

> They danc'd agyen till it was day,
> An' then went heym, but by the way,
> There was some had rare fun they say,
> An' found it nine months after – O . . . .
> (Malcolmson, 1973, p. 78)

24	Ben Jonson, *Bartholomew Fair, Ben Jonson*, vol. 6, C. H. Herford and Percy and Evelyn Simpson (eds.) (Oxford: Clarendon Press, 1938), pp. 13–141. *Country Lasses*: Act IV, scene 2, Charles Johnson (London: 1715), quoted in Malcolmson (1973), p. 78. Henry Fielding, *The History of the Adventures of Joseph Andrews . . . and An Apology for the Life of Mrs. Shamela Andrews* (Oxford: Oxford University Press, 1970 [1742]), p. 75.

25	*Bromley*: Local Population Studies Magazine and Newsletter, no. 1, Autumn 1968, p. 46, cited in Malcolmson (1973), p. 78. Daniel Defoe, *A Tour Through the Whole Island of Great Britain* (London: J. M. Dent & Sons Ltd., 1974 [1724–7]), p. 97. *Axbridge Mop*: GM., vol. 75, part 1, March 1805, p. 202. *Martinmas Hirings*: Greville J. Chester, *Statute Fairs: Their Evils and Their Remedy* (1856), p. 9. York: John Sampson *Kenilworth Advertiser*, 29 September 1877, quoted at second hand in R. Palmer (1976), p. 125.

26	*fairs*: Parham (**24**), Swindon (**40** – cattle), Llan-y-bydder (**43**), Barton-under-Needwood (**65**), Minchinhampton (**121**), Horsham (**177**? and **204** – colts), Lansdown (**241**), Bakewell (**265**) Truro (**291**), Wenlock (**335**), Bungay (**338** – cattle). Many markets may, in fact, have been fairs. An 1817 Cheshire sale (**162**), for example, occurred at Macclesfield market in late October or early November. Christina Hole notes: 'Macclesfield . . . had no less than five fairs in the year. They were held on Waters Green, and took place in . . . October and November'; Hole (1970), p. 108.

27	*pot house*: **254**. *beer shop*: **229** and **310b**. *beer house*: **258** and **310a**, c. *tavern*: **190**. *public house*: **231**, **245**, **249**, **262**, **345**, **354b**, **355**. *ale house*: **25** and **53**. *alcohol not only function*: in places like London, for example, potboys obviated the need to attend pubs for drinks by supplying these to workshops or lodgings; George (1976), p. 281. *pub tales*: Evans (1975), p. 146. *directions*: ibid., p. 145.

28 Place (1972), p. 27. *clubs*: ibid., pp. 37—8. George (1976), p. 294 (italics added). *Kindred*: Evans (1975), p. 144. *proprietor*: Charles Kindred, quoted in ibid., p. 145. *constables*: George (1976), p. 292.

29 *contractors*: Charles Kindred, quoted in Evans (1975), p. 144. *middlemen*: George (1976), p. 286. *hiring centres*: ibid., pp. 284—5; Charles Kindred, quoted in Evans (1975), pp. 143, 146. *transportation terminals*: George (1976), p. 290. *exchanges*: Kindred, quoted in Evans (1975) p. 145, *employment agency*: George (1976), p. 284. *irregular*: such as the piece-workers in the clothing trade; ibid., p. 285. This was also true of agricultural tasks such as draining and ditching; Kindred, quoted in Evans (1975), pp. 143—4. *seasonal employment*: such as harvesting or beating; ibid. *abuse quotation*: R. Campbell, *The London Tradesman* (London: T. Gardner, 1747), p. 193. *coal-heavers*: George (1976), p. 286.

30 *pay tables*: John Fielding, *Observations on Penal Law*, 2nd edn. (1768), p. 107, quoted in ibid., p. 287. *publicans and wives*: George (1976), p. 288.

31 *stallions*: Evans (1975), p. 143. *inquests and rights of commonage*: ibid., p. 146. *stables*: ibid., p. 144. *travel terminals*: George (1976), p. 290. *East Anglia*: Evans (1975), p. 140. Moritz (1795). Baldry (1976). *cattle deals*: Evans (1975), p. 145. *Kindred*: ibid., p. 144. Dickens (1968), p. 127, and (1972), pp. 196—8. *traveller*: Place (1972), p. 86; George (1976), p. 102.

32 *address*: George (1976), p. 103. *White Bear Inn*: ibid., p. 102. *farmer*: Charles Haney, quoted in Evans (1975), p. 142. *Place*: Testimony before the Select Committee on Education: *Parliamentary Report . . . on Education* (1835), p. 70, quoted in Place (1972), p. 81 note. *idlers*: George (1976), p. 290. *London Guide*: ibid. *wine licence*: ibid., pp. 295—6. Place (1972), p. 228. *press gangs*: ibid., p. 37.

33 *plays*: Hole (1949), pp. 133, 136. *sword matches*: ibid., p. 67. Francis Place, *Improvement of the Working People* (1834), pp. 19—20, quoted in George (1976), p. 281. *White*: Evans (1975), p. 146. *singing*: ibid., pp. 147—57, esp. pp. 149—50. *'settin' in's'*: ibid., pp. 156—7. *'pub talk'*: ibid., pp. 155—6.

34 *Southwark*: 25. *Shearbridge*: 310. *trade patronage*: this is especially true of those cases that involved buyers and purchasers with the same occupation. *Shoreditch*: 31. *Towcester*: 88. *Yorkshire*: 120. *Devon*: 347. *public houses*: 347 is an example. *Plymouth*: 186. *Whitechapel*: 245. *Whitehaven*: 262. *trio (Yorkshire)*: 258. *pair of men* (Cornwall): 383. *jealous husband* (Derbyshire): 345. *inns*: the following inns are mentioned specifically as rendezvous or as sites for ratifying drinks: Castle Inn (Marlborough Castle), Marlborough, Wilts (15b, c); Pelican Inn (George and Pelican), Newbury, Berks (15a), destroyed; Bell Inn, Birmingham (35); Pied Calf Alehouse, Spalding, Lincs (53), still in existence, according to a letter of Ms Sheila Robson, *Lincolnshire Free Press*, Spalding, Lincs, November 1979; Ram Inn, Smithfield Market, London (83a—c and f, 161 and 171); White Hart, Sittingbourne, Kent (129); Coal Barge, Maidstone, Kent (148); King's Head Inn, Staines, Surrey (156); White Lion, Wednesbury, Staffs (190); Black Swan, Great Grimsby, Lincs (208); Half-Moon, Smithfield Market, London (231); Blue Posts Inn, Stafford, Staffs (235); New Inn, Falmouth, Cornwall (243); public house, Holme-upon-Spalding-Moor, Yorks (249); White Hart Inn, Dulverton, Somerset (266), now the premises of Radley, Chanter and Co.; New Inn, Horwich End, Derbyshire (296); Bell Inn, Nottingham, Notts (299); Spread Eagle, Nottingham, Notts (300), destroyed; Crown Inn, Worcester, Worcs (309); Lamb and Flag, Cardiff, Glam. (315); Royal Oak, Swaffham Bulbeck,

Cambs (**336**); New Inn, Merrivale Bridge, Devon (**347**); and Royal Oak, Sheffield, Yorks (**349**), pre-1887.

35 *eleventh century*: **1**. *London parson*: **2**. *Warwickshire yeoman*: **7**. *Staffordshire case*: **10**.

36 *Inverness*: **13**. *London*: **14**. *activity*: all years in which over five wife-sale reports have been collected are noted. *1797*: **80**−**91**. *1812*: **130**−5 and possibly **136**. *1814*: **139**−**45**. *1815*: **148**−**56**. *1818*: **163**−**8**. *1823*: **191**−7. *1833*: **238**−**44** and possibly **245**. *1837*: **259**−**64**. *distortion by sources*: due to varying degrees of coverage. *multiple sales*: such as **186** (four linked attempts) and **260** (three linked sales). *final enumeration impossible*: due both to the volume of newspaper sources available and the *certainty* that even these did not report all sales.

37 *intensive wife-selling*: Menefee (1978), p. 575, and table, p. 576. *agricultural year*: Malcolmson sees the crop cycle as affecting fairs and wakes, with a concentration of those events in late spring and early summer (after sowing and before the harvest). Winter, however, was an off-season for wakes and fairs; Malcolmson (1973), pp. 24−5. *church feasts*: Hole (1961), p. 358; Jeaffreson (1872), vol. 1, pp. 285−7. The latter gives the following metrical yardstick:

> Advent marriage doth deny,
> But Hilary gives thee liberty;
> Septuagesima says thee nay,
> Eight days from Easter says you may;
> Rogation bids thee to contain,
> But Trinity sets thee free again.
>
> (ibid., p. 286)

popular tradition: ibid., p. 287; Hole (1961), p. 358. *May*: Hole (1961), p. 358; Baker (1977), pp. 53−4. *extra-marital connections*: Baker (1977), pp. 53−4; Hope (1970), pp. 167−74. *verse*: Baker (1977), p. 54. *1797*: this might, however, represent more comprehensive reporting due to increased public interest. *Horsham*: **177** and **204**. (There is no evidence as to the time of **189** and **283**.)

38 *Fotheringham*: **5**. *historical preference*: Jeaffreson (1872), vol. 1, p. 288. *Shakespeare*: Act 2, scene i, ll.305—6, William Shakespeare, *The Taming of the Shrew*, Act 2, scene i, ll.329—31. For the words 'I'm to be married o' Sunday', see Jeaffreson (1872), vol. 1, note pp. 289−90. *seventeenth century*: ibid., vol. 1, p. 291. *Victorian period*: ibid., vol. 1, p. 288. *preferred days*: Menefee (1978), p. 577, and table. *marriage rhyme*: Jeaffreson (1872), vol. 1, note p. 295; Hole (1961), p. 359. *lucky and unlucky days*: Hole (1961), p. 359.

39 *time of sales*: Menefee (1978), p. 578, and table. *approved hours for marriage*: Jeaffreson (1872), vol. 1, pp. 296−8. *clock set forward*: OCC, 22 February 1840, p. 2. *afternoon sales*: **186** (about 12.30), **116** (about 1.00), **268** (about 1.00), **231** (about 2.00), **240** (2.00), **171** (about 4.00), **190** (about 4.00), **154** (about 5.00), **333** (afternoon). *early morning sales*: **269** (4.00). *evening sales*: **33** (evening), **40** (evening), **69** (?), **78** (evening), **93** (evening), **140** (evening), **198** (evening), **215** (about 6.00), **336** (7.00), **347** (7.00), **286** (9.00), **311a, b** (night), **345** (nights), **355** (night), **304** (sale scheduled for the evening but woman sold before this time).

CHAPTER 4: CONNOISSEURS OF THE 'MERCHANDISE'

1 Wednesbury, Staffs, 190. *age*: 182 (under 20); 190 (45); 193 ('young'); 254 ('advanced age'); 257 (42); 294 (old? rheumatic pain in knee); 313 (old); 365 (elderly?).

2 *Chipping Ongar*: 195. *drunkard (Angus)*: 5. *'ill-looking' (London)*: 171. *labouring man (Staffs)*: 235. *'wretched looking' (London)*: 245. *'burly'*: 245.

3 *husband's employments (or identification)*: these include gentleman, parson, farmer, grazier, cattle dealer, maltster, blacksmith, nailmaker, brickmaker, stonecutter, weaver, tailor, shoemaker, butcher, tradesman, potter, basketmaker, publican, soldier (non-commissioned — 'a Substitute in the Army of Reserve'; Sergeant of the 95th Regiment), sailor, journeyman carpenter, journeyman blacksmith, journeyman nailer, journeymen (general), shepherd, drover, gardener, postillion, hostler, jockey, waterman, servant (at Furness Abbey, Cumb.; Lord ——'s lackey), painter, sweep, grinder, rag merchant, coal porter, porter, sand carrier, bricklayer, collier, miner (one at Flashhouse coal pit, Yorks), ironworker (steel-burner; one at Cyfarthfa Iron-works, Glam.), navvy (canal navigation man; one employed building the Shornecliffe Canal, Kent; one employed cleaning out the Old Dock at Grimsby, Lincs.; labouring banker; some employed in excavating Woodhead Tunnel, Cheshire), agricultural labourers, bricklayer's labourer, labourer (general), rat-catcher, gypsy, tinker, debtor, transport. Menefee (1978), table, pp. 581—4, and notes pp. 991—3.

4 *Thompson*: 234a, b, d, e. *Worcester*: 309. *Quaker*: 12a. *Jew*: 125; the presence of a simple form of Jewish divorce suggests that the husband may not have been a practising member of this faith. Rudé reports that the Ashkenazim (Polish and German Jews) lived and worked in Petticoat Lane at the time; George Rudé, *Hanoverian London, 1714-1808* (London: Secker and Warburg, 1971), p. 7. *'Cupid' (Staffs)*: 95. *'Grinder' (Staffs)*: 170. *'Rough'* (Staffs): 190. *'Duke' (Yorks)*: 269. *Staffordshire practice*: Mr Jon Raven reports that these nicknames, generally based on a physical characteristic, were often so closely identified with the individual that his real name was forgotten: 'Accounts of weddings, where the vicar was unable to proceed with the ceremony for want of a proper name, occur in various nineteenth-century papers', Raven (1978), p. 146. *afoul of law*: 266 (the husband had been transported for an unspecified crime).

5 *debtors*: 65, 333, 334. *owners or landlords*: 116, 230. *Thompson*: 234a, b, d. *Frost*: 273. *grazier*: 154.

6 See cases 234a, b, d, and e.

7 See case 79.

8 See case 190.

9 *ages at time of sale/length of marriage*: 15 (under 43); 24 (m. 10 years); 58 (m. 7 years); 68 (m. 5 years); 75 (38); 80 (m. 2 months); 82 (young); 109 (m. 'a few days before'); 113 (not more than 20); 117 (young); 131 (m. a few weeks); 139 (19 — m. six months); 142 (m. 11 years); 145 (m. for 'some time'); 154 (young); 158 (20—2); 160 (under 20 — m. about a year); 161 (23); 170 (young); 171 (m. 12 years); 174 (30 — m. 11 years); 182 (under 20 — m. under a month); 186 (young — m. two and a half years); 189 (m. about two years); 190 (23); 193 (m. one day); 195 (25); 209 (over 50); 210 (m. 'some years'); 231 (25 or under); 234 (22 or under); 239 (about 30 — m. six years);

245 (about 30); **254** (about 30); **257** (about 30); **263** (m. 10 years); **279** (m. two years); **290** (about 18); **294** (young); **300** (about 38); **303** (20); **310** (young — 'recently wedded'); **311** (m. three weeks); **318** (old); **329** (young); **347** (25); **357** (young). *short duration of marriage*: 80, 109, 131, 139, 182, 193 and 310 all appear to have lasted for six months or less. *wives younger than husbands*: **190** (22 years younger); **257** (about 12 years younger); **294**?; **313** (a 'good deal younger'); **347**.

10 'smart': **82** and **85**. 'pretty': **109**. 'tall': **113a**. 'very pretty and modest': **117**. *other similar descriptions*: **158** ('pretty enough'); **161** ('good looking'); and **171** ('muscular, as compared to her husband, and possessing an advantage of nearly 2' in height beyond her dwarfish companion, her countenance and manner betrayed evident signs of better sense and decency'); **170** ('good looking'); **183** ('a decent-looking woman'); **186** ('handsome'): **195b** ('her person was by no means unpleasing'); **204** ('decent looking woman', 'good looking woman'); **205** ('tidy looking'); **231** ('not bad looking'); **234a, b** ('a spruce, lively, buxom damsel'); **239** ('good looking woman'); **257** ('a well-looking young woman'); **272** ('a clean, industrious, quiet and careful woman, attractive in appearance and well-mannered for a woman in her position in life'); **274** ('smart-looking woman'); **280** ('thrifty, clean and managed a rough-tempered and rough-tongued man with great tact'); **290** ('country-looking girl'); **294** ('buxom young woman'); **310a, b** ('of prepossessing appearance', 'pretty young woman'); **318** ('a nice, clean body'). *London female*: **257**. *York*: **209**. *Staffordshire*: **303**. *Swaffham Bulbeck*: **336**. *Bungay*: **338**.

11 *Warwickshire*: **324**. *Herefordshire*: **76b**. *pit wench* (Staffs): **190**. *pot girl*: **15b**, and ms. notation mentioned in Note. *Cliffe (Sussex)*: **109**. *housekeepers*: **181** and **279**.

12 *Mrs Thompson*: **234a, b, d, e**. *1796 newspaper*: **79**. 'Moll': **170**. Worcester: **309**.

13 *Devon*: **186**. *legacies*: **30, 68** and **145**.

14 *rings*: **290** and **345**. *legal position mentioned*: **193a** ('married woman') and **213**. *Sussex girl*: **109**. *Cumberland daughter*: **131**. *Epping woman*; **239**. *sweetheart*: **372**. *fiancée*: **4**. *Yorkshire woman*; **118**. *Cheshire*: **284** ('he [the Superintendent of the Manchester and Salford Town Mission] seemed to find wife-lending less serious than he had feared because, as he put it, 'many of the women in the huts were not wives, but "tally-women", i.e. women who had followed the men as their mistresses').

15 *mulatto*: **113**. *age/marital condition (when not as given as 'unmarried' or bachelor')*: **15a, b, c** (married or widower); **20** (old?); **32** (young); **39** (widower); **75** (fifties); **90** (married); **94** (married); **115** (50—60); **140** (over 50); **161** (young); **174** (young); **190** (young); **215** (widower); **234a, b, d, e** (old? pensioner); **241** (married, which made the sale invalid); **245** (comparatively young); **248** (sixties); **257** (young); **259** (old); **296** (widower); **313** (middle-aged); **318** (about 70); **335** (thrice widowed); **337** (widower); **342** (married); **345** (young); **383** (56 — married; old — widower or separated). Pillet (1815), pp. 299—300. *Cornwall*: **254**. *Cheshire*: **94**.

16 *purchaser's occupations (or identifying terms)*: these include noble, gentleman, soldier (officer — lieutenant in Montague's regiment), artist (Sir Godfrey Kneller), farmer, horse-dealer, grazier, cattle-dealer, agent, maltster, whitesmith, blacksmith, nailmaker, brickmaker, slate pencil maker, mason, weaver, tailor, shoemaker, tanner, fellmonger, butcher,

mattress-maker, publican (one was landlord of the New Inn, Devon), soldier (non-commissioned — Barrack Sergeant; substitute in Army of Reserve; long drummer of the 4th Regiment), sailor, brewer's clerk, journeyman baker, journeyman carpenter, journeyman blacksmith, hog-driver, flower dealer, fruit salesman, gardener, coachman, carman, postillion, wagoner, ostler, painter, sweep, grinder, dustman, collier (pitman, 'butty collier') iron-worker, navvy, agricultural labourer, bricklayer's labourer, stonemason's labourer, labourer (general), tinker, pensioner, unemployed; Menefee (1978), table pp. 596—7, and notes pp. 997—1000. *classes*: for a discussion of class terminology, see E. P. Thompson (1976), pp. 9—11. *good manners*: **158** (he gave his arm to his purchase). *illiteracy*: **309**. *Lancashire*: **75**. *Sir Godfrey Kneller*: **12** and Lionel Cust, 'Kneller, Sir Godfrey', *Dictionary of National Biography*, Sidney Lee (ed.) vol. 31 (London: Smith, Elder & Co., 1892), p. 242. *Millward*: **229**. *Etty*: **249**. *drunkenness*: **253**. *wife-beating*: **340** and **347**. *assault*: **329**.

17 *prices as a guide to wealth*: most useful are those prices that, by their magnitude, suggest that the purchaser must have been a man of means. Menefee (1978), table pp. 666—82. *short of cash*: **60**. *borrowed money*: **318**. *sold watch*: **283**. *21 guineas*: **312**. *50 guineas*: **154**. *100 guineas*: **120**. Some of the earlier seventeenth-century cases also seem to indicate a fair investment by the purchaser: **6** (£6 to wife and £8 to husband), **7** (£5), **8** (£4). *home owners or occupiers*: **181**, **217**, **258**, **279**, **280** ('a cottage that was on lives'), **307** (lived in Simon Wisdom's cottages, Burford), **345** ('the couple's landlord'), **383**. *lodgers*: **116**, **230**, **355**.

18 Pillet (1815), pp. 299—300. *neighbours*: **69**, **70**, **94**, **181**. *sweethearts*: **76b**?, **160a**, **232**. *pity*: judging by the fact that in the Devonshire (**160**) case there is no evidence of subsequent cohabitation. *comrades*: **7**, **114a**. *shopmates*: **25**, **30**, **137**, **139**. *agents*: **162** (claimed as extenuation), **186**. *sale by overseer*: **65**. *chance-met*: **362** (sale made to customer in a bar). *strangers*: **6**, **361** Yorkshire auctioneer: **272**. *coal porter*: **100**.

19 *number of children/disposal of children*: **58** (one — girl of six months); **64** (one — to purchaser); **85**(one, or wife pregnant? — to purchaser); **102** (three — to purchaser); **103** (one — to purchaser); **114** (one — to purchaser), **129** (five — to purchaser); **142** (one? 10-year-old girl who may have been husband's child — to purchaser); **171** one, a daughter described as a 'good-looking young woman'); **186**, (two — one to purchaser; this was an illegitimate child that the wife was carrying. She had two other illegitimate children, one of whom was still living); **190** (one, a year-old baby, possibly the purchaser's illegitimate child — to purchaser); **210** (five — four to husband, one (youngest) to purchaser); **213** (two — one, a 5-year-old boy by former purchaser, to purchaser; one, a 7-year-old child by husband, kept by friends); **227** (one, a girl); **232** (one, 7-year-old boy — to purchaser); **258** (one — to purchaser); **262** (all children born in wedlock — to husband; presumably others to purchaser); **328** (5? — two to husband, rest to purchaser); **330** (five — to purchaser); **337** (one — to husband); **350** (one — to purchaser?); **356** (one, a boy; may have been born subsequent to sale), **359** (four, two boys and two girls — to purchaser); **380** (one baby — to husband, who did not sell 'because it was my own flesh and blood'); **381** (one — to purchaser). *Essex baptismal register*: **47**.

20 *Barton-under-Needwood*: **65**. *Epping*: **239**. *sale to officer keeper*: *JOxJ*, 15 August 1767, p. 1. *marriage to blind fiddler*: (1741), quoted in George

(1976), p. 306; further examples in *JOxJ*, 1 February 1800, p. 4, and ibid., 15 July 1809, p. 3.

21 *Sheffield*: **108**. *Kent*: **174**. *London*: **231**. *Suffolk*: **338**. *'itinerant'*: **294**. *pensioner*: **215**. *Whitechapel*: **245**. *Belper*: **333**.

22 *nine bidders*: **91**. *Yorkshire*: **294**. *Devon*: **347**. *suspect broadsides*: several such publications appear to have reported invented wife sales and may have chosen the occupations of the bidders in order to increase their own sales in various quarters. *Bristol sale*: **184**. *Scottish sale*: **215**.

23 *witnesses*: **35** (a man); **58** (four men, including a constable and possibly the husband); **93** (two married couples); **229** (three men); **248** (3 [male?] witnesses) **262** (impartial male friend — landlady of pub refused); **263** (potman); **269** (a man); **295** (two prominent local residents, at least one of whom was a man); **299** (a man, met by chance); **309** (landlord of Crown Inn); **348** (4 witnesses); **349** (two men); **354** (husband's friend, purchaser's friend and wife's parents present); **362** (three men, at least two of whom were shoemakers and the third announced that the sale had taken place).

24 *hundreds*: **119, 311**. *thousands*: **215, 312**. *Staffordshire group*: **170**. *Wednesbury*: **190**. *Frise*: **280**. *Cheltenham*: **223**. *Brighton*: **205d**. *Truro*: **291**. *Newark*: **246**. *child with father*: **216**. *child with nurse*: **76b**. *child with pony and cart*: **338**. *schoolgirl*: **271**. *Shearbridge*: **310a, c**. *neighbours and friends*: **196** (friend); **258a, b** (neighbours); **283** (friends); **362a** (party of shoemakers to which the husband belonged). *Halifax sale*: **260**. *Dulverton*: **266**. *inn sales*: **245, 345, 362a**. *Sheffield transaction*: **354b**. NQ, **317**.

25 *Heath presentment*: **11a**. *Pecke*: Peyton (1928), pp. 184, 188. *Young*: ibid., pp. 182, 183, 184. *Wednesbury*: G. T. Lawley, cited by F. W. Hackwood, *Wednesbury Ancient and Modern* (Wednesbury, Staffs: Ryder and Son, 1902), p. 108. *names*: Menefee (1978), note 57, p. 1004. *'eminent Attorney'*: **33**. *'learned clerk'*: **170**. *plaintiffs and court officials*: Menefee (1978), table in note 61, p.1004.

26 *'stout young fellows'*: **215**. *friends or associates*: **170** ('supporters'), **190** and **196**. *girl sold in Bristol*: **193**. *Sheffield woman*: **354**. *'good-looking young woman'*: **171**. *Deakin*: **32a** (this ended happily, however, as she married him shortly thereafter — **32b** and ms. entry in marriage register). *Halifax buyer*: **260**. *groom*: **313**. *childhood friend*: **329**. *foreman of granite works*: **347**. *Sadler*: **54**. *Captain Craven*: **99**. *Dartmouth girl*: **160**. *restoration to parents*: **119** and **278**. *Hambidge*: **307a**.

27 *1857 Divorce Act*: the gradual decline of the institution before this date has been discussed above. *justification for wife-selling*:

> The purchaser had long thought of making a bid, and at length decided that the act was proper and lawful. 'Well,' said he to John, groom to — of the Grange, 'I've thought of it and I'm right sure I can buy her, by law.' 'But,' said John, 'our master' (— was at the Bar) 'says you *can't*.' 'Ah,' replied Hodge, 'your master's not seen much law lately; maybe he's never read the new Divorce Act?' (313)

cost of divorce: Walker (1970), p. 90; R. Palmer and Raven (1976), p. 26. Jannoc (1866), p. 29; see also A. R. Wright (1928), pp. 26 – 7. *refutation*: P.T.A— (1939), p. 95. *examples*: **23, 50,110, 115, 142**; surprisingly, all of these date from the pre-1815 period. *military dislocation*: de Watteville (1954), pp. 129 – 30. *sailor story*: St*JC*, 8 January 1737, p. 1. *newspaperman*: **107**.

28 *smock weddings*: Menefee (1977), p. 588. *support*: a similar objective is
satisfied today by the combination of divorce with child support and
alimony payments.

29 *Knaresborough bargain*: **122**. *other dealings*: **49** (wife sold after disagreement
with husband); **127** (husband not on good terms with wife); **136** ('lived very
unhappily together'); **177**; **189** (wife 'had qualities which he could endure no
longer'); **234a, b, d, e** ('some family disputes'); **254** (husband 'having become
tired of his wife'); **275** (husband 'had lived uncomfortably a long time' with
wife); **279** ('never lived in peace' and a vain reconciliation attempted); **311a,
b** ('he had found her to be neither "worse nor better", as the parson said');
333 ('Her past conduct seems to have had a lot to do with Thompson's
disappearance'); **347** (husband dissatisfied with wife); **353** (wife 'had been
strongly advised to get rid of him' [her husband]); **357** (wife 'unruly . . . she
troubled him [the husband], and tiring of her . . . .'); **382** ('when a husband
wearied of his wife'). *three wives*: **118**. *Fleming*: **131**. *court questioning*: **239**.
Thompson: **234a, b, d, e**; this can be compared with **43**:

> She troubled me in every way, and is a curse in my household, reviling
> me when I come home every night, and she's a devilish Jezebel every
> day . . . .
>   I hope God will protect you, each and every one, from women like this
> one, who live to please themselves and to trouble their husbands who
> work themselves down to the very marrow of their bones for them.

Manchester account: **199a**. *Cornish case*: **173b**. *physical appearance*: **338**.
refusal to do housework: **76b**.

30 *Staffordshire husband*: **176**. Pillet (1815), pp. 301−2. *wife sale shortly after
birth of child*: **58**. *journeyman*: **82, 85**. *lived in same town*: **198** (the
husband's subsequent departure from town seems further evidence of this).
specific trip to purchase wife: **174, 270**. *identity known beforehand*: **53, 170,
224**. *Kent wife*: **232**. *husband's goods given away*: **249**.

31 *explicitly detailed*: **87** (wife 'had had previous connection' with the
purchaser); **140**; **156** (wife 'whose merits could only be appreciated by those
who best knew them. This the purchaser could boast from a long and
intimate acquaintance'); **215**; **218** (wife said she 'got the lad she loved'); **246**
(supposed adultery); **259** (alleged incontinence); **262** ('at last her predilection
for her paramour, the pitman, became so strong and undisguised that her
husband arrived at the philosophical determination of disposing of her'); **275**
(wife 'had been unfaithful'); **288** (sold to wife's paramour); **292** (the
purchaser was said to be the principal cause of the husband's conduct); **325**
(wife sold to supposed paramour); **345** ('it appears that the woman and this
man had been too friendly to please the husband'); **354b** ('a collier's wife
transferred her affections to another man'); **369** (purchaser's fancy for wife
reciprocated); **381** (husband sold wife to 'man with whom she had fallen in
love'). *Essex woman*: **195a**. *advertisement*: **79**. *London*: **111**.

32 *Rough Moey*: **190**. *Plymouth husband*: **186**. *living openly with lover*: **209**
(wife bought 'by a person with whom she has lately cohabited'); **239** ('she
had lived in open adultery with the man Bradley, by whom she had been
purchased'); **250** (wife purchased by man with whom she had cohabited for
four years); **264** (wife purchased by man with whom she had cohabited for
three years); **281** (wife purchased by man with whom she had been living for
several years); **337** (wife deserted husband and child and went to live with

other man). *Bradford*: **258**. *elopement*: **112, 131, 197, 263, 294**. *promiscuity*: **284** (navvy wives at Woodland Tunnel were, according to some, lent for a gallon of beer; different rumours seen to have been circulating here, however); **382** ('when a husband wearied of his wife and wished to . . . exchange her with someone who had similar "cattle" to dispose of!'). *purchaser's infatuation*: **313, 322**. Raven (1978), p. 61. *LRW*, (1777), p. 55.

33   *barrenness*: **136, 234a, b** and **c, 324**. *wife's cruelty*: **190** ('she would gently unstrap the wooden leg of the sleeping drunkard and thrash him with it to her heart's content'); **256** ('a woman beat her husband on the face till the blood flew about'). *husband's cruelty*: **113a** (wife had two black eyes); **173b** (husband frequently assaulted wife); **190** (the jealous husband 'took to beating her'); **272** ('ill-treatment'); **318** (the husband 'used to ill-treat his wife something awful'); **330** ('he had purchased Hooper's wife, as she had been badly used by her husband'); **357b** ('even though he constantly gave her good hidings she troubled him'). *drunkenness and ill-treatment*: **272** and **318**. *Falmouth seller*: **243**. *Irthlingborough case*: **362a**. *Higginson*: **25**. *Manchester couple*: **199b**. *wife's drunkenness*: **184** and **215** (these may not relate to actual cases, although it is difficult to understand why such a cause would have been invented).

34   *gambling*: **5** and **31** (wife sold for a lottery ticket, with the condition that if a blank was drawn, the woman would be returned). *extravagance*: **184**.

35   *Cornish examples*: **383**. *larcenous intent*: **40** and **322**. *York*: **272**. *Westmorland*: **372**. *Liverpool*: **353**. *Belper*: **333**. *army*: **19** and **213**. *debt*: **65, 333** and **334**. *1873 case*: **333**.

36   *Laws Respecting Women*: *LRW* (1777), p. 55. *Mercury*: **172**. *Essex man*: **239**. *Staffordshire husband*: **264**. *commonly held views*: this same approach can be used to justify both smock weddings and many of the ceremonies connected with squatters' rights. An implicit commentary on presence of the maintenance theory is given by S. C. Hall in **245** ('the sale released him from no responsibility either to the parish or the law'). *1775 sale*: **37**. *1815*: **154**. S. C. Hall and Courtney Kenny also take this view of the purchaser's actions: Hall, **245** ('the transaction freed his successor from danger of an action for *crim. con.*'); Kenny (1929), p. 495. *crim. con. in upper society*: Stone (1977), p. 506, notes that 'it was alleged at the time that some aged husbands married young wives with the deliberate purpose of making money by threats of legal proceedings against the latter's lovers.' (The abbreviation *crim. con.* stands for 'criminal conversation' rather than 'criminal connection', however.) Jarrett (1976), pp. 112–13, gives a short discussion of the Worsley case of 1782, in which the husband collected only a shilling damages because it was shown that he had 'connived at the affair'. *crim. con. at other levels*: at Thetford £5 was awarded in an action concerning a sailor's wife (this low amount was partially due to the woman's acquiescence); *LM*, 5 April 1800, p. 3.

CHAPTER 5: 'ROLL UP, AND BID SPIRITED'

1   *specific suggestions of stereotypical actions*: this is usually done with stock phrases or through mention of elements common in most sales but found lacking in the specific instance.

2   *written agreements*: while probability does not suggest that these were

specifically required for wife sales, their 'formal' legal nature makes their contents good clues to theoretical sale rules. Several, for instance, mention money, delivery in market and alcoholic extras.

3 *Essex birth register*: 47. *Moses Maggs*: 190. *Arundel man*: 200. *Cheltenham*: 223. *Derby woman*: 263. *Staffordshire*: 264. *Oxfordshire*: 327. *elsewhere*: 227. *Henry Frise*: 280. *Leeds*: 285.

4 *Staffordshire*: 170, 264, and 311a, b (compulsion used on toll-keeper). *necessity*: 262. *Frise*: 280. *foreman*: 347; perhaps this was a rationalization after court decisions had found sale participants guilty of breaking the law.

5 *Scotland*: 8. *1773 document*: 35. *London attorney*: 80. *persistence*: 186 ('she had been told by different persons that the thing could be done by public sale in the market-place on a market day'; 241 ('the bargain was not considered legal — first . . .': see quote in text); 258a, b (the wife feared that the sale would not be legal, presumably because it was not being held in public market); 263 ('deliver her, as he called it, according to law'; this was done with a halter on market day); 264; 280 (bought in market); 327 (legal if husband 'took her to market in a halter'). *necessity for public sale*: 186 and 310a ('they and their friends were so egregiously ignorant as to believe that they could secure their own legal separation by such an absurd course as this'). *Maggs*: 190. *Staffordshire man*: 264. *London husband*: 124. *Somerset*: 241. *Devon*: 347.

6 62 and 65 ('in the usual way, which has been lately practised' — halter); 69 ('in due form' — halter, witnesses?); 95a ('the usual delicate ceremony . . . was dispensed with' — no halter); 98 ('in the customary manner on such occasions' — halter); 99 ('the usual tho' disgusting form'— halter); 105 ('with the usual customs' — halter, other ?); 107 ('with the usual honourable appendage round her neck'); 111 ('general opinion which has so long pervaded the lower ranks of society, namely, that a man . . . has a right to dispose of her at a public market in the same manner as he does cattle', 'in due form' — halter?); 118 ('according to the customary *etiquette*' — halter); 122 ('equipped in the *usual style*' — halter); 125 ('with the customary appendage' — halter); 161 ('in the customary form' — halter); 172 (halter, open market); 179 ('with the customary practice' — halter); 218 ('according to the usual custom' — new halter purchased); 240 ('in the usual manner' — halter); 262 ('disposing of her not with a halter round her neck in the public market-place, but by private and solemn treaty in a public house').

7 *group of traits*: LRW (1777), p. 55 (wife's consent, market, halter, best bidder); D'Archenholtz (1789), vol. 2, p. 33 (wife's consent, halter); Pillet (1815), pp. 299–300 (sale due to adultery, public square, market day, halter, minimum price — a few shillings, witnesses); S.R— (1853), p. 209 (public place, halter); Sternberg (1853), p. 429 (market, halter); T.T.W— 'Sale of a Wife', *NQ*, series 4, vol. 6, 26 November 1870, p. 455 (halter); Harland (1973), p. 177 (halter, written receipt); A.J.M— (1881), p. 133 (wife's consent, halter — new if possible, minimum price 1s, only one sale by each husband); Andrews (1892), p. 199 (public place, halter); John Ashton, *Old Times: A Picture of Social Life at the End of the Eighteenth Century* (London: John C. Nimmo, 1885), p. 342, (1888), p. 1, and (1896), p. 295 (market, halter); GT (1903), p. 1 (nominal sum); Thomas Ratcliffe, 'T' Wife Bazaar': Childers', *NQ*, series 10, vol. 9, 23 May 1908, p. 416 (pub, halter); Bloom (1921), p. 47, and (1930), p. 54 (three tollgates, three villages, market, halter, price one to three half-crowns); Lawley (B) (sale predetermined, three

tollgates, market, halter, bidder, husband own auctioneer, written receipt); Hackwood (1974), p. 70 (tollgate, market, halter); A. R. Wright (1928), pp. 26 – 7 (wife's consent, tollgate, market, halter, minimum price 1s, written receipt, purchaser cannot resell); Kenny (1929), pp. 495 – 6 (sale predetermined, wife's consent, market, halter, minimum price 1s; A. Saxon, 'Sale of a Wife', *Notes and Queries for Somerset and Dorset*, (Sherborne, Dorset), vol. 22, June 1937, p. 141 (market, village green, halter, witnesses, money); Hole (1970), p. 7 (market, halter, minimum price — 1s); P.T.A — (1939), p. 96 (wife's consent, market, public place, halter, witnesses, written receipt); Simpson (1973), pp. 94 – 5 (public place, halter, witnesses, written receipt); Baker (1974), p. 147 (halter, money); Porter (1974), p. 28 (halter, minimum price 1s); Briggs (1974), p. 116 (sale predetermined, market, halter, minimum price 2s 6d, witnesses); Palmer and Raven (1976), p. 26 (sale predetermined, wife's consent); Jones-Baker (1977), p. 72 (market, halter, highest bidder); Raven (1978), pp. 61 – 4 (sale predetermined, three tollgates, market, new halter, price previously agreed upon, husband own auctioneer, written receipt, crying of sale).

8   *public nature of sale*: that the problems mentioned in the text were very real ones is apparent from the abuses connected with Fleet and clandestine marriages, which were at least partially rectified by the Marriage Act of 1754. *minimum price*: the supposed Yorkshire minimum price of 1s (A.J.M—, 1881, p. 133) is undercut in **78** (6d), **314** (pint of ale) and **342** (quart of beer).

9   *categories*: many causes might, of course, fall into more than one grouping.

10 *Hythe*: **113a**. *Suffolk man*: **49** *Barnsley man* **256**. *Duke of Chandos*: **15**.

11 *East Lothian*: **8**. *York husband*: **272**. *Westmorland*: **372**. *lieutenant*: **13**. *London carpenter*: **25**. *wife kept till morning*: **69, 70**. *Renfrewshire*: **248**. *Northamptonshire shoemaker*: **362a**. *Lancashire cobbler*: **318**.

12 *Parham Fair*: **24**. *Bungay Fair*: **338**. *Belper woman*: **333** (see **334** for another example). *Liverpool*: **353**. *Duke of Chandos*: **15**. *Lancashire purchaser*: **318**. *Sussex hopeful*: **283**.

13 Another reason for the rarity of newspaper advertisements may have been the social position of most husbands as compared with that of the normal newspaper advertiser, as well as the position of the potential purchaser at whom such advertisements would have been pitched. *initial cost*: after 1725 the normal charge for advertisements was 2s 6d; Cranfield (1962), p. 226. *tax*: K. Williams (1977), p. 26. This amounted to 1s for each advertisement, regardless of length, after 1712 and 2s after 1757; Cranfield (1962), pp. 225 – 6. *advertisement*: **79**. See also **71**, *rarity*: this should not be taken to indicate that they were necessarily more common at an earlier time, as there is no evidence to support this premise. *correspondence and literary ventures*: Cranfield (1962), pp. 99 – 116. *selling of items*: K. Williams (1977), p. 25.

14 *at least two cases*: **186** is another possible example, although it could also refer to the use of a bellman. *Cambridgeshire*: **336**. *Devon*: **347**. *printed libels*: Goldsworthy, (1975), fig. 29. E. P. Thompson (1976), p. 70, notes that even food-riots often 'were preceded by handwritten (and in the 1790s printed) handbills'. *call to poor*: this occurred at Tenterden, Kent, in May of that year; Jarrett (1976), p. 54.

15 *bellman*: **156** (bellman gave notice in market of sale at inn); **170; 190; 197** (bellman announced sale of eloped wife); **234a, b, d, e; 256** (bellman); **297** (town crier); **304** (town crier); **310** (town crier, bellman 'clothed in the

splendid habit of a British beadle'); possibly **186**. *'Jimmy the Grinder'*: **170**. *Moses Maggs*: **190** (division added). It is possible to see how this separation might have affected other announcements:

> The sale
> of a woman
> by public auction
> at the town hall
> in this town
> being the property
> of a jockey. (**297**)

The song 'Sally Lett' suggests a similar origin; see **385**. *Carlisle*: **234a, b, d, e**.

16 *lost pig*: as shown in commentary to 'The Town Crier', an early nineteenth-century print by William Davison, Alnwick, Northumberland (coll. of S. P. Menefee). *horse race*: Baldry (1976), p. 159. *monetary return*: ibid., pp. 159, 238. *French sailors*: ibid., p. 238. For a further description of a local bellman, see Grey (1935), p. 43.

17 *Bilston*: **170**. *elsewhere*: **190**. *Plymouth*: **186**. *exaggeration*: this may in fact be related to 'The Fortunate Purchaser' motif. *Derbyshire*: **147**. *founded rumours*: **249** and **311a**. *unfounded rumours*: **291** (rumour was rife on Saturday that a sale would occur the following Monday). *1859*: **311a**. *Truro*: **291**.

18 Pillet (1815), pp. 299—300. *London shopkeeper*: **111**. *wife impervious to threats*: **112**. *Derbyshire*: **263**. *Cumberland*: **131**. *sales after elopements*: **197** and **294** ('matters were talked over and a sale agreed upon').

19 *Huntingdonshire man*: **181**. *Louth*: **279**. *Yorkshire*: **258a, b**. *Plymouth*: **186**. *remarriage*: **115** ('after some negotiation') and **142** (a melodramatic, reworked account) are samples. *meeting known*: **80a** (according to a previous agreement); **137b** ('according to a preconcerted arrangement among the parties'); **183** (according to a previous agreement); **224** (set purchaser known); **243** (the husband met the purchaser to dispose of his wife); **262** (husband, wife, and lover met at a public house); **275** (the husband interviewed his wife's lover and agreed to sell her to him on the following Saturday); **322** (a bachelor became enamoured of the wife and 'negotiations were conducted for her purchase'); **354** ('the husband was willing to renounce his claim for suitable compensation. So the parties assembled in a public house to arrange matters' — this group included husband and purchaser, each with a friend, the wife, and her parents). *meeting inferred*: **140** (a militia man sold his wife to her adulterer in Nottingham market when there on holiday); **174** (the eventual purchaser accompanied the husband and wife to town); **264** (the woman was sold in a near-empty market within a few minutes to a man who had come from the same town and with whom she had been living three years); **270** (the purchaser had come from Sheffield to Rotherham to buy the woman).

20 *Lincolnshire*: **53**. *Renfrewshire*: **248**. *Stockport*: **229**. *lawyers*: **82** and **85**. *'the parties had consulted an Attorney'*: **80a**. *1877*: **337a** (but see **b** and **c**).

21 *Plymouth husband*: **186**. *stonecutter's foreman*: **347**. *Yorkshire labourer*: **313**.

22 *Truro*: **383**. *fair-minded husband*: **69** (the husband, however, later repurchased his wife 'at an advanced price' — see **70**).

23 *'smart'*: **82** and **85**. *'tidy'*: **205a**—**c**. *'ill-looking'*: **171**. *'of good appearance'*:

100. *'his Majesty's uniform'*: **183**. *London husband*: **257**. *Mansfield man*: **290**. *smock frock*: **183**. *Wiltshire suitor*: **40**.

24   *sold in shift*: **236**. *'respectably dressed'*: **270**. *'well-dressed'*: **134**. *'dashingly attired'*: **241**. *Berkshire sale*: **206**. *London report*: **154**. *Hereford*: **76**. *commonplace of contemporary female dress*: according to tradition, a landing by the French at Padstow was aborted when they mistook a number of women dressed in red cloaks for British soldiers (R. C. Hope, 1968, p. 32); *JOxJ*, 3 November 1810, p. 1: 'If we may judge from the *rage* for *scarlet cloaks*, the *scarlet fever* is making rapid strides among our female pedestrians'; Moritz, writing in 1782, notes: 'The women of the lower class here, wear a kind of short cloak made of red cloth' (Moritz, 1795, p. 182); in speaking of Wantage in the late eighteenth and early nineteenth century: 'The women wore red cloaks' (Agnes Gibbons and E. C. Davey, *Wantage Past and Present*, London: William Walker, 1901, p. 95); women commonly wore red cloaks 'in the days of the Georges' (G. T. Lawley, *Staffordshire Customs, Superstitions and Folklore*, n.d., p. 41, quoted in Raven, 1978, p. 132). *Gloucestershire wife*: **275**. *Wednesbury woman*: **190**. *Cumberland woman*: **234a, b, d**.

25   *Smithfield Market (London)*: **80** (Lisson Green − 5 and a half miles); **111** ('west end of town'); **123** (Chick Lane); **124** (Kensington Gravel Pits); **125** (Petticoat Lane); and **154** (6 miles). *Smithfield Market (Birmingham)*: **35** (Willenhall − 10 miles) and **247** (Coleshill Street). *distance involved*: **35, 80, 111** (for distances, see immediately above); **113** (Shorncliffe−Hythe, 3 and a half miles); **123, 124, 125** and **126** (Spitalfields−Billingsgate market); **127** (exception Bewcastle, Cumb.−Newcastle, Northumb., 51 miles); **148** (Goudhurst−Maidstone, 12 and three-quarter miles); **149** (Ferrybridge−Pontefract, 2 and a half miles); **154**; **174** (Broughton−Canterbury, 5 miles); **186** (Ivy Bridge−Modbury, 4 and a quarter miles and Ivy Bridge−Plymouth, 9 and a half miles); **193** (Rosemary St, Bristol−Bristol market); **232** (Debtling−Cranbrook, 16 miles); **234 a,b** (country−Carlisle, 3 miles); **235** (Dunston Heath−Stafford, 5 and a half miles); **243** (Mylor Bridge−Falmouth, 3 and a half miles); **246** (Southwell−Newark, 7 and a quarter miles); **247**; **254** (Branwell−St Austell, 5 and a quarter miles); **258a, b** (Great Horton−Shearbridge−planned to sell wife at Bradford, 2 miles from Great Horton); **263** (Turnditch−Wirksworth, 5 and a half miles − wife and purchaser had eloped to Whaley Bridge, 27 miles from Turnditch and 26 and a half miles from Wirksworth); **264** (Burntwood−Walsall, 8−9 miles); **294** (Thorne−Goole, 8 miles); **307** (Burford−Chipping Norton, 9 and a half miles); **311a, b** (Dixon's Green, Dudley−Hall St, Dudley); **318** (−− Moor−Blackburn); **320** (North Dovey−Chagford, 6 miles); **382** (Mobberley−Altrincham, 7 and three-quarter miles); **383** (Redruth−Helston, 10 miles; Redruth−Truro, 8 and a half miles).

26   *purchasers' habitations*: **126** (exception: Billingsgate market−Newcastle, Northumb., 274 miles − presumably on a visit to London); **177** (Horsham−Billingshurst, 7 miles); **186** (Modbury−Plymstock, 8 and a half miles; **246** (Southwell−Newark, 7 and a quarter miles); **263** (Wirksworth−Shottlegate − wife and purchaser had eloped to Whaley Bridge, 26 and a half miles from Wirksworth and 29 miles from Shottlegate), **264** (Walsall−Burntwood, 8−9 miles); **270** (Rotherham−Sheffield, 7 miles). **307** (Chipping Norton−Burford, 9 and a half miles); **383**

(Helston—Lizard Head, 11 and a half miles; Truro—Falmouth, 8 and a half miles). *another market town used.* **246**, **264** and **307**. *previous agreement*: **264**.

27 6*Cumberland sale*: **127**. *Somerset sale*: **241**. *Devon woman*: **186** (the towns were 11 miles apart). *oft-sold Cornish wife*: **383**. *Smithfield market*: **257** (the markets were 1 and a half miles apart). *Kent husband*: **148**.

28 *halter about neck*: Menefee (1978), p. 648, and note 35, p. 1020. *waist*: ibid., p. 648, and note 36, p. 1020. *arm*: **183** and **318**. *Epping*: **239**. *Walsall*: **264**. *positioning of halter not specified*: Menefee (1978), p. 648, and note 40, pp. 1020—1. *Belper debtor's wife*: **333**. *Liskeard husband*: **197**. *Boston husband*: **218**.

29 *Sussex*: **200**; italics added. *Warwickshire*: **386b** (see also **a**). *London*: **17**. *legality of rough music*: Hole (1961), p. 288. *Lincolnshire informants*: Rudkin (1973), pp. 53—4. It may be recalled that the demonstration against a Burford wife purchaser lasted three nights (**307**). *Yorkshire*: Hole (1940), p. 23. *Harpenden*: Grey (1935), pp. 161—2. *Wiltshire*: F. A. Carrington, 'Of Certain Wiltshire Customs', *Wiltshire Archeological Magazine*, vol. 1, 1854, pp. 88—9. *Carmarthenshire*: D. C. Williams, 'Casgliad o Lên Gwern Sir Gaerfyddin', *Transactions of National Eisteddfod of Wales, Llanelly, 1895* (1898), p. 303, quoted in Owen (1968), p. 169. *Charlecote*: *Folk-Lore*, (London), vol. 24 1913, p. 241, cited in R. Palmer (1976), pp. 96—7. *Headington*: ODFS, (1951), p. 14. *formal aspects*: Menefee (1977), pp. 871, 990. *prize fights*: W. H. Barrett, *Tales from the Fens*, Enid Porter (ed.) (London: Routledge & Kegan Paul, 1963), pp. 58—63. *three blows*: in this case the wife was lashed three times with a whip for her treatment of an illegitimate child; *BH*, 27 July 1878, cited in E. P. Thompson (1972), p. 297, and note 51. *smock wedding* (Rhode Island, USA): Earle (1898), pp. 53—4. *divination*: Menefee (1974), pp. 248—52. In Northern Ireland on May Eve churns were washed in 'three landlord's waters' before a libation was poured to the fairies; Sheila St Clair, *Folklore of the Ulster People* (Cork, Co. Cork: Mercier Press, 1971), p. 39.

30 *Wednesbury*: **190**. *Dudley*: **311**.

31 *Yorkshire*: **258**. *other cases*: **186** and **263**. *Mobberley husband*: **196b**; this may be paralleled by the escorts mentioned in **170**. *Dartmouth*: **160**. *man named Barnes*: **202**. *false pretences*: **223**.

32 *Boston*: **218**. *Plymouth*: **186**. *Smithfield*: **154** (husband and wife, however, are described as being a cut above the normal sales participants). *Islington*: **257** (the husband is described as of 'shabby-genteel exterior'). *Shropshire*: **252**.

33 *Maidstone*: **148**. *appearance at agreed hour*: **234a, b, d** and **240**. *Truro*: **291**. *Yorkshire*: **157**. *Smithfield*: **171**. *John Nash*: **193**. *Derbyshire debtor's wife*: **333**.

34 *Stafford*: **235**. *Canterbury*: **174**. *halter bought*: **218, 255, 263, 290**. *halter borrowed*: **333**. *placed on woman*: Menefee (1978), p. 652, and note 7, p. 1022. *price*: **218, 255**. *Sheffield*: **108a**. *Kent man*: **174**. *London wife*: **231**. *Epping*: **239**. *Suffolk husband*: **338**.

35 *sales room*: **129** and **336**. *open space*: **137, 242a, 246a, 310a, c**. *post*: **113a**. *railing*: **80, 83, 139, 147, 231, 257** (tied to what is not specifically stated). *Pillet*: **139a, 147**. *Bilston*: **170**. *Carlisle woman*: **234a, b, d, e**. *Devon*: **347** (table). *Yorkshire*: **272** (table) and **294** (chair). *Swaffham Bulbeck*: **336**. *Wednesbury*: **190**.

36 *not characteristic*: **95** specifically mentions the halter's absence. *halter around neck*: Menefee (1978), p. 654, and note 4, pp. 1023—4. *waist*: ibid., p. 654, and note 5, p. 1024. *arm*: **222**; see also note 28. *double loop*: **239** and **264**. *silk*: **154** and **241** ('covered with silk'). *ribbon*: **277** (white ribbon) and **310b**. *decorated with ribbons*: **310a, c**. *Wales*: **43**. *specific inclusion in purchase price*: **65, 89, 290, 300b**. 'Magician and His Pupil': a widespread international tale type (Grimm, no. 68, Aarne-Thompson, no. 325). This story is found in both Ireland and Scotland. Briggs (1970—71), part A, vol. 1, pp. 162—4 ('The Black King of Morocco') and pp. 347—9 ('The King of the Black Art'). See J. G. McKay (ed.), *Gille A' Bhuideir: The Wizard's Gillie and Other Tales* (London: St Catherine Press, n.d.), pp. 13—31 (the hero resumes his proper form when he rubs the bridle from his head, but it appears, by analogy with his previous transformations, that he *becomes* the bridle as an interim step and then changes to a man when this touches the ground). The specific Stith Thompson number given to this belief is C. 837 (*Tabu: losing bridle in selling man transformed to horse*), Briggs (1970—71), p. 163. *France* (at Cornimont, in the Vosges): Mauss (1969), p. 64. *wearing of colored ribbons*: Williams and Lloyd (1969), p. 124. *quotation*: ibid., p. 99. *college cap*: S. Baring Gould *et al. Songs of the West*, C. J. Sharp (ed.), revised edn. (London: Methuen, n.d. [1889]), notes p. 2. *red ribbons*: ibid., p. 9.

CHAPTER 6: SIGNED, SEALED AND DELIVERED

1 *political speeches*: Goldsworthy (1975), pp. 41—2, gives some examples. *Wednesbury*: **190**. *tinker's wife*: **336**. *Bungay Fair*: **338**. *Warwickshire*: **324**. *Carlisle*: **234a, b, d, e**. *mad dog*: at this time no cure was available for rabies, Harold N. Johnson, 'Rabies', *Encyclopaedia Britannica* (1964), vol. 18, pp. 862—4. Period newspapers are full of morbid cases concerning those who were bitten by such animals and succumbed to hydrophobia. *cholera morbus*: an epidemic of this disease started about October 1831 (in Sunderland, Durham) and had spread to London by January 1832. The mention would have been readily recognizable from references in period newspapers. Additionally, several popular broadsides on the subject existed — one, 'The Cholera's Coming', was sung to the tune of 'The Campbells are Coming'. Another, 'Cholera Humbug or The Arrival and Departure of the Cholera Morbus', includes the following verse:

> In every street as you pass by,
> 'Take care', they say, 'or you will die;'
> While others cry, 'It's all my eye,
> There is no cholera morbus.'

Obviously, the disease was a topical matter; R. Palmer (1974), pp. 156—9. *Mount Etna*: a serious eruption occurred here in 1830; 'Etna, Mount', *Encyclopedia Britannica*, vol. 9 (London: Encyclopaedia Britannica Inc., 1910), p. 852. *four parts*: this formalism, however, could have resulted from broadside improvements. *catchword*: **234a, b, d** and **e, 190**. *humorous nature*: **170**; compare this with **385**. *capacity for drink*: **170** and **190**. and **234a, b, d, e**. *York*: **272**. *London woman*: **161**. *London male*: **158**. *Lincolnshire*: **220**. *Nottingham*: **300**.

2 *few people*: **264**. *Staffordshire*: **190**. *Bilston*: **170**.
3 *stated price/actual price*: **43** (£3:£1); **95** (1d:5s 6d); **100** (£1 1s:£1 1s); **108a** (£1 1s:£1 1s); **140** (3d:6d); **149** (1s:11s); **158** (15s:15s); **200** (£3:£2); **220** (2s:2s); **233** (£1:£1); **234a, b, d, e** (£2 10s:£1 10s and a Newfoundland dog); **239** (1s 6d:2s 6d); **243** (£50:10s); **246** (£1 10s:£1); **248** (£20, Scots: £20, sterling); **300a** (2s 6d: 1s); **345** (glass of ale: glass of ale); **353** (£3?:£7); **354b** (£3: £1 10s); **370** (1s 6d: withdrawn); **236** (£1 — ?). *withdrawn*: **370**. This may also be true of **241** (woman bought in at 5s). *fixed minimum*: minima are stated by several authors without citing authority. *London*: **158**. *Yorkshire*: **108a**. *haggling*: **43**, **89**, **231**, **300a**. *Sheffield*: **354b**. *pre-selected purchaser forced to bid*: **170** and **318**. *bidding*: **86a** (two bidders); **91** (nine bidders); **95** (several bidders); **129** (more than one bidder?); **161** (more than one bidder: 6d, 9d — 3d increases); **171** (more than one bidder; 2s 6d); **176** (more than one bidder); **184** (four bidders: 5s, 10s, 15s — 5s increases); **186** (more than one bidder: 5s, 10s, 15s — 5s increases); **201** (a 'few' bidders); **215** (five bidders: £1 10s, £1 10s 6d, £1 12s 6d, £1 15s — 6d minimum increases); **239** (more than one bidder); **240** (more than one bidder: 4s, 4s [4s 6d?] — 6d increases); **249** (2 bidders: 1s — 1s increase); **347** (three bidders: coat, pick — bids in kind); **254** (two bidders, in tandem: 2d — 2d increase); **257** (several bidders: initial bid 5s — wife bought for £1 6s); **270** (several bidders); **294** (more than one bidder: 3d, 1s); **311** (more than one bidder: 1½d); **318** (more than two bidders: 6d, 7d, 2s, 2s 1d); **336** (more than one bidder: 6d, 1s, 1s 6d, 2s — 6d increases). *Lancashire*: **199**. *Cambridgeshire*: **336**. *two purchasers*: **254**.
4 *no acceptable bids*: **241** and **370**. *hung on hand*: **100**. *Cornish bidder*: **166**. *prices*: earlier examples included £14 (£8 to the husband, £6 to the wife), £5, £4, £52 10s and £20. In later sales, prices were more commonly 5s, 2s, 6d, 1s, and 6d. The actual record is, of course, mixed, with some cheap early sales prices and some expensive late ones, but the growing tokenism of prices is an accurate generalization; Menefee (1978), table pp. 666 — 82. *Yorkshire*: **120**. *Repurchase and resale*: **260**. *London*: **158**. *Devon*: **347**. *Towcester*: **88**. *Newcastle*: **89**. *Smithfield*: **107**. *Holme-upon-Spalding Moor*: **249**.
5 *Ashby-de-la-Zouch*: **224**. *Devon wife*: **186**. *Rough Moey*: **190**. *Cambridgeshire tinker*: **336**. *Nottingham*: **140** (the woman was put up for 3d and sold for 6d). *Herefordshire husband*: **76**. *Newark*: **246**. *Horsham*: **283**.
6 *sale by weight*: **11** (2d per lb); **18** (three-farthings per lb); **33** (5½d per lb). *Hannah Hull*: Earle (1894), p. 43: *guess*: **18**. *alcoholic beverages*: Menefee (1979), table pp. 694 — 6. *food*: **19** (bread); **20** (leg of mutton); **346** (dinner). *tobacco*: **122** and **366**. *animals*: **24** (bullock); **154** (horse) **234a, b, d**, 3 (Newfoundland dog); **381** (horse and van). *lottery ticket*: **31**. *barter or sale*: **24** (bullock sold) and **381** (horse and van exchanged for 1962 Jaguar, which was then exchanged for £60 and a motorcycle).
7 *price/return*: **80** (10s 6d:£20 in bad [Birmingham] halfpence); **97** (5s:2s 6d); **277** (5s:6d); **288** (1s:1½d). *London publican*: **80**; period newspapers report that some tradesmen refused to accept these coins. *Suffolk*: **273**. *gown*: **51** (£1 1s). *coach*: **78** (£1 1s for trip to Manchester). *body clothes*: **79**. *furniture*: **103** and **129**. *bed and bedding*: **138**. *other items*: **129** (horse and cart). *social factors*: the husband would obviously prefer to retain legitimate rather than illegitimate children, while a mother would be more necessary for the welfare of younger children. *economic factors*: both husband and wife would desire to retain children who were capable of contributing to the family income rather than being a drain on its resources; Stone (1977), pp. 468 — 9, 472 — 3.

8   *market toll*: 35 (1s [toll?] entered in market book); 65; 78 (clerk of market received 4d); 195 (purchaser paid 1d market toll); 205 (husband paid 1s toll, which was entered in the market book by the clerk of the market); 239 (6d toll paid); 254 (husband paid 1d toll). *payment entered in toll book*: 35 (Bell Inn), 65, 205. *Whitehouse*: 35. *Brighton*: 205.

9   *Fittleworth*: 87. *Brighton*: 205 (paid by husband). *London*: 231. *Yorkshire*: 269. *resale of halter*: 250 (6d) and 290 (halter purchased for occasion).

10 *written contracts*: 93 ('the articles of separation and sale were formally signed by the contracting parties, and witnessed by two wedded couples'); 148 (? — a 'deed and covenant', which was witnessed); 217 (bargain drawn up and signed by respective parties); 235 (? — transaction ratified at Blue Posts Inn); 248 (contract drawn up and signed by three witnesses); 258 ('all the persons present signing their hands as witnesses to the deed of transfer'); 300 (articles of agreement signed at an inn); 302 (purchaser produced certificate showing he had bought wife for £1); 343 (document with receipt stamp); 348 (four people present signed document as witnesses); 355 (purchaser took a receipt for his money); 377 (agreement signed by purchaser to take over wife 'with all appurtenances'); 380 (a document given to the purchaser). *inns*: 170, 229, 235?, 258, 300, 354. *professional assistance*: 170. *Somerset*: 29; parson's signature and that of a witness follow. *Millward*: 229; drawn up on a 1s. 6d. stamp. *Middleton*: 309. *Boothroyd*: 349; the signatures of the participants and those of two witnesses follow. *Taylor*: 354. *Belfast*: 346. *Bodmin*: 302. *Yorkshire court*: 343.

11 *lack of writing skills*: 309. *Whitehaven*: 262. *Nottingham*: 299. *transaction*: 295 and 362 (an oral arrangement made, giving the names of two witnesses). *delivery*: 69. *non-liability for debt*: 58.

12 *liability*: the same problem of liability was responsible for the use of smock weddings. *Balls advertisement*: 58; the names of several witnesses follow. *Yorkshire advertisement*: 168. *Irthlingborough*: 362. *Lancashire*: 230 (done the day after delivery). *London*: 14.

13 *Oxfordshire*: 11. *bargain 'struck'*: 200, 243 and 299. *Fittleworth*: 87. *Oxfordshire*: 60. *Derbyshire*: 345. *Mansfield*: 290. *Islamic divorce*: Mair (1977), pp. 182, 191 — 6. *Dudley*: 311a, b. *kissing*: 7, 53 (former husband also kissed), 60, 190. *Goole*: 294. *Bristol*: 184. *smock weddings*: Menefee (1977), pp. 586 — 686. *Buckinghamshire*: 198.

14 previous agreement: 181, 183 and 230 (next day). *prior payment*: 207 (after purchase price — ale — consumed), 231, 275 and 337. *total transfer*: 33 (in one week's time) and 183. *partial transfer*: 13 and 120. *Renfrewshire*: 248. *Yorkshire*: 269. *Rotherham*: 270. *Derbyshire*: 296. *Scotland*: 8. *Wales*: 43. *Staffordshire*: 235. *Pillet*: 147. *delivered thus equipped*: in almost all these cases, the halter was placed around the wife's neck; Menefee (1978), p. 691, and note 63, p. 1031. *Jackson's Oxford Journal*: 60a. *transfer after completion of payment*: 170 and 281. *Spalding*: 53. *Derbyshire*: 263. *white ribbon*: 277. *Wath Bowling-Green*: 38.

15 *Derbyshire*: 147 *Herefordshire*: 76. *Suffolk*: 105; this latter is reminiscent of the Sussex street crossings felt necessary to establish a smock wedding as official — *SWA*, 5 March 1770, p. 4, and ibid., 10 November 1794, p. 3. The same view was held in the United States — Earle (1898), pp. 54 — 7. *purchaser's house*: 94 and 325. *Frise*: 280. *Aston*: 335. *removed*: 170. *retained*: 234a, b, d, e (he used it for the dog he had acquired in trade). *Newark*: 246. *horse*: 215. *conveyance*: 257 (coach). *Blackfriar's Bridge*: 100.

16 See 318.

17 *alcoholic payment*: Menefee (1978), table pp. 694 – 6. *beer*: ibid. *gin*: **69, 70, 102, 126, 132, 232, 239, 347** (Plymouth gin)). *punch*: **59, 104** and **117.** *brandy*: **231.** *whisky*: **243.** *cider*: **255.** George (1976), p. 52. *assessment*: a weaver (**126**), a sand carrier (**232**) and a stonemason (**347**) are listed as husbands receiving gin. The same weaver and a journeyman carpenter (**68**) are the only men whose occupations were specifically associated with porter. It should be noted that there is no evidence — perhaps the consequence of a lack of cases — from the major period of gin drinking, 1720 – 51; George (1976), p. 41. *quantities in excess of 1 gallon*: **145** (6 gallons), **190** (3 gallons) and **347** (2 gallons). *total sales price*: Menefee (1978), pp. 697 – 8, and table pp. 694 – 6.

18 *1808*: **123.** *weaver*: **126.** *Staffordshire*: **190.** *Bilston*: **170.** *post-sale drinking sessions*: **126?**; **152**; **161**; **170**; **176** (the expense was stood by both the husband and the purchaser); **190**; **207**; **208** (the parties retired to an inn to 'settle the purchase'); **218** (the husband 'drank to the luck of the purchaser'); **220** (they retired to a public house 'to quaff the heavy wet'); **231**; **235** (the parties went to an inn 'to ratify the transfer'); **239** (? — the purchaser and wife went to a public house and the husband got drunk, but the evidence does not make clear whether this took place at the same inn); **258** (at the purchaser's house); **262** (they spent the evening together, 'as merry as grigs'); **300?**; **309**; **316.** *Nottingham*: **207.** *Worcester*: **309.** *drink not specifically supplied*: **218, 231, 239, 243?, 282, 292?** There appears to have been no ceremonial consumption in the two questioned cases. *London*: **231**; *Epping*: **239.**

19 *friends and helpers*: **190.** *witnesses*: **299.** *wife and purchaser*: **195a** ('regaling themselves with some strong brown'); **254** (wife with her two purchasers); **283** (with 'friends'); **355.** *husband*: **142, 184, 234a, b** and **d** 'indulging in the effusions of Bacchus and repeatedly exulting in his happy release from bondage'), **245** (? — wife and purchaser are reported to have walked away). *'row'*: **152.** *1817*: **161.**

20 *'moisten'*: **309.** *'wet'*: **161.** *'musicing' newlyweds*: John Greaves Nall, *Great Yarmouth and Lowestoff*, etc. (London: Longman, Green, Reader and Dyer, 1860), pp. 182 – 3; Porter (1974), pp. 26 – 7. *mock punishments*: *JOxJ*, 12 January 1754, p. 2 (repeal of the Naturalization Bill); ibid., 26 January 1793, p. 3 (hanging and burning of Tom Paine's effigy). A correlation appears to exist between this distribution of liquor and those punishments 'approved of' by influential individuals within the community, which would relate this to political largesse. *mock mayor ceremony*: revenue was collected from bystanders for this celebration; Raven (1978), p. 122. *toast ale*: this was given by 'butty colliers' for all the men employed at their pits and the apprentices; G. T. Lawley, *Staffordshire Customs, Superstitions and Folklore*, cited in ibid., p. 88. *reward/bribe*: Menefee (1977), pp. 987 – 8.

21 *contracts*: it is interesting that many cultures use the sharing of salt, the smoking of tobacco or the consumption of alcohol or a meal as methods of sealing bargains or contracts; see Mauss (1969), p. 3, for a possible explanation in terms of the *social* meaning of exchange. *change of state*: Arnold Van Gennep, *The Rites of Passage*, M. B. Vizedom and G. L. Coffee (trans.) (London: Routledge and Kegan Paul, 1977 [1908]), p. 29; George (1976), p. 284. *'Footings'*: A. Smith (1969), p. 16, and newspaper cuttings, vol. 6, pp. 19, 20 (West Bromwich Library, Staffs), cited in Raven (1978), p. 163. *Parliamentary Report*: Mr Hickson, *Reports from Commissioners 1840*,

vol. 9, *The Condition of the Hand-Loom Weavers*, Parliamentary Report, vol. 24 (London: William Clowes and Sons, 1840), pp. 58−9. *father*: A. Smith (1969), p. 16.

22   *1684: Sessions Book, Cal.*, Middlesex, 1783−84, quoted in George (1976), p. 388. *1722: Sessions Book*, Westminster, quoted in George (1976), p. 284. *1806: Sessions Book Ap.*, Westminster, 1806, quoted in George (1976), p. 388. *birthday celebrations*: personal observation, 1973−7.

23   *Franklin*: the additional levy was complied with after an unsuccessful resistance; *The Autobiography of Benjamin Franklin*, H. A. Davidson (ed.) (Boston, Mass.: D. C. Heath, 1908), pp 65−6. *'banging out'*: A. Smith (1969), pp. 15−16. *table*: ibid., p. 34.

24   *quotation*: J. D. Burn, *A Glimpse of the Social Conditions of the Working Classes during the Early Part of the Present Century*, p. 39, quoted in George (1976), p. 283. *survival*: Charles Booth, *Life and Labour of the People in London*, 2nd series; *Industry* (London: Macmillan, 1903 [1896]), pp. 27−8. *tailor*: Charles Booth, *Life and Labor of the People of London*, 1st series: *Poverty*, vol. 4, *The Trades of East London Connected with Poverty* (London: Macmillan, 1902), pp. 143−4.

25   *table*: Francis Place, *Fines and Forfeits imposed by journeymen coopers on a young man coming out of his time in the year 1780*, ms 1825. (British Library, ADD. MSS 2783, fo. 213, cited in George (1976), p. 283. The 'celebration' imposed for doing a piece of work for the first time suggests interesting anthropological parallels: Gregory Bateson, *Naven*, 2nd edn. (Stanford, Calif.: Stanford University Press, 1958 [1936]). *subsequent history of fines*: George (1976), p. 283. *building jobs*: A. Smith (1969), p. 12. *Shottesbrook*: ibid. *harvest lord*: George Ewart Evans, *The Farm and the Village* (London: Faber & Faber, 1969), pp. 70, 124−5. *'dew beer'*: Baker (1974), pp. 26−7; Porter (1974), p. 66. *Essex*: W. R. Lethaby, *House and Country Arts* (1924), cited in Baker (1974), p. 26. *Suffolk*: Baker (1974), p. 26.

26   *Yorkshire*: **42**. *Lincolnshire*: **53**. *Shearbridge*: **258**. *Belfast*: **346**.

27   *Iver*: **34**. *Suffolk*: **51**. *Somerset*: **210**. *lightning*: Hole (1961), p. 41; Thomas (1971), p. 31. *banished evil spirits*: Hole (1961), p. 41. *travellers*: M. G. Hobson and K. L. H. Price, *Otmoor and Its Seven Towns*, (Oxford: TRUEXpress, 1961), pp. 33−8. *sunken bells*: Hole (1961), pp. 42−3; Briggs (1971), part B, vol. 2, pp. 158−60, 389−90; R. C. Hope (1968), pp. 129−32. *ringers*: for a good description of such a group and its workings, see George Ewart Evans, *Ask the Fellows Who Cut the Hay*, second edn. (London: Faber and Faber, 1972 [1962]), pp. 140−7. *funeral bell*: often cited as a source for the proverb 'Nine tailors [i.e. tellers, or strokes] make a man' − Wilson (1970), p. 567. *weddings*: Baker (1977), pp. 106−7. *major holidays*: Raven (1978), pp. 77, 107, 135; Lawley (1893), p. 115 (Guy Fawkes Day); *Restoration*: RM, 6 June 1748, p. 1; for Staffordshire, Lawley (1893), pp. 117−18. *royal birthdays*: Cheshire, Haworth (1952), p. 55; London, *LNJ*, 16 August 1783, p. 2 (twenty-first birthday of Prince of Wales). *military victories*: Andrews (1892), p. 200; Cheshire, Haworth (1952), p. 49 (King of Prussia's victory over the Queen of Hungary in 1757), p. 55 (Trafalgar in 1805, Waterloo in 1815 and the ending of the Second World War in 1945); Staffordshire, G. T. Lawley, *Bilston in the 17th Century* (1920), p. 67, cited in Raven (1978), p. 179. Lawley (1893), pp. 122−3 (surrender of Limerick in 1691, naval victory in 1622/23, Ramillies in 1708). *political victories*: Bristol,

PA, 27 April 1797, quoted in Shyllon (1977), p. 240 (defeat of the Slave Trade Bill); Wiltshire, *JOxJ*, 12 January 1754, p. 2 (repeal of the Naturalization Bill); Staffordshire Lawley (1893), p. 123 (union of England and Scotland in 1707). *winning race horse*: Andrews (1892), p. 200. *success in lottery*: *AR 1767*, p. 149 (at Abingdon, by Mr Alder, a cooper and publican who had won £20,000). A wife-selling jingle is associated with the bells of one Hertfordshire church.

28 *Times*: **91a**. *Macclesfield*: **94**.

29 *Shoreditch publican*: **31**. *Sussex wife*: **109**. *Kent husband*: **148**. *Caerleon*: **182**. *Cheshire*: **284a, b**. *denial*: **284c**.

30 *Smithfield market*: **86a, b, d**. *Bath*: **241**. *Devon*: **370**. *dislike of purchaser*: **193** and **199**. *Bradford*: the sale took place on the way to market, at a pub at Shearbridge (**258a, b**). *impetuous purchaser*: **304**.

31 *Plymstock*: **186**. *Shearbridge*: **310a, c**. *Bewcastle*: **127**. *Cheltenham*: **223**. *Barnsley*: **256**. *Hull*: **116**. *Somerset*: **266**. *London*: **257**. *Shearbridge*: **310**. *Rotherham*: **270**.

CHAPTER 7: THE HUZZAS OF THE MOB

1 *validity believed*: **136** (husband 'readily agreed' to appear before the magistrates), **181, 186**. *justification*: **194, 357, 358, 363**. *Heath*: **11**.

2 *Somerset wife*: **29**. *Exeter woman*: **328**. *Yorks ne'er-do-well*: **272**. *Suffolk farmer*: **273**. *wife received back*: **298**. *repurchase*: **69, 70**. *Yorkshire blacksmith*: **260**.

3 *Warwickshire yeoman*: **7**. *Inverness*: **13**. *Lincoln husband*: **52**. *London husband*: **25**. *Biddulph policeman*: **369**. *Essex man*: **4**. *Newark husband*: **246**. *Irish husband*: **346**.

4 *Carpenter*: **86a** (see also **b** and **d**). *second sale*: **241**. *Great Torrington*: **370**. *Wiltshire*: **40**. *Devon*: **322**. *Cornwall*: **383**.

5 *Cornwall*: **173b**. *positive reactions*: **51** ('happy to think he had made a good bargain'); **166** ('to the great apparent satisfaction of her late owner'); **218** (drank to the luck of the purchaser); **263** (wished his wife and her purchaser 'all the good luck in the world'); **264** (husband glad to get rid of wife at any price). *Hadleigh*: **273**. *Edinburgh*: **215**. *Thompson*: **234a, b, d, e**. *other man*: **257**. *Louth*: **279**. *Portsmouth*: **142**. *Holme-upon-Spalding Moor*: **249**. *London*: **245**. *Ansty*: **217**. *lost opportunities*: **318**. *attendant mockery*: **311a** and **318**. *left town*: **18** and **19**. *Aylesbury*: **198**.

6 *newspaper disclaimers*: **58** and **168**. *cried disclaimers*: **14, 230** and possibly **362**. *court excuse*: **331**. *obligations ended*: **328**. *Hampshire*: **142**. *Blackwood*: **380**. *St. Austell*: **254**. *Goole*: **294**.

7 *manifest approval*: **134** ('The woman declared it was the happiest moment of her life'); **240** (wife carried off, 'nothing loth'); **173b** (wife 'had cheerfully welcomed the prospect'); **197** (led 'unresisting' to market cross); **193b** (wife apparently satisfied with first purchaser); **210** (wife 'seemed very willing that the sale should take place!'); **234a, b, d, e** (wife appeared pleased about forthcoming exchange); **238** ('the fair one . . . seemed quite agreeable'); **292** (wife particularly pleased 'at obtaining a new master'). *Boston*: **218**. *Devon*: **186**. *Wednesbury*: **190**. *Edinburgh*: **215**. *Carmarthenshire*: **43**.

8 *Bradford*: **258a, b**. *Rotherham*: **270**. *Ripon*: **343**.

9   *Dartmouth*: 160. *dragged to market*: 202. *driven to market*: 382 (urged on by friend with stick). *London*: 171. *Cheltenham*: 223. *cry*: 296. *entreat on knees*: 212. *Barnsley*: 256. *Newcastle*: 127. *Grassington*: 120. *Devon*: 320. *Scots*: 248. *Bristol*: 193b. *Chris*: 372. *Ashton*: 294.

10 *left with siblings*: 11 (brother in London). *left with parents*: 119 (bought by father) and 278 (delivered in halter to her parents). *Horsham*: 283. *property claimed*: 251. *Suffolk*: 273. *Devon*: 347.

11 *full confession*: 6. *agent*: 162. *Yorkshire*: 329. *appeal of verdict*: 248.

12 *delight of purchaser*: 90 ('led home his bargain in high spirits'); 134 ('the purchaser said that he would not take 10l for his *bargain*'); 231 ('highly pleased'); 166a ('led off his bargain in triumph'); 232 ('The purchaser was so well pleased with his bargain . . . .'); 246 ('eagerly snapped at'); 279 (purchaser 'purposing to snap the bargain of what he called so "amiable and agreeable a creature"'); 287 (apparently satisfied with investment); 296. *Lancashire*: 318. *Coventry*: 324. *purchaser disappeared*: 353. *resold*: 177, 189, 193, 213.*given away*: 54. *deserted*: 285 (after 25 years) and 340 (after 28 years). *returned to husband*: 44. *London*: 123. *pelting*: 199c. *attack by females*: 179 (see *IJ*, 26 May 1821, p. 3). *Colchester*: 99. *Burford*: 307a. *Brighton*: 185. *attack*: 260. *wives displaced*: 191, 342, 383. *Sheffield*: 78. *Alfreton*: 345.

13 *protection of children*: 146. *death of former husband*: 115. *solemnization of common-law union*: 75 and 115. *Bodmin*: 302.

14 *Bradford*: 258. *satisfaction*: 39 ('all parties seemed very well satisfied'); 53 (the remainder of the day was 'spent with harmony and mirth agreeable to all parties'); 65 ('the parties returned home seemingly well satisfied'); 264 ('all the parties seemed satisfied'); 88 ('the parties seemed much pleased with this kind of barter, each returning home well satisfied'); 148 ('to the apparent satisfaction of all parties'); 174 (all were 'equally well satisfied'); 161 ('all the parties appeared satisfied'); 281 ('all parties seemed well satisfied'); 316 (both husband and wife seemed satisfied). *Sudbury*: 179 (see *IJ*, 26 May 1821, p. 3). *Sussex*: 200. *Manchester*: 199a (see also b). *good relation of wife with purchaser*: 154 ('seemingly nothing loath to go'); 245 ('I saw the newly united pair walk off, the man with an air of bravado, and the woman with a sniff in the air'); 234a, d, e ('happy couple'); 249 (left 'arm in arm'). *Bilston*: 170.

15 *meaning of term*: Rudé (1973), pp. 293–4 Jarrett (1976), p. 18. Rudé (1973), pp. 309–10.

16 *traditionalism*: Rudé (1973), p. 22; see also Jarrett (1976), p. 14. Jarrett, p. 199 citing E. P. Thompson ('The Moral Economy of the English Crowd in the Eighteenth Century', *Past and Present*, vol. 50, 1971, pp. 76–136) says that some have 'seen the riots of the eighteenth century as part of a continuing dialogue between propertied and labouring men over traditional rights'. *themes*: Rudé (1973), pp. 311–15. Place (1972), p. 16. Moritz (1795). Letter from Hans Stanley to the Earl of Huntingdon, 15 June 1776, quoted in Historical Manuscripts Commission Reports 78, *Hastings*, vol. 3, pp. 173–4, and secondarily in Jarrett (1976), p. 18. *scientist*: Grosley (1772), p. 85. *fashions*: ibid., p. 16; *JOxJ*, 19 April 1803, p. 4 (foreign ladies in slight clothing hooted out of park by crowd of young men); see also Jarrett (1976), p. 16. For other examples of crowd abuse, generally directed against the French, see Grosley (1772), pp. 84–8.

17 *Bilston*: 170. *Wednesbury*: 190.

18 *arrival in market*: 170. *Brighton*: 205a–c. *St Albans*: 216. *Bristol*: 193a. *1819*

exchange: 170. 'joey': term for a fourpenny (and later a threepenny) piece. *Wednesbury*: 190. *Carmarthenshire*: 43. *Herefordshire*: 76. *Bungay Fair*: 338. *Yorkshire*: 260. 'huzzas': 100; see also 59 ('to the wonderful Amusement of the Populace'); 102 ('amidst the shouts and huzzas of the mob'); 166a; 195a ('amidst the shouts of the idle rabble'); 239 ('amidst the shoutings of the assembled multitude'). *Cheltenham*: 223. *Blackburn*: 318. *Liverpool*: 353. *Belper*: 333.

19 *Derbyshire*: 147. *Cornwall*: 286. *Hertfordshire*: 216. .*Staffordshire*: 170. *Blackburn*: 318. *Norfolk*: 236. *Warwickshire*: 386. *Devon*: 371. *Yorkshire*: 261b.

20 *Carmarthenshire*: 43. *Canterbury*: 174. *Cumberland*: 262. *London*: 171. *Horsham*: 204a. second occurrence (*Horsham*): 283. *Dulverton*: 266.

21 *Dartmouth*: 160. *Hull*: 329. *London*: 171. *Bristol*: 193b. **Boston**: 218. *London*: 240. *Yorkshire*: 249a and 259. *Nottinghamshire*: 290. *Belper*: 333 (there were also no bidders in 334). *Newark*: 246 (small boys would, in any case, have been attracted to such activities — in 190 'ragged urchins' are said to have followed the town crier). *Blackburn*: 318. Briggs (1971), part B, vol. 2, p. 342, gives 'Cuckold's' instead of '—'. *Dudley*: 311a.

22 *Truro*: 291. *Lincolnshire*: 279.

23 *Yorkshire*: 149. *Manchester*: 199a (see also c). *London*: 240. *Somerset*: 244. *1763*: punished for sodomy: GM, vol. 33, April 1763, p. 198. *1780*: punished for sodomy; *JOx*], 15 April 1780, p. 1; *The Speeches of the Right Honorable Edmund Burke in the House of Commons, and in Westminster-Hall*, 4 vols. (London: Longman, Hurst, Rees, Orme and Brown, 1816), vol. 2, pp. 156 – 7. *Bristol*: CS, 9 April 1737, p. 2. Another Bristol example occurs on the same page. A woman who attempted to extort money from a slave by imposing a baby on him as his own (she had 'artfully smutted a borrowed Child over for that purpose') was 'most miserably pelted for some time, but the Mob turning their Showers of Dirt, &c. on themselves, the Officers and People, she escap'd the Danger of her Life'. *Duke of Wellington*: R. Palmer (1974), pp. 36 – 7. *Bible Society*: Carrick-on-Suir: *JOx*], 28 January 1826, p. 2. *Middlesex*: the woman's house was suspected of being a bordello because of its green doors, window frames and shutters; ibid., 31 October 1807, p. 2. *Suffolk*: ibid., 21 October 1820, p. 1. *70-year-old man (Yorks)*: MC, 8 August 1797, p. 3.

24 *Manchester*: 199a, c. *Dublin*: 21. *Suffolk*: 179, see also the reactions of people to a wedding held in the town the year before (note 23). *Scottish invasion (Edinburgh)*: 215. *New Sneddon*: 248. *Leicestershire*: 224a. *food riots*: E. P. Thompson (1976), p. 70 and Malcolm I. Thomis, *The Luddites: Machine-Breaking in Regency England* (Newton Abbot, Devon: David & Charles, 1970), pp. 22 – 3, 109, 185. *Perth*: G. Penny, *Traditions of Perth* (Perth, Perthshire: 1836), quoted in R. Palmer (1977), pp. 105 – 6.

25 *Dublin*: 21. Smith (1969), p. 34. *House of Lords*: *JOx*], 25 April 1840, p. 4. *hat dyer*: AR 1770, p. 74; similar treatment was afforded a hatter's worker who worked at cut-rate prices in 1696 (Sidney and Beatrice Webb, *The History of Trade Unionism*, revised edn., London: Longmans, Green, 1920, p. 28). *Woolwich*: *Greenwich and Deptford Chronicle*, 12 March 1870, p. 2. *ribbon maker*: in 1818, *Reports from Commissioners, Corporations, England and Wales*, Parliamentary Reports, vol. 25 (London: House of Commons, 1835), p. 1834. *Plymouth*: *JOx*], 16 September 1854, p. 3. *less homogeneous groups*: cock-fight betters unable to settle their debts were

often placed in a basket and drawn to the ceiling for the duration of play (*T*, 23 September 1797, p. 2); a man accused of trying to seduce a girl was sentenced by the villagers of Up-Street, Kent, to hang by his heels from a beam for 20 minutes and to drink 4 pints of onion broth, two before and two *during* the punishment (*JOx*], 20 December 1817, p. 4). *Cheltenham*: **223**.

26   *Oxford*: **32b**. *cleavers and marrowbones*: see Jeaffreson (1872), vol. 2, p. 112, who mentions a 'marrowbone-and-cleaver club'; William Conner Sydney, *England and the English in the Eighteenth Century*, 2 vols., 2nd edn. (Edinburgh: John Grant, 1891), vol. 1, p. 69; letter from Horace Walpole to Sir Horace Mann, 1 November 1742, Horace Walpole, *Selected Letters*, William Hadley (ed.) (London: Dent, 1967), pp. 56—7 (at Lord Carteret's); *JOx*], 19 May 1770, p. 1 (from Carnaby Market: serenading Wilkes when he visited a mistress ?); ibid., 22 April 1797, p. 4 (marriage of Prince of Wirtenberg with Royal Princess); ibid., 20 March 1847, p. 4 (marriage); ibid., 15 October 1831, p. 4 (fourth marriage). *Chipping Norton*: **307**. *Yorkshire*: **313**. *Bury*: **325**. *result of adultery*: E. P. Thompson recognizes this connection (E. P. Thompson, 1972, p. 294), but I have found no evidence supporting his statement that the connection occurs only in particularly flagrant examples (ibid., note p. 304). He seems to be right, however, about the rarity of cases in which the two institutions intersect (ibid.).

27   *Staffordshire*: **170** and **190**. *interference*: **257** (the sale was removed to another locale, 'several persons interfering') and **310a** (the sale was unfinished, as 'some disturbance was created by a crowd from a neighbouring factory'; see also **b**). *disturbance of the peace*: **147** and **270**. *Yorkshire*: **258a, b**; that fear may have been related to the Bradford crowd reaction shown one year later (**259**). *1815*: **152**. *1817*: **161**. *political mobs*: Rudé (1973), pp. 296—7. *card-playing*: *JOx*], 23 February 1754, p. 1. *Harrow*: Historical Manuscripts Commission Reports 61, *Du Cane*, pp. 230—1, cited in Jarrett (1970), p. 71. *widow*: *JOx*] 28 May 1808, p. 1; there may well be a thematic connection between breaking windows and pelting.

CHAPTER 8: 'WHERE WERE THE MAGISTRATES?'

1   *saleable news*: K. Williams (1977), p. 11. *Warwickshire*: *popular tabloids*: David Bradbury, 'Who'll buy this wife?', *Daily Mirror* (London), 27 January 1978, p. 6; for earlier tabloid treatment, see *DM* (1899), *GT* (1903), *NOW* (1924).

2   *Civil War*: K. Williams (1977), pp. 8—10. *restricted range*: ibid., pp. 7—16. *'cut and paste'*: ibid., p. 25. *out of date*: Williams has made a partial study of the time reports took to reach London from various locales in the eighteenth century; ibid., p. 18. *new papers*: ibid., pp. 16, 32. *Stamp Act*: ibid., pp. 23, 24. *loopholes*: ibid., pp. 24, 26, 29. *taxes*: ibid., pp. 23—5. *reduction*: ibid., pp. 25, 28. Moritz (1795), p. 267; Boswell patronized London coffee houses for this purpose (James Boswell, *Boswell's London Journal 1762—1763*, Frederick A. Pottle (ed.), New York: McGraw-Hill, 1950, p. 23), and Cranfield (1962), p. 11 quotes another example. *weeklies*: this does not necessarily imply that coverage was always sketchy. During the Civil War London had no fewer than 11 newspapers, at least one of which was issued every day of the week except Sunday; K. Williams (1977), pp. 8, 9. *first*

daily: ibid., p. 19. *1709*: ibid. *provincial press*: ibid., pp. 23−32. In 1710 there were 13 papers (in nine towns); in 1723, 24 papers; in 1740, 31 papers; in 1744, 36; in 1745, 41; in 1753, 32; in 1754, 36; and in 1760, 35. After 1719 the number of provincial papers was never less than 20. After 1737 the number was never less than 30. By 1760 55 towns had at least one newspaper and many others several more. While the selection of specific towns was due to such factors as population, location and commerce, there was a general expansion of the press from south and south-west England to the north and the Midlands (Cranfield, 1962, pp. 17, 18, 21, 22, 22−3, 25, 27). *'soft news'*: as opposed to 'hard news' (wars, government activity and foreign affairs). *'hard news'*: K. Williams (1977), pp. 24−5.

3   *wives refusing to return*: 7 and 25a. *buyers returning purchases*: 44. *husbands retaining sold wives*: 13. *buyers refusing to return wives*: 52. *unusual prices*: 20 (leg of mutton), 31 (lottery ticket) and 24 (ox).

4   *normal sales*: 18, 19, 33, 34, 35, 39, 40, 42, 49, 50, 51, 53, 54, 59, 60, 64, 65, 69, 70 (picked up by the London press when the wife was repurchased for a larger price), 78. *1797*: 80a, 81, 82, 83a−c and f, 84a, 85, 86a, b and d, 87, 88, 89, 90, 91, 82, 87, 85a−c, 89. *'encreasing value'*: 84c (see also a). *'mistake'*: 84d (see also e). A monthly report appeared in several newspapers giving information about the state of the livestock market. *'bucks'*: 83h. *'right to sell'*: 83i (see also g). *'advertisements'*: 83x, aa. *'horned cattle'*: 83y; another reference to the market report. *'divorce-notes'*: 83z. *'demand'*: 83ff this may refer to the Babylonian marriage market or it may be related to the following comment:

> That the daughters of parents who keep gaming houses should elope with their *creditors*, is a matter so easily foreseen, and so regular in the course of business, that we could advise such parents not to lay claim to the *pity* of the public, lest, in return, they meet with its contempt. The difference between a gaming-house and a brothel is merely the difference between *cause* and *effect*. (*JOxJ*, 12 August 1797, p. 2)

'forestaller': 86j. forestalling was a contemporary market complaint mentioned in various newspapers in 1797; see, for example, *LNJ*, 10 March 1797, p. 2; 21 April, p. 3; 15 June, p. 3; 19 June, p. 3. The general problem is discussed in John Ashton, *The Dawn of the XIX Century in England* (New York: G. P. Putnam's Sons, 1886), pp. 16−22, 240−1. *'Christie's'*: 88d; the well-known and expensive auction house, where high-priced objects were sold, would have been deemed an appropriate locale for the price paid in 88. *'go-off'*: Partridge (1961), p. 336, notes that this refers to the disposing both of women in marriage and of goods by sale (17th to 20th century). *currency depreciation*: 83bb mentions the 'late havock made among old proverbial sayings' and, in addition, in a reference to wife-selling, says, 'It is no compliment to say that a man is as "*good* as the *Bank*".' 'Safe as the bank', a proverbial phrase used to indicate reliability (Wilson, 1970, p. 691), was ironic because the Bank of England had had recent financial problems. On 26 February 1797 the threat of a gold drain on the Bank was met by an Order in Council suspending payments in coin but allowing the Bank to issue paper currency without limit. This Order was confirmed by Act of Parliament on 3 May (Hill, 1966, p. 147). *divorce*: 83dd (mention of the Court of King's Bench); 86e (reference to Westminster Hall, the location of the Court of King's Bench, where the verdict at law necessary for a parliamentary divorce

was usually obtained); **86f** (mention of Westminster Hall). *desertion*: **83x**.
arranged marriages: **83ff**, **86f** (marriage brokers supposedly feel threatened
by wife sales); **86m** (mentions setting up a *'Marriage-Shop'* in connection
with 'The genuine *Smithfield* principle'; a possible parallel to this is the
agency for 'virgins, widows, and the placing of dowries' run by one
Monsieur Liardot in Paris at this time or very early in the nineteenth century
— Nina Epton, *Love and the French*, London: Cassell, 1959, p. 286).
dowries: **83n**.

5   Andrews (1892), p. 199. *'popular cause'*: Raven (1978), p. 62.
6   *throwing at cocks*: GM, vol. 7, January 1737, pp. 6—8; letter from J. S—,
     Essex, 20 January, GM, vol. 20, January 1750, p. 19; letter from F—, GM:
     vol. 21, January 1751, p. 8 ('barbarous and unmanly custom . . . infamous
     and iniquitous custom, a custom which conduced to promote idleness,
     gaming, cruelty, and almost every species of wickedness . . . . put an end to
     this horrid enormity . . . a practice which is as absurd as it is offensive both
     to God and men, and which perhaps cannot be equal'd by any among the
     most ignorant and barbarous nations in the universe'); 'To the Publick', GM,
     vol. 23, January 1753, p. 5 ('wretched custom . . . . A progress towards the
     suppression of this evil is already made in some places'); *Sheffield Weekly
     Journal* (Sheffield, Yorks), 17 February 1756, cited in Cranfield (1962), p.
     207; letter from Paul Gemsege, GM, vol. 26, January 1756, pp. 17—18;
     letter, GM, vol. 31, May 1761, p. 202 ('the most inhuman and infamous
     practice . . . notwithstanding the laws by which it may be restrained, arising
     from the negligence of those who should enforce them, and their inattention
     to the enormity of the crime'); NM, 1 March 1762 ('scandalous and inhuman
     practice'), quoted in Malcolmson (1973), p. 121; letter from A—, 28 January,
     GM, vol. 32, January 1762, pp. 6—7; ABG, 5 March 1764, cited in Langford
     (1870), vol. 1, p. 143; JOxJ, 28 February 1767, p. 3; ABG, 10 February 1777,
     cited in Langford (1870), vol. 1, p. 257; letter of 10 February, GM, vol. 51,
     February 1781, p. 72 (including extracts from a religious tract against the
     practice; NM, 2 February 1788 ('a practice too common at this Season . . . to
     the Credit of a Civilized People, [it] is annually declining'), quoted in
     Malcolmson (1973), p. 121; 'The Projector', no. XI, GM, vol. 72, pt. 2,
     November 1802, p. 998. *bull-running*: LSM, 14 November 1788 ('a custom
     which has too long disgraced the town of Stamford'), quoted in Malcolmson
     (1973), p. 127; LSM, 20 November 1812 ('People of *respectability* follow the
     bull at Stamford, who would be affronted with the imputation of doing
     anything else on a party with such a proceeding'), quoted in Malcolmson
     (1973), p. 134; LSM, 12 November 1814 ('Such a custom might comport with
     the barbarism and darkness of past ages . . . might suit the genius of an
     uncivilized and warlike race; but surely, must be regarded as an indelible
     stain upon the history of an enlightened and professedly christian people'),
     quoted in Malcolmson (1973), pp. 135—6. *boxing*: NM, 11 June 1791, p. 3
     ('the duty of every magistrate, as well as every man, to use their utmost
     endeavours to repress so disgraceful, so dangerous, & so increasing an evil'),
     quoted in Malcolmson (1973), p. 145. *fairs*: T, 31 August 1797, p. 3 ('It is
     astonishing at [sic] among so many liberal and merchantile men as compose
     the City Magistracy, some of them have not applied to Parliament for its
     suppression'). *bear-baiting*: LM, 6 September 1800, p. 3 ('an example worthy
     the imitation of every magistrate in the kingdom . . . suppressing the
     inhuman custom'). *bull-baiting*: LSM, 10 November 1826 ('barbarous

diversion which has been happily declining in public favor for some years past'), quoted in Malcolmson (1973), p. 125; *JOx*], 21 October 1837, p. 3 ('Thame is no longer the scene of that brutality which once cast a blemish over its inhabitants'), quoted in Malcolmson (1973), p. 125; *ABG*, 30 September 1839 ('cruel and barbarous practice'], quoted in Malcolmson (1973), p. 126. *Street football: Derby and Chesterfield Reporter*, 23 February 1832 ('a sport at once so useless and so barbarous'), quoted in Malcolmson (1973), p. 143. *heaving*: newspapers (Staffs c. 1800−50), cited in Raven (1978), p. 92. *considerations*: *LSM*, 13 November 1789, quoted in Malcolmson (1973), p. 135. *selective nature*: Malcolmson (1973), p. 152. *double standard*: ibid., pp. 152−6. *pragmatic realism*: ibid., p. 157.

7 *spread*: see, for example, **61**:

> As instances of the sales of wives have of late frequently occurred among the lower classes of people who consider such sale lawful, we think it right to inform that, by a determination of the courts of law in a former reign, they were declared illegal and void, and considered (a light in which religion must view them) as mere pretence to sanction the crime of adultery.

After the report of a Hertfordshire sale (**64**), the *London Chronicle* notes, 'Shame on the morals and follies of the day.' As late as 1872 a Yorkshire sale (**329b**) is described as 'disgraceful' and one participant as 'without any sense of decency'. *advertisement*: **79a**. *favourable comparison*: **69a**. *elopement*: **83t**. *'vulgar' error*: **60** ('vulgar Mode of *Divorce* lately adopted'); **111** ('the general opinion which has so long pervaded the lower ranks of society'); **124−6** ('This very shameful traffic has lately become . . . prevalent among the lower orders'); see also **79a**.

8 *'disgusting'*: **235**. *'degrading'*: **78**. *'depraved'*: **83 a−c, f**. *'disgraceful*: **116b, 122a and b, 179, 230a, 235, 310a, 311a and b, 328, 329b**. *borrowed verbatim*: **114a and b, 116b, c and d, 122a and b**; the squibs in the *Annual Register* were usually taken from London newspapers. *printing without comment*: *Jackson's Oxford Journal*, **124−6 and 134**. *Times*: **157 and 162a**; to some extent this may have been due to copying. *plight of wife*: **160a and 171**. *plight of husband*: **174, 249**. *queries*: **183** ('The magistrates have the power to stop this kind of nuisance') and **200** ('Why did not the Magistrate interfere?'). *whipping*: **95** (? − 'we could mention a way in which a rope might very properly reward the persons concerned'), **114a and 218a**. *noose*: **95?** and **205a**.

9 *Norfolk*: **191**; this was also included as a separate news item in a non-wife-selling context (*JOx*], 18 April 1818, p. 4). *slave market*: italics added (ibid., 7 June 1817, p. 1). A letter quoted in *OCC*, 24 October 1840, p. 1, includes the following: 'I was grieved to find these [Egyptian] markets thronged with slaves as heretofore . . . the unfortunate creatures still subjected to the same cattle-like treatment and examination of their persons.' *Mercury*: **172**. *generalities*: **86k**. *newly established practice*: **60**.

10 *'usual manner'*: **65** ('usual way'); **98** ('customary manner'); **99** ('usual . . .form'). *'lately practised'*: **60** ('lately adopted'); **61** ('have of late frequently occurred'); **65** ('which has been lately practised'). *previous sales*: **111, 186, 192a**. *economic tally*: **80j, 84b** (price has risen); **83dd** ('the market has been dull of late'); **86f** ('slow of late'); **91a** ('poor shew'); **88b, c** ('*Advance in the*

Market'); **89** ('an indifferent price'). *London*: **107**; see, for example, **83a** (price of £3 8s).

11 *1797 statement*: **85c**. *1832 letter*: **234c** (this was in reference to **b**). *House of Correction*: **83e**. *fornication*: **83ee**. *lawyers' petition*: **86i**; it is difficult to tell whether this was meant as a joke or was a completely straightforward piece of reporting. If the latter, then it is interesting that the illegality of selling a wife, the sanctity of marriage or the resultant fornication were not given as equally valid reasons for voiding the sale (conversation with Professor R. Needham, All Souls College, Oxford 1977).

12 *debt disclaimers*: **58** and **168a** (see also **b** and **c**). *advertisements*: **79a, b, c**.

13 *ecclesiastical courts*: **3, 4, 5, 6, 8, 11**. *convictions*: In the Essex case (**5**) there appears to have been conflicting testimony. *Cheken*: **2**; as 1553 fell in the reigns of (Protestant) King Edward VI and (Roman Catholic) Queen Mary, and as Catholic clergy were not allowed to marry, this could represent Queen Mary's disciplining of an 'undesirable' Protestant. *Eliel chapel*: **75**. *Gazette*: **61**.

14 *sacrament*: This reinforces the interpretation that wife-selling was equivalent to the preceding (secular) contract. *Chandos*: **15a, c** (**b**, however, identifies the Duke as James Brydges, and dates the subsequent marriage to 1736). The entry from the register of Mr. Keith's proprietary chapel, Mayfair, which refers to this is mentioned in **15 note**. *Pillet*: **146**. *Halifax*: **115**. *York*: **272**. *Cockerham*: **75**. *church ceremony*: although these couples had been living in adultery, neither party had a living married partner. *Isle of Wight*: **110**.

15 *marriage vow*: **32b** and **255**. But see **311a**. *Observer*: **258a** (see also **b**). *Lincolnshire*: **277**. *Quarter Sessions*: **165a**.

16 **Essex**: **47** ('Amie Daughter of Moses Stebbing by a bought wife delivered to him in a Halter'). It appears that the curate, Thomas Shaw, who recorded this entry may not have known how to treat this union. It is not entered in the normal form ('John Son of Samuel & Jemima Cottiss' — 26 May 1782), but does not appear to have been considered a illegitimate birth (as in 'Mary Humphreys base born Daugr: of Peter and Mary Hawkes' — 2 June 1782) (both entries from the Perleigh Parish Register, Essex Record Office). *Devon*: **280**.

17 See case **163**.

18 *glosses*: Ellis (1926), pp. 3—4. *Cnut*: promulgated in 1027; translation, A. J. Robertson, *The Laws of the Kings of England* (Cambridge: Cambridge University Press, 1925), pp. 212—13. *not proof*: Bates (1872), p. 468. The women could have been girls or widows under the control of kinsmen. *relation/derivation*: the connection of wife-selling with cattle sales is reminiscent of other cultures in which brideprice is often quoted in terms of livestock.

19 Blackstone (1836), vol. 4, §. 64. *indecent exposure*: (1663) *Le Roy versus Sr Charles Sidley*. ibid., note 31; 1. *Sidderfin* 168. *ostensible apprenticing*: (1763) *Rex versus Sir Francis-Blake Delaval, William Bates, and John Fraine*. Blackstone (1836), vol. 4, § 64, note 31; 3 *Burrows* 1438. *assignment of a wife*: (before 1763) Blackstone (1836), vol. 4, §64, note 31; 3 *Burrows* 1438. *assignment of a wife*: (before 1763) Blackstone (1836), vol. 4 §64, note 31. *enticement*: (1682) 3 *State Trials* 519. Blackstone (1836), vol. 4, § 64, note 31. *summation*: 3 *Burrows* 1438. Kenny (1929), p. 495, notes that the apparent social class of the offender referred to would suggest his knowledge of the agreement's essential invalidity (except as a protection against *crim. con.*).

20   *case*: Tried on 27 July 1818; **163**. *footnote*: Blackstone (1836), vol. 5, § 64, footnote to note 31. The author continues citing *Porter's Case*, Cro. Car. 461, as his authority.

21   *Laws Respecting Women*: LRW (1777), p. 55. *Cabinet Lawyer: The Cabinet Lawyer*, quoted in **231a**. Note that *R. v. Delaville* is identical with R. v. Delaval in note 19. Similar coverage is found in *The Cabinet Lawyer: A Popular Digest of the Laws of England*, etc., 13th edn. (London: Simpkin, Marshall, 1846), p. 372; 15th edn. (Longman, Brown, Green, and Longmans, 1852), pp. 415 – 16; 16th edn. (1853), p. 447; 17th edn. (Longman, Brown, Green, Longmans and Roberts, 1857), pp. 456 – 7; 18th edn. (1859), pp. 460 – 1; 20th edn. (Longman, Green, Longmans, Roberts and Green, 1865), p. 488; 22nd edn. (Longman, Green, Reader, and Dyer, 1867), p. 506; and 23rd edn. (1871), p. 522. Wife-selling is not mentioned in the 24th edn. (1874). *Magistrate's Pocket-Book*: John Frederick Archbold, *Dr Robinson's Magistrate's Pocket Book* 2nd edn. (London: J. Richards, 1842), p. 407, citing Chitty (1837), vol. 2, p. 235. *Burn's*: Chitty (1831), vol. 5, p. 1025. *sample indictment*: letters represent the names of the individuals cited — A.B. is the husband, C.D. his wife, E.F. the (potential) purchaser; the fourth count covers sale to an unknown purchaser, the fifth, sale to avoid maintenance and the sixth, an incomplete sale. *query*: **288a**. *Mears*: (1851) *Reg. v. Mary Anne Mears and Amelia Chalk*: 4 *Cox*, 247; 4 *Criminal Law Cases*, 423. *Howell*: (1864) *Regina v. Simeon Howell and Mary Bentley*: 4 *Foller & Finlason*, 160. Kenny (1929), p. 494. *Hall*: (1695) *Hall & al' Executors of Tho. Thynne v. Jane Potter Administratrix of George Potter*: 1 *English Reports* 52.

22   *London*: **2**. *ecclesiastical connections*; see note 13. *husband and wife as unit*: Tobias notes, 'A married woman was in certain circumstances not answerable for offences committed in the presence of her husband, on the supposition that she acted under his direction . . . .' Tobias (1972), p. 104. *Stirling*: **6**. *confession*: **6**. *explanation*: **8** and **11**. *conflicts in testimony*: **4**. *examination of witnesses*: **8** and **11**. *Humbie*: **8**. *passed on*: **5**. *penance*: **3**, **6**, **8**, **11** (commuted — Hair, 1972, p. 20, notes that this was an occasional practice).

23   *assizes*: P. N. Walker (1970), pp. 29 – 32. *cases*: **13** (1730: refused to honour contract); **357** (Leeds Assizes, 1895 — bigamy); **358** (1895 — bigamy); **363** (Leeds Assizes, 1900 — bigamy); **378** (Devon Assizes, 1926 — divorce case). *not common venue*: I am indebted to Dr J. Hackney, Wadham College, Oxford, for this suggestion (communication of June 1978).

24   *Quarter Sessions*: Walker (1970), pp. 53 – 6. *cases*: **50** (1785 — assault on wife; during the court proceedings the husband agreed to sell his wife, who had remarried in his absence); **155** (1815 — wife sale; pillory and three months' imprisonment for husband); **162** (Chester Q.S., 1817 — wife sale); **164** (Leominster Q.S., 1818 — wife sale); **165** (Rutland Q.S., 1819 — wife sale; purchaser fined 1s and expenses); **173** (1820 — wife sale; fine of 1s and three months' imprisonment for purchaser; husband unavailable); **205** (wife sale; orders were given by the local magistrate to secure the individuals for the next quarter session, but, for whatever reason, the case seems never to have come to trial); **214** (West Kent Q.S., 1828 — wife sale; husband, wife, and purchaser all received one month's imprisonment); **242** (Marlborough Q.S., 1833 — husband imprisoned for 3 months and fined £1); **261** (West Riding Q.S., 1837 — wife sale; husband received one month's or two months' hard labour). *theoretical authority*: **311c** does cite the 1837 West

Riding Q.S. case (261) as a general proof of illegality. Dr J. Hackney suggests that this lack of citation is the norm (perhaps as a consequence of the provincial nature of the cases, in contrast to the London origin of most case law (communication of June 1978). *Clipsham* (Rut.): 165b.

25   *magistrates' courts*: P. N. Walker (1970), pp. 56−8. *cases*: 29 (1768 − disturbing the peace); 136 (petty sessions, 1828 − non-support of wife and children; postponed for a determination of jurisdiction); 147 (before 1815 − disturbance of the peace; imprisonment, failed), 161 (1817 − wife sale or disturbing the peace); 162 (wife sale; husband, wife, and purchaser committed to House of Correction until Quarter Sessions); 181 (1821 − wife sale; husband, wife, and purchaser bound over for good behaviour); 186 (1822 − wife sale; husband and wife bound over to answer charge at next Sessions); 191 (1823 − wife sale or non-support; husband's wife returned, and purchaser told to support his own wife); 193 (1823 − wife sale or refusal of wife to honour contract; dismissed); 199 (1824 − wife sale; husband and wife remanded and discharged with a warning); 204 (1825 − wife sale; participants disappeared before action could be taken); 205 (1826 − wife sale; toll collector examined for his part in the transaction and warrants issued for the buyer and seller for indictment at the next Sessions); 224 (1830 − preventing disturbance of the peace; husband and wife imprisoned); 239 (petty sessions − desertion; husband imprisoned); 241 (1833 − disturbing the peace; husband imprisoned); 248 (1834 − disturbing the peace; husband and purchaser (et al. ?) dismissed with warning); 276 (1842 − assault or disturbing the peace; husband bound over to keep the peace); 279 (1842 − wife sale or disturbing the peace; husband, wife, and purchaser bound over £5 each to keep the peace); 280 (before 1843 − wife sale; no action taken); 289 (1847 − wife sale; wife taken into custody and warrant for husband's arrest issued); 285 (1871 − non-support; purchaser ordered to pay 6s 6d a week toward wife's support); 328 (Exeter police court, 1872 − non-support of children; dismissed); 329 (Hull police court; 1872 − assault; purchaser fined 50s and costs); 330 (Clerkenwell, 1872 − assault; dismissed); 346 (1882 − assault); 350 (1891 − non-support of children); 359 (police court, 1896); 365; 367 (Marlborough Street police court, 1903); 369 (1904 − assault or disturbing the peace); 340 (1908 − ill-treatment and non-support); 374 (Southend police court, 1920); 377 (1924 − persistent cruelty); 379 (1926); 380 (1928). *preliminary hearing*: 162, 186, 205; no substantiating Quarter Session evidence has been found to date. Pillet: 147. *Renfrewshire*: 248. *Exeter*: 328. *London*: 330..

26   *court proceedings*: 186 and 205. *initial arrest/detention*: 147 and 162. *imprisonment*: 83d ('a man may be sent to the House of Correction for the public indecorum of selling his wife'). *treadmill*: 136 and 246. *capacity*: Dr J. Hackney has noted that in normal circumstances this was not a notoriously successful defence (communication of June 1978). *show trials*: this suggests a possible parallel with newspaper campaigns against sports and customs. *petty officials*: 205; in connection with this, it is interesting to speculate on the possible personal considerations of the judges − Godfrey Kneller, for example, was a purchaser who was also (although perhaps not at the time of his purchase) a Justice of the Peace; 12.

27   *county courts*: P. N. Walker (1970), pp. 75−9. *cases*: 331 (before 1873 − non-support of wife) and 342 (Sheffield County Court, 1881 − non-support of purchaser's wife; adjourned for more evidence); 343 (beak, 1881 −

truancy of purchaser's son); **349** (Sheffield County Court, 1887). *police action*: **58** (constable served as witness for debt disclaimer); **117** (interference — protection of husband); **147** (arrest of wife and purchaser — prevention of a disturbance of the peace); **161** (arrest of wife and purchaser — prosecution for wife sale or disturbance of the peace); **171** (interference — protection and release of wife); **186** (arrest of husband and wife — prosecution for wife sale); **193** (arrest of wife and purchaser); **197** (interference); **199** (detention of wife and arrest of husband — prosecution for wife sale or, perhaps, for disturbing the peace); **223** (prevention of recurrence; prevention of wife sale or pumping of husband); **246** (*refusal* to interfere); **248** (arrest of husband and purchaser and, perhaps, prevention of disturbance of the peace); **270** ('made their appearance' — prevention of disturbance of the peace); **279** (interference — prevention of wife sale); **346** (testimony — conviction of husband for assault); **369** (interference — prevention of a disturbance of the peace). *formation of police forces*: these developed from community law enforcement officers such as the Watch. Jarrett (1976), p. 57, notes that London did not have a police force until 1829 and that it was not until about 1860 that the rest of the country followed suit. *attorneys*: **33** ('The agreement was drawn up by an eminent Attorney') and **85** ('agreeably to an engagement drawn up by an Attorney'). *squib*: **86k**; a later example in which articles of sale were said to have been drawn up at a solicitor's was alternatively explained by the husband involved as being a settlement to prevent proceedings (**337**). *valid and binding*: a more pragmatic interpretation is that these lawyers were trying to create a side-business of their own at the expense of the laymen, without regard to the greater issues involved, much as today pre-nuptial agreements of dubious legality may be drawn up.

28   *Thackeray*: William Thackeray [M. A. Titmarsh, pseud.], 'Jerome Paturot', *Fraser's Magazine for Town and Country* (London), vol. 28, September 1843, p. 439. *'ordinary' unnatural vice*: such unbalanced views of the British still persist in France. A Scottish teacher reports that students there cherish 'such a caricature of the British, especially the Scots. I don't know how many times I've told them that we don't all wear kilts, live in haunted castles and drink whisky with breakfast, lunch & dinner' (letter from Miss S. MacGregor, October 1977). D'Archenholtz (1789), vol. 1, title page. *wife sale*: **56**. Pillet (1815), pp. 299–306, including **139**, **140**, **146** and **147**. *Statesman*: **140**. *ancient origin*: Pillet (1815), p. 299, 301–2. *quotation*: ibid., p. 302. *de Fauconpret*: **158**. *1857 sale*: **309a** (see also **b**). White (1891), p. 24. Sternberg (1853), pp. 429–30. Baring-Gould (1926), pp. 58–9. The case referred to is probably **280**, which fits the *curé*'s requirements. Baring-Gould was also familiar with **347**, which did not occur in market. The 'books of the highest authority' presumably included Colin de Plancey's *Legends and Superstitions Connected with the Sacraments*, cited by Baring-Gould, p. 58 as having several pages devoted to this topic. J. Collin de Plancy, *Légendes des Sacrements* (Paris: Henri Plon, 1861), however, makes no mention of wife-selling. *cartoon*: *Punch*: cited in Kenny (1929), p. 494. *Brigadier Gerard*: from 'How the King held the Brigadier', telling of Gerard's escape from a French prisoner-of-war camp on Dartmoor; Sir Arthur Conan Doyle, *Adventures of Gerard* (London: Pan, 1977 [1896]), p. 108. *1850*: G.L.B— (1850), p. 217. *1857*: the author attributes this to ignorance and hard feelings after the war (*which* war is unspecified). See also **333**. K.P.D.E— (1856), p. 420. *1858*: K.P.D.E— (1858), p. 490. *1863*: K.P.D.E—

(1863), p. 486. *1891*: White does not deny that some sales took place (White, 1891, p. 24). Chambers (1869), vol. 1, p. 487:

> Rather unfortunately, the occasional instances of wife-sale, while remarked by ourselves with little beyond a passing smile, have made a deep impression on our continental neighbours, who seriously believe that it is a habit of all classes of our people and constantly cite it as evidence of our low civilization.

Ashton (1888), p. 1, notes the factual basis of wife-selling. *French wife sale*: *T*, 27 November 1866, p. 10.

CHAPTER 9: SMITHFIELD BARGAINS

1   *verse*: John Nathan Hutchins, *Hutchins Almanac* (New York: Hugh Gaine, 1759), quoted in Marion Barber Stowell, *Early American Almanacs: The Colonial Weekday Bible* (New York: Burt Franklin, 1977), pp. 265 — 6. *1815*: **154a**. *quips*: **83g, t** ('Talk of a Smithfield bargain!') and **bb**. *1604*: Wilson (1970), p. 746. *meaning*: ibid. *Smithfield Market*: while the proverb refers to London's Smithfield, markets in Manchester and Birmingham were subsequently given the same name (wife sales are known to have taken place in the latter). *London cases*: **80, 83, 84, 86, 91?, 96?, 100, 106, 107, 111, 117, 123, 124, 125, 132, 134, 152, 154, 158, 161, 171, 187, 211, 231, 257**. Hall: **245**.

2   *'Horn Market'*: Pillet (1815), p. 303. *cuckoldry*: Brand (1890 — 93), vol. 2, pp. 181 — 8. *Charlton (Kent):* this fair was traditionally believed to have been granted by King John to a miller who found the monarch kissing his wife. Held on 18 October, the fair was marked by a pair of horns affixed to a pole. R. W. Muncey, *Our Old English Fairs* (London: Sheldon Press, 1935?,) p. 74. Hole (1975), pp. 164 — 5 nc es that it also formerly included a procession of men and women wearing horns and that every stall was surmounted by a gilded pair; see also Hole (1976), p. 105, and Brand (1890 — 93), vol. 2, pp. 194 — 5. *Ebernoe*: Jacqueline Simpson, *The Folklore of Sussex* (London: B. T. Batsford, 1973), pp. 124 — 6; Hole (1975), p. 164, and (1976), p. 105. *Hardy*: Hole (1975), p. 157; F. B. Pinion, *A Hardy Companion*, reprint edn. (London: Macmillan, 1974 [1968]), p. 506. *Weyhill Fair*: Wendy Boase, *The Folklore of Hampshire and the Isle of Wight* (London: B. T. Batsford, 1976), pp. 146 — 7; Hole (1941), pp. 93 — 4, and (1975), pp. 157 — 8. *ballad*: 'The Blind Sailor' (June 1794), quoted in John Holloway and Joan Black, *Later English Broadside Ballads* (London: Routledge & Kegan Paul, 1975), pp. 29 — 30, and note p. 30. *procession*: **38**. *bons mots*; **83cc, dd**.

3   *Smithfield*: **83y**. *Sheffield*: **108a**. *cow*: Partridge (1961), vol. 1, p. 185. *John Bull*: Jarrett (1976), pp. 22 — 4, 200. *newspaper advertisement*: **79**. *north country husband*: **277**; see also **86n** ('If a husband could say like a horse dealer, *parting with her for no fault*, he could not fail to make a fortune'), and Borrow (1969), pp. 268 — 9, who claims that women were known as 'mares' and has his character claim that they were treated as such in old English law. *financial dealings*: **83u, z** ('it is thought they will quite supersede the *ready-money business* in Smithfield'); **86g, h** (middlemen), **j** (forestallers) and **n**. *squib*: **65**.

4 *marriage market*: **191**; a similar version, not quoted in connection with a wife sale, occurs in *JOxJ*, 18 April 1818, p. 4. The original account of this occurs in Book 1 of Herodotus' *Histories* (**196**) — see *The Histories*, Aubrey de Sélincourt (trans.), reprint edn. (Harmondsworth, Middx: Penguin Books, 1.68 [1954]), p. 93. Today the practice is probably best-known from the painting 'The Babylonian Marriage Market', first displayed by Edwin Long in 1875.

5 *brideprice cited*: Hole (1961), p. 363. *destined bride*: *Notes and Queries on Anthropology*, 6th edn. (London: Routledge and Kegan Paul, 1971 [1874] p.116. *dowry*: ibid. *based on:* Nadel (1951), p. 241. *Africa*: Mair (1977), pp. 50−68. *sale of rights*: ibid., p. 50. *external pressures*: Nadel (1951), p. 241. *cattle quotation*: Mair (1971), p. 54. Claude Lévi-Strauss, *The Elementary Structures of Kinship*, James Hare Bell and John Richard von Sturmer (trans.), revised edn. (London: Eyre & Spottiswoode, 1969 [1949]), pp. 469−70. *divorce*: Mair (1977), pp. 61, 182−4; Nadel (1951), p. 241. *cattle*: Mair (1977), pp. 51−6.

6 *Britons*: Pillet is quoting the theory of a contemporary magistrate (**147**). *Anglo-Saxons*: P.T.A— (1939), p. 96, gives this theory but questions its accuracy. Hole (1961), pp. 363−4. Udal (1970), pp. 197−8. Sherren (1902), p. 20. *continuity*: apart from the 1073 mention (**1**), no certain reference to wife-selling seems older than the sixteenth century.

7 *Fittleworth*: **87**. *chattel*: I am indebted for this suggestion to Dr J. Hackney, Wadham College, Oxford, (conversation of July 1976).

8 *Carlisle*: **234e**. *Oxford*: **60**. *Mansfield*: **290**. *Derbyshire*: **345**.

9 *handfasting quotation*: italics added. *The Statistical Account of Scotland* (1793), vol. 10, pp. 537−8, quoted in A. D. Hope (1970), p. 157.

10 *Russian slave*: Rushworth (1722), vol. 2, p. 468, quoted in Shyllon (1977), p. 17. *East Indian domestics*: Shyllon (1977), p. 122. *1555*: John Lok returned to England with five slaves in this year (Shyllon, 1977, p. 6). *1553*: two dozen slaves were supposedly sold in England; Cedric Dover, *Hell in the Sunshine* (London: 1943), p. 159, quoted in Shyllon (1977), p. 6. *1440*: Martha Warren Beckwith, *Black Roadways* (Chapel Hill, North Carolina: 1929), p. 3, quoted in Shyllon (1977), p. 6. *dormant*: Shyllon (1977), p. 7. *quotation*: ibid., *newspaper*: *Mercurius Politicus* (London), 11 August 1659, quoted in ibid., p. 10.

11 *popular acceptance*: the mob on occasion sided with blacks who were being reclaimed although they had been baptized or married an English citizen (Shyllon, 1977, pp. 17−20, 97, 223−4). *non-legality*: ibid. pp. 19−20, 97. *court decisions*: such as *Butts v. Penny* (1677) and *Gelly v. Cleve* (1694) (Shyllon, 1977, p. 17); on the other hand, in *Chamberlain v. Harvey* (1698), *Smith v. Browne and Cooper* (1701) and *Smith v. Gould* (1706) slavery was not recognized (Shyllon, 1977, p. 17). *legal limbo*: the legal position on slavery in the latter part of the eighteenth century can only be described as confused. Apparently, although the institution could not exist in England, a slave-owner was not considered to have waived his former legal rights should a slave leave the country with him. While in England a slave was not entitled to wages gained from his work and was not considered a hired servant (and thus entitled to poor relief). Opinions varied as to whether slaves could be forced to depart the country (ibid., pp. 19−20). *Somerset case*: ibid., pp. 24−5; a separate legal system governed Scotland, where slavery was ruled illegal in 1778 (*Knight v. Wedderburn*) — ibid., p. 26.

forced exportation of blacks: 1773, Shyllon (1977), p. 25; 1790 (a girl), ibid., p. 25; 1792, ibid., p. 25; 1823 (Grace Jones), ibid., p. 27; 1809 (nine blacks), ibid., p. 32; 1826 (twenty-five blacks), ibid., p. 28. *abolishment of slave trade*: Plumb (1975), p. 159. *1440*: the importation of slaves does not necessarily imply their sale. *1553 wife sale*: **2**. *period of greatest activity*: precise figures on slave sales are not available, the 1660—1772 estimate being only approximate and based on evidence given by Shyllon (1977).

12   Shyllon (1977), pp. 13, 122. *Kirke*: (London, March 1685), quoted in G. Williams (1897), p. 477. *Indian*: presumably an East Indian. *LGaz.*, 1688, quoted in Shyllon (1977), p. 11. *'Tannymoor'*: Shyllon suggests the reading 'tawny-moor'. *LGaz.*, 1694, quoted in Shyllon (1977), p. 11. *'Caesar'*: *LGaz.*, 25 January 1696, quoted in Shyllon (1977), p. 77. *Dyer*: LA (1756), quoted at second-hand in Shyllon (1977), p. 14. Additionally, the essayist Richard Steele quotes the following complaint from a black child named Pompey: 'the parrot who came over with us from our country is as much esteemed by her as I am. Besides this the shock dog has a collar that cost as much as mine' (the analogy appears to have been more than accidental); quoted in the *Tatler* (London), 1710, and secondarily in Shyllon (1977), p. 29.

13   *'To be sold'*: LA, 1756, quoted in G. Williams (1897), p. 478. *'healthy Negro Girl'*: *Public Ledger* (London), 31 December 1761, quoted in G. Williams (1897), p. 478. *'TO BE SOLD'*: *Liverpool Chronicle* (Liverpool), 15 December 1768, quoted in Plumb (1975), p. 159. *'from Africa'*: 1771 sale at Litchfield, Staffs; G. Williams (1897), p. 479.

14   *1756 slave sale*: boy sold in London; *LA*, quoted at second-hand in G. Williams (1897), p. 478. *1756 wife sales*: **20** and **21**. *1763 slave sale*: boy sold in London; Shyllon (1977), p. 13, supposedly quoting *GM*, vol. 33, 1763. *1763 wife sale*: **23**. *1771 slave sale*: boy sold at Richmond, Yorkshire; *LSM*, 1771, quoted in G. Williams (1897), p. 479. *1772 estimate of slave's worth*: per capita estimate by Lord Mansfield (*Somerset case*) of the cost of freeing all slaves in England; Shyllon (1977), p. 101. *1788 slave sale*: from a letter to John Tarleton, Liverpool slave merchant. The (high) price was per head for 262 slaves; Liverpool Papers, 25 June, ms., British Library, Add. MSS. 38416 fol. 134, quoted in Shyllon (1977), p. 14. *1789 estimate of slave's worth*: estimate of loss of value to British owners from run-away slaves; G[ilbert] Francklyn, *Observations, occasioned by the attempts made in England to effect the Abolition of the Slave Trade* . . . (London: 1789), pp. xi—xii, quoted in Shyllon (1977), p. 76. *1789 wife sales*: **58**, **59** and **60**, **63**. *1792 slave sale*: girl sold at Bristol; *Bonner's Bristol Journal* (Bristol), 8 December 1792, quoted in Shyllon (1977), p. 25. *slaves sold by weight*: in Boston Samuel Pewter offered to sell slaves at a fee of sixpence a pound (horses, however, were sold at a flat rate) — *Weekly Rehearsal* (Boston, Mass.), 1737, cited and quoted in Earle, 1894, p. 89. Earle also notes specifically (ibid.) that Negro children were sold by the pound.

15   *'Perhaps'*: Shyllon (1977), p. 13, supposedly quoting *GM*, vol. 33, 1763. *'shocking*: *LSM*, 1771, quoted in Shyllon (1977), p. 14. *views on wife-selling*: **229a** ('A more disgraceful affair never took place in a country where the traffic of slaves is unknown'). *not contemporaneous*: slave sale criticisms occurred in the 1760s and 1770s. Adverse newspaper reactions to wife sales appeared in the 1790s and continued into the first half of the nineteenth century. *Somerset case*: groups of blacks attended each hearing, with a larger number appearing at Westminster Hall on the day of judgement. A

few days later some 200 attended a ball held to celebrate the verdict; Shyllon (1977), pp. 79–80. *Parliament*: during discussion of Dolben's Bill in 1788 (regulating the carrying of slaves to the plantations), delegations of free blacks attended several of the debates and the examination of witnesses. Some wrote letters supporting the measure to Dolben, Pitt and Fox, which appeared in contemporary newspapers; ibid., pp. 229–30, 269–70. *wife-selling*: no direct legislative discussion of the problem is known, but see **344** ('As late as 1881 a case was mentioned in Parliament of a man selling his wife for a quart of beer').

16 *husband sale*: Pillet (1815), pp. 305–6, supposedly quoting *Stm*, 11 March 1814 in translation. *parallel apparently accepted by the Frenchman*: ibid. (text in French). *Goole*: **294**. *Liverpool*: **353**.

17 *Birmingham*: William Bates, 'Selling a Wife', *NQ*, series 1, vol. 7, 18 June 1853, p. 603.

18 *Deal*: *JOxJ*, 26 December 1823, p. 2; compare this with the following 1823 wife-sale prices: **191** (£6 10s); **192** (5s, average price: £1 1s); **193** (6d: 9d); **194** (3s); **195** (10s), **196** (1s 6d).

19 *unappealing nature of work*: not only was this work seasonal in character, but it was also considered socially demeaning (not without reason, as sweeps were often associated with begging and theft). There were dangers of burning, suffocation, broken bones and cancer of the scrotum; George (1976), pp. 239–40, 378; Jarrett (1976), p. 76. *no apprenticing fee*: despite the payment of premiums by parish authorities mentioned by Jarrett 1976, p. 76, newspaper evidence shows that this was not the case for most parents or 'guardians' from which boys were 'purchased'. *lack of inducement*: general apprenticing fees were often paid in two instalments, making it worthwhile for the employer to concern himself with an apprentice's health in the interim; George (1976), pp. 237–8; Jarrett (1976), p. 76. For mistreatment, see George (1976), pp. 239–42, 378. *regulatory Acts*: in 1767 and 1778; Jarrett (1976), p. 76. Judge (1979), pp. 41–5, gives the following dates and Acts, however: Act of 28 George III, c.48 (1788), Act of 4 and 5 William IV, c.35 (1834); Act of 3 and 4 Victoria, c.85 (1840); Act of 27 and 28 Victoria, c.37 (1864); and Act of 28 and 29 Victoria, c.70 (1875). *Society for Improving the Condition of the Infant Chimney-Sweepers*: George (1976), pp. 241, 378. Judge gives the title as 'The Society Superseding the Necessity of Climbing Boys, by encouraging a New Method of Sweeping Chimnies, and for Improving the Condition of Children and Others, Employed by Chimney Sweepers' and dates its foundation from 1803; Judge (1979), p. 42. *1773*; Jonas Hanway, *The State of Young Chimney-Sweepers' Apprentices* (1773), quoted in George (1976), p. 240. *quotation*: Hanway (1785), p. 25. *Porter*: *Commons Journals*, 1 May 1788, quoted in George (1976), p. 240. *remark*: David Porter's information to *Second Report of the Society for Bettering the Conditions of the Poor*, p. 153, quoted in George (1976), p. 242. *1827 prosecution*: BCh, 5 February 1825, p. 4. *Bennett* (Derbyshire): ibid., 21 April 1827, p. 4; see also *JOxJ*, 8 November 1817, p. 4 (complaint to the magistrates by Jonathan Ogle about his theft and subsequent sale to a sweep). Other cases of theft may have been the basis for the 'Myth of the Lost Climbing Boy', treated at length in Judge (1979), pp. 45–52. *1785 sweep sale*: Hanway (1785), p. 25. *1785 wife sale*: **50**. *1825 sweep sale*: BCh, 5 February 1825, p. 4. *1825 wife sales*: **201**, **203**, **204**. *1827 sweep sale*: BCh, 21 April 1827, p. 4. *1827 wife sales*: **209** and **210**.

20   *baby-farming*: Pearsall (1972), pp. 313, 362. Place (1972), pp. 87−8. *prices*: Pearsall (1972), pp. 360, 361, quotes a general price of £20. In 1885 William T. Stead was supposedly offered 100 virgins for £25 each by a Member of Parliament during investigations on the subject. Eliza Armstrong was offered to Stead for £5; ibid., p. 371.

21   *agreement*: from a court case, in which it was noted that Shaw sold his 16-year-old daughter to a collier named Cudman; *DM* (1899), p. 7. *Oxfordshire*: *JOx]*, 19 September 1767, p. 2 The gypsies may have been a pair arrested in Maidenhead, Berks, in May, 'accused of stealing Farmer's Children about the County, and selling them to Beggars'; ibid., 16 May 1767, p. 1. Not perhaps coincidentally, two gypsies were taken up at Barnes, Surrey, in December, 'charged with stealing children in that Neighborhood and selling them to Beggars in Kent-street, in the Borough'; ibid., 19 December 1767, p.3. Compare this with a 1767 wife-sale price of 5s 3d and a gallon of beer (**30**). *1822*: the sale was between the wife of a Caistor innkeeper and a hawker who had called by for refreshment. The child, aged three months, was later found about 3 miles away, in Gratsby, 'where the man had left it, the child having become excessively troublesome, from the want of its accustomed nourishment'; *G*, 31 August 1822, p. 4; *JOx]*, 7 September 1822, p. 4. *1896*: newspaper, September 1890, (Miller Library, Colby College, Waterville, Maine, USA).

22   *Grateful Dead*: G. H. Gerould, *The Grateful Dead* (London: David Nutt, 1908). *judged to be illegal*: Elliott v. Vorley et al. (1811). W. O. Woodall, 'Arresting a Dead Body for Debt', *NQ*, series 8, vol. 9, 28 March 1896, pp. 241−2. *cases*: Fife, 1669 − George R. Kinlock (ed.), *The Diary of Mr. John Lamont of Newton, 1649−1671* (Edinburgh: Abbotsford Club, 1830), pp. 211−12; quoted in John Ewart Simpkins, *Examples of Printed Folk-Lore Concerning Fife With Some Notes on Clackmannan and Kinross-shires*, County Folk-Lore, vol. 7 (London: Sidgwick and Jackson, 1914), p. 189; Berkshire, 1689 − parish register of Sparsholt, Berkshire, quoted in Andrews (1890), p. 167; Derbyshire, 1724 − Andrews (1890), pp. 166−7; Hertfordshire, 1784 − *GM*, vol. 54, pt. 1, June 1784, pp. 477−8; London, 1794 − *T*, 5 September 1794, p. 2, *JOx]*, 6 September 1794, p. 3, and *GM*, vol. 64, pt. 2, October 1794, p. 952; 1811 − *T*, 15 October 1811, p. 3, ibid., 17 October 1811, p. 3, and ibid., 18 October 1811, p. 2; 1875 − *Evening Standard* (London), 4 October 1875, p. 5.

23   *difficulty*: Douglas (1974), pp. 15−26. *necromancy*: it was believed that babies' fat was used in witches' ointment. The 'Hand of Glory', made from the hand of a suicide or an executed felon, could be used for cures, or in sorcery or to abet theft (it was supposed to stupefy all those to whom it was displayed); Hole (1961), pp. 124−6, 179−80. *religious scruples*: one idea was that all parts of the body must receive burial for a 'quiet grave' or a successful resurrection; Hole (1961), p. 70. For a story of the danger of tampering with a burial in Wiltshire, see Leslie V. Grinsell, *Folklore of Prehistoric Sites in Britain* (Newton Abbot, Devon: David & Charles, 1976), p. 117. *riots*: Linebaugh (1975), pp. 69−78. *'resurrectionists'*: Douglas (1974), pp. 15−26. *Burke*: ibid., generally. *1791*: *T*, 21 October 1791, p. 3. *c. 1750 corpse sale*: Douglas (1974), p. 17 (the child involved was murdered by the women). *pre-1754 corpse sale*: Bath, Somerset, *JOx]*, 23 March 1754, p. 2. *1791 corpse sale*: *T*, 21 October 1791, p. 3. *wife sales*: **72, 73**. *1825 corpse sale*: *JOx]*, 31 December 1825, p. 4 (deceased husband a hackney

coachman). *1825 wife sales*: **201**, **203**, **204**. *1827 corpse sales*: Douglas (1974), pp. 33 and 35 (killed by Burke and Hare). *1827 wife sales*: **209** and **210**. *1828 corpse sales*: Douglas (1974), pp. 37, 39, 42, 46, 47, 48, 54 (£10 was the 'winter rate', £8 the 'summer rate'; killed by Burke and Hare). *1828 wife sales*: **214**, **215** and **216**. *1831 corpse sale*: Douglas (1974), p. 155 (murdered). *1831 wife sales*: **228**, **229** and **230**. Additionally, Dr Knox of Edinburgh is known, on at least one occasion, to have paid £26 5s for a corpse; Douglas (1974), p. 26. *Brighton*: **185**; this calls to mind similar uses to which waiting coffins are put in the Bahamas and elsewhere, a spin-off of the status that accrues to a 'proper' (i.e., expensive) burial. The Burial Societies that are responsible for these arrangements appear to be descended from English antecedents; George (1976), p. 391.

CHAPTER 10: PEACOCK FEATHERS AND THE KING'S SHILLING

1   *'Change'*: a poem concerning the (forthcoming) autumnal fair at Henley-on-Thames, Oxfordshire; *JOxJ*, 22 September 1827, p. 3.
2   fairs: Hole (1975), p. 166, and (1976), p. 97. These were also known as 'Stattit Fairs' (Hole, 1949, p. 120) or the 'Statty' (Jones-Baker, 1977, p. 162). *Statute of Labourers*: Hole (1975), p. 167, and (1976), p. 97; This was passed in 1349 (Rowling, 1976, p. 149). *repeal*: Hole (1975), p. 167, and (1976), p. 97.
3   *Woodforde (Norfolk)*: 3 October; James Woodforde, *Diary of a Country Parson*, Beresford (ed.), vol. 3, p. 303, quoted in Malcolmson (1973), pp. 23−4. *Warwickshire*: between two and three thousand people travelled 25 or 30 miles on foot to this statute fair; William Marshall, *The Rural Economy of the Midland Counties* (London: G. Nichol, 1790), vol. 2, p. 19. *dress*: T. E. Kebble, *The Agricultural Labourer: A Short Summary of the Position*, new edn. (London: W. H. Allen, 1887), pp. 177−8. *ballad*: *A Collection of Broadsides and Ballads*, (British Library, ms. 1875, d.13), quoted in Malcolmson (1973), p. 87. *allotted place*: Hole (1976), p. 97. *row*: Chambers (1869), vol. 1, p. 645. *separate groups*: Hone (1878b), p. 87. *Cumberland*: F. W. Garnett, quoted in Rowling (1976), p. 149. *straw*: Chambers (1869), vol. 1, p. 645. *feathers*: Hole (1961), p. 260.
4   Hardy (1912a), p. 43. *indications*: shepherd − crook (Hole, 1941, p. 95, and 1975, p. 167), wool in hat (Grey, 1935, p. 60; Briggs, 1974, p. 35; *JOxJ*, 22 September 1827, p. 3; Bloom, 1930, p. 107); cowherd/cowman − straw (Hole, 1941, p. 95), cow hair (*JOxJ*, 22 September 1827, p. 3), cow hoof or horn on smock (*CWN*, 12 December 1924, quoted in Porter, 1969, p. 139); groom − brightly coloured whip (Bloom, 1930, p. 107), sponge (Jones-Baker, 1977, p. 162, and Bloom, 1930, p. 107); horsekeeper − whip or whipcord in hat (*CWN*, 12 December 1924, quoted in Porter (1969), p. 139; carter − whip (Burne (1973−74), vol. 2, p. 464), whipcord in hat (Jones-Baker, 1977, p. 162; Briggs, 1974, p. 35, and *JOxJ*, 22 September 1825, p. 3), horsehair (Hole, 1975, p. 167); waggoner − whipcord in hat (Hone, 1878b, p. 87); ploughboy − whipcord in hat (ibid.); gardener − flowers (ibid.); day labourer − plaited hay (Bloom, 1930, p. 107); thresher − sheaf of grain (*JOxJ*, 22 September 1827): Thatcher − woven straw (Hardy, 1912a, p. 43); milkmaid/dairymaid − milk pail (Hole, 1975, p. 167), cowhair on breast

(Sir Frederick Eden, *Survey of the Conditions of the Poor in the Famine of the Years 1795—1796,* 1797, vol. 1, p. 32, quoted in Baker, 1974, p. 127, and Hole, 1975, p. 167); housemaid — broom (Jones-Baker, 1977, p. 162, and Burne, 1973—74, vol. 2, p. 464), mop(Jones-Baker, 1977, p. 62), pail (ibid). *broadside*: York, Yorks: Kendrew; British Library, 1870. c.2 quoted in R. Palmer (1974), p. 105. *Warwickshire mops*: Hone (1878b), p. 88. *Kendal*: quoted in Brand, (1893—4), vol. 2, pp. 455—6, *Canterbury*: M. C. Baker, *Memories of a Sussex Childhood, 1894—1905,* ms. quoted in Baker (1974), p. 129. Chambers (1869), vol. 1, p. 645.

5   *half a year*: Rowling (1976), p. 149. *one year*: Burne (1973—74), vol. 2, pp. 462—3; Hole (1975), pp. 166—7. *Lake District*: Rowling (1976), p. 149. *elsewhere*: R. Palmer (1974), p. 108; Hole (1975), p. 167. *change of mind*: R. Palmer (1974), p. 108. *Warwickshire*: reminiscence of Mr Lusby of Wellesbourne, who was hired (at Warwick) when aged 11; R. Palmer, *The Painful Plough: A portrait of the agricultural labourer in the nineteenth century from folk songs and ballads and contemporary accounts* (Cambridge; Cambridge University Press, 1972), p. 18. *Shropshire*: Burne (1973—74), vol. 2, p. 462. *Oswestry*: ibid., p. 463. *Runaway mops*: Hole (1975), p. 167. *spending of earnest*: Burne (1973—74), vol. 2, p. 463. *Hertfordshire*: Jones-Baker (1977), p. 162. *Warwickshire*: Hone (1878b), p. 88.

6   *poem*: *JOxJ*, 22 September 1827, p. 3. *Clare*: stanza 61, quoted in Malcolmson (1973), p. 23. Francis Heath, *Peasant Life in the West of England* (1883), p. 69, quoted in Ralph Whitlock, *The Folklore of Wiltshire* (London: B. T. Batsford, 1976), p. 63.

7   *quotation*: 'The Scarlet and the Blue'; R. Palmer (1977), p. 60. *'take the shilling'/'collar a shiner'*: 'Muddley Barracks'; R. Palmer (1977), pp. 93, 95.

8   Jackson served from 1803—14 (his recruiting stint was in the summer of 1812); Thomas Jackson, *Narrative of the Eventful Life of Thomas Jackson, late Sergeant of the Coldstream Guards* (Birmingham: 1847), cited in R. Palmer (1977), pp. 10, 290. *Recruiting Officer*: George Farquhar, *The Recruiting Officer* (1704), quoted in R. Palmer (1977), p. 9. *Winchester*: R. Palmer (1977), pp. 10—12. *anti-war song*: c. 1849—52 (Birmingham: Wm Pratt); R. Palmer (1977), p. 41. Edwin Mole, *A King's Hussar* (1893), quoted in R. Palmer (1977), pp. 51, 53—4. *blandishments*: 'The Recruiting Sergeant'; R. Palmer (1977), pp. 55—6. *Perth*: G. Penny, *Traditions of Perth* (1836), pp. 60—1, quoted in R. Palmer (1977), p. 10. In addition to this, cash bonuses were often given to ˙volunteers. The following rates applied: American War — man (long-term) £16 16s, boy (long-term) £12 1s 6d, man (short-term) £11 11s, boy (short-term) £8 8s, anyone supplying a recruit, £3 3s (Royal Marine recruiting poster, R. Palmer, 1977, p. 159); 1793 — £8 8s (R. Palmer, 1977, p. 30); 1795 — £26 5s (*JOxJ*, 3 January 1795, p. 3; this appears to have been a special case); 1803 — £6 (R. Palmer, 1977, pp. 2—6; this compares with contemporary wife-sale prices of £1 1s in case **108** and £5 5s in case **109**); 1853 — 10s (R. Palmer, 1977, p. 45; this compares with contemporary wife-sale prices of £1 in case **302** and 6d in case **303**.

9   *recruitment*: *JOxJ*, 3 January 1795, p. 3. *Chelsea Pensioner*: 1847, quoted in R. Palmer (1977), pp. 12, 288. *MacMullen*: *Camp and Barrack Room: or, the British Army as it is* (1846), quoted in R. Palmer (1977), pp. 12, 291.

10 *sex boundaries*: some girls were apprenticed to carpenters or breeches makers; George (1976), p. 231. *Act of 1601*: ibid., p. 221. *sent˙to other*

parishes: ibid. *Staffordshire*: **65**. *fees*: George (1976), p. 221. *revocation*: ibid., pp. 225, 233, 235. *differences in parish apprenticing*: ibid., p. 222.

11 *temporal range*: the Statute of Apprentices was passed in 1563. Parish apprenticeship continued until about 1844; George (1976), p. 256, and E. P. Thompson (1976), p. 279 (who refers to the Statute as the Statute of Artificers). *social advancement*: George (1976), p. 222; compare the seven-year preliminary to the seven-year absence popularly believed to be sufficient for a divorce. *working of systems*: George (1976), pp. 222−3. *money as master's property*: there are even cases in which the prize money of apprentices who had been impressed was paid to their masters; ibid., pp. 231, 237, 375, 377. *matrimony*: marriage often resulted in the payment of a fine; ibid., pp. 272, 385. *Grey Coat School*: Catharine Cappe, *An Account of Two Charity Schools for the Education of Girls: And of a Female Friendly Society in York* (York, Yorks: William Blanchard, 1800), p. 18. *impressment/kidnapping*: George (1976), p. 227. *'out-door'*: George (1976), p. 234. *'clubbing'*: ibid. *trial apprenticeships*: ibid., p. 245, and Place (1972), pp. 71, 83−4. *Hanway*: George (1976), p. 237.

12 Place (1972), pp. 71, 72.

13 *definition*: Alderman (1975), p. 24. *similarity to apprenticeship*: ibid., p. 77. *decline*: Alderman sets the decline in Virginia from about 1726−88; ibid., pp. 48, 65. *tobacco*: ibid., pp. 24, 61. *elsewhere*: ibid., p. 24. *survival beyond 1800*: ibid., pp. 27, 75.

14 *voting*: Virginia later allowed the vote if a poll tax and tithes were paid; Alderman (1975), pp. 61−2. *marriage*: this was true in Pennsylvania, Maryland and Virginia; ibid., pp. 86, 75, 61. *extra servitude*: amounting to an extra year in Virginia and Pennsylvania; ibid., pp. 61, 86. *punishment for marrying indenturee*: ibid., pp. 61, 86. In 1662 a Virginia minister who had married two such servants was fined 10,000 pounds of tobacco; ibid., p. 61. *forbidden to trade*: ibid., pp. 61, 75. *selling of indentures*: ibid., pp. 75, 84. *limits*: usually four or five years; ibid., pp. 58, 74. *'custom of the country'*: ibid., pp. 57, 74. *access to court*: ibid., pp. 61−2, 69, 89. *renegotiation of contracts*: ibid., pp. 61, 75.

15 *Irish*: Alderman (1975), pp. 27, 48. *Scots*: ibid., p. 48. Other indentured servants came from the Continent, especially the German states; ibid., generally. *England*: ibid., p. 24. *ordinances*: ibid., pp. 33, 35. *debtors*: Pennsylvania; ibid., p. 87. *Pennsylvania*: ibid., p. 86.

16 *London*: Alderman (1975), p. 29. *location of 'spirits'*: ibid., pp. 30−3. *quotation*: ibid., p. 33. *baits*: mentioned by 'The English Rogue'; Alderman (1975), p. 35. *music*: ibid., p. 49. *'safe house'*: ibid., pp. 32−3. *formal indentures*: 1624, ibid., p. 57; *1636*, ibid., p. 24. *terms lengthened*: ibid., p. 58.

17 The following gives a general idea of servant prices; 1649 − £3, including spirit's fee and cost of food (Alderman, 1975, p. 35); 1672 − £10, average price for a 'redemptioner', a person who paid part of his passage and contracted for the remainder after his departure from the country (ibid., pp. 26, 73−4); before 1746 − £16, the price of a Scot with seven years' servitude in Pennsylvania (ibid., p. 50); 1770 − £30, average price for a redemptioner, including £6−13 for passage (ibid., p. 76). One spirit (at St Katherine's) who had operated for 12 years, claimed that he purchased his quota for an average of £1 5s each and resold them for £2; ibid., p. 36.

18 Anne C. Wilson, *Food and Drink in Britain* (Harmondsworth, Middx:

Penguin Books, 1973), pp. 88−9. *rings*: Bloom (1930), p. 107. *memorandum book*: quoted in *Byegones*, April and May 1883, and requoted at second-hand in Burne (1973−74), vol. 2, note p. 463. *forestalling*: *DSJ*, 22 May 1795, p. 4. *petition*: ibid., p. 1. Andrew Blaikie, *A Scottish Farmer's Ride Through England 100 Years Ago*, Jennie Lang Blaikie Lang (ed.) (Selkirk, Peeblesshire: George Lewis, 1906), pp. iv, 1. *quotation*: 19 April; ibid., pp. 24−5.

19   *Lees v. Weaver*: 'just as . . . Smithfield Market' − italics added; *JOxJ*, 14 October 1809, p. 4. The action for return was successful. *livestock prices*: cattle (1795), Shropshire, 4−4½d per lb (*JOxJ*, 21 February 1795, p. 3), London, 4½d (*DSJ*, 16 January 1795, p. 3), 3¾d (ibid., 19 June 1795, p. 4), 3¼d (ibid., 7 August 1795, p. 3), 3¼d (ibid., 9 October 1795, p. 3), 3d (ibid., 11 December 1795, p. 3), (1796) London, 2¾−3¼d (*LNJ*, 7 October 1796, p. 4), 4½d (ibid., 11 November 1796, p. 1), 5d (ibid.); horses (1788), Lancashire, 4½d (*RM*, 17 March 1788, p. 4); sheep (1795), London, 3¼d (*DSJ*, 19 June 1795, p. 4), 3¼d (ibid., 9 October 1795, p. 3), 3d (ibid., 11 December 1795, p. 3); (1796), London, 3¼−3¾d (*LNJ*, 7 October 1796, p. 4), 3¾d (ibid., 11 November 1796, p. 1); hogs (1796), London (ibid.).

20   *underestimation*: this was not acceptable to the seller; *RM*, 17 March 1788, p. 4. *Cheshire*: Hole (1970), p. 22. *spitting*: ibid. *description*: ibid. *Yorkshire*: **42**.

21   *Connecticut*: italics added; this was published under the heading '*An Act against, and for the punishment of Adultery in Connecticut, passed in May 1784*'. One is strongly reminded of Nathaniel Hawthorne's *The Scarlet Letter*. *Hales*: Henry M. Brooks, *Some Strange and Curious Punishments*, the Olden Time Series no. 5 (Boston, Mass.: Ticknor, 1886), p. 36. *court records*: Francis Brown, for stealing goods (1763), ibid., p. 2; Thomas Kendry, for breaking into a store and stealing goods (1786) ibid., p. 48; Catharine Derby, for stealing from a shop (1787?), ibid., p. 22; James Ray, for stealing from the same shop (1788), ibid., p. 5; Lewis Humphries and John Boyd, for stealing (1784), ibid., pp. 46−7. *Dove*: de Watteville (1954), pp. 124−5. *militia*: *LC*, 30 September 1797, p. 314.

22   *miner*: *JOxJ*, 16 September 1854, p. 3. *Staffordshire*: italics added; *Derby Mercury* (Derby, Derbyshire), March 1850 quoted in *Weekly Sentinel* Summer 1912, p. 18, and secondarily in Raven (1978), p. 65.

23   *ballad*: Child (1965), vol. 2, pp. 346−55. *gypsies*: E. B. Lyle, review of Eleanor Long's '"The Maid" and "The Hangman"', *Folklore* (London), vol. 83, Summer, 1972, pp. 169−70. *Led Zeppelin*: 'Gallows Pole'. *first quotation*: version B; Child (1965), vol. 2, p. 351. *second quotation*: version B; ibid. *third quotation*: version A; ibid. p. 351.

24   *1622*: quoted in H. A. Kennedy, 'Hanging or Marrying', *NQ* series 4, vol. 4, 13 November 1869, p. 417. *1686*: Edward Skelton; Linebaugh (1975), p. 114. *1722*: John Hartley, alias 'Pokey', hung for robbery in the streets; the Ordinary's *Account*, 4 May 1722, *Proceedings*, 6 April 1722, and *Weekly Journal or Saturday Post*, 5 May 1722, all cited in Linebaugh (1975), p. 114. *Vassa*: Gustavus Vassa (alias Oladah Equiano); *The Interesting Narrative of the Life of Oladah Equiano, Gustavus Vassa, The African*), 4th edn., enlarged (Dublin: W. Sleater, 1791 [1789]), pp. 337−8. *festive dress and attitude*: Linebaugh (1975), pp. 112−15. M. Mission, *Memoirs and Observations on his Travels over England* (1719), p. 124, quoted in ibid., p. 112. *Thomas*: *GEP*, 25 March 1735, p. 3. *Weskett*: the Ordinary's *Account*,

11 June 1764, quoted in Linebaugh (1975), p. 112. 'Wicked Lord Ferrers': The Life and Times of Selina Countess of Huntingdon, vol. 1 (1839), pp. 401−8, quoted in Linebaugh (1975), p. 112. 'hanging-match': Linebaugh (1975), p. 112.

CHAPTER 11: 'PAY HEED TO MY DITTY'

1   animals inside stones (or other objects): S, 22 September 1797, p. 3, and MC, 23 September 1797, p. 3 (frog found inside stone); WFP, 28 September 1818, p. 4 (lizard inside lump of coal); JOxJ, 24 June 1837, p. 2 (live toad in heart of oak tree); ibid. 23 August 1851, p. 1 (live toad in flint). sheep thieves hanged: Annual Register, or a View of the History, Politics, and Literature for the Year 1762, vol. 5, 5th edn. (London: J. Dodsley, 1787), p. 122; LNJ, 1 January 1796, p. 3, DSJ, 1 January 1796, p. 3. divine judgments: AR 1766, p. 72 (man wished flesh might rot and eyes not shut if he lost the next game of loo − he died of gangrene); WFP, 18 June 1787, p. 3 (man struck dumb and killed for profanities and threat to murder his wife); NM, 11 June 1791, p. 2 (man who swore struck dumb and died); LNJ, 16 September 1796, p. 3 (man struck dead, when he swore he wasn't married); JOxJ, 19 June 1797, p. 3, (man struck dead for swearing falsely about debt); ibid., 2 November 1816, p. 4 (farmer killed for impiously commenting on blighted ear of corn). treasure: JOxJ, 25 February 1797, p. 2. raven leading man to safety: AR 1766, p. 55.

2   well-known personalities: in this, they follow the example of jokes, which often cluster around prominent figures − political (Rev. Ian Paisley, Gov. George Wallace), religious (the Pope) or academic (Sir Maurice Bowra, Professor Bull Warren). Chandos; 15. English lord: 146; see also 12, involving the painter Sir Godfrey Kneller. ms. notation: the antiquary Shaw stated that 'she was chambermaid of the inn at Newbury'; 15a. Through the help of Dr J. S. C. Riley-Smith, the 'old peerage in the library of Queens' College, Cambridge' can be identified as A. Collins, The Peerage of England, 4th edn. (London: H. Woodfall et al., 1768), vol. 2, p. 258. After the identification of the Duke's second wife as 'Mrs Anne Welles' is an 'X': 'The X is in ink − and at the bottom of the page is written in ink "chamber maid at an inn at Newbury Berks. He. . . ." It looks as tho' retrimming of the page at some time has cut off the last line of the note.' Dr Riley-Smith reports that the volume was given to the college in 1774 by Henry Morris, a former fellow (Dr J. S. C. Riley-Smith, Queens' College, Cambridge, letter of April 1978). dismissal 15d. aristocratic involvement: in 154 a silk halter was used, suggesting wealth or fine birth. Lord Ferrers was traditionally believed to have been hanged in 1760 (for the murder of his steward) in a silken halter; G. R. Russell Barker: 'Shirley, Lawrence', Dictionary of National Biography, Sidney Lee (ed.), vol. 52 (London: Smith Elder, 1897), pp. 134−6.

3   James (1974), pp. 120, 120−1. penny fiction: ibid., pp. 115−20, 123, 132−4, 187−9. The same theme is also found in Buckstone's play Luke the Labourer (1826); ibid., p. 120. ballads: this is particularly true if one includes courtship by soldiers; Cox (1967), pp. 316−17 ('A Pretty Fair Maiden') and p. 355 ('The Orphan Girl'), James N. Healey, The Mercier Book of Old Irish Street Ballads, vol. 1 (Cork, Co. Cork: Mercier Press, 1967), pp. 298−300 ('The Maid of Lough Gowna Shore'), and Sharp (1966), vol. 2, pp.

226–7 ('Loving Nancy') and pp. 249–51 ('The Courting Case'). *suicides*:
WFP, 4 January 1790, p. 3. *James quotation about heiresses*: James (1974), p.
130. 'Master and Servant': Menefee (1974), pp. 92–3, 115, 280, 284, 389
class dream: another example of this sort of belief is 'The Lost Climbing Boy',
a memorat fully discussed by Roy Judge in his *Jack in the Green* (1979), pp.
45–52. In this story a boy who is stolen when a child becomes a climbing
sweep, and is afterwards recognized by his family, which holds a celebration
for all chimney sweeps on 1 May in memory of the event. 'The myth in fact
combined the nostalgic glories of May-day with the romance of the outcast
who comes into good fortune. It satisfied a whole spectrum of emotional
needs, offering origin, structure and justification for the whole activity',
ibid., p. 49. Sternberg (1853), pp. 429–30.
4   *London*: **30, 68** and **145**. *Plymouth*: **186**. *gypsy tale*: **318**. *Suffolk*: **273**.
5   '*Loathly Lady*': these include 'The Weddynge of Sr Gawen and Dame
Ragnell' (Percy Folio), 'The Marriage of Sir Gawain', 'King Henry', 'The
Wife of Bath's Tale' (in Chaucer's *Canterbury Tales*), a story in Gower's
Confessio Amantis and 'The Daughter of King Under-waves' (in Campbell's
Popular Tales of the West Highlands); Child (1965), vol. 1, pp. 288–300.
fairy gifts: Briggs (1970–1), part B, vol. 1, p. 235. *Swaffham Peddler and
similar stories*: ibid., part B, vol. 2, pp. 234–5, 298–303, 364–6, 385–6.
6   *London*: **25**. *Brough Hill*: **372**.
7   *Cornwall*: **383**. *lack of logic*: as the husband would have been considered an
accomplice in the murder of the first purchaser, it is most unlikely that he
would have revealed this part of the story. The same is true for the
subsequent murder of the wife. *repertoire of tales*: these included stories
about a well that produced barrenness, a murder near Crowntown, a woman
who put crockery in her husband's pastry and a couple starved in a cage for
murder and ritual cannibalism; letter to Mr Tony Dean in December, 1967,
pp. 5–9, from a xerox copy supplied by Mr Deane, May 1977.
'*Marrowbones*': also known as 'An Old Woman's Story'; Cox (1967), p. 464.
'*The Twa Sisters*': Child Ballad no. 10; Child (1965), vol. 1, pp. 118–41;
Cox (1967), pp. 20–2; Sharp (1966), vol. 1, pp. 26–35; Foxworthy (1976),
pp. 32–3 ('There Was an Old Man in the West Countrie'). *The String of
Pearls*: by Thomas Peckett Prest? James points out that Catnach was
imprisoned for libel in 1818 for intimating that a butcher made his sausages
from human flesh; James (1974), pp. 190–2. Dickens's Tom Pinch, in
Martin Chuzzlewit hoped that no one would think he had been made into
meat pies; Dickens (1968), pp. 650–1. That this belief had earlier popular
grounding is shown by a 1753 incident in which an apprentice was paraded
through the streets of Lincoln to show that he had not been baked, 'as some
had reported', *JOxJ*, 3 November 1753, p. 1. *Burke and Hare*: Douglas
(1974). *Burkers*: Briggs (1970–1), part B, vol. 2, pp. 14–20, 274–5. '*Long
Pack*': ibid., part B, vol. 2, pp. 254–6. In a parallel factual practice,
'resurrectionists' sometimes sold live bodies to unsuspecting surgeons, who
were left holding an empty sack or box the next morning; Douglas, 1974, pp.
20–1. *murderous hosts*: Briggs (1970–1), part B, vol. 2, pp. 14–20,
274–5. In a related story impoverished parents mistakenly murder their
own son when he lodges with them; ibid., part B, vol. 1, pp. 516–17, and
vol. 2, pp. 304–5, and Robert Hunt, *Popular Romances of the West of
England or the Drolls, Traditions & Superstitions of Old Cornwall* (London:
Chatto and Windus, 1923), pp. 442–4. '*Mr Fox*': also called 'The Robber

Bridegroom'; Briggs (1970−1), part A, vol. 2, pp. 390, 405−6, 446−8, 448−50, 457−62, and part B, vol. 2, pp. 87−8, 103, and Katharine M. Briggs and Ruth L. Tongue, *Folktales of England*, Folktales of the World (London: Routledge & Kegan Paul, 1965), pp. 90−4.

8   *story*: trans. by Seán O'Súilleabháin, from an account written by Doncha O Floinn from Conchobhar O Síoháin; ms. vol. 1672, pp. 51−5 (Irish Folklore Commission). *Märchen Der Europäischen Völker* (Rheine, Wesphalia, West Germany: Gesellschafte zue Pflege des Märchengutes der europäischen Völker e. V., 1975), pp. 1−3. *Danaher*: Dr Danaher, Department of Irish Folklore, University College, Dublin, notes that such stories are rare and typically international folktales (letters of May and June 1978).

9   *anchor*: it has been noted that the aristocratic residences of many Scottish ballads, for instance, resemble nothing so much as the prosperous rural farmsteads of the period; David Buchan, *The Ballad and the Folk* (London: Routledge & Kegan Paul, 1972), pp. 79−81. *'Aristocratic Purchaser'*: These examples come from **15**.

10 *Hatfield church*: Jones-Baker (1977), p. 72. *Warwickshire*: Northall (1892), p. 293, and R. Palmer (1976), p. 97. *Staffordshire*: Northall inexplicably cites Bede (1879), p. 510, as his source; Northall (1892), p. 293. *Nebuchadnezzar*: *Daniel* 1−5 in the Bible. Nebuchadnezzar's madness was popularized by William Blake's print on the subject. *Babylon*: 'Here's a poor widow from Babylon', Fraser (1975), p. 124, and 'How many miles to Babylon?' Opie (1952), pp. 63−4. *Queen of Sheba*: Fraser (1975), p. 30; for a general discussion of topical rhymes, see Iona and Peter Opie, *The Lore and Language of Schoolchildren* (Oxford: Clarendon Press, 1959), pp. 98−120. *Worcester*: Bede (1879), p. 510. *Thomas*: *John* 11:16 in the Bible. *'Little Dicky Dilver'*: Opie (1952), p. 148; see Jeaffreson (1872), vol. 1, note p. 291, for another version. *'Bought a wife . . .'*: Jeaffreson (1872), vol. 1, note p. 290; this is similar to 'Tom married a wife on Sunday' (Opie, 1952, p. 410, and plate XX) and to several Irish ballads (Healy, 1969, pp. 130−4). It seems to be more distantly related to 'Solomon Grundy' (Opie, 3952, pp. 592−3). It is interesting to note that such a chain of events is not limited to the nursery. In Lanark

> Eliz. Fairy was proclaimed (in order to marriage) on sunday, was accordingly married on monday, bore a child on tuesday, her husband stole a horse on wednesday, for which he was banished on thursday, the heir of the marriage died on friday and was decently interr'd on saturday: all in one week. (*GSJ*, 5 February 1736, p. 3).

11 *Hutton*: Rev. Alexander Gordon, 'Hutton, William', *Dictionary of National Biography*, Sidney Lee (ed.), vol. 28 (London: Smith, Elder, 1891), pp. 361−3. *poem*: Lawley (A). *possible sale*: 77. *Cox*: Z, letter to the editor, dated 2 May, *GM*, vol. 59, part 1, May 1739, p. 432.

12 'The Hopeful Bargain: Or a Fare for a Hackney-Coachman, giving a Comical relation, how an Ale-draper at the Sign of the Double-tooth'd Rake in or near the new Palace-yard, Westminster, sold his Wife for a Shilling, and how she was sold a Second time for five Shillings to JUDGE; My Lord ——['s] Coachmen, and how her Husband receiv'd her again after she had laid with other Folks three Days and Nights, etc.,' Thomas D'Urfey, *Wit and Mirth: or PILLS to Purge Melancholy; Being a Collection of the best Mery Ballads and Songs, Old and New* (London: W. Pearson, 1719), pp. 258−60.

13   'Smithfield Bargain': T. Jones, *Vauxhall Songster* (c. 1790—99), British
     Library, no. 9. Bl 1876 e 20 p. 71, from a xerox supplied by Mr Roy Palmer,
     May 1978). See also *The Vocal Magazine*, no. 8 (London: Hay and Turner),
     1 August 1815, pp. 50—2; no. 1533, *Voc. Lib.*, 1822, p. 569; *Oliver's* (18—),
     pp. 280—1. *Emery*: John Emery (1777—1822) came of a theatrical family,
     performing in Yorkshire in the early 1790s; 'Emery, John', Highfill *et al.*
     (1978), p. 82. In September 1798 he entered into a contract with Covent
     Garden: 'Although obliged in these early years to act mostly inferior
     characters, Emery was slowly establishing a line of old men and country
     rustics. In the latter he was eventually to hold "an absolute and undisputed
     supremacy"'; ibid., p. 84. For a general discussion of Emery, see ibid., pp.
     82—90, and John Knight, 'Emery, John', *Dictionary of National Biography*,
     Leslie Stephen (ed.), vol. 17 (London: Smith, Elder, 1889), pp. 352—3. '*John
     Hobbs*': *The New London Laughable Songster for 1812* (London: Momus,
     ℤ1812?]), pp. 31—2, sung by Mr Lovegrove in *Any Thing New*, Theatres
     Royal (?). William Lovegrove, 1778—1816, was an actor who appeared in
     1810 at the Lyceum with the Drury Lane company and remained with them
     until his retirement; Joseph Knight, 'Lovegrove, William', *Dictionary of
     National Biography*, Sidney Lee (ed.), vol. 12 (London: Smith, Elder, 1909),
     p. 163. *Any Thing New*, an operatic farce, was first produced at the Lyceum
     on 1 July 1811; Nicoll (1955), vol. 4, p. 383. See also no. 1756, *The Vocal
     Library* (1818), quoted in S.H.W— 'Wife selling', *NQ*, series 4, vol. 10, 9
     November 1872, p. 378; *Voc. Lib.* (1822), p. 647; *Pop.Voc.* (n.d.), p.
     72 ('*A celebrated Comic Song, sung by Mr. Harley, at the Theatres Royal*');
     The little English warbler, quoted in Palmer and Raven (1976), p. 25; song
     quoted in C. C— 'Wifeselling', *NQ*, series 4, vol. 10, 19 October 1872, p.
     311; *All the Year Round*, London, 20 December 1884, p. 255; song noted
     down from singing of Mrs Glover, Shropshire, by Mrs J. H. Blunt, June 1907
     (Foxworthy, 1976, p. 18); Palmer and Raven (1976), p. 25. '*miraculous
     recovery*': the husband, in a surprise twist, hangs himself by a rope rather
     than leading his wife to market with it but is cut down and revived. Compare
     this with 'Johnny Bell', a song about a parish clerk who hanged himself in the
     steeple because of a noisy wife but who was also cut down and resuscitated;
     no. 539, *Voc. Lib.* (1822), p. 208. '*Poor Will Putty*': Ulverston (1812), pp.
     175—6; see also *Oliver's* (18—), pp. 98—9. '*Easter Monday*': Ulverston
     (1812), pp. 136—7; see also '*Easter Monday for Ever; or, The Cobbler at
     Greenwich*', *The Melodist, and Mirthful Olio*, 3 vols. (London: H. Arliss,
     1828), pp. 158—9 (sung to the tune 'John Grouse and Mother Goose'), and
     Oliver's (18—), pp. 13—15. '*knock down*': referring to assault and to the
     selling of goods by an auctioneer; See **170** and **245**. '*spare ribs*': involving a
     pun on the cut of meat and use of the term 'rib' as slang for 'wife'; Partridge
     (1961), p. 696 (based on the story of Adam and Eve in *Genesis*); see **118** and
     157. '*Peg Briggs and her Pigs*': *The British Melodist; or National Song-Book*,
     2nd edn. (London: Longman, Hirst, Rees, Orme, and Brown [1819]), pp.
     195—6; see also 'The Queer Little Woman', Mr Bryant, *Hodgson's New
     Skylark; or Theatrical Budget of Harmony* (London: Hodgson, 1823), pp.
     93—4, and *Poc. Melo.* (n.d.), p. 12. *quotation*: *Poc. Melo.* (n.d.), p. 12.
     '*Mrs Mullins*': *Mrs. Mullins; or, Grunt and Gaby* was an operatic farce
     written by Charles Dibdin, Jr, and produced at Sadler's Wells Theatre on 2
     October 1815; Nicoll (1955), vol. 4, p. 293. *ditty*: *Roundelay or the New
     Siren* (London: W. Lane, n.d.), pp. 165—6. *Fawcett*: probably John Fawcett,

Jr, 1768—1837. He played at Covent Garden, where he was the theatre's stage manager from approximately 1818 to 1828 and was extremely popular from 1805 until the early 1820s. 'For nearly forty years he was one of the leading portrayers of low comedy, rustic, and eccentric characters especially those which required singing'; 'Fawcett, John Jr.', Highfill *et al.* (1978), pp. 198—9. *Staffordshire* (a) fragment of an eighteenth-century ballad, recited by an old man to G. T. Lawley, Lawley (A) (Bilston Public Library, Staffs); (b) 'Sally Lett, or, A Wife for Sale', Lawley (B) (Bilston Public Library, Staffs), also in Raven (1978), pp. 63—4. Mr Roy Palmer reports that a nineteenth-century copy of this appears to exist (letter of January 1980).

14   '*Account of the Sale of a Wife*': Shepherd (1823), and **193**. *Catnach version*: Catnach (1832). *Catnach*: Charles Hindley, *The Life and Times of James Catnach*, reprint edn. (Detroit, Mich.: Singing Trees Press, 1969 [1878]). *Catnach catalogue*: Leslie Shepard, *The History of Street Literature* (Newton Abbot, Devon: David and Charles, 1973), p. 221. *newer offerings*: the song itself is undoubtedly older, although this version might have originated with Catnach. *Pratt's versions*: 'Particular and Merry Account/ of a Most Entertaining and Curious/ Sale of a Wife!/ Of a Pretty Young Woman, who was Sold to a Gallant Young Fellow for £15 and a Dozen of wine, this morning, together with the Wedding Song' (Birmingham: [William] Pratt, [1849—56]) (Birmingham Reference Library, Birmingham), marked 'Price One Penny', and Pratt (1849—56). *Pratt*: Victor E. Neuberg, *Chapbooks*, 2nd edn. (London: Woburn Books, 1972 [1964]), p. 56. *Walker's version*: 'Sale/ of/ a Wife', Song 221 (Otley, Yorks: Walker, [post-1810]) (Northampton Central Library, Northants). *second song*: see also Livsey (n.d.); 'Sale of a Wife' (Manchester: Pearson [1870?]), volume of broadsides, p. 10 (Central Reference Library, Manchester); Kidson Collection (n.d.), 'Sale of a Wife/ in This Neighbourhood — Mrs. You-Know-Who', quoted in Hindley (1969), vol. 1, p. 40; fragment of song (Sheffield, Yorks), quoted in Leader (1901), p. 42. The relationship of these versions is difficult to determine, but the Pratt and Livsey versions and the Yorkshire fragment may be earlier because of their smoother rhythm. They use specific locales for the sale and the post-sale feasting and have sellers with four-syllable occupations (Livsey and the fragment both use cotton-spinners). Pearson, the Kidson broadside, Walker and Hindley all share two-syllable occupations (the former two tailors the latter two, masons) and use a generalized milieu. Walker and Hindley also both delete the word 'smock'. *Walker*: M. J. Preston, M. G. Smith, P. S. Smith, 'The Lost Chapbooks', *Folklore* (London), vol. 88, no. 2, 1977, p. 173, note 8. *third broadside*: 'Wife for Sale' ('The Ship carpenter's wife'?), apparently from Sam Henry Collection, quoted in R. Palmer (1974), pp. 196—7; H. Such (n.d.); 'Sale of a Wife' (c. 1798—1838), quoted in Ashton (1888), pp. 1—3 (this also appears in Ashton (1896), pp. 295—7, with minor variations in punctuation and spelling); and 'A New Song Called The Sale of a Wife', collected from an Irish source and quoted in Healy (1969), pp. 137—9. *crossing to Ireland*: Healy (1969), p. 100.

15   *blanks*: Hindley (1969), vol. 1, p. 40. In broadsides such as 'County Statutes' blanks were actually left for the name of the relevant fair to be supplied; R. Palmer (1974), pp. 105—6, 108. The more people and places a single ballad could cover, the better would be its sale. *variation of locales*: such as London's Ratcliffe Highway and Denison Street in Liverpool; Such (n.d.),

and Ashton (1888), pp. 1—3, respectively. Ratcliffe Highway had the reputation of being a dangerous neighbourhood; George (1976), p. 93. Now known simply as 'The Highway', it was formerly 'full of pubs and "dives", its pavements cluttered with drunks, pimps, crimps, and prostitutes. . . .'; Hugill (1966), p. 202. This location was the subject of the sea chanty 'Ratcliffe Highway', which ends:

> Now all you young sailors take a warnin' I say,
> Take it aisy, me boys, when yer down that Highway,
> Steer clear of them flash gals, on the Highway do dwell,
> Or they'll take up yer flipper an' yer soon bound ter Hell!
>   (ibid., pp. 200—1)

Denison Street appears in at least one sea chanty, from L. V. Briggs, *Around Cape Horn to Honolulu on the Bark 'Amy Turner'* (Boston, Mass.: Charles E. Lauriat, 1926), p. 89:

> Oh, as I was awalking up Dennison Street. . .
> Oh it was a young jaunt that I chanced to meet—

The location of Denison Street was supplied by Mr Hugill (letter of June 1980). 'Sale of a Wife' mentions the Casino in a Manchester version, and the Horse and Jockey in a Birmingham broadside; Livsey (n.d.) and Pratt (1849—56), respectively. The Casino, known also as the 'Cass', was a low-class music hall in nineteenth-century Manchester; Partridge (1961), p. 131. *sexual responses*: for a discussion of the place of obscene songs in English society, see Place (1972), pp. 57—9; Stone (1977), p. 621—2. *quotations*: Hindley (1969), vol. 1, p. 40. *stock types*: it is noteworthy that no one is ever described as raising his bid; multiple bids, however, occur in each of the three broadside types. *exaggerations*: Hindley (1969), v9l. 1, p. 40.

16   *carts*: R. Palmer (1974), pp. 196—7. *carrying on back*: ibid. *multiple sales*: R. Palmer (1974), pp. 196—7. *female intervention*: Pratt (1849—56). *collective purchase*: Catnach (1832).

17   Although each song must have had an author, most writers were probably hacks whose greatest asset was their ability to pander to popular tastes. Anything produced for the mass market was a fairly accurate reflection of popular culture.

18   Act III, scene ii: 11. 1—4. William Shakespeare, *Measure for Measure*, J. W. Lever (ed.), Arden edition (London: Methuen, 1966), pp. 81—2.

19   *The Phoenix*: Act I, scene iv; Middleton (1885), vol. 1, p. 127. The play was produced in 1607; ibid., vol. 1, pp. xxvii—xxviii. Other examples of such plays are Webster's *The White Devil* and *The Duchess of Malfi*, Tourneur's *The Revenger's Tragedy*, Middleton's *The Changeling* and Shakespeare's *Titus Andronicus*. Dr William Power, 'The Sale of a Wife', *NQ*, new series 4, vol. 202, October 1957, p. 455. The presence of anachronisms in Elizabethan drama is well attested to; F. E. Halliday, *A Shakespeare Companion*, revised edn. (Baltimore, Md.: Penguin, 1964), p. 30. *quotation to Phoenix*: Act I: scene iv; Middleton (1885), vol. 1, p. 127. *written agreement*: Act II: scene ii; ibid., pp. 143—5.

20   *bawdy passages*: Act II, scene ii. Middleton (1885), vol. 1, pp. 143—5. *real document*: compare this phrasing with the memorandum used to assign a Somerset wife in 1766 (29).

21   *Love the Leveller*: Nicoll (1955), vol. 2, p. 221; Gevest's criticism is echoed

by Nicoll (ibid.). *plot basis*: ibid., note p. 188. *Wife to be Lett*: ibid., p. 188.

22   *advertisement*: *The Times* of 2 August had a similar advertisement, except that it is for the third performance. Another on 7 August mentioned no specific performance. Advertisements for the play also appeared in the *Morning Chronicle* on 31 July and 2, 4 and 7 August; 83l−t, w−x. *topic of conversation*: **83**, **84** and **86**. *entertainment explained*: 83l; as the price of admission decreased during the evening, it maximized profits to ensure that people attended the theatre at an early hour. *Morning Chronicle quotation*: **83n**. *run of play*: apparently from 31 July − 7 August; there were no Sunday performances. *puffs*: such as the 'Cabinet of Monkies', who started their new engagement with Astley, 'a Manager who knew their worth too well to let them slip through his fingers. Of the other Stage Amusements, report speaks particularly favourable of The Escape, The Female Soldier, A Trip to Burgundy, and The Siege of Troy'; *T*, 4 July 1797, p. 3. See also ibid., 14 July 1797, p. 3; 8 August 1797, p. 3; 11 August 1797, p. 3; 5 September 1797, p. 4; *MC*, 8 August 1797, p. 4; 29 August 1797, p. 3. It was common to have multiple pieces lasting the better part of an afternoon or evening. *Kit*: Dickens (1972), pp. 375−6, and illustration. There was also a song 'A Peep at Astley's' sung to the tune of 'Yankee Doodle'; *Pop. Voc.* (n.d.), pp. 121−2, and illustration. *suitability*: such as

> an Intermezzio called St. Bartholomew Fair, intended principally for the amusement and information of those persons who, though they might occasionally like to see the humours of Smithfield at this time, are not over-fond of crowding it with bakers, barbers, chimney sweepers and the like . . .
>
>   (*MC*, 5 September 1797, p. 4)

novelty: *T*, 11 August 1797, p. 3. *happily adapted*: ibid., 5 September 1797, p. 4. 'The Female Soldier', mentioned above, for example, was a topic of many broadside ballads. *talk of the town*: while there were frequent comic references to wife sales in period newspapers, it is hard to gauge whether these preceded or followed public interest in the institution. *quotation from play*: **83p**. *Wife to be Sold*: Nicoll (1959), vol. 4, p. 351. Sternberg (1853), pp. 429−30.

23   *street theatre*: sales took place on raised platforms, often in inn courtyards, before large audiences. They often included colourful auctioneer's patter and audience participation, and in some cases the wife seems almost to have been acting out a role. *quotation*: **83p**.

24   Borrow (1969), pp. 268−9; background information, ibid., pp. 260−1.

25   Hardy (1912b), pp. 7−13. *three examples*: **205b**, **210a** and **220a**. These accounts were copied into *Facts: from Newspapers, Histories, Biographies and other chronicles (mainly local)* (Dorset County Museum); Winfield (1970), note p. 224 and p. 225. *preface*: Hardy (1912b, p. vii) states:

> The incidents narrated arise mainly out of three events, which chanced to range themselves in the order and at or about the intervals of time here given, in the real history of the town called Casterbridge and the neighbouring country. They were the sale of a wife by her husband . . . .

The view that Hardy's account was based on an actual Dorset sale is supported by writers such as Kenny (1929), p. 495. Winfield (1970), pp. 225−7.

26 *location*: Hardy (1912b), pp. 1−7. *quotation*: ibid., pp. 8−9. *London wife sale*: **25 note**. *return of ring*: Hardy (1912b), p. 12. *Lincolnshire*: **53**. *family names*: Florence Emily Hardy, *The Life of Thomas Hardy 1840−1928* (London: Macmillan, 1975), p. 6. *sparse representation*: **356** and **375**.

27 Lady Catherine Milnes Gaskell, *Prose Idylls of the West Riding* (London: Smith Elder, 1907), pp. 198−250. *quotation*: ibid., p. 198.

28 Hugh Walpole, *Rogue Herries* (London: Macmillan, 1930), pp. 158−61. Beatrice Tunstall, *The Shiny Night* (London: William Heinemann, 1931), p. 64. Alison Uttley, *The Country Child* (Harmondsworth, Middx: Penguin, 1977 [1931]), pp. 115−16. Rosalind Laker, *Warwyck's Wife* (London: Methuen, 1979), pp. 7−20. Ms Laker notes of her sources: 'I knew of wife-selling from all I have heard of old country customs in the county of Sussex in which I live, and over the years I had simply dotted down a line here and there where it was mentioned . . . .' She was familiar with both the Hardy and Walpole accounts from fiction (letter of April 1980). *Aubrey*: Patrick O'Brian, *Desolation Island* (London: Fontana, 1979 [1978]), p. 5.

29 *Gerard*: Sir Arthur Conan Doyle, *The Exploits of Brigadier Gerard* (London: Pan, 1977 [1896]), p. 108. *fox hunting*: Sir Arthur Conan Doyle, *Adventures of Gerard* (London: Pan, 1976 [1903]), pp. 59−73. Sternberg (1853), pp. 429−30. Guy de Maupassant, *Short Stories*, Marjorie Laurie (trans.) (London: J. M. Dent & Sons, 1971 [1934]), pp. 73−7.

30 *faro*: many mentions of this game occur in *The Times* and the *Morning Chronicle* for 1797; see, for example, *T*, 3 February 1797, pp. 2 and 3 (including anecdotes, a poem, and a discussion of the penalties attaching to the game); *MC*, 13 March 1797, p. 3 (court case), and 21 March 1797, p. 3 (court case). Gillray's print is 'Discipline à la Kenyon'; Hill (1966), fig. 86. A caricature of 'A Sale of English-Beauties, in the East-Indies', however, comes close to wife-selling (ibid., figs. 78 and 79), and Gillray treats politicians as cattle in a Smithfield market context in 'Market-Day'; Draper Hill, *The Satirical Etchings of James Gillray* (New York: Dover Publications, 1976), fig. 14.

31 *exception*: even here, many ballads were unillustrated or carried pictures in no way related to their subject matter. 'Sale of a Wife', printed by Livesey, shows two crude wood blocks, one of a bellman (?) discovering a sleeping boy by a haystack, the other, of a donkey; Livsey (n.d.). Another, 'Sale of a Wife', depicts a woman seated before a kitchen fire with two little girls; Kidson Collection (n.d.). *Bristol*: the printer was Shepherd, who appears to have used the same block a year later — 'Account of the Sale of a Wife'; see **184** and **193b**. Ashton (1888), p. 1, also illustrated in Palmer and Raven (1976), p. 28. (Mr Palmer confirmed that Ashton was the source for this in a letter of January 1977.) See broadsides reproduced on pp. 206 and 68.

32 See Catnach (1832); see also broadside reproduced as frontispiece.

CHAPTER 12: A CUSTOM OBSERVED BY THE PEOPLE

1 Place (1972), p. 91; see also George Eliot, *Adam Bede* (New York: New American Library, 1961 [1859]), p. 176.

2 The problems of localized studies are discussed in depth by Macfarlane (1977), pp. 1−25.

3 Evans-Pritchard (1951), pp. 28—43, and introduction to Robert Hertz, *Death and the Right Hand*, Rodney and Claudia Needham (trans.) (London: Cohen & West, 1960), pp. 12—14; Beattie (1964), pp. 8—10; Godfrey Lienhardt, *Social Anthropology*, 2nd edn. (Oxford: Oxford University Press, 1966 [1964]), pp. 25—8; Mair (1972), pp. 47—53. For a specific discussion of the comparative method, see Harris (1969), pp. 150—65.

Select Bibliography

A—, P. T. (1938), 'Matrimonial Sales', *Notes and Queries* (London), series 15, vol. 175, 29 October, p. 314

A—, P. T. (1939), 'Matrimonial Sales', *Notes and Queries* (London), series 15, vol. 176, 11 February, pp. 95—6

ABG: Aris' Birmingham Gazette (Birmingham)

Addy, S. O. (1973), *Folk Tales and Superstitions* [1895], reprint edn. (East Ardsley, Wakefield, Yorks: E. P. Publishing)

Alderman, C. L. (1975), *Colonists for Sale: The Story of Indentured Servants in America* (New York: Macmillan)

Andrews, W. (1880), *The Derbyshire Gatherer of Archaeological, Historical, Biographical Facts, Folk-lore, etc.* (Buxton, Derbyshire: J. C. Bates)

Andrews, W. (1892), *Bygone England: Social Studies in its Historic Byways and Highways* (London: Hutchinson)

Andrews, W. (1975), *Old Church Lore* [1891] (East Ardsley, Wakefield, Yorks: E. P. Publishing)

AR 1766: The Annual Register, or a View of the History, Politics, and Literature for the Year 1766, vol. 9, 5th edn. (London: J. Dodsley, 1793)

AR 1767: The Annual Register, or a View of the History, Politics, and Literature for the Year 1767, vol. 10, 5th edn. (London: J. Dodsley, 1796)

AR 1770: The Annual Register, or a View of the History, Politics, and Literature for the Year 1770, vol. 13, 5th edn. (London: J. Dodsley, 1794)

Ashton, J. (1888), *Modern Street Ballads* (London: Chatto & Windus)

Ashton, J. (1896), *When William IV was King* (London: Chapman & Hall)

Ashton, J. (1899), *Social England under the Regency* [1890], new edn. (London: Chatto & Windus)

Atiyah, P. S. (1971), *An Introduction to the Law of Contract* [1961], 2nd edn. (Oxford: Clarendon Press)

B—, G. L. (1850), 'Wives, Custom of Selling', *Notes and Queries* (London), series 1, vol. 2, 31 August, p. 217

Baker, M. (1974), *Folklore and Customs of Rural England* (Newton Abbot, Devon: David & Charles)

Baker, M. (1977), *Wedding Customs and Folklore* (Newton Abbot, Devon: David & Charles)

Baldry, G. (1976), *The Rabbit Skin Cap* [1939], the Norfolk Library, Lilias Rider Haggard (ed.), reprint edn. (Ipswich, Suffolk: Boydell Press)

Banks, M. M. (1941), *British Calendar Customs: Scotland*, vol. 3 (London: William Glaisher)

Baring-Gould, S. (1926), *Devonshire Characters and Strange Events* [1908], later edn. (London: Bodley Head)

Bates, W. (1872), 'Wife-Selling', *Notes and Queries* (London), series 4, vol. 10, 14 December, pp. 468−9

BCh: Berkshire Chronicle (Reading, Berks)

Beattie, J. (1964), *Other Cultures: Aims, Methods and Achievements in Social Anthropology* (London: Cohen & West)

Bede, C. (1879), 'St Thomas, surnamed "Didymus"', *Notes and Queries* (London), series 5, vol. 12, 27 December, p. 510.

BG: Boston Gazette and Lincolnshire Advertiser (Boston, Lincs)

BH: Buckinghamshire Herald (Aylesbury, Bucks)

Blackstone, Sir W. (1836), *Commentaries on the Laws of England*, 19th edn. Hovenden and Ryland (eds.) 4 vols. (London: S. Sweet)

Bloom, J. H. (1921), 'Warwickshire Folklore', *Notes and Queries* (London), series 12, vol. 9, 16 July, p. 47

Bloom, J. H. (1930), *Folklore, Old Customs and Superstitions in Shakespeare Land* (London: Mitchell Hughes & Clarke)

BM: Bristol Mercury and Monmouthshire, South Wales and West of England Advertiser (Bristol)

Bond, R. (1891), 'Some Events of Seventy Years', *Transactions of the Lancaster Philosophical Society*, 1890−91, pp. 66−91

Borrow, G. (1969), *The Romany Rye* [1906], reprint edn. (London: J. M. Dent & Sons)

Brand, J. (1890−93), *Observations on the Popular Antiquities of Great Britain*, Sir Henry Ellis (ed.), 3 vols. (London: George Bell & Sons)

Briffault, R. (1927), *The Mothers*, vol. 2 of *A Study of the Origins of Sentiments and Institutions*, 3 vols. (London: Allen & Unwin)

BrG: Brighton Gazette and Lewes Observer, etc. (Brighton, Sussex)

Briggs, K. M. (1970−71), *A Dictionary of British Folk-Tales in the English Language*, 2 parts, 4 vols. (London: Routledge & Kegan Paul)

Briggs: K. M. (1974), *The Folklore of the Cotswolds* (London: B. T. Batsford)

Brown: P. F. W. (1951), 'Wife Selling', *Notes and Queries* (London), vol. 196, 31 October, p. 460

Burne, C. S. (1973—74), *Shropshire Folk-Lore: A Sheaf of Gleanings* [1883], 2 vols., reprint edn. (East Ardsley, Wakefield, Yorks: E. P. Publishing)

Burstow, H. (1911), *Reminiscences of Horsham, being Recollections of Henry Burstow the Celebrated Bellringer and Songster* (Horsham, Sussex: Christian Church Book Society)

Catnach, J. (c. 1832?), 'Particular and merry Account of a most Entertaining and Curious SALE OF A WIFE, Of a pretty young WOMAN, who was Sold to a gallant young Fellow, For FIFTEEN Sovereigns, and a Dozen of Wine, this Morning, Together with the Wedding SONG' (London: J. Catnach) (London: British Library, Broadsides LR 271 a 5, vol. 4, p. 290)

Cawte, E. C. (1978), *Ritual Animal Disguise* (Cambridge: D. S. Brewer)

Ch: Champion, or Evening Advertiser (London)

Chambers, R. E. (1869), *The Book of Days: A Miscellany of Popular Antiquities*, etc. [1862—64], 2 vols., later edn. (London: W. & R. Chambers)

ChC: Chester Chronicle (Chester, Cheshire)

Child, F. J. (1965), *The English and Scottish Popular Ballads* [1882—98], 5 vols., reprint edn. (New York: Dover Publications)

Chitty, T. (1837), *Burn's Justice of the Peace and Parish Officer*, 6 vols., 28th edn. (London: S. Sweet)

Chitty, T. (1845), *Burn's Justice of the Peace and Parish Officer*, 6 vols., 29th edn. (London: Sweet, Maxwell & Son)

Claverhouse [pseud.] (1905), *Gretna Green and its Traditions* (Paisley, Renfrewshire: Alexander Gardner)

CoC: County Chronicle and Weekly Advertiser for Essex, Herts, Kent, etc. (London)

Coleman, T. (1968), *The Railway Navvies* [1965], rev. edn. (Harmondsworth, Middx: Penguin)

Cox, J. H. (1967), *Folk-Songs of the South* [1925], reprint edn. (New York: Dover Publications)

Cranfield, C. A. (1962), *The Development of the Provincial Newspaper 1700—1760* (Oxford: Clarendon Press)

CS: Common Sense (London)

CWN: Cambridge Weekly News (Cambridge, Cambridgeshire)

D'Archenholtz, M. (1789), *A Picture of England: Containing a Description of the Laws, Customs and Manners of England*, 2 vols., trans. from French (London: Edward Jeffrey)

DCC: Dorset County Chronicle (Dorchester, Dorset)

DeC: Derby Chronicle (Derby, Derbyshire)

de Watteville, Col. H. (1954), *The British Soldier: His Daily Life from Tudor to Modern Times* (London: J. M. Dent & Sons)

DG: Doncaster Gazette (Doncaster, Yorks)

Dickens, C. (1968), *The Life and Adventures of Martin Chuzzlewit* [1843 – 44] (Harmondsworth, Middx: Penguin)

Dickens, C. (1972), *The Old Curiosity Shop* [1841] (Harmondsworth, Middx: Penguin)

DM (1899): 'Daily Magazine. The Trade in Wives', *Daily Mail* (London), 1 March, p. 7

DoC: Doncaster Chronicle (Doncaster, Yorks)

Douglas, H. (1974), *Burke and Hare* [1973] (London: New English Library)

DSJ: Dorchester and Sherborne Journal and Taunton and Somersetshire Herald; Dorchester and Sherborne Journal and Western Advertiser (Dorchester, Dorset)

DT: Daily Telegraph (London)

E—, K. P. D. (1856), 'Notes on Wife Selling', *Notes and Queries* (London), series 2, vol. 1, 24 May, pp. 420 – 1

E—, K. P. D. (1858), 'Wife Selling', *Notes and Queries* (London), series 2, vol. 6, 11 December, p. 490

E—, K. P. D. (1863), 'Wife Selling', *Notes and Queries* (London), series 3, vol. 3, 20 June, p. 486.

Earle, A. M. (1894), *Customs and Fashions in Old New England* [1893] (New York: Charles Scribner' Sons)

Earle, A. M. (1898), *In Old Narragansett: Romances and Realities* (New York: Charles Scribner's Sons)

EC: Essex Chronicle (Chelmsford, Essex)

Ellis, T. P. (1926), *Welsh Tribal Law and Custom in the Middle Ages* (Oxford: Clarendon Press)

Evans, G. E. (1975), *The Days That We Have Seen* (London: Faber & Faber)

Evans-Pritchard, E. E. (1951), *Social Anthropology* (London: Cohen & West)

Fenn, H. E. (n.d.), *35 Years in the Divorce Courts* (London: T. Werner Laurie)

Fleming, W. (1812), Diary and Commonplace Book, ms., 27 – 8 January, (microfilm copy, Harold Cohen Library, University of Liverpool, sheets 2405 – 6)

Foxworthy, T. (1976), *Forty Long Miles* (London: Galliard and English Folk Dance and Song Society)

Fraser, A. S. (1975), *Dae Ye Min' Langsyne?* (London: Routledge & Kegan Paul)

G: Globe (London)

G— (1847), Correspondence, *Justice of the Peace*, 20 March, p. 223

Gainer, P. W. (1975), *Witches, Ghosts and Signs: Folklore of the Southern Appalachians* (Grantsville, West Virginia: Seneca Books)

George, M. D. (1976), *London Life in the Eighteenth Century* [1925] (Harmondsworth, Middx: Penguin)

GEP: General Evening Post (London)

GM: Gentleman's Magazine and Historical Chronicle (London)

Goldsworthy, E. (1975), *Recollections of Old Taunton* [1883] (Taunton, Somerset: Barnicotts Publications)

Green, J. R., and Roberson, G. (1901), *Studies in Oxford History Chiefly in the Eighteenth Century*, C. L. Stainer (ed.), Oxford Historical Society (Oxford: Clarendon Press)

Grey, E. (1935), *Cottage Life in a Hertfordshire Village* (St Albans, Herts: Fisher, Knight)

Grosley, M. (1772), *A Tour to London; or New Observations on England and Its Inhabitants*, Thomas Nugent (trans.) (London: Lockyer Davis)

GSJ: Grub Street Journal (London)

GT: Globe and Traveller (London)

GT (1903), 'Wife Selling', *Globe and Traveller* (London), 16 November, pp. 1−2

HA: Hull Advertiser (Hull, Yorks)

Hackwood, F. W. (1974), *Staffordshire Customs, Superstitions and Folklore* [1924], reprint edn. (East Ardsley, Wakefield, Yorks: E. P. Publishing)

Hair, P. (ed.) (1972), *Before the Bawdy Court: Selections from Church Court Records* (London: Paul Elek)

Hanway, J. (1785), *A Sentimental History of Chimney Sweepers in London and Westminster* (London: Dodsley)

Hardy, T. (1912a), *Far from the Madding Crowd* [1874] (London: Macmillan)

Hardy, T. (1912b), *The Life and Death of the Mayor of Casterbridge: A Story of a Man of Character* [1886] (London: Macmillan)

Harland, J., and Wilkinson, T. T. (1973), *Lancashire Legends, Traditions, Pageants, Sports*, etc. [1873], reprint edn. (East Ardsley, Wakefield, Yorks: E. P. Publishing)

Harris, M. (1969), *The Rise of Anthropological Theory: A History of Theories of Culture* (London: Routledge & Kegan Paul)

Harrison, B. (1971), *Drink and the Victorians* (London: Faber & Faber)

Haworth, D., and Comber, W. M. (eds.) (1952), *Cheshire Village Memories* (Malpas, Cheshire: Cheshire Federation of Women's Institutes)

HE: Halifax Express, Halifax and Huddersfield Express (Halifax and Huddersfield, Yorks)

Healy, J. N. (1969), *The Mercier Book of Old Irish Street Ballads*, vol. 4 (Cork, Co. Cork: Mercier Press)

Hewett, S. (1973), *Nummits and Crumnits: Devonshire Customs, Characteristics and Folk-lore* [1900], reprint edn. (Norwood, Penn.: Norwood Editions)

Highfill, P. H., Jr, Burnim, K. A., and Langhans, E. A. (1978), *A Biographical Dictionary of Actors, Actresses, Musicians, Dancers, and Other Stage Personnel in London 1660−1800*, vol. 5, *Egan to Garrett* (Carbondale, Ill.: Southern Illinois University Press)

Hill, D. (1966), *Fashionable Contrasts: Caricatures by James Gillray* (London: Phaidon Press)

Hindley, C. (1969), *Curiosities of Street Literature*, 2 vols. [1871], reprint edn. (London: Seven Dials Press)

HJ: Hereford Journal Advertiser for the Counties of Hereford, Brecon, Radnor, etc. (Hereford, Herefordshire)

Hole, C. (1940), *English Folklore* (London: B. T. Batsford)

Hole, C. (1941), *English Custom and Usage* (London: B. T. Batsford)

Hole, C. (1949), *English Sports and Pastimes* (London: B. T. Batsford)

Hole, C. (1961), *Encyclopaedia of Superstitions* [1948], rev. edn. (London: Hutchinson)

Hole, C. (1970), *Traditions and Customs of Cheshire* [1937], reprint edn. (East Ardsley, Wakefield, Yorks: S. R. Publishers)

Hole, C. (1975), *English Traditional Customs* (London: B. T. Batsford)

Hole, C. (1976), *British Folk Customs* (London: Hutchinson)

Hole, C. (1977), *Witchcraft in England* (London: B. T. Batsford)

Hone, W. (1878a), *The Every Day Book; or a Guide to the Year*, 2 vols. [1826−27] (London: William Tegg)

Hone, W. (1878b), *The Table Book of Daily Recreation and Information* [1827] (London: William Tegg)

Hone, W. (1878c), *The Year Book of Daily Recreation and Information* [1832] (London: William Tegg)

Hope, A. D. (1970), *A Midsummer Eve's Dream* (New York: Viking Press)

Hope, R. C. (1968), *The Legendary Lore of the Holy Wells of England* [1893], reprint edn. (Detroit, Mich.: Singing Tree Press)

HT: Hereford Times, and General Advertiser, for the Counties of Hereford, Monmouth, Glamorgan, etc. (Hereford, Herefordshire)

Hugill, S. (1966), *Shanties from the Seven Seas* (London: Routledge & Kegan Paul)

IJ: Ipswich Journal (Ipswich, Suffolk)

James, L. (1974), *Fiction for the Working Man 1830−50* [1963], reprint edn. (Harmondsworth, Middx: Penguin)

Jannoc (1866), 'Selling a Wife', *Notes and Queries* (London), series 3, vol. 10, 14 July, p. 29

Jarrett, D. (1976), *England in the Age of Hogarth* [1974] (St Albans, Herts: Granada)

Jeaffreson, J. C. (1872), *Brides and Bridals*, 2 vols. (London: Hurst & Blackett)

Jones-Baker, D. (1977), *The Folklore of Hertfordshire* (London: B. T. Batsford)

JOx]: Jackson's Oxford Journal (Oxford, Oxfordshire)

Judge, R. (1979), *The Jack in the Green: A May Day Custom* (Cambridge: D. S. Brewer)

K: Kaleidoscope (Liverpool)

KBJ: Keene's Bath Journal (Bath, Somerset)

Kenny, C. (1929), 'Wife-Selling in England', *Law Quarterly Review* (London), vol. 45, October, pp. 494—7

KG: Kentish Gazette (Canterbury, Kent)

Kidson Collection (n.d.), 'Sale of a Wife', (Glasgow: Mitchell Library, Kidson Broadside Collection, no. 41)

L., J. (1887), 'Sale of a Wife', *Gloucestershire Notes and Queries* (London), vol. 3, p. 675

LA: London Advertiser (London)

Landwor, (1880), 'Wife-selling', in Thomas Hughes (ed.) *The Cheshire Sheaf, Being Local Gleanings, Historical and Antiquarian, From Many Scattered Fields*, (Chester, Cheshire: Courant Steam Printing Works), vol. 1, pp. 245—6

Langford, J. A. (1870), *A Century of Birmingham Life* [1868], 2nd edn. (Birmingham: W. G. Moore)

Lawley, G. T. (A), 'South Staffordshire Stories. Wife Selling', newspaper (Bilston, Staffordshire: Public Library)

Lawley, G. T. (B), 'South Staffordshire Stories', newspaper (Bilston, Staffordshire: Public Library)

Lawley, G. T. (1893), *A History of Bilston in the County of Staffordshire* (Bilston, Staffordshire: John Price)

LC: London Chronicle (London)

Leader, R. E. (1901), *Sheffield in the Eighteenth Century* (Sheffield, Yorkshire: Sheffield Independent Press)

LG: Lancaster Gazette (Lancaster, Lancashire)

LGaz.: London Gazette (London)

LinC: Lincolnshire Chronicle and General Advertiser (Stamford and Lincoln, Lincolnshire)

Linebaugh, P. (1975), 'The Tyburn Riot Against the Surgeons', in D. Hay *et al., Albion's Fatal Tree: Crime and Society in Eighteenth Century England* (New York: Pantheon), pp. 65—117

LivM: Liverpool Mercury, or Commercial, Literary and Political Herald,
subsequently *Liverpool Mercury and Lancashire and Cheshire Advertiser* (Liverpool)

Livsey (n.d.), 'Sale of a Wife', (Manchester: Livsey) Central Reference Library volume of broadsides, p. 44

LM: Leeds Mercury (Leeds, Yorkshire)

LNJ: Leicester and Nottingham Journal (Leicester, Leicestershire)

LRW (1777): *The Laws Respecting Women, As they Regard their Natural Rights, or their Connections and Conduct,* etc. (London: J. Johnston)

LSM: Lincoln, Rutland and Stamford Mercury (Stamford, Lincolnshire)

M—, A. J. (1881), 'Wife Selling', *Notes and Queries* (London), series 6, vol. 4, 13 August, p. 133

Macfarlane, A. (1970), *The Family Life of Ralph Josselin, a Seventeenth-Century Clergyman* (Cambridge: Cambridge University Press)

Macfarlane, A. (1971), *Witchcraft in Tudor and Stuart England, a Regional and Comparative Study* (New York: Harper & Row)

Macfarlane, A. (1977) (in collaboration with S. Harrison and C. Jardine), *Reconstructing Historical Communities* (Cambridge: Cambridge University Press)

MacNeil, Máire (1962), *The Festival of Lughnasa* (Oxford)

Maid Gaz.: Maidstone Gazette (Maidstone, Kent)

Mair, L. (1972), *An Introduction to Social Anthropology,* [1965] 2nd edn. (Oxford: Clarendon Press)

Mair, L. (1977), *Marriage* [1971], reprint edn. (London: Scolar Press)

Malcolmson, R. W. (1973), *Popular Recreations in English Society 1700—1850* (Cambridge: Cambridge University Press)

Mauss, M. (1969), *The Gift* [1954], I. Cunnison (trans.) (London: Cohen & West)

MC: Morning Chronicle and London Advertiser (London)

Menefee, S. P. (1974), 'Divination in the British Isles' (ms. in Bodleian Library, Oxford)

Menefee, S. P. (1977), 'Informal Institutions in British Society', dissertation draft, University of Oxford

Menefee, S. P. (1978), 'Wife-Selling: An Informal Institution in British Society' (ms. in Bodleian Library, Oxford)

MH: Morning Herald (London)

Middleton, T. (1885), *The works of Thomas Middleton,* A. H. Bullen (ed.), 8 vols. (London: John C. Nimmo)

MJ: Maidstone Journal and Kentish Advertiser (Maidstone, Kent)

MM: Manchester Mercury (Manchester)

Money, W. (1895), 'The Duke of Chandos and Shaw House', *Transactions of the Newbury District Field Club* (Newbury, Berkshire), vol. 4, pp. 12—15

Moritz, C. P. (1795), *Travels, Chiefly on Foot Through Several Parts of England, in 1782*, trans. by 'a Lady' (London: G. G. and J. Robinson)

Nadel, S. F. (1951), *The Foundations of Social Anthropology* (London: Cohen & West)

NC: Norfolk Chronicle, or Norwich Gazette (Norwich, Norfolk)

NDB (1884): *Nottingham Date Book* (Nottingham, Nottinghamshire: H. Field), vol. 2

Nicoll, A. (1955), *A History of English Drama 1660–1900*, 3rd edn. (Cambridge: Cambridge University Press)

NM: Northampton Mercury (Northampton, Northamptonshire)

Nonagenarian [pseud.] (1876), 'Hereford in the Olden Time. Selling Wives in Hereford', *Hereford Times, and General Advertiser, for the Counties of Hereford, Monmouth, Glamorgan*, etc. (Hereford, Herefordshire), 20 May, p. 16

Northall, G. F. (1892), *English Folk-Rhymes, a Collection of Traditional Verses Relating to Places and Persons, Customs, Superstitions etc.* (London: Kegan Paul, Trench, Trubner)

NOW (1924): 'When Wives Were Sold', *News of the World* (London), 6 January, p. 9

NQ: Notes and Queries (London)

NWG: Nottinghamshire Weekly Guardian (Nottingham, Nottinghamshire)

O: Observer (London)

OCC: Oxford City and County Chronicle (Oxford, Oxfordshire)

ODFS (1951): 'Some Instances of "Rough Music" in Oxfordshire', *Oxfordshire and District Folklore Society Annual Record* (Oxford), no. 3, pp. 13–14

Oliver's (18—): *Oliver's Comic Songs* (Edinburgh: Oliver & Boyd)

Opie, I. and P. (1951), *The Oxford Dictionary of Nursery Rhymes*, (Oxford: Clarendon Press)

Owen, T. M. (1968), *Welsh Folk Customs* [1959], 2nd edn. (Cardiff: J. D . Lewis)

PA: Public Advertiser (London)

Palmer, K. (1976), *The Folklore of Somerset* (London: B. T. Batsford)

Palmer, R. (1974), *A Touch on the Times: Songs of Social Change, 1770 to 1914* (Harmondsworth, Middx: Penguin)

Palmer, R. (1976), *The Folklore of Warwickshire* (London: B. T. Batsford)

Palmer, R. (1977), *The Rambling Soldier* (Harmondsworth, Middx: Penguin)

Palmer, R., and Raven, J. (1976), *The Rigs of the Fair: Popular Sports and Pastimes in the Nineteenth Century Through Songs, Ballads and Contemporary Accounts* (Cambridge: Cambridge University Press)

Partridge, E. (1961), *A Dictionary of Slang and Unconventional English* [1937], 2 vols., 5th edn. (London: Routledge & Kegan Paul)

Pearsall, R. (1972), *The Worm in the Bud: The World of Victorian Sexuality* [1969], paperback edn. (Harmondsworth, Middx: Penguin)

Peyton, S. A. (1928), *The Churchwarden's Presentments in the Oxfordshire Peculiars of Dorchester, Thame and Banbury* (Oxford: Oxfordshire Record Society) vol. 10

Pillet, R. (1815), *L'Angleterre vue à Londres et dans ses provinces* (Paris: Alexis Eymery)

Place, F. (1972), *The Autobiography of Francis Place (1771 – 1854)*, Mary Thale (ed.) (Cambridge: Cambridge University Press)

Plumb, J. H. (1975), *England in the Eighteenth Century* [1950], Pelican History of England, vol. 7, reprint edn. (Harmondsworth, Middx: Penguin)

Poc. Melo. (n.d.): *The Pocket Melodist; or Dramatic Musie* (London: Hay & Turner)

Pop. Voc. (n.d.): *The Popular Vocalist* (London: T. Duncombe)

Porter, E. (1969), *Cambridgeshire Customs and Folklore* (London: Routledge & Kegan Paul)

Porter, E. (1974), *The Folklore of East Anglia* (London: B. T. Batsford)

Pratt, W. (c. 1849 – 56), 'Sale of a Wife by Auction' (Birmingham: Wm Pratt) Oxford: Bodleian Library, Harding Collection)

Puckle, B. S. (1926), *Funeral Customs: Their Origin and Development* (London: T. Werner Laurie)

R—, S. (1853), 'Selling a Wife', *Notes and Queries* (London), series 1, vol. 8, 27 August, p. 209

Raven, J. (1978), *The Folklore of Staffordshire* (London: B. T. Batsford)

Rayner, S. (1881), 'Wife Sales in Yorkshire', in *Old Yorkshire*, William Smith (ed.), vol. 1 (London: Longmans, Green)

RM: *Reading Mercury and Oxford Gazette* (Reading, Berkshire)

Roberts, H. A. (1957), Correspondence, *Hertfordshire Countryside* (Letchworth, Hertfordshire), vol. 11, Spring 1957, p. 146

Rowling, M. (1976), *The Folklore of the Lake District* (London: B. T. Batsford)

Rudé, G. (1973), *Paris and London in the Eighteenth Century, Studies in Popular Protest* [1952] (New York: Viking Press)

Rudkin, E. H. (1973), *Lincolnshire Folklore* [1936], reprint edn. (East Ardsley, Wakefield, Yorks: E. P. Publishing)

Rushworth, J. (1680 – 1722), *Historical Collections of Private Passages of State*, etc. (London)

S: Star (London)

SDT: Sheffield Daily Telegraph (Sheffield, Yorkshire)

Sharp, C. J. (1966), *English Folk Songs from the Southern Appalachians* [1932], Maud Karples (ed.) 2 vols, reprint edn. (London: Oxford University Press)

Shepherd (1823), '"Account of the Sale of a Wife", by J. Nash, in Thomas-street Market, on the 29th May, 1823' (Bristol: Shepherd) (Avon County Library, Miscellaneous Broadsides)

Sherren, W. (1902), *The Wessex of Romance* (London: Chapman & Hall)

Shyllon, F. O. (1977), *Black People in Britain 1555—1833* (London: Oxford University Press)

Simpson, J. (1973), *The Folklore of Sussex* (London: B. T. Batsford)

Smith, A. (1969), *Discovering Folklore in Industry* (Tring, Hertfordshire: Shire Publications)

Smith, P. C. (1957), 'The Sale of a Wife', *Notes and Queries* (London), new series 4, vol. 202, December, p. 548

ST: Sunday Times (London)

Sternberg, V. T. (1853), 'Selling a Wife', *Notes and Queries* (London), series 1, vol. 7, 30 April, pp. 429—30

StJC: St James's Chronicle, or British Evening Post (London)

Stn: Statesman (London)

Stone, L. (1977), *The Family, Sex and Marriage in England 1500—1800* (London: Weidenfeld & Nicolson)

Such, H. (n.d.), 'The Carpenter's Wife' (London: H. Such) (Oxford: Bodleian Library, Harding Collection)

SWA: Sussex Weekly Advertiser, or Lewes Journal (Lewes, Sussex)

T: The Times (London)

Thomas, K. (1971), *Religion and the Decline of Magic: Studies in Popular Beliefs in Sixteenth and Seventeenth Century England* (London: Weidenfeld & Nicolson)

Thompson, E. P. (1972), '"Rough Music": le charivari anglais', *Annales* (Paris), vol. 27, no. 2, March—April, pp. 285—312

Thompson, E. P. (1976), *The Making of the English Working Class* [1963], rev. edn. (Harmondsworth, Middx: Penguin)

Thompson, T. W. (1915), Notebook, ms., vol. 10 (Leeds, Yorkshire: Institute of Dialect and Folk Life Studies, School of English, University of Leeds)

Thornton, W. H. (1906), 'The Devonshire Matrimonial Market', *Devon Notes and Queries* (Exeter, Devon), vol. 4, pp. 54—5

Tobias, J. J. (1972), *Crime and Industrial Society in the Nineteenth Century* [1967] (Harmondsworth, Middx: Penguin)

Tongue, R. L. (1965), *Somerset Folklore*, County Folklore, vol. 8 (London: Folklore Society)

Tudor, J. R. (1883), *The Orkneys and Shetland: Their Past and Present State* (London: Edward Stanford)

Udal, J. S. (1970), *Dorsetshire Folk-Lore* [1922], 2nd edn. (St Peter Port, Guernsey: Toucan Press)
Ulverston (1812): *The Ulverston New Poetical Miscellany* (Ulverston, Lancashire: G. Ashburner)

Voc. Lib. (1822): *The Vocal Library* (London: Sir Richard Phillips)

W—, E. (1870), 'The Duke of Chandos Buying a Wife', *Notes and Queries* (London), series 4, vol. 6, 27 August, p. 179
Walker, J. W. (1939), *Wakefield, Its History and People*, vol. 2, 2nd edn. (Wakefield, Yorkshire: privately printed)
Walker, P. N. (1970), *The Courts of Law: A Guide to their History and Working* (Newton Abbot, Devon: David & Charles)
WB: West Briton and Cornwall Advertiser (Truro, Cornwall)
Westermarck, E. (1921), *The History of Human Marriage* [1891], 3 vols., 5th edn. (London: Macmillan)
WFP: Western Flying Post, or Sherborne and Yeovil Mercury and General Advertiser (Sherborne, Dorset)
White, C. A. (1891), 'Smithfield', *Notes and Queries* (London), series 7, vol. 12, 11 July, pp. 24 – 5
Whitfeld, H. F. (1900), *Plymouth and Devonport in Times of War and Peace* (Plymouth, Devon: E. Chapple)
Williams, G. (1897), *History of the Liverpool Privateers and Letters of Marque with an Account of the Liverpool Slave Trade* (London: William Heinemann)
Williams, K. (1977), *The English Newspaper: An Illustrated History to 1900* (London: Springwood Books)
Williams, R. Vaughan, and Lloyd, A. L. (1969), *The Penguin Book of English Folk Songs* [1959], reprint edn. (Harmondsworth, Middx: Penguin)
Wilson, F. P. (1970), *The Oxford Dictionary of English Proverbs* [1935], 3rd edn. (Oxford: Clarendon Press)
Winfield, C. (1970), 'Factual Sources of Two Episodes in *The Mayor of Casterbridge*', *Nineteenth Century Fiction* (Berkeley, Calif.), vol. 25, no. 2, September, pp. 224 – 31
Wood, E. J. (1869), *The Marriage Day in all Ages and Countries*, 2 vols. (London: Richard Bentley)
Wright, A. R. (1928), *English Folklore* (London: Ernest Benn)
Wright, E. M. (1913), *Rustic Speech and Folk-Lore* (London: Oxford University Press)

YCh: York Chronicle (York, Yorkshire)
YG: Yorkshire Gazette (York, Yorkshire)
YH: York Herald, County and General Advertiser (York, Yorkshire)

Index